Bradbury Beyond Apollo

Jonathan R. Eller

Bradbury Beyond Apollo

**UNIVERSITY OF
ILLINOIS PRESS**
Urbana, Chicago, and Springfield

Library of Congress Cataloging-in-Publication Data
Names: Eller, Jonathan R., 1952– author.
Title: Bradbury beyond Apollo / Jonathan R Eller.
Description: [Urbana]: University of Illinois Press, [2020] | Includes
    bibliographical references and index. |
Identifiers: LCCN 2020013179 (print) | LCCN 2020013180 (ebook) | ISBN
    9780252043413 (cloth; acid-free paper) | ISBN 9780252052293
    (ebook) Subjects: LCSH: Bradbury, Ray, 1920–2012. | Authors,
    American—20th century—Biography. Classification: LCC PS3503.
    R167 Z655 2020 (print) | LCC PS3503.R167 (ebook) | DDC 813/.54—dc23
LC record available at https://lccn.loc.gov/2020013179
LC ebook record available at https://lccn.loc.gov/2020013180

Frontispiece:
Photo © by V. Tony Hauser. Courtesy of Ray Bradbury Literary Works; used by permission.

For Bettina Bradbury

1955–2019

Whose success as a writer

made her father most proud.

What shall we whistle as we stroll in our rocket, hoping to make it by the vast darkness where shadows wait to seize and keep us?

Follow me.

I know a tune.

Here . . . *listen*.

—Ray Bradbury, Afterthoughts: *Mars and the Mind of Man* (1971)

Contents

Acknowledgments

"You have words, my soul, you have fine words in your mouth and at your elbow, jumping out of your typewriter, speaking I imagine in your sleep." Poet Helen Bevington's April 1986 letter to Ray Bradbury offered this emotional response to reading his books; her words serve to highlight the very insubstantial margin dividing the realities from the reveries that, together, shaped his creative world. Bradbury's complicated and unpredictable inner world constantly spilled over into his adaptations for stage and screen, into his poetry, essays, book reviews, hundreds of interviews, and over time, flowed into the minds of architects, generations of Disney's Imagineers, prominent illustrators, and above all, into the learning lives of untold numbers of students, teachers, librarians, general readers, and those who shaped the Space Age. I'm profoundly grateful for the decades when he shared that world with me in conversations, interviews, and countless hours navigating the files and artifacts that eventually took over most of his Los Angeles home and a fair portion of his Palm Springs residence as well.

Bradbury's mind constantly exploded with ideas, and his complex files—together with the many thousands of papers and letters that were never filed at all—represent the consequences of an amazing and largely self-taught interdisciplinary imagination. The inner logic of his filing strategy is largely unfathomable, and at times his fast-paced life resulted in layers of accumulation with no order at all. Ray Bradbury: The Life of Fiction, Becoming Ray Bradbury, and Ray Bradbury Unbound all benefited from his presence and advice, but Bradbury Beyond Apollo was written after his passing. Yet the myriad trails of paper radiating out from his life did not die with him, thanks largely to Donn Albright, Bradbury's longtime friend and principal bibliographer. Bradbury Beyond Apollo would not have been possible without Donn Albright's generosity and foresight, combined with the love and generosity of Ray Bradbury's family.

In the late 1980s, Ray Bradbury urged me to contact Donn, who was in the midst of his 53-year career as a professor of illustration at the Pratt Institute. "If you want to learn about my work and life, you must learn from Donn Albright. He knows me better than I know myself." Albright received, through Ray Bradbury's bequest, the manuscripts of his works in all media, as well as Bradbury's author copies of all the magazines and books in which his works ever appeared, including a formidable arsenal of foreign editions. Donn immediately gifted, in turn, Bradbury's bequest, including his working library, to the Center for Ray Bradbury

Studies at Indiana University's School of Liberal Arts on the Indianapolis campus (IUPUI). Donn's memory and insights have been invaluable in this book and all of my earlier books, and I'm profoundly grateful for his support and for the encouragement of his daughter, Elizabeth Nahum Albright, who learned, early in life, how to document—through photography and words—the remarkable writer who was her godfather.

The Bradbury family's parallel gift of artifacts, office, awards, photographs, and audio recordings also included other papers and correspondence, and this rich legacy arrived at the Bradbury Center together with the Albright gifts in the fall of 2013. The staging and packing of these combined gifts would not have been possible without the on-site support of Bradbury's daughter Alexandra, who spent months assisting with the sorting of countless books, papers, and artifacts. She was often joined by her sisters Susan Nixon, Ramona Bradbury, and the late Bettina Bradbury in planning and granting the family gift, which was made on behalf of all.

None of my books would have been possible without the support of Don Congdon Associates in New York. Altogether, the late Don Congdon and his successor, Michael Congdon, have represented Ray Bradbury and his estate for over seventy years. Michael Congdon and Cristina Concepcion have provided access to the Congdon-Bradbury correspondence as I wrote all three volumes, and I continue to benefit from access granted to the agency's archival deposit of Bradbury-related papers at the Butler Library of Columbia University.

James W. Sullivan, manager of Ray Bradbury Literary Works, LLC, has granted permission to quote from published and unpublished works and letters and given permission for the illustrations; his colleagues Cheryl Carter and Ann Crane have also been extremely helpful and encouraging as this final volume took shape. I'm grateful as well to Bradbury Centennial planner Larry Schiller for his work in facilitating clearances for some of the photographs included in *Bradbury Beyond Apollo*.

Dr. Phil Nichols of the University of Wolverhampton, U.K., the leading scholar on Bradbury's media adaptation history, has been immensely helpful in reading drafts and in guiding my research through the massive but sometimes fragmentary record of Bradbury's stage, film, and television work. I owe Phil a great debt for his insights into Bradbury's unproduced screenplays as well as the history of *The Ray Bradbury Theater*. I'm grateful to Brian Sibley, well-known author of literary adaptations and documentaries for Britain's BBC Radio, for providing access to his trans-Atlantic correspondence with Ray Bradbury. Annette Kirk, wife of the late Russell Kirk and director of the Russell Kirk Center for Cultural Renewal, graciously provided the important portions of the correspondence record between Bradbury and her husband.

I was often sustained by the encouragement and advice of prize-winning poet and essayist Dana Gioia, who was instrumental in Bradbury's continued prominence in American Letters during his long tenure as Chair of the National Endowment for the Arts. Pulitzer Prize–winning critic Michael Dirda provided advice that helped me balance the duties of running the Center for Ray Bradbury Studies while simultaneously researching and writing *Bradbury Beyond Apollo*.

Film professor John Tibbetts of the University of Kansas and California journalist-biographer Gene Beley willingly provided research copies of their interviews with Bradbury and others over the course of many years. Novelist and former film writer and producer, Steven Paul Leiva, who continues to honor Bradbury's legacy through various events and observances, offered steady encouragement and provided important background on Bradbury's concept work for Gary Kurtz on what later became *Little Nemo in Slumberland*.

I'll always be grateful to William F. Nolan, one of Bradbury's oldest writer-friends, for his early advice and interviews as I began the biography trilogy in the late 1990s and early 2000s. His pioneering *Ray Bradbury Companion* and its forerunner checklists opened the way to all bibliographical scholarship on Bradbury's often bewildering publishing history. I also had the advice of Stephen E. Ammidown, curator of the Bradbury-Nolan Collection at Bowling Green State University. All roads also lead back to Bradbury's hometown of Waukegan, Illinois, and this book would not have been complete without the assistance of Ty Rohrer and his Waukegan Historical Society staff.

During the final months of writing, I was able to tie up a number of loose ends and solve more than a few mysteries through the work of the Bradbury Center's professional interns (Dr. Catherine Walsh and Katie Watson) and staff volunteers (Nancy Orem and Debi Eller). My wife Debi has been a constant source of encouragement and strength, providing wise counsel as I made the revisions that transformed *Bradbury Beyond Apollo* into whole cloth.

The presence of Ray Bradbury looms large over all of these years of research and writing. In the late 1980s, I accompanied him to a conference panel where he and other science fiction writers spoke to a large public audience. The first question came from a young boy with thick black-rimmed glasses not unlike Bradbury's own. "Mr. Bradbury," the youngster said, "What will your work mean to us after you're dead?" Bradbury leaned down from the table, raised his eyebrows above the rim of his glasses, fixed the boy with eyes of wonder, and said, "Oh, son, you don't understand—when I die, you all will disappear." Above all, I'm grateful that Ray Bradbury has left us here a bit longer on this planet, so that we can follow his vision and cautions into a future yet unknown.

Bradbury Beyond Apollo

Introduction

> "When you reach the stars, boy, yes, and live there forever, all the fears will go, and Death himself will die."
> —Ray Bradbury, *The Halloween Tree*

Ray Bradbury passed away on the evening of June 5, 2012, just as astronomers were recording a rare solar transit of Venus, but his first great posthumous honor centered on the Red Planet he had loved all his life. In early August 2012, the successful planetfall of Curiosity, the most sophisticated Martian rover ever built, led the Jet Propulsion Laboratory (JPL) scientific team to name the landing site after Ray Bradbury. His creativity had already arrived on Mars, however; in 2008, the Phoenix lander brought a small digital library, including *The Martian Chronicles*, to the far northern arctic latitudes. If Phoenix represented the past and present, Curiosity represented everything that Bradbury hoped for the future. Through its years of exploration, Curiosity has confirmed that Mars once held bodies of water—large ones. Curiosity continues to move on through the varied terrain of Gale Crater from "Bradbury Landing," a site named after a man who, like Edgar Rice Burroughs and H. G. Wells, had dared to write about his dreams.

For Bradbury, his abiding dreams of Mars were not really about sentient Martians at all, although the exotic, golden-eyed creatures of his *Martian Chronicles* have captivated mainstream readers in edition after edition since its first publication in 1950. For decades, the stories he had woven into *The Martian Chronicles* would stand as the defining fiction of the Red Planet—not because of the book's imaginary encounters, but because it was about *our own* dual potential for towering achievement and planetary-scale destruction. When he first published the *Chronicles*, he privately observed that many would follow the initial explorers and "go off to Mars, just for the ride, thinking they will find a planet like a seer's crystal, in which to read a magnificent future. What they'll find, instead, is the somewhat shopworn image of themselves. Mars is a mirror, not a crystal."

Fifteen years later, he would remain right on message as Mariner IV's rather barren photographic images reached the public eye. During the summer of 1965,

Bradbury was not dismayed by the conclusions drawn from these few photo-graphs, but rather by the way prominent Americans—from the White House to Hollywood—felt that everything was different. He was far more annoyed at Hollywood, where imagination and reality could blend, than he was with Wash-ington. It all played out as he finished a four-year sequence of *Chronicles* scripts for two producers and several major studios; forty years later, he reflected on this frustration in a private interview: "The month I turned in the *Martian Chronicles* script, late in the summer of 1965, we had our first photographic assays of Mars. And the studio said, 'There's no life on Mars, so let's not shoot the film.' How stupid! I mean, that's all the reason to do it, if there's no life there—*we're* the life, aren't we?"

Television eventually provided the visual legacy for his *Chronicles*—first, through a 1980 NBC miniseries shaped by other hands, and eventually through sixty-five cable TV episodes of his own *Ray Bradbury Theater*. His six seasons of award-winning adaptations (1985–1992) reprised a broader range of his sci-ence fiction stories, as well as many of his fantasies, tales of suspense, and the magical realism of his Green Town memories—mostly older Bradbury classics, a few newer stories, together representing his most sustained broader-market success in controlling the performed dramatic legacy of his fiction.

But the prodigious output of stories that had defined "Ray Bradbury" in our culture was no longer defining his path into the future. Was the mysterious chan-nel from the subconscious to his typing fingertips slowly fading, or was he simply distracted by "being" Ray Bradbury? For every creative project he accomplished with film studios and museums, many others remained unfulfilled. Looking back, he once observed in private conversation that "I've had a lot of fun in my life around the edges of things that never happened." The striking originality and impact of his best early fiction surfaced less frequently over time, and we may never be sure how increasing distractions, advancing age, or shifting authorial intent combined in this process. What is sure is that all of his widely scattered creative ventures from the late 1960s onward were stabilized and sustained by his growing presence as a witness and celebrant of the Space Age. Burroughs, Lowell, and Wells had only imagined Mars; Bradbury would arrive there, through the mementos and machines of true space travel.

Bradbury Beyond Apollo completes the tale begun in *Becoming Ray Bradbury* and continued in *Ray Bradbury Unbound*. Even in three volumes, the storyteller's story is so complex and so full of unrelenting (and sometimes uneven) creativity that one must pass over some of his lesser adventures altogether. These volumes represent a biography of the mind, recording life as he experienced it, not nec-essarily how the public saw it. Like the earlier volumes, *Bradbury Beyond Apollo* chronicles a number of ventures that the public knows little about; yet these were things that *he* cared a great deal about, whether they succeeded in grand fashion or failed to reach the public eye at all.

: : :

To follow the creative trail from mid-career on to the end of his life, one has to regard his celebrated past as prologue. This is a difficult proposition, as his forward progress was masked by countless ghosts of the past. In spite of the significant things to come, the stories and fables that define Ray Bradbury's twenty-first-century legacy were almost all written during the first two decades of his seventy-year career.

Between 1941 and 1962, a fraction of his amazing output during those early years gave life to the nine story collections, novels, and novelized story cycles that define his role as one of the best-known and best-loved storytellers of our time: the dark and sometimes enchanting fantasies that populated first *Dark Carnival* and then *The October Country* with the chilling Otherness of the autumn people; the edgy and emotionally powerful science fiction that shaped *The Martian Chronicles* and *The Illustrated Man*; the antiauthoritarian brilliance of *Fahrenheit 451*; the fantasies and magical realism that emerged from *The Golden Apples of the Sun* and fairly exploded out of *A Medicine for Melancholy*; the mixed terrors and joys of childhood summers vividly recalled in *Dandelion Wine*; and *Something Wicked This Way Comes*, Bradbury's first true novel and his first sustained exploration of the uncertain boundaries between good and evil, life and death.

By the end of the 1960s he had taken an unmistakable turn down other paths that extended many of these early tales and books into adaptations for dramatic and musical stage, television, major studio motion pictures, and a wide range of graphic forms. His Space-Age dreams took him into a wider range of nonfiction writing and public lectures than he had time for, and what little time remained for his Muse was almost always channeled into Hollywood. He would return time and again to the safe harbors of his early success over the remaining four decades of his life, still refashioning what were rapidly becoming contemporary classics, but also producing occasional new works that extended his creativity into innovative and powerful forms of fictional narrative.

These significant later works included *The Halloween Tree*, a playful fantasy of the history behind all traditions of death and renewal; the murder mysteries *Death Is a Lonely Business* and *A Graveyard for Lunatics*, long-deferred explorations of his own early career as a writer and screenwriter; late-life fulfillments of major prose projects mapped out half a lifetime earlier, such as *From the Dust Returned*, *Farewell Summer*, *Somewhere a Band Is Playing*, and *Leviathan 99*; the surprising appearance of a precious few resurrected stories from his most creative early years, previously uncollected or never before published at all; and a few newer gems that stand out from most of his later-life tales, stories such as "The Toynbee Convector" that reveal the visceral core of his settled philosophies better than the more mediated filters of his engaging public lectures, interviews, and speculative essays.

These achievements—some new, and some buried surprises from the far past—were all on the horizon as the 1970s opened, and they would all be sustained and crafted within the greater fabric of his deepening engagement with the American space program. By 1969, which he dated in much of his correspondence as "Apollo Year 1," he had become a cultural icon whose legacy would shine a light deep into the next century. Yet remarkable projects still lay ahead; his career was not yet half over, but it is here where the final chapters of his life begin to unfold.

Part I

The Inherited Wish

The great thing about my life is, God gave me the capacity to recognize a metaphor when I saw one. You can give all these metaphors to other writers, and they wouldn't necessarily write a story. They'd say, "Ohm, that's a nice idea," but they wouldn't get excited. So I have this genetic capacity to erupt, to let my volcano go when I see a good idea. But that's a thing I was born with; you can't teach that.

—RB, October 25, 2002

1 Prometheus Bound

In the weeks leading up to the July 1971 launch of Apollo 15, the crew named the lunar features in the vicinity of the descent module's designated landing zone. Some of their Houston Spaceflight Center colleagues helped out, and the various reference points soon had names drawn from works of science fiction and fantasy.[1] Commander David Scott and Lunar Module Pilot Jim Irwin, who would both make the descent from Al Worden's orbital position in the Command Module, named one large crater "St. George," after the wine bottle carried by Jules Verne's intrepid travelers in *From the Earth to the Moon*.

The title of Frank Herbert's *Dune* provided the name for another crater, and several features were named after various locales in Tolkien's *Lord of the Rings* Trilogy. Heinlein's blind poet Rhysling, from *The Green Hills of Earth*, and Arthur C. Clarke's novel *Earthlight* identified other craters. Allusions to Ray Bradbury would seem best suited for the terrain of Mars; nevertheless, the astronauts named one of the smallest craters to the far south of the landing zone "Dandelion," in honor of Bradbury's *Dandelion Wine*.

These designations were announced in passing by the media on the launch date, July 26th, but only mission personnel and those relatively few beyond NASA who were interested in the navigational details of the lunar landing would ever know the significance that Bradbury's tiny "Dandelion" landmark would play in the mission itself. Apollo 15 was the first of the extended expeditionary missions, with a Rover stowed aboard their Lunar Module. Scott and Irwin spent three days on the lunar surface and made three extravehicular activity excursions in their Rover. Surface features like "Dandelion" proved to be invaluable markers—the selected landing site was a geologically complex region along the eastern edge of the vast Mare Imbrium, and the descent from orbit proved challenging. The Apennine Mountains loomed above them to the east, and the landing trajectory had been the steepest yet attempted for an Apollo mission.

The second EVA excursion would prove to be the longest, a seven-hour run south from the landing site on August 1, 1971. Scott navigated using a detailed topographic traverse chart, and the two astronauts made their way to "Dandelion" and its conjoined neighbor "Front," which formed the designated turnaround station and a walking point. "Dandelion" was on the front slope of the

Partial enlargement of Apollo 15 commander David Scott's topographical chart for the second lunar rover EVA event, August 1, 1971. The Lunar Module (LM) location is top left; Bradbury's "Dandelion" crater, bottom right, identifies the terminal turnaround station and furthest walking site for the longest EVA of the mission. Scott and Lunar Module Pilot James Irwin found the Genesis Rock along this route.

Apennines, and the two men had to negotiate a path to and from "Dandelion" between a crater-pocked downslope to the northeast and a very steep and extended rise to the southwest. During the run out to "Dandelion/Front" and back, Scott and Irwin discovered and retrieved what became known as the Genesis Rock. It proved to be the oldest sample ever taken from the moon, dating back more than four billion years to the period just after the formation of the moon's crust.

The facts read like a science fiction story opening—on that day, NASA's science met Ray Bradbury's fiction in a dream turned reality. Bradbury soon learned what only a few members of the broader reading public would ever know—that his "Dandelion" naming honor was also a crucial navigation point on Mankind's first extended journey across the surface of another world. Here was tangible proof of what he had sensed when he first met most of the astronaut core in January 1967: "They had read my books growing up. They were glad we were 'working' together. So it seemed that while I wasn't going into Space, some small part of my writing past was."[2]

Mission commander David Scott remained in contact with Bradbury after the successful completion of the Apollo 15 mission. "Many thanks for your inspiration," Scott wrote, "and for your guidance through the lunar 'stratigraphy.'"[3] Along with Tolkien's "Uttermost West" and Heinlein's "Rhysling," the "Dandelion" crater would become a permanent lunar feature, and not just a mission navigation coordinate. Time and again in the coming years, America's space program would pull Ray Bradbury into key moments of exploration as a validating witness and celebrant—and perhaps also as a talisman. His ever-expanding relationship with NASA, the Jet Propulsion Laboratory, and eventually the highly influential Planetary Society illuminated the way that Bradbury's remaining four decades would play out beyond Apollo. The teller of tales had now entered the Great Tale itself.

: : :

For more than a quarter-century before the success of Apollo 15, Bradbury's unusual brand of science fiction—powerfully emotional studies of the human heart and mind mounted on a barely perceptible armature of science and technology—had inspired many scientists, engineers, and astronauts who would play roles in the Great Tale. His Space Age presence was constantly renewed by additional printings of the Bantam mass-market editions of *The Martian Chronicles* and *The Illustrated Man*, periodically reissued with new and eye-catching cover art. Doubleday's infrequent but well-advertised revivals of his hardbound editions also kept the lights burning in the Bradbury universe, and his science fiction constantly appeared in commercial and textbook anthologies.

The best of his subsequent 1950s space stories, along with a few previously uncollected 1940s stragglers, wound up in *R Is for Rocket* (1962) and *S Is for Space* (1966). Ironically, his last significant space-age fiction had appeared well before the first Mercury manned suborbital and orbital missions of 1961; a heavily revised version of his early 1940s story "R Is for Rocket," plus "Icarus Montgolfier Wright," "The End of the Beginning," and "The Strawberry Window" all focused on the human anticipation of space travel and the emotional challenges facing first voyagers during the jolting transition from dream to reality. He considered the characters of the last two stories to be central to his dream as it evolved during the mid-1950s—the aging parents of an astronaut destined to build the first space station in "The End of the Beginning," and the little family of Martian colonists transporting their most cherished memory of Earth to a new planet in "The Strawberry Window." In a summer 1969 letter to Don Congdon, his longtime New York literary agent, Bradbury identified these two tales as "my raison d'etre for space-travel and the future, of man in and among the stars."

Yet in the late 1960s, as successive Apollo missions first moved out beyond near-Earth orbit, Bradbury's active participation in the Great Tale moved away from the short fiction that had made him famous. His new audiences were drawn in by his older fiction and by his ever-increasing number of lectures at Caltech and other institutions, but the new Bradbury work they encountered would be essays, poetry, interactive multimedia projects, stage plays, and even orchestral projections of his Space-Age dreams. Apollo 8's striking photographs of a distant planet Earth, and the crew's December 1968 reading of *Genesis* broadcast from Lunar orbit, coincided with the first performance of Bradbury's *Christus Apollo* cantata, set to music by Academy Award–winning composer Jerry Goldsmith and performed in UCLA's Royce Hall. In 1973, award-winning film and television composer Lalo Schifrin would set Bradbury's *Madrigals for the Space Age* to music in The Los Angeles Music Center's Dorothy Chandler Pavilion.

As he moved through these new media frontiers, Bradbury's experimentation with the essay form had the most impact nationally. His three *Life* magazine articles of the 1960s anticipated the conquest of the moon as the first step toward planetary settlements that would focus technological advances toward his real dream: taking mankind to the stars. The pure vitality of this new voice was not just for public display, however; he also privately noted the Apollo era's greatest tragedy on the first full draft of his 1967 award-winning *Life* magazine essay "An Impatient Gulliver above Our Roofs." Bradbury signed and dated the completion of this draft in his sprawling hand on Thursday, January 26, 1967. The red ink was scarcely dry when he appended, in black ink, "Friday—Jan 27th—Grissom, White, Chaffey killed in flash fire—Cape Kennedy." He then turned to the third page of his draft and somberly changed the nation's 1969 projection for the first moon landing to "1970 or 1971."

The ability of NASA scientists and engineers to learn from the tragedy, reconfigure systems, and reach the surface of the moon in the summer of 1969 reenergized Bradbury's many public lectures on the subject. He would always consider Apollo 11 to be the greatest single event in the history of Mankind—indeed, in the deep-time history of all terrestrial creation. Yet on some level, Bradbury and other close observers of NASA's political fortunes realized that the safe return of Armstrong, Aldrin, and Collins marked the beginning of the end for the entire Apollo program. The Kennedy challenge had been met, and there was no longer a clear consensus in Congress, or even in the popular mind, that the remaining nine missions should be launched at all.

Bradbury's sense of the sheer awe and wonderment of these missions never waned. Who else but Ray Bradbury would begin to date his 1969 correspondence as "Apollo Year 1"? It was heartbreaking that his new Age of Apollo, publicly celebrated in the "Christus Apollo" cantata, would have such a short life. All the moon landings occurred within the incredibly short span of thirty-nine months, and none of his letters are dated in celebration beyond "Apollo Year 3." For the rest of his long life, no human would ever again leave the relative safety of low-Earth orbit or set a course for other worlds. There would be no more fire on the Moon.

: : :

In 1970, as Bradbury began to feel the momentum bleeding off from the Apollo program, he was able to generate a degree of creative momentum through his first extended working experience with the Disney Imagineers. The December 1966 passing of Walt Disney did not deter Disney executives like John Hench and Marty Sklar from plans for the Florida complex centered on Disney World and EPCOT. But plans had to be modified, and as the Imagineers began to adjust, Marty Sklar discovered Ray Bradbury's early defense of Disneyland in the June 28, 1958, issue of the *Nation*, where he effectively counteracted Julian Halevy's claim that Disneyland was no better for children than Las Vegas. In 1970, Sklar brought in Bradbury to work with Marc Davis, a legendary animator, to develop a new historical adventure ride a continent away in Disney World.

Davis had been a character designer and animator for such Disney classics as *Fantasia, Bambi, Sleeping Beauty, Cinderella*, and *101 Dalmatians*, and would come to be known as one of the legendary "Nine Old Men" who launched so many of the enduring films and park concepts. Disney's "Carousel of Progress" at the 1964–65 New York World's Fair was populated by Marc Davis's animatronic actors; Bradbury, who had authored the narration for the Fair's United States Pavilion, took his family through the Carousel during the summer of 1964. The "Carousel of Progress" moved to a permanent site in Disneyland after the Fair closed, and Sklar eventually set Davis and Bradbury to work on a similar tour for the new Disney World park in Florida—a larger tour of human progress that would move through deep time, from prehistory and on into the future.

Bradbury's working concept carried into development as "The Yestermorrow Time Machine." Davis's watercolor tableaus gave visual life to Bradbury's words and his central narrative image of fire as the life force of mankind's entire existence; Bradbury's surviving 1970 draft includes the observation that "The emergence of Man from Fire, his survival by Fire, and his Continuance in the Future with Fire, are the Central facts of our time machine drama." The Monsanto Corporation was the targeted sponsor, and when Bradbury came in to Disney headquarters for the presentation, John Hench convinced him to make the pitch. Bradbury was at the top of his visionary game, but the Monsanto executives were dismayed by the pervasive use of fire when their preferred corporate expression of progress centered on the concept of "energy." Bradbury's immediate comeback was that you can't have a cave man holding up a burning torch in triumph, yelling "Energy! Energy!"

It was no use; Hench and everyone involved at Disney felt that the Davis-Bradbury team had made an excellent presentation, but Monsanto walked away from the table. In the end, Disney executives had to fall back on an existing sponsored attraction instead. The Carousel of Progress was moved cross-country from Disneyland to Disney World and reconstituted, in a much-diminished form, under GE sponsorship.

By the end of 1970, the fires of the "Yestermorrow Time Machine" were extinguished, and the fires of Apollo would soon follow into history. In Bradbury's mind, one flame required the other—the inherited dream as projected by Disney, and the actualized dream of the conquest of space through Apollo. For Bradbury, ever the spinner of myth-based wonderment, Prometheus was indeed bound, and without the saving satisfaction that the Promethean gift of fire would ever light the way to other worlds. But as H. G. Wells had observed, there were always "things to come"; it was simply a matter of choices. The future was yet unknown, but over the next decade, the essential core of Bradbury and Davis's "Time Machine" would evolve into the Bradbury-narrated "Spaceship Earth," the EPCOT centerpiece of Disney World.

2 | The Darkness between the Stars

Bradbury entered the fray surrounding the Apollo program cutbacks in early 1972, but only after his frustration simmered throughout the two-year process of reducing the number of launches. The ten projected lunar landing missions had been predicated on the fact that ten of the massive Saturn V and V-B stages had been contracted and built; Apollo missions 12 through 20 would be carried aloft on the fires of the remaining nine. But the Skylab program loomed just beyond the Apollo timeline, and continuing unrest over the Vietnam Conflict and domestic social tensions led President Nixon to remove NASA's priority budget consideration. For years to come, NASA's budget would shrink; on January 4, 1970, NASA's new director, Thomas O. Paine, canceled Apollo 20 so that the first Skylab mission could be scheduled for a Saturn V launch in the coming years.

This left eight missions on the books: four more of the Apollo 11–style short-stay missions and four J-missions—longer duration journeys, each carrying an Extended Lunar Module and a Lunar Rover for extravehicular surface exploration. In April 1970, the high drama of Apollo 13's onboard explosion, which had expended one of the Saturn V rockets without achieving a lunar landing, offered a very public reminder that tragedy was always just seconds away in the unforgiving vacuum of space. In September 1970, NASA canceled one of the two remaining short-stay missions, as well as one of the longer duration J-missions, and redesignated the remaining missions to eliminate Apollo 18 and 19. The great logistical success of Apollo 15's extended mission led President Nixon to consider cancelation of 16 and 17 entirely; ironically, the last victory for the Apollo program occurred on the ground, when the President was persuaded to stay the course, for now.

In late April 1972, Kenneth Reich, editor of the *Los Angeles Times* op-ed page, gave Bradbury his first chance to defend Apollo in a syndicated column by inviting him to write on "the deterioration of the American Space Program."[1] Reich had recently launched an editorial initiative soliciting "diverse views on public issues . . . strongly expressed," and that's exactly what he received from Bradbury. The May 17th issue of the *Times* printed Bradbury's editorial, illustrated by the prominent political cartoonist Ranan Lurie, under the unmistakable Bradbury title "Apollo Murdered: The Sun Goes Out."

Bradbury used the image of our descendants, a billion years from now, living on other worlds, wondering if we knew, in our time, the cosmic significance of Apollo 11: "The special day when, after three billion years of genetic waiting, genetic dreaming, Man reached up to Touch Space, Touch Moon, Touch Eternity?" He went on to rehearse the common-sense–based generalizations he would use for years: the money isn't thrown into a crater on the Moon, it employs scientists and technicians and manufacturers on Earth; the money we spend on Space exploration is a fraction of the money spent on foreign wars. And he also offered the most chilling image of the cosmic alternative that he would ever write in essay form:

> Go out and look at the stars tonight.
> Let the darkness between the stars warn you.
> There is more dark than light in the Universe.
> We must be part of those small touches of fire that fill an otherwise empty Space.
> We must choose Light and not delay. Otherwise, Darkness chooses us.

For Bradbury, a deeper knowledge of the space between the stars was simply irrelevant; his metaphor offered truth, not fact, and it would compel regardless of subsequent discoveries of dark matter, dark energy, or even the more measurable electromagnetic phenomena of solar wind and the broader interstellar medium of gas and dust. It was all about the survival of humanity long into the future of the Cosmos; to abandon the first step beyond Earth was to abandon life itself.

Bradbury's editorial, along with commentary by other writers, set the stage for debate as the final Apollo missions played out. The public was aware of the gradual cancelations of Apollo 18 through 20, but the launch of Apollo 17 sparked a final media debate over the rapidly approaching end of lunar exploration. In December 1972, as the Apollo 17 crew prepared for a daring nighttime launch, Time magazine found it difficult to express the magnitude of this remarkable decision: "Historians will have a difficult time explaining the decision to abandon the Apollo program. . . . Barely three years after the first lunar landing, the nation that made it all possible has turned its thoughts inward and away from space."

Time's lead article in the December 11th issue turned to Ray Bradbury to explain the human dilemma at the heart of the matter, and Bradbury offered the best summation he knew: the closing scene of H. G. Wells's 1936 film, Things to Come, where an antiscience protest gathers at the launch pad of the first lunar mission: "We don't want mankind to go out to the moon and the planets! . . .

We shall hate you more if you succeed than if you fail. Is there never to be calm and happiness for man?"

As a teenager, Bradbury had been riven by the existential implications of Wells's novel and film, and the *Time* article continued on with what Bradbury had given them, ending with a loose version of the lines that had fueled Bradbury's passion for endless exploration since the age of sixteen: "Man must first conquer 'this little planet, its winds and ways, and all the laws of mind and matter that restrain him. Then the planets about him, and at last out across the immensity to the stars.'" Bradbury's observations prompted *Time* editors to present the abandonment of Apollo as a fundamental conflict between those who strive to dominate nature and those who wish to live in harmony with it.

: : :

Bradbury sensed that the Soviet program was in no position to take over lunar exploration. Sometime in 1972, Apollo 12's Alan Bean, soon to command the Skylab 3 mission, sent him sketches of the Saturn V's Soviet equivalent, which Bean found to be smaller than expected.[2] Bradbury's hopes were now pinned on America's unmanned planetary probes and orbiters that would dominate deep space discoveries well into the twenty-first century. These robotic children, as he would call them, were primitive at first, and no match for the human eye. He had learned that lesson early on, through the misleading photographic assays of Mariner IV in July 1965.

Mariner IV was a great achievement, validating that a spacecraft could navigate and orient itself during deep space missions, but this brief flyby represented little more than a hurried shot in the dark. Only 1 percent of the Martian surface was covered, and these first photographs happened to image some of the most barren and featureless spots on the planet. Yet that was enough to convince various Hollywood executives, for a time, that *The Martian Chronicles* had no future as a film.[3]

The headlines said that Mars was a dead world, little different from our own moon. But as the photographic images came in, JPL planetary scientist Bruce Murray was beginning work on the geological data collected in various ways from the brief Mariner IV mission. He was the architect of the entire Mariner series and would become a close friend of Bradbury's. In the fall of 1971, just weeks after Apollo 15 put "Dandelion Crater" on the lunar map, Murray planned for the imminent orbital insertion of Mariner 9 around the planet Mars. Bradbury would be a key part of these plans.

On November 12, 1971, the day before Mariner 9 entered Martian orbit, Murray and Carl Sagan faced off against Bradbury and his good friend Arthur C. Clarke in a friendly debate about Mariner's likelihood of finding evidence of life, past or present, on the Red Planet. Moderator Walter Sullivan was science editor for the *New York Times*, leaving Bradbury as the only participant without scientific training beyond his lone semester of high school astronomy, taken back in the fall of 1937. But the evening seemed to focus the discussion on the Human race rather than Mars; following Sagan's opening survey of the centuries-old search for scientific truth about Mars, Bradbury took aim at the historical present:

> But at this moment in history, it looks as if I must semi-retire to the wings, along with Greek and Roman authors, and hope to become part of some strange new mythology. This is probably true of many science fiction authors this week, this year, and in the immediate years ahead. . . . A few years ago I was worried about going out of existence completely once we hit Mars. But then I realized that what I was doing was writing fairy stories—writing a mythology, doing a Bible really. *The Martian Chronicles* is very much akin to the childhood influences on me of the Old and the New Testament.

The mythological context of Bradbury's remarks is not surprising. In his 1969 cultural study, *Enemies of the Permanent Things*, Russell Kirk had already placed Bradbury among such mythopoeic writers as C. S. Lewis and J. R. R. Tolkien: "The trappings of science-fiction may have attracted young people to Bradbury, but he has led them on to something much older and better: mythopoeic literature, normative truth acquired through wonder. Bradbury's stories are not an escape from reality; they are windows looking upon enduring reality."

For Bradbury, that reality was now headed to the stars, and he would take a further step into the Great Tale the following evening, November 13, 1971, when he joined Wernher von Braun and members of the Mariner 9 mission team at the Jet Propulsion Laboratory to witness transmission of the first close-up images of Mars. Von Braun commemorated the meeting by inscribing a note, "For Ray Bradbury, who had it all figured out, long ago." The meeting was more emotionally complicated for Bradbury, who summed it up the next day in a letter to Don Congdon: "The irony of life; here was Hitler's number one rocket man, now responsible to the Human Race and its billion-year future in Space. I accept von Braun, as I must accept myself."

: : :

Nearly a year later, Bruce Murray and the other distinguished Mariner 9 panelists reacted to the surprises revealed by the orbiter's photographic surveys. Mariner 9 had revealed the four massive equatorial volcanoes of Mars, the largest with a caldera greater than the entire big island of Hawaii itself. An extensive equatorial canyon system dwarfed any geological feature on the much larger Earth. And there was now some evidence of wind and water erosion dating from an indeterminate period of the planet's deep history.

By the time that Bradbury's final thoughts on Mariner 9—as well as those of his friends Carl Sagan, Arthur C. Clarke, Walter Sullivan, and Bruce Murray—were gathered for publication, the orbiter's photographic eyes were closed forever. In October 1972, with no remaining fuel to adjust its alignment to the sun, it was shut down just before its solar cells failed. It remains an artifact for future explorers to reflect on, or perhaps retrieve.

Murray edited the original transcripts from the November 1971 discussion, as well as new comments by all, and in the final months of 1972 he prepared a book of this record, complete with many Mariner 9 photographs, under the overarching title *Mars and the Mind of Man*. Bradbury wrote the Foreword, "On Going a Journey," and his new post-Mariner comments formed the final section of the book. In the Foreword, he offered "Dark They Were, and Golden-Eyed," a Martian tale *outside* of his *Chronicles* saga, as the core metaphor for what we will become:

> In that Martian story, I told of a man and his family who helped colonize Mars, who eat of its foods and live in its strange seasons, and stay on when everyone else goes back to Earth, until the day finally comes when they find that the odd weathers and peculiar temperatures of the Red Planet have melted their flesh into new shapes, tinted their skin, and put flecks of gold into their now most fantastic eyes, and they move up into the hills to live in old ruins and become—Martians.
>
> Which is the history I predict for us on that far world. . . . We are, then—at this moment, because we dream it so—Martians. We wish to be that thing and so will be it.

Bradbury's invocation of the Great Dream—the blueprint for the Great Tale he was now living—set up what he would say in the long closing section of *Mars and the Mind of Man*: "Toynbee speaks of the challenge and response of various tribes, nations, and racial groups in the long history of man. Those who refuse the challenge, who will not respond, become the detritus of history. The universe will not accept mediocre lunacy save to tread upon it, grind it under, and go on to other yeasting experiments."

In the British historian Arnold Toynbee, Bradbury had found a key to understanding how a dream of the future and the focused effort to extend that dream represents the key to survival for any human civilization. Here, and in more fully developed essays and stories of the 1980s, he would return to Toynbee's defined need to believe in the dream and turn it upward, to the stars. But first, he wanted to conclude *Mars and the Mind of Man* as a storyteller, offering a time-honored metaphor to defeat the darkness between the stars:

> The journey is long, the end uncertain, and there is more dark along the way than light, but you can whistle. Come with me by the wall of the great tomb-yards of all time which lie a billion years ahead. What shall we whistle as we stroll in our rocket, hoping to make it by the vast darkness where shadows wait to seize and keep us?
>
> Follow me.
>
> I know a tune.
>
> Here . . . *listen.*

3   A Teller of Tales

In the spring of 1971, Ray Bradbury spoke at Citrus College in Glendora, California, just a few blocks north of old Route 66—the road that had first brought him to Los Angeles in 1934, a thirteen-year-old boy riding in his father's road-weary 1928 Buick. As a speaker, he was no stranger to the many colleges around Glendora, Azusa, Pomona, and Claremont, but this particular visit apparently triggered reflections on that early journey west and his ever-lengthening ride into the future. The night before his presentation, he wrote a three-stanza poem on death, burial, and remembrance. That thirteen-year-old boy had fallen in love with the Pacific, and the fifty-year-old man's closing stanza asked for final rest "Where the dawn wind blows from the sleeping west":

> Slumber me there with the twilight sails
> That go where the wanderer wants to be
> In an endless night on a rimless sea
> In a crying of gulls and nameless birds.
> But name me for those with the gift of words
> Say that I was a teller of tales.

He already sensed that his legacy would derive from those final four words, just as it had for Robert Louis Stevenson, whose verse Bradbury greatly admired—the Samoan people had named Stevenson "Tusitala," "teller of tales," during his final dying days in the islands. Yet Bradbury held this poem out of the three major poetry volumes and various compilations he would publish over the next forty years; the single ephemeral publication was in the June 4, 1971, issue of the *Citrus College Clarion*, under the title "Say That I Was a Teller of Tales."

This elusive publication history hid a significant irony, for Bradbury was hardly telling any tales at all during these years. Between 1940 and 1969, he had published more than 260 professional stories, crafting many of these into novelized story cycles and story collections, but throughout 1970 he published but one story—a sentimental Irish tale published overseas in the *Irish Press*. Only two stories reached print in 1971, and just one would appear in 1972.

Given his other priorities, it's a wonder he published any tales at all; Ruth Alben, who started handling his speaking engagements in 1969, was building an ever-increasing calendar of engagements throughout the West Coast and nationally. He was also writing more verse, and Knopf was close to committing to a poetry volume contract. Two significant stage play productions were in the offing for 1972 as well. But he was also deeply engaged in transforming a story fragment and an unproduced animated screenplay into his first novel in a decade—*The Halloween Tree*.

: : :

Given his spontaneous methods of writing and reshaping his fictions, it was almost inevitable that Bradbury would leave a rich trail of precursors. The extended story line was triggered by a partial draft of an unfinished "Halloween Tree" story dated 1959. The following year, a visual interpretation surfaced in the form of a remarkable Bradbury painting of an organic "Halloween Tree" full of pumpkins. In this painting jack-o-lanterns are hanging from the tree, and others have fallen from their branches along with golden leaves to complete the outline of a leafy human body on the ground. Bradbury would later call this composition a visual metaphor for the root system of death.[1]

Renewed enthusiasm for the Halloween project was fired by his reaction to the 1966 animated Halloween television special, *It's the Great Pumpkin, Charlie Brown!* which Bradbury felt had bypassed the imaginative power of Halloween in story and legend. His good friend Chuck Jones challenged him to create an alternative that celebrated the entire tradition. By this time, Jones was a producer and director with MGM's animation and visual arts department, and, with his encouragement, Bradbury began to script an animated history of Halloween that would trace the branching evolution of this ancient celebration down through history.[2]

Here, just as in developing his NASA space program features for *Life* magazine, he would need research guidance. Members of the MGM research department provided Bradbury with background material on Halloween traditions in the Western world. He conducted further library research on his own, making notes to check Celtic and druid references in Sir James Frazer's *The Golden Bough* and Bulfinch's *Mythology*, as well as the June 1960 Stonehenge feature in *National Geographic*.[3] He also relied on the oldest source in his own home office library— Ruth Edna Kelley's 1919 study, *Book of Halloween*. It would serve to evoke the mood and practices of the 1920s Waukegan Halloween practices that formed some of his earliest memories.[4]

By the summer of 1967, Chuck Jones had seen Bradbury's remarkable Halloween Tree painting and urged him to center the screenplay on the tree and its magic. Although Jones was thinking of a half-hour special, Bradbury favored a feature-length animated screenplay with a personification of death orchestrating the action. Over the next two months, he conceived the exotic and vampirelike Carapace Clavicle Moundshroud and placed him in a forbidding gothic mansion inspired by two houses near his childhood home in Waukegan, Illinois. In the completed form of the screenplay, boys in Halloween costume begin their journey through time from this house and its glowing Halloween tree.

With Moundshroud as guide, the children journey back in time to observe the ritualized burials of the ancient Egyptians and even witness the primitive life and death cycles of neolithic man. From these origins, Moundshroud brings the boys through successive cultural manifestations of Halloween, from the Celtic druids and their Roman conquerors to various Roman Catholic traditions that spring from these pagan roots. Notre Dame and its gothic gargoyles, an enchanted broom factory and its resulting medieval witchcraft, Irish folklore, and Mexico's annual Day of the Dead observances at Lake Patzcuaro conclude their adventures through time. Back in Moundshroud's mansion, the boys discover a museum of Halloween traditions rising floor by floor through all the time periods they visited. In this way they learn the origins of their costumes and enjoy Moundshroud's dual "trick and treat" to full measure.

Bradbury revised the script throughout 1968, but production of The Halloween Tree was canceled when MGM closed down animation production. Once again Jones formed a new production company, and soon developed The Curiosity Shop series for ABC. Meanwhile Jones and Bradbury remained committed to The Halloween Tree, and during the fall of 1971 they submitted the screenplay to ABC Television. The Halloween Tree generated immediate interest at ABC, but the network was already committed to an educational run of monthly children's specials for the 1972–73 season; network executives also felt that the holiday-focused material of the story would severely limit the rerun potential and declined the project.[5]

This situation soon became more of an opportunity than an obstacle, for Bradbury had a proven ability to adapt his work across most genres and media forms. As the new decade opened, he was already negotiating with his new publisher, Alfred A. Knopf, for a contract to bring The Halloween Tree forward as a short novel for young readers "of any age." During the summer of 1971, Bradbury contracted to write a 30,000–50,000-word "juvenile fiction" version of The Halloween Tree for publication the following year. By the fall of 1971, he had completed a sustained 118-page draft of the book.[6]

Bradbury kept all the action and much of the original script dialog intact, but he added a new boy, Joe Pipkin, a natural leader who suffers a burst appendix just before Halloween and may not survive. His spirit is trying to evade

Mr. Moundshroud, and he spins back through time to avoid Death. As the boys set out to explore the history of Halloween with Moundshroud, they are also searching for their wounded leader. At every stop, they catch a glimpse of Pipkin, caught in the rituals of ages past.

In his final draft revisions, Bradbury added one new adventure to the concluding chapter—a visit to the catacombs of Guanajuato, where Pipkin's spirit must run a race through the famous gallery of disinterred mummies. While Pipkin tries without success to overcome his fears, Moundshroud asks the other boys to shorten their own lives by a year each in order to save their friend. This pact, sealed with eight boy-sized bites from Pipkin's candy skull apple, gives Pipkin the courage to win his race with death. "That humanized the whole concept," Bradbury would later observe.[7] Pipkin successfully runs the gauntlet, and when his friends follow his spirit home to Green Town they find that he has indeed survived his emergency appendectomy. In this way, Bradbury revisited his 1945 trip through these same catacombs and transformed his own abiding uneasiness with his experience into the climactic episode of his Halloween fantasy.

As The Halloween Tree evolved from screenplay to novel form, Bradbury strove to accommodate young readers without excluding older ones. In early March 1972, Knopf's editors styled Bradbury's submitted typescript for publication and also made deeper revisions to favor a younger reading audience. A reference to cork-popping champagne bottles was eliminated, and Bradbury's "poisonous sweets" (meant in the medieval sense of enchantment) were changed to "incredible sweets." A few brief narrative asides were eliminated, and some of Bradbury's trademark taffy-string phrases were repunctuated. A couple of longer descriptive passages were also lost in the editorial process of tightening the narrative, including a remarkable moment when the candle-lit mouths and eyes of the Halloween Tree's jack-o-lanterns shine on the boys below:

> The boys' faces, looking up, had, printed on them as by shadow-show lantern-light, every kind of grimace, gape and smirk, from every kind of pumpkin mouth.
>
> And in each of their eyes printed bright, was an even stranger reflection of a frightened pumpkin eye.
>
> Tom looked over and saw a thousand images of pumpkin faces trembling on the blind masks of his friends."[8]

Fortunately, only a few such descriptive gems were lost to Knopf's editing. Many of the suggested cuts certainly improved the pace of the plot; no episodes were eliminated, and for the most part Bradbury accepted the changes without argument. Much to his relief, there was greater editorial consensus concerning *The Halloween Tree*'s eye-catching illustrations.

Bradbury's friend and illustrator Joe Mugnaini created many pieces of line art, including chapter headpieces and a number of full-page illustrations that captured Bradbury's aesthetic in ways that only Mugnaini could accomplish.

Masking and unmasking is at the heart of all Bradbury fantasy, and each chapter opens with a highly stylized Mugnaini mask that both reveals and conceals. Many of the masks serve as visual epigraphs, bearing designs that foreshadow the myths and creatures at the center of their respective chapters. Others are more enigmatic, and taken together they all work to extend Bradbury's sense of mystery across the pages of the entire novel. Mugnaini's illustrations accentuate the sense that this novel, perhaps more than any other Bradbury work, focuses the three central elements of his fictions: myths, masks, and metaphors.[9]

Bradbury had once again returned to supernatural fantasy, one of the safe harbors of his earliest success as a teller of tales, but *The Halloween Tree* was much more than a creative refuge—it would also become one of the first significant markers in the final phase of his long career; among his longer works, it remains Bradbury's most playful and life-affirming book of fiction. Here, as in so much of his writing of this period, Bradbury's notion of the ultimate purpose of Mankind was never far below the surface. Tom Skelton's final question—"Will we ever stop being afraid of nights and death?"—is answered by Moundshroud's final telepathic words to him: "When you reach the stars, boy, yes, and live there forever, all the fears will go, and Death himself will die."

: : :

Moundshroud's final words in *The Halloween Tree* could have formed an epilogue as well for Bradbury's opening presentation in the 1972 "Cosmic Evolution" public lecture series, a summerlong program held in San Francisco's Palace of Fine Arts Theatre and Exploratorium. He would be followed by eleven weeks of scientific speakers, including the distinguished MIT physicist Philip Morrison, all addressing aspects of "Man's Descent from the Stars." The series was sponsored by the NASA/Ames Research Center in northern California, the City College of San Francisco, and the Astronomical Society of the Pacific. NASA/Ames became the fourth major NASA facility with which Bradbury had worked; he would eventually engage with at least six of NASA's major research and operations facilities across the United States.

On July 10, 1972, over 3,000 attendees heard Bradbury open the "Cosmic Evolution" series by offering "The Cosmic Perspective"; he previewed his presentation in his usual off-trail style, designed to both showcase and defend his layman's background: "I will be participating as minor-poet and sub-minor philosopher, seeking to explain our age and the great three-billion-year age ahead. Religion will be part of my bent as well as the new shapes of God and Man fusing themselves before us under the impact of technologies."[10] This kind of interrogation of God's creativity and Man's exploring soul would inform many of Bradbury's public lectures through the 1970s and well into the 1980s, as he worked out his settled views on human destiny in the cosmos.

In 1972, he began to slip naturally into an entirely different kind of lecture relationship centered on the world of creative writing. Bradbury's entire seventy-year career was predicated at times on good luck and good timing, and the early 1970s generated an unforeseen moment when the Teller of Tales began to interact with new generations of writers on a more personal level than an isolated lecture could ever provide. In 1972, writer and longtime friend Sid Stebel drove Bradbury up to Squaw Valley, site of the 1960 winter Olympics, for the second year of the writing workshops that would eventually evolve into the Writer's Community at Squaw Valley. During the workshops, the two met San Francisco writer Barnaby Conrad and his wife Mary, beginning a friendship that would last for the rest of all their lives.[11]

Conrad had his doubts about writer's conferences where only published writers were usually invited, and he decided to strike out on his own the following summer with a conference at the Cate School in Santa Barbara. He was a man of wide interests—an accomplished artist, a best-selling novelist, and an experienced matador who had competed in Spain and Latin America. Over time, his charm and his dedication to nurturing writers attracted a number of major authors as workshop directors and guest speakers. The Conrads convinced Bradbury to participate in the 1973 inaugural conference as keynote speaker, and Bradbury would return in this role nearly every year for the rest of the twentieth century. Even after his 1999 stroke, he continued to appear when he could; in 2005, he was finally too ill to attend anymore; his brief "Santa Barbara Beginnings" keynote, recounting more than thirty years of memories, was delivered in absentia.[12]

For nearly all of the intervening years, his keynote provided a reliable ingredient of the Santa Barbara magic. In this way he would interact with Eudora Welty, whom he had read since his early '20s, and Gore Vidal, whom he had met at age 30 in mid-century Manhattan. He came to know William F. Buckley, Charles Schulz, Ross Macdonald, Jonathan Winters, Budd Schulberg, Robert Mitchum, and the influential writing instructor John Leggett at Santa Barbara as well. Yet each of his keynotes represented far more than a ceremonial appearance.

Bradbury would stay at the conference, from its earliest beginnings at the Cate School to a quarter-century residence at the Miramar Hotel in nearby Montecito. He interacted with the up-and-coming attendees, many of whom would have professional careers.

Bradbury's engagement with writing conferences in the early 1970s ran parallel to a very different kind of annual conference presence, one that radiated out through popular culture from the very successful mid-century adaptations of his stories by the accomplished graphic artists of EC Comics. It was a two-way relationship; in childhood, he had learned to read at the breakfast table from the newspaper comic strips, and accounts of his early systematic collecting of these strips, preserved in more than two dozen scrapbooks, were well known. San Diego Comic Convention founder Shel Dorf made sure that his first Con, then a statewide event hosted in San Diego during early August 1970, would include Ray Bradbury among the well-known artists and writers in attendance. As it turned out, Bradbury was a major attraction for participants from around the country, especially from the East Coast comic art establishment.[13]

Bradbury continued to attend as the Comic Convention grew into the national event known simply as ComicCon, offering his help as Dorf overcame problems with some of the early conference sites in and around San Diego. He enjoyed his interaction with young readers who often entered the world of literature through comics, and his support was rewarded by the chance to see old friends who also shared this world, including his favorite mentor-couple, Leigh Brackett and Edmond Hamilton, A. E. Van Vogt, Jack Kirby, and the ever-popular Milton Caniff.

Up-and-coming writers and artists also interacted with Bradbury at the early ComicCons, including Greg Bear, already a Bradbury correspondent during his high school and early college years. Bear was a key planner with the inaugural 1970 Con; later, as a Hugo and Nebula Award–winning author, he became a founding member of the Association of Science Fiction Artists as well, occasionally painting works inspired by Bradbury's science fiction and horror classics. His long friendships with Bear, Greg Benford, and David Brin brought Bradbury in contact with California writers who held doctoral degrees in science, and he appreciated their various efforts to explore humanity in contact with profoundly alien worlds—a challenge that Bradbury perhaps valued above all other science fiction themes.

4 The Prisoner of Gravity

The transformation of *The Halloween Tree* from an unproduced screenplay into a published novel had extended through all of 1971 and
most of 1972; however, this important milestone did not represent the major
distraction from short-story writing, for the plot and much of the text derived
from his preexisting screenplay. The time he might have spent completing and
revising the story ideas that continued to well up from his subconscious was
consumed instead by a half-dozen major projects centered on stage and screen
adaptations. His attraction to success in these forms was no less mysterious to
Bradbury than gravity itself had been to astronomers before Newton; the man
with his eyes on the stars could not break free of earlier projects centered on
his storytelling success with supernatural terrors, magical realism, Midwest
memories, and riders to the stars.

Dark suspense resurfaced first, in the form of a feature-length television adaptation of "The Screaming Woman," originally a 1951 story of a little girl who
cannot get anyone to believe that she can hear the cries of a woman buried alive
in a vacant lot. This project grew out of a Universal Television deal for three
Bradbury stories, initially targeted for Rod Serling's new *Night Gallery* series. That
was Bradbury's expectation, at least, but the deal only led to "The Screaming
Woman," which expanded into a 72-minute made-for-TV movie production that
aired instead as an *ABC Movie of the Week* on January 29, 1972. The expanded format
and budget allowed for a John Williams score and a distinguished cast of film
greats and TV veterans, including two-time Oscar winner Olivia De Havilland,
Joseph Cotton, Walter Pidgeon, and Ed Nelson. Bradbury initially worked on the
project, but the expansion of the story into a full-length film plot was crafted
by scriptwriter Merwin Gerard. The film received critical praise, but very few
elements of Bradbury's edgy tale remained.

: : :

To this point in his career, Bradbury's most sustained attempt to dramatize his
fiction centered on what had become, in 1962, the novel *Something Wicked This
Way Comes*. His powerful tale of a predatory carnival, a terrifying inversion of
all the traveling entertainments of traditional tents and sideshows, had first

surfaced in his imagination in the mid-1940s, but by the early 1970s this work had reached a new stage of intensity. His earlier intermittent efforts to interest a variety of producers and directors had been hampered by Sam Goldwyn Jr.'s hold on rights to adaptation, but by 1971 Bradbury was able to pay back the final $5,000 installment on Goldwyn's original $25,000 option. Now he had a new version of the screenplay under way, and he had attracted the interest of Broadway stage producer Andre Goulston, who was preparing to venture into motion pictures. In early March, Goulston had extensive discussions with Bradbury over possible directors; he had already made contact with British director Jack Clayton and favored Hollywood's Stanley Donen or Robert Wise as well.

Clayton was an old Bradbury friend, having been one of John Huston's assistant directors when Bradbury was scripting *Moby Dick* in 1953–54. He had hoped to work with Clayton again some day, possibly on *Something Wicked*. But Bradbury also knew Robert Wise and sent him a copy of the script as the Goulston discussions continued. Both directors were proven talents in the kind of direction that Bradbury's supernatural tale would need—Bradbury was a great admirer of Clayton's *The Innocents*, an adaptation of Henry James's *The Turn of the Screw*, and he was coming to believe that Wise's *The Haunting*, where the great brooding forces of darkness are ever-present but never seen, was the best film ever made in this genre.

Bradbury went a step further, and suggested Sam Peckinpah, who had already expressed interest in the project. And he could not resist dreams of securing Sir David Lean, whose Academy Award–winning films had captivated him for nearly two decades. It didn't help that a Lean documentary aired just as his discussions with Goulston were in full swing. "The other night I saw the David Lean Special on TV," he wrote to Congdon on March 12th, "and with each of his old films shown I wept with my old love for him. I feel the same way today about Lean that I did when I was 33 and loved Huston, before I got burned. I suppose I shall never grow up."

The intense discussions of March 1971 slowed significantly through the next year, although the rugged Peckinpah and Bradbury met periodically for lunch or dinner. Good food and better alcohol fueled enthusiastic discussions of the film, prompting Peckinpah to describe how he would shoot the book by stuffing the pages directly into the camera. "I have lived in Bradbury country a good part of my life," he asserted during an early June 1971 lunch. "There are Bradbury touches in all of my films." Indeed, *Something Wicked* offered the cold and calculating indifference of predatory evil showcased in so many Peckinpah films; when Bradbury reported this conversation to Congdon, he added, "How can I resist him?"

Peckinpah's directorial career was in high gear, but *Something Wicked* was never far from his mind in the early 1970s. He invited Bradbury and Maggie to a studio film screening followed by dinner at a nearby restaurant, where Peckinpah's surprise guest turned out to be Jason Robards Jr., who played the title role in *The Ballad of Cable Hogue*—an uncharacteristically mild Peckinpah western. Robards was introduced to the Bradburys as the lead character in Peckinpah's vision of *Something Wicked*. Robards would indeed play the lead adult role as Charles Halloway, a decade after Peckinpah and Bradbury parted ways.[1]

The central problem was that Bradbury could not get a firm commitment and, at some point in 1972, he finally offered Peckinpah production and direction rights for a dollar.[2] This was an earnest offer, and perhaps the only way for Bradbury to break through the director's heavy working schedule. Peckinpah was in the midst of releasing five feature films in a six-year span—including *The Wild Bunch*, *Straw Dogs*, and *The Getaway*—and navigating the controversy that the violence of each film would generate. As Bradbury told Congdon, he simply couldn't get the director to hold still long enough to make serious plans. Goulston eventually disengaged and Bradbury optioned *Something Wicked This Way Comes* to Chartoff-Winkler with hopes that Jack Clayton would remain interested in directing. His only mistake was not keeping Peckinpah fully informed, especially given the fact that he had introduced Bradbury to the Chartoff-Winkler production team.[3] Upon hearing the news, he sent Bradbury a small cactus plant and a jar of Vaseline, with instructions for use.

A more tempestuous scenario is hard to imagine, but his hopes for realizing a successful national stage production of *The Wonderful Ice Cream Suit* proved even more aggravating than Peckinpah's gesture. The original story, first published as "The Magic White Suit" in the October 4, 1958, issue of *The Saturday Evening Post*, focuses on a plan by five young Mexican American Los Angelinos to share a strikingly beautiful white suit; each will have to share the cost, but each then gets a magical hour to wear the suit during an evening of dancing.

By the early 1970s, Bradbury thought he had a chance to bring the story to life as a stage musical. He had twice tried, unsuccessfully, to turn this trick with *The Martian Chronicles*, and he had actually succeeded with a small-stage version of *Dandelion Wine* at Lincoln Center. Now he found that Neil Simon was producing as well as writing plays and asked Congdon to send the story on to him. He soon found himself at a private dinner with Simon, hosted at the home of Hollywood's Esther Williams and Fernando Lamas. As often happened, there was enthusiasm but no commitment; nevertheless, by the summer of 1971 he was able to engage pop composer Gary Geld and lyricist Peter Udell, who had just launched their musical *Purlie* on Broadway.

The spring through autumn run of *Purlie* would earn a Tony nomination, but Bradbury's great enthusiasm for the stage managed to corral the team for a two-week stint of work in May that resulted in Bradbury's final 94-page stage book and about 35 minutes of songs by Geld and Udell. On June 2nd, Peter Udell left for New York to pitch the musical to theater-chain owner and film producer Ted Mann, but there were already indications of trouble that would run on for months. The romantic plot and rich Latino setting of "The Wonderful Ice Cream Suit" was bursting with musical potential, but could it survive the personalities involved in creating it?

In the end, Bradbury would be as much to blame for these problems as his lyricist and producer. He was predisposed to get along with his composers, and Gary Geld was no exception. This followed a pattern of respect that originated in his teenage meetings with Sigmund Romberg, Victor Young, and other studio-era composers when he was still climbing over studio walls and prowling the gates for autographs, and this admiration carried over as well into his subsequent working relationships with prominent symphonic Hollywood composers like Miklós Rózsa, Bernard Herrmann, and Jerry Goldsmith. But in Bradbury's mind, the genius behind a successful lyric was another matter entirely. "In the history of song-writing," he wrote to Congdon, "there are only a few lyricists whose work you can sit down and *read*. Cole Porter, Hammerstein, Frank Loesser on occasion, Lerner on occasion, and Noel Coward's "Mad Dogs and Englishmen Go Out in the Noon Day Sun."

Four years earlier, his disputes with his *Dandelion Wine* lyricist Larry Alexander had almost exploded that collaboration, and it was a near-miracle that it reached a 1967 reading production at Lincoln Center. He now transferred the same frustrations to Udell, noting to Congdon that "every lyricist is a frustrated novelist or short story writer, full of beans and dumb. We have had some near-fights already." Bradbury wanted time to polish his newly expanded version of "The Wonderful Ice Cream Suit" as a stage book, and see it walked through on stage before he made cuts. But Udell and Geld had a show running a continent away on Broadway, and Udell wanted to save time and make cuts to the text as he wrote song lyrics. Both men had a point, but the uneasy relationship became even worse when Ted Mann bought into the project.

Mann was the dynamic cinema-franchise owner and entrepreneur who would soon buy one of Bradbury's favorite Hollywood landmarks, Grauman's Chinese Theatre and place his own name on the marquee. He had also moved into film production, and his first producing credit was Warner Brothers' 1969 production of *The Illustrated Man*—a project where Bradbury had felt as if he were an outsider in all aspects of production. Warner Brothers had contracted only for rights, not for a Bradbury script, but he was deeply disappointed in the *Illustrated Man* script that Mann's partner, Howard Kreitsek, wrote for the production, prompting Bradbury to focus many of his frustrations with the film directly on Mann. *The Wonderful Ice Cream Suit* would prove to be an equally frustrating second act to the Bradbury-Mann relationship, but this time Bradbury made the mistake of assuming some of the aspects of a producer that he had long-hated in others.

In mid-July 1971, Mann's list of controlling conditions led Bradbury to demand a contract where cuts or revisions to his stage-book version would be shared—and where he himself would have overall control. His explanation to Congdon exceeded what any writer might expect: "I would like to retain some sort of super voting privilege, if possible, for I sense that my taste is superior to the others committed to this project. That sounds awful, I know, but, damn, it's true. Peter Udell has taste like my foot. Gary Geld is better, nearer to myself. But Mann? I fear him and want a final veto over most of what he does."

In ten years of stage productions, Bradbury's successes were still limited to the adaptations he had produced with his own acting company in the Los Angeles area. His ventures with outside producers and collaborators had either closed early or never been staged at all. The fate of his "Ice Cream Suit" musical would be the same; on October 2nd, he reported to Congdon that even Gary Geld had joined Mann and Udell in affirming what he called the "'fire Bradbury when convenient' clause." The project imploded at that point; Bradbury dropped the Geld-Udell songs, but he continued to work with the underlying stage book. As always, he took the long view. The widely popular actor-singer Harry Belafonte had taken an option on the property before, and he would do so again during the 1970s, but an actual musical production would remain a dream until 1990, when Bradbury formed a durable working relationship with singer/composer José Feliciano.

For now, however, Bradbury felt compelled to fill the void left by the "Ice Cream Suit" failure, and by the fall of 1971 he had turned back to his earlier Billy Goldenberg and Larry Alexander collaboration on the *Dandelion Wine* musical. It's not clear how much of the original score and libretto remained, but he worked with Goldenberg to write five new songs of his own. In part, these lyrics emerged from his expanding passion for writing poetry and were stimulated as well by working, once again, with a composer he admired and trusted. On some level, he knew that his composer was providing most of the magic. In early February 1972, he would report to Congdon that "Billy Goldenberg *beams* at me—his new student. Grand fun." Here also was a rare chance to sidestep his perennial irritation with lyricists; his own lyrics were neither refined nor enduring, and his February summation for Congdon suggests that he had enough sense to know it: "I have finished the complete rewrite of *Dandelion Wine* from start to finish and done five new songs, which have turned out nicely, and in one or two cases super-fine."

He had crafted the *Dandelion Wine* musical revival on his own terms, but who would direct? Bradbury engaged actor Kirk Mee to pull it all together on the California State College campus at Fullerton. Mee proved to be a gifted director who emphasized the camaraderie of the stage, and this talent became clear during the first week of March 1972, just before the curtain went up on opening night, and just as Bradbury stepped backstage:

> The cast and crew, 70 of them, cheered, yelled, stomped, whistled until tears leapt from my eyes. They wouldn't shut up. It went on for two or three minutes and then we joined hands in a great love-circle and our director, Kirk Mee, talked to all of us for a few minutes before the curtain went up on our Premiere performance. And I knew why I keep coming back to the theatre . . . Suddenly there weren't 70 people there with me, but only one person, a vast body of love immensely dedicated and full of joy . . . it was transcendent and beautiful. [ellipses Bradbury's]

He sent this note to Don Congdon the next day, and it captures one of the best moments that Bradbury would ever know in the theater. Here was the same kind of magic that he had known nearly a decade earlier when his Pandemonium Players had staged his triple bill of one-acts at the Coronet Theater. During his teenage years, his passion for acting and writing for the stage at times surpassed his passion for writing fiction. His lifelong attraction to theater was like gravitational force; he couldn't remember a time in his life when the attraction wasn't there, and he would try for the rest of his life to stay within its orbit.

∴ ∴ ∴

The spring 1972 regional success of *Dandelion Wine* seemed a good omen for his next production. Bradbury had learned in the 1960s that audiences in Los Angeles favored the highly emotional focus he could bring to his imaginary journeys into the space age, and he had already decided to take the starship adventures of *Leviathan 99* beyond its initial radio play success and on to the stage itself. Bradbury's success in adapting *Moby Dick* for film eventually led to outlines for a retelling of the story in a novel of his own, played out in deep space, across a sea of stars. He found success with a 1968 BBC radio production in Britain featuring his friend Christopher Lee as Ahab, the blind and driven commander of an interstellar expedition to intercept and destroy the rogue comet that had taken his sight during an earlier encounter.

Less than a year later, unexpected reinforcement for his abiding fascination with leviathans came through his first experience with flight. For decades critics had made much of Bradbury's refusal to drive a car or travel by air, but in January 1969 he accepted an invitation to whale-watch from one of the Goodyear blimps. The combination of first flight—and the low 300-foot cruising altitude along the southern California coast—amplified the experience, and the next day he described the emotional impact of his first whale sighting in a letter to Don Congdon:

> Jesus, it was beautiful. . . . We saw at least 40 pilot whales, two or three hundred dolphins, and finally, two gigantic grey whales, each about fifty feet long and weighing as much as 30 to 50 tons each . . . we circled them low and followed them as they surfaced, blew their spouts, fluked the water, and submerged. I haven't been so excited in years. Old MOBY is just as great and holy and mysterious and beautiful as Melville said. I felt privileged to be aloft in my own helium whale looking down on the miracle.

In the aftermath of his cetacean epiphany, Bradbury completed the refashioning of his *Leviathan 99* radio play into a stage version. True to form, he immediately tried to secure an actor he had always dreamed of writing for—in this case, Sir Laurence Olivier, the actor he had wanted John Huston to sign for *Moby Dick* in the role of Ahab. Bradbury had corresponded with Olivier at great intervals and had actually met him in 1957 in London and again, as Charles Laughton's guest, on the Hollywood set of *Spartacus* in 1960. Olivier politely declined, as did his other choices, Richard Harris and Richard Boone. In the end, Bradbury was able to secure the talents of William Marshall as the space-age incarnation of Ahab. The casting of Marshall would, in the end, prove to be the sole saving grace of the *Leviathan* production.

Marshall was nearly six-and-a-half feet tall, and his commanding presence combined with his powerful operatic bass voice had won international praise for his title role performances in various productions of *Othello*. Bradbury had followed Marshall's career from Broadway to film and television for decades and was aware of his remarkable range as an actor; in 1968 alone, Marshall had starred in an episode of *Star Trek* and in the remarkable *Catch My Soul*, a jazz musical adaptation of *Othello* performed at the Ahmanson Theatre in Los Angeles. Bradbury was able to secure the Samuel Goldwyn Studio Stage 9 Theater for the production; casting was completed on Friday, October 13, 1972, and rehearsals began the following Wednesday for a late November opening.

After all the near misses with media ventures of the past, Bradbury wanted to take as much overall control of the *Leviathan 99* production as he could. He had raised enough to open, but the venue was expensive and, overall, he was far more exposed financially than he had ever been before. On Friday, November 24th, a few hours before the opening, he wrote to Congdon to express his doubts about three key members of his crew—Michael Shere, his expensive and often distracted scenic and lighting director; Joseph Steck, his producer; and even his longtime friend, Charles Rome Smith, who had directed many Bradbury plays for nearly a decade.

Bradbury was characteristically stoic, but he had no illusions about his chances for success: "It will either be a disaster, for technical/casting reasons, or will shamble through to be a moderate success." For all his talent and experience, William Marshall did not immediately settle into the complexities of Bradbury's refashioned Ahab, and there were problems with the technical effects throughout. The *Los Angeles Times* review by Dan Sullivan magnified these shortcomings in a brief and unnecessarily brutal judgment, and that ended all hopes for *Leviathan 99*. Both Charles Rome Smith, who was dealing with his mother's serious illness, and the producer, Joe Steck, left the production before the December 7th closing, leaving Bradbury to direct the final performances and deal with the creditors. Steck had no production experience and disappeared without accounting for the backing money expenditures; by his account, Bradbury would never be able to find him again. In all, Bradbury lost $40,000 on *Leviathan 99* and various investors lost another $20,000.

In all his stage ventures, his great strength centered on his natural optimism and an overarching reflex ability to fix what he could fix during a production run. With three performances remaining, Bradbury reminded William Marshall of Hamlet's famous advice to the players who would perform the fateful play-within-the-play:

> I said, do you remember the directions Hamlet gave the actors? He said, "Yes, I do." I said, "Now, for the next performance, will you 'use all gently,' please? And save your energy for the last scene of the play. But 'use all gently,' and don't gesticulate a lot." He said, "I'll do that," and that night he gave a brilliant performance. I sat there in the audience and I wept. It was too late; the reviews were already in. But I thanked him anyway. And for the next week after that, we had three performances for children from various schools, and they loved it.[4]

In retrospect, Bradbury would feel that he should have designed the entire show for a young audience. And that was it; about forty-eight hours of depression, and then on with the show. A few weeks later, in his end-of-year summary for Don Congdon, he summed it up this way: "I have to balance the disaster of *Leviathan 99* with the lovely memory of *Dandelion Wine*. I can't carp about anything else, really. I am happy about finishing and publishing the Halloween Tree . . . my new poems are coming out fine."

Tellingly, Bradbury did not allude to his almost total lack of story production. What was also left unsaid was his determination to never again expose himself to such a theatrical risk. His unrestrained desire for stage and screen success made him vulnerable to self-styled producers with little or no production experience, and this had cost him dearly. In the future, he would generally rely on such institutional venues as the Eugene O'Neill Theater at Yale or the Arena Stage in Washington, D.C., for larger-scale productions, but these would be few and far between. And he would always bleed funds to some degree, and sometimes even significantly, as he continued to put on local area plays with his Pandemonium Players well into the twenty-first century.

Even larger psychological issues were at play as 1972 came to a close. It was proving harder and harder to move ahead in time simply as "Ray Bradbury," already one of the best-known writers and visionaries of his age. He kept returning to the Past to reconfigure the Now; the various media projects of 1971 and 1972 were all drawn from work imagined—and largely created—between 1945 and 1960. Only his local production of *Dandelion Wine* succeeded and, even then, the play itself and much of the musical structure had been completed and staged during the 1960s. Hardly any new stories were reaching print, and there would be no Bradbury letters dated Apollo Year 4.

But Apollo was now an enduring fact of history, and he had imagined the significance of Mankind's lunar landings long before the concept of Apollo was even conceived. Bradbury's 1956 story, "Next Stop, the Stars," better known as "The End of the Beginning," suggested how the Age of Gravity was about to end: "A billion years Gravity kept us home, mocked us with wind and clouds, cabbage moths and locusts," says a father on the night his son will launch with the first rocket crew into space. "That's what's so god-awful big about tonight . . . it's the end of old man Gravity and the age we'll remember him by, for once and all." Bradbury was part of the Great Tale, and the most effective way he could move into the future would be as a witness and celebrant of the robotic missions already mapped out for the rest of the twentieth century.

5 | Witness and Celebrate

During the 1960s, Bradbury had become more and more comfortable with the observer's role, writing to witness and celebrate the achievements of the Space Age, and it was only natural that by the 1970s he would turn to nonfiction prose and, eventually, to poetry to reach the ever-widening audience that shared his dreams. In February 1972, Apollo 12's Alan Bean wrote asking Bradbury to consider ways for long-mission Skylab crews to maintain "energy, enthusiasm, creativity, and a resourceful attitude on the same level on the 30th or 40th day as it is on the first day." Bradbury would indeed explore such questions in dramatic presentation form, but these verse and choral experiments would take a distinctly different turn from the seemingly endless adaptations of his older work that Bradbury had tried in his stage and film projects.

One of the only verse projects to ricochet cleanly through all of the unconsummated media projects of the early 1970s was *Madrigals for the Space Age*, which was essentially completed between January and August 1970. It was the result of his work as a board member and eventually as president of the California Chamber Symphony, conducted by his good friend Henri Temianka. The Symphony had already found sponsorship and performed his *Christus Apollo* cantata collaboration with composer Jerry Goldsmith at UCLA's Royce Hall, and this success encouraged Bradbury to create a similar mixture of choral and narrated lyrics for a deeper interstellar dream—one that touched on the darker psychological challenges of deep space that had remained beneath the surface of his earlier Apollo celebration. The lone star–bound astronaut of *Madrigals*, frozen in suspended animation, has only the thin thread of remembrance to anchor his sanity:

> Earth falls away
> And suddenly there is no night nor any day
> Nor dusk or sweet sunrise
> And all the cries of children and of men
> Are lost.
> Such is the cost of traveling in Space:
> All memories unraveling,
> All simple sums erase;

Nothing persists.
With Earth now just a star among stars
Suddenly
I do not believe
That Chicago *exists.*

The potential of these lyrics attracted Lalo Schifrin, an established Hollywood composer whose ability to cross-pollinate classical and jazz forms had resulted in distinctive and popular television themes (*Mission Impossible, Mannix*) and feature film soundtracks (*Cool Hand Luke, Bullitt, Coogan's Bluff*). As Schifrin began his long tenure scoring Clint Eastwood's *Dirty Harry* film franchise, he also composed a madrigal score for piano, chorus, and narrator around Bradbury's madrigal lyrics.

Bradbury continued to revise under Schifrin's guidance, and for the most part this involved shortening and eliminating the stream-of-consciousness intervals such as the "Chicago" passage. In the end there were five verse sequences spoken by the narrator, alternating with five performance madrigals for the chorus, accompanied by piano. Bradbury's narrative passages were essentially mood pieces, held together by repeating moments observed between planets and across interstellar intervals:

I walk in Space
I tread the Stars.
I move in emptiness
From Earth to Moon
And then beyond to Mars.
I move, I go, I seek,
I look for answers in the Pleiades.

The verses were now ritualized, serving as recursive moments of space-time reverie, designed to serve as prelude to and intervals between the main performance elements built on Schifrin's music. The Bradbury words sung by the chorus may not have really mattered, in the sense of sequential lyrics; it was sound that mattered, voice and keyboard.

The finished creation was clearly experimental as Schifrin conceived it, and in February 1973 he set the transformed *Madrigals* within his Latin Night concert at the Dorothy Chandler Pavilion. To emphasize the space-age context of the *Madrigals*, Bradbury brought in Apollo 7 astronaut Walt Cunningham, the first civilian astronaut to log space hours on an Apollo mission, to read the narrative intervals. Latin compositions preceded and followed the *Madrigals*, and Schifrin concluded with his own "Rock Requiem."

Arlen Walter wrote the primary review for the *Los Angeles Times*, and he was not impressed by the eclecticism of the evening.[1] There was plenty of criticism to go around, and every composition felt a critical blow based on tempo or balance of the sound that evening. He was very dismissive of the *Madrigals*, which he categorized as "simple kitsch." He liked some of Schifrin's "instrumental effects," but overall the *Madrigals* paid the price for the evening's various digressions from the Latin music that Walter expected to hear. But Cunningham enjoyed his chance to work with Bradbury that evening; he left his reading copy of the score with Bradbury, inscribed in the cover with the opening verses of "High Flight," the time-honored anthem poem of all aviators and astronauts.

The criticism was irritating, but not as devastating for an author who really had very little control over how his concept was finally performed. He had worked with one of the most up-tempo theme composers of the day, and he greatly enjoyed the experience. For this kind of specialized production, Bradbury could maintain with truth that critical acclaim was never a personal goal; he wrote to celebrate his own loves, not to reinforce the intellectual paradigms or aesthetic temperaments of the reviewers. His payoff centered on audience response, and his abiding desire to connect with playgoers who loved the same things he loved about life and human nature.

∶ ∶ ∶

Bradbury's increasingly defiant articles on the termination of the Apollo program culminated not with another jeremiad, but with a sermon, published in the December 1972 issue of *Playboy* magazine, just days after Apollo 17 brought home the last astronauts to walk on the surface of the moon in that first era of space exploration. "From Stonehenge to Tranquility Base" offered the best image he had yet developed to convey the tiny period of cosmic time where Humanity began to reach for the heavens. His central image was vivid:

> Stonehenge. Tranquility Base.
> Try these last on your tongue. Say them aloud.
> Why? Because the shadow of winter ape men on England's ancient moors has reached up to fit an astronaut's shoes and stir the strange dust of the moon. The history of all mankind is in such shadows and such dust. The time span we speak of began three billion years before this morning and will not end ten billion years beyond tonight. But, in mid-stride hamstrung, we have shot down Apollo.

His anthropologist friend Loren Eiseley would have reminded him that the builders of Stonehenge were not fire-wielding apes, but the overall structure of this sermon was otherwise remarkably seamless. His newer arguments of national budgetary priorities remained generalizations, but they were framed for the first time within a larger whole: "It is surely apparent from all I have put down so far that I look upon space not as an experiment in paramilitary physics but as a *religious* enterprise. The proper study of mankind is man. The proper study of God is space. All wheel about one another in concentric gravities. All are one."

He was still fitting his cosmic metaphors together, in much the same way that Johannes Kepler sought a correspondence between gravity and the Holy Spirit centuries earlier. It would be eight more years before Bradbury would finally define his own Space-Age Trinity in an equally intriguing 1980 *Omni* magazine article, "Beyond Eden."

From the mid-60s on, his wonderment with the Cosmos, and indeed his impulse to celebrate many of the miracles of human history and human nature, found primary release through verse. During the high hopes of the Apollo years, as he fully novelized *The Halloween Tree*, he was also preparing the first of three collections of verse he would publish for Knopf between 1973 and 1981.

His influences ran from the nineteenth-century verse of Gerard Manley Hopkins to contemporary poets Phyllis McGinley and Helen Bevington. He was open to all kinds of poetic experiences, from the Metaphysical Poets to anonymous doggerel verse and sea shanties. He thought highly of Eliot, but never completely fathomed his major poems. The sonnets of Shakespeare, the poems of Poe, Robert Louis Stevenson, and Dylan Thomas went right to his heart.

With Thomas, his appreciation was based on sound rather than substance. "I don't know what in the hell he's writing about half the time, but he sounds good, he rings well" (Dylan Thomas had no such problem reading Bradbury, who was one of the Welsh poet's favorite fantasy writers).[2] Bradbury's fair knowledge of the British Romantic and Victorian poets owed a lot to his early mentor Edmond Hamilton. His further reading of the American "Fireside Poets" and the great innovators Dickinson and Whitman came through his own public library browsings and the recommendations of his well-read wife Maggie, whose knowledge of American, British, and European literature ran far deeper than he would ever venture.

By the late 1960s, his early morning reveries, which he sometimes called "the hidden theatre of the mind," had been augmented by a return to writing verse. The odd experiments in poetry that he had sent out to various literary magazines in the early 1940s had lapsed as he matured as a fiction writer, and now a far less self-conscious mode of poetic contemplation held sway during these quiet mornings as he rounded the age of 50. But his poems were no less mysterious than the metaphor-rich prose that welled up in unexpected moments, a process he no longer questioned or tried to force.

He knew his limitations as a verse-writer, but he took his subjects and inspiration most seriously; these ranged from gentle insights about his daughters, aging, or the passage of time all the way to celebrations of scientists, great writers, and our first steps into the Cosmos. Some critics mistook his enthusiasm for ideas as an unwarranted poetic hubris, but his new Knopf editor knew better. Bob Gottlieb, now head of Alfred A. Knopf, had overseen I Sing the Body Electric! and The Halloween Tree; in the early 1960s, during his Simon & Schuster years, Gottlieb had also edited Something Wicked This Way Comes. He encouraged Bradbury's desire to break away from genre labels (he considered him "one of nature's good guys"), but he decided to pass editorship of the new poetry volume over to Nancy Nicholas, who was editing poetry and a wide range of prose authors for Knopf at that time.[3] Bradbury's first letter to Nicholas offered no illusions about his approach to composing verse: "I think you should know now that of course I do not know, on a conscious level, what I am doing. I have loved poetry since I was a child and it has taken me roughly 35 years to begin to let the wonderful stuff come out my fingertips unhampered."[4]

For Bradbury, the working dynamic was different for poetry; he was literally writing the volume as he went along, and Nicholas established an easy process of markup and return until there were enough poems of interest for a slim volume. Nicholas would recommend a sequence, and it all seemed to work out. In a private interview, she recalled how different this was from editing a poet of reputation: "He understood that he really wasn't a poet, that he was writing verse, and he was enjoying it, and he was apparently able to do it very easily and very quickly. And he had his friend, Joe Mugnaini doing jackets. And so it was all a sort of cottage industry. With poetry you never expect to have best sellers, so this was something we could all enjoy doing, because there wasn't a lot riding on it one way or another."

The first volume's title poem recalled his childhood memory of hanging the area rugs out in the yard on clotheslines, like textured elephants waiting to be bathed and cleaned. The title, "When Elephants Last in the Dooryard Bloomed," represented homage to Whitman's Lincoln elegy that was a bit too much for some critics, but critical reception had nothing to do with why he wrote poetry. He was at ease with the process, and Nicholas appreciated his attitude: "He was a model author, he took advice, he didn't get huffy, he knew what he wanted, he understood what I wanted and did it to the best of his ability. It was not dramatic, because he's such a nice guy, and a pro."

She would edit two more volumes of verse, with equally startling titles: *Where Robot Mice and Robot Men Run Round in Robot Towns* (1977), and his final Knopf volume of poems, *The Haunted Computer and the Android Pope* (1981). Nicholas would also edit his next story collection and novel before she moved on to Simon & Schuster in the late 1980s. Bradbury would continue to write verse at intervals for the rest of his life, a creative exercise and an affirmation of life without any illusions of excellence. He just wanted to express and celebrate ideas in ways that he could, occasionally, read at public events. More often than not, these readings would focus on his Apollo-inspired Space Age verse.

In the closing days of 1972, Bradbury found that his cultural achievements across all genres made him a prime candidate for the most elusive cultural exchange program of the day. On December 15, the director of the State Department's Office of Eastern European Programs offered Bradbury a chance to make an official visit to the Soviet Union.[5] This would be a monthlong journey under the Bilateral Exchanges Agreement, and Bradbury would have a choice of cities and venues. He already had summer plans in place for 1973; when he declined, the State Department offered him sponsorship for 1974, urging him to consider a fall or spring trip in language that carried a touch of intrigue: "More interesting people are likely to be available then."

Given his abiding interest in Soviet films and the interest of Soviet filmmakers in his fiction, the Moscow Film Festival was high on his list. He was told that the United States no longer officially participated in this event, and he would have to attend on his own as a private citizen; that complication, along with continuing Soviet intransigence over Don Congdon's repeated requests for reasonable royalty considerations, deferred, at least for now, further discussions of a Russian visit.

A more direct travel sponsorship soon emerged from another—and far older—empire. Writing under the high patronage of Her Imperial Majesty Farah Pahlevi, Empress of Iran, the director of the Eighth Teheran International Festival of Films for Children and Young Adults invited Bradbury as guest of honor for this autumn 1973 event.[6] The focus of the festival greatly appealed to Bradbury, but he was still an earthbound traveler and connections by sea and rail were far too time-consuming to consider. The president of the California Center of Films for Children represented him instead, but Bradbury's beautiful invitation offered a reminder of the politics at the margins of his international fame; the invitation had been opened, and resealed, somewhere between Teheran and Los Angeles.

6   The Sleep of Reason

Bradbury's pace of writing never slowed, but most of his time at the typewriter was devoted to new adaptations of his stories for stage, television, and film. Newer versions of older adaptations inevitably involved a great deal of new writing as well. There were consequences, of course; Bradbury published no new stories at all in 1974. Over the previous four years he had published only six new stories, but the last of these held deep personal meaning. The December 1973 issue of *Woman's Day* contained "The Wish," a story of his father's final days in the fall of 1957, and his final secret words to his grieving son.

It had languished in the magazine's queue for more than a year prior to publication, but that didn't matter to him at all; what did matter was that the magazine had purchased it on the ancient holiday that connected him with all who had come before. "This is, after all, All Hallows Day itself," he told Congdon, "the day that we dedicate to departed Souls . . . so if you had sold the story either on Halloween, or today, or tomorrow, all part of the three-day dark/light celebration, I would have been happy. This is the best sort of news in memory of my Dad."

Bradbury was in his mid-thirties before he really understood how much this quiet and sometimes gruff man had loved him, leaving very little time before death separated father and son. Characteristically, the bond remained with Bradbury in ways that sometimes bordered on the eccentric, and perhaps even the superstitious. "I am a very foolish person about all this," he continued to Congdon. "My Dad subscribed to the *National Geographic* sixteen years ago, before his death. The subscription is still running, and coming to our house, under his name, Leonard S. Bradbury. I haven't had the heart ever to make the final cutting of the invisible thread between life and death. As long as the magazine shows up each month with his name still on the mailing label, I feel reminded of his presence in my genetics anyway."

In such ways, Bradbury's life sometimes offered faint echoes of his early supernatural tales, where Reason abandoned Fantasy altogether—often with terrifying results. "The sleep of Reason produces monsters," observed Goya, whose paintings Bradbury knew well.[1] Toward the end of his life, as Bradbury revisited the "invisible thread between life and death," the monsters were sometimes absent. A major step toward one of these more gently crafted final works played out quietly behind the scenes, as Katharine Hepburn brought him together with director George Cukor to discuss a new film project in the summer of 1974.

Hepburn already knew Bradbury's work; his spring 1971 gift of a book led to an invitation to meet during her stage run of *Coco* in Los Angeles. Meeting backstage after the performance, Hepburn was charmed by Bradbury's third daughter, sixteen-year-old Tina. A second backstage visit, this time with her younger sister Alexandra, began an occasional written correspondence with Hepburn that Tina would always cherish. Bradbury himself already had deep roots in the Hollywood community, but these meetings awakened the young boy who had often climbed the studio walls, now still buried deep within the man. "Hepburn was so kind and direct and lovely," he wrote to Congdon. "Seeing her up close was one of those rare dreams come true. I imagine I have been in love with her for well over 35 years."[2]

Katharine Hepburn had already won three of her four Academy Awards, and during the summer of 1974 she was working once again with George Cukor, a close friend who had directed ten of her films. But Cukor was faced with a challenging project—a groundbreaking Cold War feature film collaboration between American and Soviet filmmakers. The compromise subject was to be an adaptation of Maurice Maeterlinck's 1908 fantasy stage play *The Blue Bird*, and Hepburn advised Cukor to ask Bradbury to write the screenplay. The three met and discussed the project over lunch.[3]

The allegorical heart of the play is the quest for happiness by two children, who search across a vast fantasy panorama for the bluebird of happiness, only to find that it had always been in their own backyard. But through their journeys the children also discover the graveyards of children and even siblings born to an age where child mortality was an accepted tragedy of family life. Bradbury argued against making the film at all, maintaining that even if some parts of the world still buried too many children—and he had seen too much of that himself in Mexico, in 1945—the younger generations in America would not identify with the darker side of *The Blue Bird* at all.

To make his case for the film, Cukor asked Hepburn to read passages of the play aloud to them; Bradbury gently objected, noting that she could read from anything—including the phone book—and he would try to write a script for it. The joke passed, but when she finished reading, Hepburn herself said, "You know something, George? Ray's right." Bradbury would, at rare intervals, offer *The Blue Bird* as a contrast to the gift of longevity bestowed by medical science in more recent times. He spoke once to Cal Tech freshmen on this subject, but in 1982 he offered his most incisive statement for "The Mind and Supermind" series at Santa Barbara City College:

> When the play was written and produced for the first time, how did we spend our Sunday afternoons to visit your family? . . . [I]f you wanted to visit your family, they were in the graveyard! You've forgotten, because you never knew. You are alive, and you don't know what an obligation you have to life, because you are alive tonight because of the medical revolution! My sister is a dead person; one of my brothers is dead. You do not know. In those days, you went to the graveyard to sit and commune with your dead relatives. That's all changed. That's a revolution. I went back to George Cukor and said, "I can't write the screenplay. It's no longer valid."[4]

Hepburn would eventually drop out of the project, which was in fact filmed and released in 1976. Even without Hepburn the cast was formidable; it included Elizabeth Taylor, Ava Gardner, Jane Fonda, and prominent Russian stars. But Cukor had to work with a largely Russian and European crew, often communicating through sign language, and the film was not well received. Bradbury saw Cukor again in November 1980, as they waited in the green room to tape separate sessions of Dick Cavett's PBS *Late Night* television show. Cukor entered the room, went directly to Bradbury, smiled, and said, "You were right."[5] He loved his actors, for he was known as a director who privileged actors over his own reputation, but the enterprise had been more of a political rapprochement than a manageable work of art.

Nevertheless, the 1974 luncheon with Hepburn and Cukor remained one of the best memories of his many years in Hollywood. Afterward, he left to hail a cab, but Hepburn intervened. He was headed to an engagement in Beverly Hills, and she drove him on a meandering route and pointed out homes where she had lived over her forty-year career. As he climbed out of her car, he turned and said, "You know, I hate this, but I'm going to do the cliché thing—I love you very much." She gave him a kiss in appreciation.[6] He would never have a chance to work with her again, but the sleep of reason now released a new dream—the living Kate Hepburn merged in his imagination with the screen star he had admired for decades. In this dual form, she would inhabit Nef, the immortal central character of *Somewhere a Band Is Playing*, a slowly evolving work of magical realism that would take nearly a half-century to bloom.

:   :   :

Other aspects of Bradbury's sense of immortality and creative purpose surfaced in television appearances he would make in 1974. He spoke in a rather limited way about these dreams when he appeared on Tom Snyder's *Late Night*, but that was a three-way conversation that included Gene Roddenberry and Harlan Ellison. Bradbury's fully articulated sense of the cosmos emerged in a remarkable interview with James Day on the television show *Day at Night*.

This two-season widely broadcast PBS series sustained an interview schedule of national and global significance; besides Bradbury, the fifty-three weekly interviewees included composers Richard Rodgers and Aaron Copland, Dr. Jonas Salk, controversial nuclear physicist Dr. Edward Teller, U.N. Secretary General Kurt Waldheim, Muhammad Ali, Jacob Bronowski, Billie Jean King, Agnes De Mille, and writers Katherine Anne Porter, Irving Stone, Christopher Isherwood, and Ayn Rand. Host James Day had been president of two major program-producing PBS stations (San Francisco's KQED and New York's WNET), and his ability to bring out the best of his subjects was masterful. For Bradbury, *Day at Night* "was easy to do," he told his Knopf editor, Nancy Nicholas, after she had seen the broadcast in New York, adding "He is a very relaxing man to work with."[7]

Bradbury's discussion with Day was broadcast on January 21, 1974, and it featured unfettered and concise statements on the existence of humanity as "part of the universe waking up. In this part of the universe, God is wakened, on this planet, and shaped Himself the way we are shaped. We are the flesh of the universe which wishes to know itself." Here was a very narrow beam of light surrounded by the darkness of mystery, but it revealed exactly what he believed. "Everything ends in mystery. Scientists have theories, and the theologians have myths. . . . Religion takes up where the mystery begins."

He had often been just as cryptic in describing the mysteries surrounding his conviction that a writer must bring out all the truths by indirection, through fiction. In his conversation with James Day, he opened up in revealing ways: "Intellect is a danger to creativity, a terrible danger because you begin to rationalize and make up reasons for things instead of staying with your own basic truths." This point of departure led him to describe his intuitive methods with unusual clarity:

> You must never think at the typewriter, you must *feel*. Your intellect is always buried in that feeling anyway. You do a lot of thinking while you are away from your typewriter, but at the typewriter you should be *living*, it should be a living experience. . . . The worst thing you do, when you think, is lie. You can make up reasons that are not true for the things you did. What you are trying to do, as a creative person, is surprise yourself, find out who you really are, and try not to lie—try to tell the truth all the time. . . . Be very active, be very emotional, and get it out of yourself. Making lists of things that you hate and

things that you love. You write about these intensely, and when it's over, then you can think about it, then you can look at it and see if it works or it doesn't work . . . and then if something is missing you go back and re-emotionalize that, and so it's all of a piece. Thinking is supposed to be a corrective in our lives, it's not supposed to be at the center of our lives.

For Bradbury, the typewriter and the occultist's ouija board were one and the same, "your hands move on it and reveal things about yourself you don't know." Aspects of his intuitive method had surfaced in his essays on writing since the mid-1950s, eventually gathered in his *Zen in the Art of Writing*. But this mysterious method emerged most clearly and fully in conversation, and never reached print. The *Day at Night* interview may be the best example that survives. Beyond his interviews, however, Bradbury's often-overlooked book reviews also provide another largely hidden source of self-revelation.

"I have been accused on several occasions of being anti-intellectual," Bradbury observed in opening his 1974 *Los Angeles Times* review of Stan Lee's *Origins of Marvel Comics*. "I plead guilty to the charge." There are perhaps no better exemplars of Ray Bradbury's half-century tightrope walk between popular culture and intellectual acceptance than his wide-ranging 1970s book review selections for the *Times*. His initial reviews included three murder mysteries by Ross Macdonald and equally insightful reviews of Loren Eiseley's best-selling essay volumes, *The Unexpected Universe* and *The Night Country*. Bradbury's long-standing friendships with both Eiseley and Macdonald (the best-known pen name of Kenneth Millar) underscore the literary and cultural abyss that he often bridged.

Two of his 1974 reviews illustrate the range of his appreciation of visual art. In reviewing Archie Lieberman's *Farm Boy*, a twenty-year photographic chronicle of a farm family in northern Illinois, Bradbury avoided the hyperbole he brought to some of his reviews: "The photographs in this book, then, are not brilliant or stunning. That is not their purpose. The book is accumulative in its simple surprises, just as life accumulates in all of us and decides to speak its truths."[8]

Lieberman was a noted photojournalist whose images often appeared in *Life*, *Time*, and *Look*, and Bradbury was able to use his broader knowledge of photojournalism as contrast to his subject's quiet strengths: "Lieberman has not tried for the instant surprise, the intuitive hummingbird flash of a Henri Cartier Bresson who knew just which movements to trap with his camera and so keep truth forever. Bob Capa did the same, in war, and managed to hold terror still to be printed in a darkroom."

Bradbury had met the celebrated Robert Capa in Paris in 1953, just months before Capa's combat death in the last days of French Indochina. Now, nearly thirty years later, he saw Lieberman's study of enduring farm life as an anodyne for the malaise caused by the aftermath of a war without victors, the resignation of an American president, and economic uncertainty. Bradbury, who had voted Republican for the first time in his life to support Nixon as the Democrats cast about for a strong leader, refrained from the political digression that sometimes hobbled his lectures; his review of *Farm Boy* made an indirect but healing reference to these events: "This book is a calm mirror for us to look at in a time of disquiet. With neither distortion toward darkness nor flattery toward the light, it tells us that all things pass and end and all things begin again."

Not surprisingly, he saw Lieberman's talent as a way to exorcise his own demons; in 1978, they would collaborate on a book, *The Mummies of Guanajuato*, a photographic return journey to the visual horrors that had left Bradbury paralyzed with fear during his 1945 travels through central Mexico. His initial attempt to work through the trauma, the very fine realistic 1947 thriller "The Next in Line," formed the centerpiece for *The Mummies of Guanajuato*, but working in tandem with Lieberman's images would finally bring closure.

Bradbury's measured and meditative review of Lieberman's *Farm Boy* appeared in the August 25th issue of the *Los Angeles Times Book Review*. The December 8th issue published Bradbury's review of Stan Lee's new book, which exploded out of the front page of the *Calendar* section under the title "Unleashing the Beast That Makes Men Human." He quickly added fuel to his anti-intellectual guilty plea, sparing neither the Right nor the Left:

> I have no patience with intellectuals who hate horror films.
>
> I would gladly draw and quarter pretend liberals who wind up being reactionary conservatives against rockets and space travel.
>
> And now, with Stan Lee's book *The Origins of Marvel Comics* in my hands, I realize I have one more to add to the list: intellectuals who don't understand comic strips, never read the stuff and advise against it.

Bradbury's bias was not simply based on his own early reading passions (he had in fact learned to read through the Waukegan and Chicago newspaper comics); as Russell Kirk and others had already pointed out, Bradbury's core aesthetic bias was locked deep within his inherent mythopoeic sensibilities. He brought this more refined bias to Lee's defense:

> The premise behind many comic strips is the same one behind most of the Greek and Roman myths: Man cannot control his environment or his life, try as he may. He must then ask help of the gods for superstrength, ask for

magic, ask for controls. In the old myths he got or did not get such controls, depending upon his moral life in the recent past.

In terms of taste, Bradbury's version of the Middle Way had previously surfaced in his occasional sallies against the Museum of Modern Art,[9] and he now refined his merged polarities in great detail:

> If I were asked to describe my ideal "intellectual-with-a-small-i" I would do it thus: a person who can start an evening with Shakespeare, continue with [Fu] Manchu and James Bond, jog further with Robert Frost, cavort with Moliere and Shaw, sprint with Dylan Thomas, dip into Yeats, watch All in the Family and Johnny Carson and finish up at 1 in the morning with Loren Eiseley, Bertrand Russell and the collected cartoon works of Johnny Hart's B.C.

For readers and critics who knew Bradbury's work, the credibility of his "small-i" intellectual catalogue rested in the simple fact that he had read *all* of these authors, and had committed to an overarching respect that, in his mind, leveled *all* genre and cultural biases. Yet in the heat of his argument, Bradbury did not lose track of the inherent value of Lee's history of Marvel. He phrased this value as honest counterpoint to what he called the "great art" pretensions of "the Lichtenstein/ Warhol flimflam":

> I'm not saying the work collected in this book is great art . . . The artwork here is somewhat better and surely no worse than stuff seen in a thousand other comic magazines the past 30 years. What I am saying is that here is some sort of beginning, or for many of you a continuation, of interest in a relatively new medium. . . . Stan Lee's comics are better than Lichtenstein can ever hope to be, because they lack pretension and wind up being just what they set out to be: the creative beast prowling men's cities, knocking down walls for a few hours, so we can go on being and remaining human.

Although Bradbury enthusiastically engaged the Renaissance, Romantic, Impressionist, and Surrealist traditions at home and abroad, his disdain for abstract expressionism at times approached the irrational. But he did understand the history of art in its broader outlines, and he understood the evolving comic tradition of the twentieth century, both as a collector and as the subject—through the efforts of EC and eventually Byron Preiss—of some of the most talented graphic artists of his time.

Bradbury's balancing act between high and popular culture was made even more apparent over in the *Book Review* section of the same December 8th issue of the *Times*, where he also published a review of *Himalayas*, the best-known art book by Japanese photographer Yoshikazu Shirakawa. Bradbury was no doubt drawn to the book by Arnold Toynbee's preface (he admired Toynbee's Challenge and Response philosophy), and Sir Edmund Hillary's introduction (he had met Hillary in London shortly after the Everest ascent).

But the Shirakawa review also reflected Bradbury's understanding of the sublime and the terrifying, the impressionistic and the surreal, which bridged his abiding preference for the beauty of the human form in Renaissance art and his parallel appreciation of natural grandeur in landscape painting and photography. If Bradbury took on the intellectual establishment from time to time, as he had once again done in the Stan Lee review, he did not do so in darkness.

7 The Inherited Wish

"I have the feeling that I was born to be me." This is how Ray Bradbury interpreted the essence of Sir Laurence Olivier's explanation of his own life, which Olivier viewed as an inherited wish, a biological imperative translated, over time, from his genetic heritage into a distinguished life in theater. Bradbury had seen Olivier offer this explanation in a January 1973 interview with Dick Cavett on ABC's *Late Night* show; a few weeks later he tried to parse Olivier's words to fit his own life as he drafted "The Inherited Wish," an introduction for Bill Nolan's *The Ray Bradbury Companion*.

Nolan's *Companion* was published in 1975, an oversize boxed bio-bibliography that documented Nolan's quarter-century sideline as a comprehensive chronicler of his close friend's career. In a sense, it was a proto-biography and it offered the author a chance to look back through the lens of his "Inherited Wish" introduction. Bradbury interpreted Olivier's observation not as a single beginning, but as a recursive process of renewal: "If someone slapped me on the back the hour I was born, causing me to yell, then every morning I feel the same slap and know some sort of rebirth, simply because I know I am alive for another day and able to write down yet another surprise."

This passage was considerably toned down from his near-final draft ("Jesus Christ, I must have been delivered in the Notre Dame belfry when the Hunchback was ringing changes and wild sportive rambles on Bach with the damn bells"). Yet even the restrained final draft opened the door to a hyperbolic romp through the catalog of obstacles facing the 1940s genre writers who would bring the weird and the science fictional into the literary mainstream. "The Inherited Wish" was simply intended to entertain and to celebrate the things he loved and wrote about, but there were moments of well-phrased insight as well. Bradbury compellingly captured the mid-century turning point where intellectual tyranny had even the most scientific of the science fiction authors facing this unbearable possibility:

> What if what the bright apes said at their literary teas was true? What if science fiction, after all, wasn't even so much as a crippled shadow on the far outside wall of Plato's much-talked-about cave?

What if instead of reality being compassed by our imaginative flights, it had always escaped us, and we were merely kidding ourselves about Space, Time, Eternity, mankind and his robots, humanity and its dreams?

He went on to chronicle how he and others began to squeeze out from under the hostile American pastime of "labeling-in-order-to-conveniently-dismiss-and-forget." This would not be his first brush with the intellectual establishment, nor would it be his last. "The Inherited Wish" celebrated what had been overcome early in his career, but it remained to be seen how he would break out of the growing perception among his friends and publishers that his storytelling powers were now feeding lesser work in other genres.

In early 1975, and for the second year in a row, Bradbury opened the year with a quality television interview experience for public broadcasting distribution. On January 28th, almost exactly a year after his well-received interview for James Day's *Day at Night* program, the influential poet and memoirist Maya Angelou interviewed Bradbury for Portland's KOAP television's widely distributed series, *Assignment America*. Angelou, whose stage, television, and film successes were in full swing, knew the world of media adaptation that had distracted Bradbury from his true calling as a teller of tales. Once again, Bradbury found himself comfortable within the programmatic parameters of public television.

This time, however, there were no carefully styled studio walls to confine him; Angelou interviewed Bradbury in Magic Castle, one of Bradbury's favorite stops in Hollywood since his teenage years. He offered Angelou a variation on what he had told Day about his settled views on faith and science: "There's really no split between science and religion. Where facts stop, faith has to take over."[1] Clearly, he was shaping this notion into a more concise, portmanteau talking point. His discussion with Angelou may also represent the first time he used, at least in broadcast form, what would become one of his most famous catch phrases: "We're an impossibility in an impossible universe."[2]

An even more intriguing cultural encounter came a few months later in the spring of 1975, when Bradbury attended a performance by the world-renowned mime Marcel Marceau at the Schubert Theater in Los Angeles. Afterward, he went backstage in hopes of a meeting. Marceau hurried out, saying, "You may know me, but I *know* you." Bradbury quickly discovered that Marceau had read a number of his books and was interested in creating a mimed stage show around some of his stories.[3] They met for several late dinners (Marceau never took a meal before performances and dined close to midnight). The artist was headed to New York for performances at City Center, and Bradbury asked Congdon to meet him and make contact with his agents there.

The plan was to develop a show in mime to be performed sometime in the next twelve or eighteen months, and Bradbury created an intriguing concept around four of his tales of space travel—the opening "Rocket Summer" bridge from *The Martian Chronicles*, "Kaleidoscope" from *The Illustrated Man*, and two more *Chronicles* tales, "The Third Expedition" ("Mars Is Heaven!") and "Night Meeting." Bradbury wanted to contrast the alternating brilliance and fathomless blackness of outer space, under the two-line working title

Dark Worlds & Light
Light Worlds & Dark

He even designed a logo for the cover page that reflected the collaboration:

Marceau	Bradbury
Bradbury	Marceau

Bradbury had once planned an illustrated *Dark Carnival* novel without words; now, with Marceau, he was enchanted with the idea of, in effect, a stage play without words. He typed up a three-page description of the stories as mime. The closing "Night Meeting," an encounter across thousands of years of time between the spectral image of an ancient Martian and Gomez, an equally ephemeral present-day Earth colonist on Mars, showed the depth of Bradbury's understanding of the show's potential:

Each can see through the other. They can pass their hands through each other, so neither knows whether the other is a ghost or real. This act could be pantomimed by using the black-magic techniques of Victorian stage illusionists; that is with one dancer being reflected in a large clear pane of glass. In reality the Martian would be dancing off-stage. We would see only his reflection on the stage itself in the pane of glass, where he would fade or come clear as we raised or lowered the light on him, off-stage. The use of his reflection in this manner, would allow the real dancer, Gomez, on center-stage, to "pass" through the illusion of the Martian on occasion, simply by passing through the "reflection."[4]

Marceau continued his American tour through New York and Boston, but he also kept in touch with Bradbury at least through May. The plan was to develop the show for a Paris premier; this was the heart of Marceau's territory, and Paris would also attract Bradbury's strong French following in Surrealist artistic and literary circles. Unfortunately, there is no record of Marceau's response to Bradbury's outline, and no other correspondence survives. The project would remain, like the Earthman and the Martian of "Night Meeting," mute and ephemeral reflections of what might have been.

Even though he was not able to collaborate with Marceau, he would soon be able to reprise his collaboration with Lalo Schifrin through a second performance of *Madrigals for the Space Age*. For the 1973 premier, Schifrin had embedded *Madrigals* within an evening of Latin symphonic pieces by various artists that the *Los Angeles Times* reviewer considered devoid of continuity and at times out of balance with the choral accompaniment. *Madrigals* returned to the Dorothy Chandler Pavilion, but this time the work would have a completely different environment. On January 17, 1976, the Los Angeles Master Chorale and Sinfonia Orchestra selected *Madrigals* for a bicentennial concert featuring the distinguished American composer Aaron Copland as guest conductor. Copland opened with two of his own works and a new choral composition by Paul Chihara; after intermission, Copland conducted *Madrigals for the Space Age* and closed the bicentennial concert with more of his own compositions and his signature arrangements of old American songs.

Along with Aaron Copland, the best-known concert participant was veteran actor James Stewart, who performed Bradbury's narration for *Madrigals*. "Thanks for the wonderful words," Stewart would inscribe on Bradbury's program. The new setting made all the difference in bringing out the best aspects of Schifrin's music, which the program notes described as "the lean economy of means" with chorus and piano-only orchestration. Bradbury was thrilled by the turn of fortune for *Madrigals*, and he did not fail to present his Space Age vision once again in his own contribution to the program notes. "I have been astounded over the years, to see little being done in the musical field having to do with mankind's destiny in Space. Up until this year, very few lyricists or composers have entered the field. *Aniara*, the Swedish opera, is the only title that comes to mind."

He was an admirer of the twentieth century's mystical and mythological compositions of Gustav Holst and Vaughan Williams, but in music, as in literature, Bradbury wanted contemporary composers to bring humanity directly into the mix. Ever passionate and occasionally combative on this theme, Bradbury closed his program note by locking horns with what he continued to see as the principal cultural obstacle that had prompted him to write the *Madrigal* poems in the first place: "When the final history books are written (and I stake my heart and soul on this) it will be said that I was right in my guess, my intention, my inspiration, and my will, while the intellectual mob which turned its face away from Space, was deeply wrong."

Other major stage productions of his story adaptations were performed in other cities during the mid-1970s. Bradbury allowed writer/producer Peter John Bailey to tour a "story theater" version of *Dandelion Wine* for winter 1975 performances in New York and eventually for a March–May 1976 run in Chicago. Performances also ran at the 500-seat Kreeger Theatre of the Arena Stage complex in Washington, D.C.; Bradbury was not able to see these versions, and he was somewhat frustrated by his lack of creative control. He was, however, pleased that the Arena Stage productions were strengthened by modifications introduced by founder Zelda Fichandler and her production company.

From November 1975 through March 1976, the Chicago-based Organic Theatre Company reprised the company's original 1973–74 production of *The Wonderful Ice Cream Suit*. The remarkable original cast returned for the 1975–76 run; this ensemble included stage veteran Joe Mantegna, on the threshold of his distinguished film career, and two actors destined for prominent television careers—Dennis Franz and Meshach Taylor.[5] Bradbury was able to attend one of the final Chicago performances along with Harry Belafonte, who had explored stage adaptation rights for *The Wonderful Ice Cream Suit* story in the late 1960s.

Shortly after seeing the March 1976 Organic Theatre production, Belafonte began another series of negotiations to produce his own stage version. Like Bradbury, a range of projects kept his schedule in constant flux, but Belafonte remained enthusiastic about transforming the story into a stage musical centered on empowerment within the Latin cultures of the New World. He was eventually able to lay the foundation for his concept with writers and composers who knew the cultural milieu, but Belafonte's many other projects prevented the option from becoming a reality. As time permitted, he actively sought backing for two more years, even circulating Bradbury's traditional stage version as well as his own musical to see which approach resonated in New York.[6] Bradbury had great respect for Belafonte's talents and vision, but he was never comfortable with politicization of a story and play that he had always considered a romance. He gently advised Belafonte against pursuing yet another option window, and the two remained friends in spite of these unfulfilled dreams.

: : :

Bradbury's early 1976 trip through Chicago for the final *Ice Cream Suit* performances represented the return leg of a railroad odyssey from California through Florida, where he was able to set eyes on Disney World and see the recently renewed planning for EPCOT. He was now part of the Disney planning forums, but the high point of the trip would be a couple of hours away, where he was honored with a tour of Cape Canaveral and the unimaginably vast main Rocket Assembly Building.

The experience had such an impact that, at first, he had no idea how to write about it. "I arrived there," he later told his British publisher, Sir Rupert Hart-Davis, "and stood weeping with amazement and happiness, but unable to find the metaphor to write about the incredible experience of being up on the gantries looking down at the Apollo rockets below me like immense toys. Then, on the way to my train I said it's like walking around inside Shakespeare's mind! . . . it was only a few minutes before the enclosed long poem exploded onto paper as I rode cross country on a night train!"[7]

The poem he sent Hart-Davis, "Thoughts on Visiting the Main Rocket Assembly Building at Cape Canaveral for the First Time," was full of childlike wonderment conveyed through a constant barrage of images, but the central conceit was intriguing:

> "Othello's Occupations?
> Here they lie—in countries where the spacemen
> Flow in fire and much desire the Moon
> And reach for Mars."

No room for quiescent Hamlet here; Othello's backstory of achievement was more apt, allowing Bradbury to run his own catalogue of future achievements and close with a Shakespearean command to "Act out the Universe!" It would appear as "Thoughts on Visiting Canaveral" in his 1977 collection of poetry, *Where Robot Mice and Robot Men Run Round in Robot Towns.*

Bradbury also read this poem at the July 2, 1976, NASA symposium held just weeks before the Viking I landing on Mars. He was in good company; the other panel participants included best-selling novelist James A. Michener, MIT physicist Philip Morrison, and undersea explorer Jacques Cousteau, all gathered in Cal Tech's Beckman Auditorium to discuss the timely topic, "Why Man Explores."

Moderator Norman Cousins, longtime editor of the *Saturday Review*, contextualized Bradbury as the leading visionary of Space-Age exploration, prompting Bradbury to define his role as he saw it. "I can service the cause by trying to find metaphors to fit what we are doing. . . . That's my business—to find the metaphor that explains the Space Age, and along the way write stories." Characteristically, he went on to criticize the roadblocks that technology-driven culture had created. "We Americans suffer from too much data, from too many facts, at times. . . . We have been given the facts over and over again, and they are always diminished by what I call the aesthetic of size. Television diminishes everything it touches and makes it small."[8]

Jacques Cousteau agreed. "There was nobody like Ray Bradbury to force NASA to make really striking films," he maintained, and went on to label NASA's detail-oriented public relations, ponderous organization, and red tape as "the enemies of exploration that are there immediately as soon as a big exploration tries to organize." What Cousteau knew from long experience, Bradbury was now beginning to research on his own. During his recent trip to Cape Canaveral, he had researched the comparative budgets of NASA and the Department of Defense.

He was by no means a numerate thinker, but the proportional comparisons cut through the details in compelling ways.

From this point on, he began to identify the "enemies of exploration" in just such terms whenever he spoke of the Great Tale. Over time, Bradbury would be aided in defending NASA's funding by the introduction of larger flat-screen televisions that he and other writers had foreseen since mid-century, and by images from the great orbital eyes of the Hubble and Kepler telescopes projected into millions of homes. He would live to see both instruments serve as NASA's greatest publicists of the new century.

∴ ∴ ∴

On many fronts, 1976 was a good year for Bradbury. At such times, he always assessed how his publishers were responding, or not responding, to his broader successes. His long-term paperback contracts with Bantam and Ballantine provided a significant and dependable flow of royalty income, even if half of all of his Bantam sales income had to be shared with the originating hardback trade publishers of his books, who periodically let his hardbound editions fall out of print. That was the custom of the book trade, and not Bantam's fault; but, lately, Bradbury had detected diminishing enthusiasm in Bantam's editor-to-editor discussions with Knopf over the pending paperback rights to Long After Midnight.

In late July 1976, he wrote to his longtime Bantam editors Oscar Dystel and Marc Jaffe about this. His objective was to trigger a healthy cash advance and royalty percentage for Long After Midnight, and to get Bantam to spin up what he perceived as a low-energy marketing and reprinting effort for his paperbacks, which were among the steadier selling titles, if not best-selling. He certainly understood this distinction ("Do you realize there are times in my life when I wake up and actually wish I were Louis Lamour? God, what a dream that was!"), and he knew that his cultural significance rose in part from the successive generations of readers who encountered his books in this format.

In the end he received his usual terms through Knopf for the Bantam paperback of the new collection, and his five-year renewals on his other titles continued, for now, for his earlier Doubleday, Simon & Schuster, and Knopf titles. Bantam also expanded their illustrated boxed-set issues of his works, with three slightly different five-book combinations marketed over the next two years in the United States and Britain. Bradbury's sometimes unreasonable ego burned through the paper of his letter, but his relationship with most of his editors was strong enough to bear the occasional tirades. "Is this the talk of an elitist? It damn well is. I get spoiled by high school and college kids who tell me they love me and want me to live forever. That kind of talk is heady and wondrous."

8 | *Long After Midnight*

The selection of stories for Long After Midnight set the pattern for all of the Bradbury collections that would follow during the second half of his career. He had published very few stories since the 1969 release of I Sing the Body Electric!; he gathered seven for the new collection, and added two more recent stories that had not placed in magazines at all. Bradbury would need more than twenty tales, and he began to survey uncollected stories published further back in time. He turned to Bill Nolan, whose long history as friend and chronicler combined with his recent deep research for the Bradbury Companion to offer a full command of all the uncollected stories that remained from the deep past. This familiarity, as well as his own instincts as a successful short story writer, led to the selection of some of the strongest stories that remained uncollected.

Nolan was perhaps too close to the older stories, both professionally and as a friend, and he came up with a total of thirty-five in his initial file search for the collection.[1] Eventually, twenty-three tales went to Nancy Nicholas and Bob Gottlieb for review at Knopf. Bradbury was worried about "I, Rocket," one of the Nolan choices and the earliest published story selected. This survivor from the May 1944 issue of Amazing Stories had the trademark Bradbury off-trail quality that early readers found intriguing—a combat rocket with personified intelligence and a deep love for its combat crew narrates its own story. It predated his better science fiction of the later 1940s, however, and his attempt to hand-revise the galley sheets proved fruitless.[2]

The twenty-two remaining stories went forward without any apparent sequence of old and new or even a hint as to the vintage of each tale. The overarching title was a favorite that he had preserved like a lambent flame for more than a quarter century; "Long After Midnight" had been the working title for "The Fireman," the earliest complete version of Fahrenheit 451; that working title remained unused in print until 1962, when he bestowed a variant, "The Long-After-Midnight Girl," on an unremarkable tale buried in the winter 1962 issue of Eros. For the new collection, he retitled the story "Long After Midnight" and made it the volume's title tale.

Knopf's dust jacket made Long After Midnight the perfect title—the choice of John Henry Fuseli's 1781 oil, "The Nightmare," combined to create a masterful dust-jacket cover effect. But the title story itself was an underdeveloped mood piece, evocative of an unsolvable noir murder with the legendary Bradbury twist ending, yet without the detail and texture of his better work. Six of the older stories were strong, however, a testament to the magic that the combined Bradbury-Nolan memory banks had resurrected, as were four of the newer ones. These ten would have to carry the collection, and they did so by evoking the observation that Bradbury had placed in the midst of his 1970s tale "The Wish": "God gives us dreadful gifts. The most dreadful of all is memory."

Most of the ten tales explored memories of the inexorable pull of death in life, seen from different chronological points in his already long career. The collection led off with "The Blue Bottle," a Bill Nolan favorite originally published in the Fall 1950 issue of *Planet Stories* as "Death Wish." "The Blue Bottle" may have been Bradbury's original intended title, for it evokes the irresistible attraction to death that the Blue Bottle decants whenever it is found and tasted by the lonely treasure hunters roving the barren terrain of Mars. Ever one to generalize about human nature, Bradbury was convinced that only men exhibited the death wish, and here only one of the five desperate wanderers who find it, a happy man of no imaginative powers at all, is free of the death wish compulsion. He only sees and tastes what he searches for—a wonderfully distilled bourbon blend.

"Drink Entire: Against the Madness of Crowds" was one of the best of the new stories, offering an updated exploration of death and life through a big-city variation on a timeless tale of enchantment. The forlorn commuter, worn down by his corporate job, is offered everything he desires if he marries the unseen witch in the shadows of her back-alley shop. He is greatly tempted by this once-only offer, but he fears the unseen too much to accept. He tells a friend at work, who accepts. Fates are set in motion, and the ending is vintage Bradbury.

But the great dark tale at the center of the collection was the deceptively titled 1954 story, "Interval in Sunlight." There is no true sunlight in sun-filled Mexico for the young American writer; her husband's constant and abusive efforts to control every aspect of her life ruined the vacation before it ever started. She is trapped in the marriage, trapped in Mexico, and traumatized by the cruel indifference of her husband and the land itself. The writer is unnamed, but the events reflect all the trauma of Bradbury's three-month automobile odyssey through Mexico in the early fall of 1945.

"Interval in Sunlight" was actually written in 1947, shortly after Bradbury completed his far better known "The Next in Line," which reveals the horrific climax of the wife's entrapment when she encounters the famed Mummies of Guanajuato. "Interval," in effect, represents a prequel that lays out all the interpersonal dynamics of Bradbury's 1945 trip. His friend Grant Beach suggested the trip to collect native masks for the Los Angeles County Museum; Beach had a car and could drive, and Bradbury had a windfall from three stories he had recently sold to the major market magazines. They traveled on Bradbury's money, and Beach's increasingly menacing dominance and his constant hypochondria exacted a far greater price.

At times during the journey they traveled with his Aunt Neva's friend, photographer Anne Anthony, and writer Renee Tallentyre, who were researching a potential Mexican article for *National Geographic*. The constant presence of poverty and death in a culture where Bradbury could not speak the language took its toll. "None of us belonged in Mexico," he reflected six decades later. "It wasn't the right place to be." In both stories, the writer is a blend of two realities. "I took the identity of the woman, who's a composite of Anne, and my own fears, of course. So it was a nightmare."[3]

Two of the stories that Bradbury had sold to finance the trip to Mexico were also pulled into *Long After Midnight*. "One Timeless Spring" (*Collier's*) and "The Miracles of Jamie" (*Charm*) were both published in April 1946, accelerating his postwar move into the mainstream magazines. The other strong stories from his early career were "Forever and the Earth," his resurrection of Thomas Wolfe in the far distant future, and "A Story of Love," capturing that moment when a high school student falls in love with a teacher. Both of these stories cycle back to the grave, as does "The Wish," representing one of the great wish fulfillments of his life—a chance to see his father again, so that they could both say the word that never passed between them in life.

Long After Midnight was released on August 31, 1976. New and old, a few gems peaked out from Bradbury's otherwise unrefined ore. But of the newer stories, only "The Wish," his Martian tale "The Messiah," his supernatural chiller "The Burning Man," and "Drink Entire" were on the level of the six strongest older tales. Were they enough to carry the verdict of the reviewers for all twenty-two?[4] His old friend and fellow writer, Theodore Sturgeon, tallied the score in his *Los Angeles Free Press* review, cautioning "whether, for any one reader, the hauntings plus the celebrations will add up to 22, is a highly individual thing. Some of the stories might strike the reader as wishful whimsies." Sturgeon was frustrated by the hidden evolution of the stories showcased here, wishing that the collection had been arranged chronologically.

Other reviewers also criticized the somewhat bricolage nature of the compilation. The *Baltimore Sun* found it to be "a pickup collection of new stories from Bradbury mixed in with much older work as yet unanthologized," counting only seven stories worthy of the master. The very negative *Boston Globe* review, which revealed more about the reviewer than it did about Bradbury, valued only three of the old pulp stories and classified the overall contents as "out-takes from previous gatherings" that "crept up from Bradbury's wastebasket." This was in part another reaction to the veiled provenance of the collection; even the copyright page was abbreviated. The *Harper's* magazine reviewer also questioned the selection strategy but conceded more of the gems: "This collection underlines Bradbury's weaknesses as well as his strengths. The book is a catchall, and not all its choices are wise."

It was problematic that *Long After Midnight*, like many of his later collections, garnered very few major reviews. Besides the savage *Boston Globe* review and the short *Harper's* notice, there were positive reviews in the *St. Louis Post-Dispatch* and the *Los Angeles Times*. The *LA Times* guest reviewer was Sid Stebel, a writer and well-known teacher of writing who had been close to Bradbury since the late 1940s. Stebel digressed a bit to tell the stories behind some of the Bradbury stories and conceded that some of the tales were unresolved, yet he offered a reminder that Bradbury's "style and technique, his use of language and metaphor" offered much "for those who would seek to match him."

One final review of note appeared after the spring 1977 British release of *Long After Midnight*. In May, Tom Hutchinson of the *London Times* singled out "Interval in Sunlight" as a masterpiece of "the horror of claustrophobic relationships." Hutchinson was guarded about the rest of the collection, but he found the underlying Bradbury to be "the best kind of primitive. He hits hardest at the heart, not the head. That is why so many pay him so much regard. That is why he is still a master—but one to whom we should pay the compliment of being wary, to see that he does justice to us as well as to himself."

Both Stebel and Hutchinson offered implicit reminders that Bradbury's relevance would not be undermined by his diminishing output of new short fiction. But Sturgeon's *Free Press* review offered an observation about Bradbury's storytelling voice that could be problematic if this diminishing trend continued. "Not everybody in a Bradbury story talks like Bradbury-the-Narrator, but a great many do." Often this worked, but as his late-century stories became more and more underdeveloped and anecdotal, this characteristic became more of a liability. As Sturgeon also pointed out, readers either love Bradbury or dismiss him. In spite of the stronger tales mixed into this collection, *Long After Midnight* did little to change the score.

The larger reason that *Long After Midnight*'s reception did little damage rested in the longevity of the early Bradbury titles that continued to sell in sturdy little Bantam and Ballantine mass-market paperbacks. Parents sometimes lost the urge to read his stories, reinforcing, in a way, Bradbury's abiding sense that, like insect and chrysalis, adults and children were two distinctly different forms of life. In his *LA Times* review, Sid Stebel posed this perennial phenomenon in the form of a rhetorical question: "What parent has not had a child thrust a Bradbury book into his hands, announcing a 'discovery'? What do these children know—sense, feel—that parents do not?"

: : :

The final days of 1976 capped a yearlong resurgence of involvement with the Disney World EPCOT project that had been set aside when Monsanto declined to sponsor the original "Yestermorrow Time Machine" concept that Bradbury had put together with Disney artist-designer Marc Davis in 1970. The successful 1971 opening of Walt Disney World's Magic Kingdom had proven the viability of the East Coast theme park, and by the mid-1970s, Disney's Marty Sklar brought the WED's (later Walt Disney Imagineers) creative focus back to building the EPCOT concept. In 1975, Imagineer Peggy Fariss began a series of conferences to define how the "Experimental Prototype Community of Tomorrow" would merge entertainment with the aspects of progress that defined American life going forward.

Bradbury was an early and prominent invitee to these conferences, known as EPCOT Forums. Here he would enter lasting relationships with such designers as John DeCuir Jr., an architect by training who was a project designer for EPCOT, Spaceship Earth, and related attractions. DeCuir, like his father, John Sr., worked on many major film productions, but as an architect he and prominent mall designer Jon Jerde would later bring Bradbury back into the perennial public discussions on the use of communal space throughout the Los Angeles region. At this point, however, Bradbury was still focused on extending his "Yestermorrow Time Machine" history of Mankind storyboard narrative into more expansive visual snapshots for the emerging Spaceship Earth interior ride concept.[5]

By December 1976, Bradbury had built in a long digression highlighting the Centennial of 1876 as a major milestone in the American journey, imagining Andrew Carnegie proclaiming his vision through Old Testament allusions: "Against the night, let's build a fortress wall of books! With bankroll, thus! I strike the prairie rocks! Let books gush forth! 11,000 libraries, now, rise! New caves where men can warm their souls and cook Ideas!" Famous book characters shout down from the shelves, invoking a cavalcade of classic novels. Some months later, Bradbury would actually write to the Carnegie Corporation, discovering that his imaginary Andrew Carnegie built far too many libraries, and built them years ahead of the actual Carnegie Library era.[6] WED's Imagineers would help him compress the narrative of his "EPCOT Theatre Concepts" to fit the actual 1982 Spaceship Earth experience; even then, it was too abstract and poetic, requiring further revisions several years after the great sphere opened,[7] but Bradbury's core emotional message—his faith in humanity, and his desire to celebrate human potential—always remained at the heart of the ride's narrative.

But 1976 marked an important advance in the design of EPCOT and the transition from EPCOT Theatre to Spaceship Earth. To finish the year, Marty Sklar and John Hench brought Bradbury down to the WED labs in the "MAPO" building to focus the vision. Just two days before Christmas 1976, Bradbury addressed a large gathering of Imagineers, interpreting his charge from Hench and Sklar as a mission "to come up here and explain you to yourselves."

He compared his 1954 discovery of the Renaissance world in Rome, Florence, and Venice to his equally astonishing discovery, just a few months later, of the Sleeping Beauty production art stored at the Disney Studio. Here were the magnificent *Sleeping Beauty* background paintings of Disney artists such as Eyvind Earle, whose work Bradbury would begin to collect in years to come. Looking back from the vantage point of 1976, he gave his blessing: "And so, really, what you are is Renaissance People. If ever there was a Renaissance organization, this is it. . . . the whole world's going to be looking at you."[8]

He went on to compare the equally impressive mechanical wizardry of the Imagineers to the nineteenth-century precursor technologies he discovered in 1969, when he first encountered the grand Victorian Age mechanisms curated in London's Victoria and Albert Museum. This was high praise indeed for Disney's fabricators of animatronic wonders, but it was Bradbury's overarching proclamation of "Renaissance People" that endured in the minds of this entire generation of Imagineers, and all that would follow.

9 A Mailbox on Mars

Just weeks before his *Long After Midnight* story collection was published, Bradbury found himself in the Jet Propulsion Laboratory control room for the landing of Viking 1. It was, in fact, long after midnight when he arrived—3:45 A.M.—on the morning of July 20, 1976. Mars was his world, in a cultural sense, both nationally and internationally (young Russian readers joined Bradbury clubs all over the Soviet Union), and he found himself toasted as much as *Viking* was as it landed and began sustained surface contact with JPL. All of the major NASA players were there; once again he met Wernher von Braun, who was retiring from NASA and would in fact die less than a year later.

The television and film luminaries who joined Bradbury at JPL included longtime space-program proponent Johnny Carson, *Star Trek* producer Gene Roddenberry, and actress Nichelle Nichols. Both Roddenberry and Nichols were interviewed by journalist Jon Lomberg during the final twenty minutes of *Viking*'s descent from its orbiter. Immediately after touchdown, Lomberg captured Bradbury's thoughts on the significance of the moment: "We should go to Mars just as we do all the wonderful and exciting things we do in life, so we can survive. Everything is survival—*everything* is survival, which enables us to exist in this universe of ours."[1]

In an unusually candid aside, Bradbury alluded to the lack of cosmic awareness in the everyday world, a problem that had been a prime motivator for his passion since his childhood: "I sometimes am astounded when I think of the average person who doesn't realize that we live in this universe, that we live in a star system, that we're incredible, that we're miraculous, that we're impossible." Normally, he would simply have said "We are an impossibility in an impossible universe," and glossed over the potentially tragic human preoccupation with self in the narrow confines of day-to-day existence.

Other portions of Bradbury's Viking 1 landing interview were consistent with the progression of his Space-Age message as it evolved through the 1970s. In his 1969 broadcast interview during the Apollo 11 landing, Bradbury had focused on turning away from wars and uniting humanity in a new war against the vast and cold indifference of the cosmos. Those words had been uttered at the height of the Vietnam Conflict; now, as Viking was transmitting its first image of the

Martian surface, Bradbury turned instead to the idea he had articulated two years earlier in his *Day at Night* radio interview—the converging purposes of science and religion on the threshold of interplanetary travel:

> We must move out to the stars. We are responsible to the gift of life in the universe, in this part of the universe. We're the only things alive right around here, hmmm? As far as we know. That's a lot of responsibility. And space travel is a responsible way of reacting to the gift of life that we have. So we're suddenly talking theology here, aren't we, and that's not science, not politics, and anything of that sort. It's being responsible to our position in the Milky Way.

By 8:00 A.M., when Bradbury finally departed the control room, he had given a number of direct television and radio interviews for stations in Rome, London, and New York. "Felt very much loved and wanted," he wrote to Congdon later that day. "In tears quite often. After all, that IS my country up there. Bless us all. What a day!"

Bradbury's old friend, the distinguished radio-broadcasting pioneer and innovator Norman Corwin, later explained why Bradbury could feel that way about a national triumph. "And what has Bradbury done that his name comes ahead even of his country's in our consciousness of Mars?" In his regular media column, Corwin proceeded to answer the question:

> What *did* he do then? Well, all he did was write. He is an artist, and he got to Mars before the scientists. Long before. His words, his *Martian Chronicles*, the beauty and vibrance of his imagery, his imagination, carried us to a Mars that heretofore had been only a cold body of astronomical details and inconclusive telescopic observations. No matter that Ray's landscapes were richer than what the *Viking* looked around and saw. No matter that there are no somber cities on Mars, nor any ectoplasmic populations. Mars was, to the best of man's intents and purposes, captured by Ray Bradbury. He colonized it with his poetry. No amount of scientific data, no logs and extrapolations of computer codes, will ever dislodge him from that planet.[2]

The first Viking 1 photographs had been received and processed before Bradbury left the building, transmitted from the landing zone on the Chryse Planitia. These "Golden Plains" were not selected by mission planners to evoke Bradbury's golden-eyed Martians, but they do. Viking 2 landed on another region of the northern hemisphere on September 3rd, and both missions raced against time to transmit the images and measurements of the primary mission before Mars entered its superior conjunction and passed behind the sun on November 15, 1976.

While the Viking program's race against time ran its successful course on the Martian surface, Bradbury returned to the Jet Propulsion Laboratory at Caltech to open an October 8, 1976, symposium on "The Search for Life in Our Solar System." He was there, of course, to inspire and set the tone for the distinguished speakers who followed, including Dr. John Billingham, chief of programs for the Search for Extraterrestrial Intelligence, soon to be popularized under the acronym SETI.

Bradbury's presentation, "Evolution of Our Cosmic Perspective," led into lectures on the Viking Project and updates on planning for future unmanned probes as well as manned exploration missions.[3] Soon after the Viking landings, Bradbury was already building metaphors to describe their magic, extending observations made the day that Viking I landed: "There is life on Mars, and it is us—extensions of our eyes in all directions, extensions of our mind, extensions of our heart and soul have touched Mars."

The first Viking mission would continue to transmit for another six years, but there was an image in many of Earth's newspapers that preceded most of Viking 1's history-making photographs. The syndicated cartoonist Frank Interlandi's commemoration of the Viking 1 landing broke through all of the bicentennial celebrations with an image of the surface of Mars. "The scene is desolate," Norman Corwin noted, "except for one feature standing sharp and clear: a mail box. The name on the box is Ray Bradbury. . . . His mailbox, like those first firm footprints on the moon, will stand there forever."

: : :

The Viking landings coincided with fast-paced developments that brought *Something Wicked This Way Comes* closer to film production than it had been at any time since Gene Kelly first explored the possibility with Bradbury's earliest script in the mid-1950s. By the mid-1970s, Walter Mirisch's perennial interest in producing the film had shifted to *The Martian Chronicles*, and the Chartoff-Winkler option on *Something Wicked* was expiring. Bradbury had rewritten the script yet again during that option period, describing the process through a playful metaphor: "I am happy with the job I've done of, late in the years, swimming over my own eggs to refertilize them," he wrote in a sidebar to Knopf's Robert Gottlieb. "A strange, asexual or should I say bisexual act, eh? Write a book one year, then twelve years later come back and refertilize yourself."[4]

In the short term, there was no real chance to continue with Robert Chartoff and Irwin Winkler, who were finishing up their Oscar-winning film *Rocky* and had other pictures (*Rocky II* and *Raging Bull*) on the horizon. But in late 1975, Peter Douglas introduced himself to Bradbury on the street outside Hunter's

Bookshop in Beverly Hills, setting off a seven-year pathway to the making of *Something Wicked This Way Comes*.[5] This was one of Douglas's favorite novels from high school days, and he had periodically discussed the idea of making the film with his father, Kirk Douglas, who had known Bradbury since the 1950s.[6]

Early in 1976, Peter Douglas was able to set a deal in motion soon after he and Bradbury had agreed on Bradbury's choice of Jack Clayton as director; by great good fortune, Clayton was over from England, and Douglas persuaded him to direct the project over breakfast.[7] He didn't have to wait long to find a studio. Clayton happened to be meeting Paramount president David Picker later that morning, and the two meetings actually overlapped.

Picker had already read the novel, liked it, and knew it had possibilities; by April 1976, Peter Douglas had a $50,000 option secured from Paramount. Clayton wasted no time getting to work; he studied Bradbury's overlong 1974 screenplay and offered a written critique with a 30-page treatment outline that would guide Bradbury through a much more cinematic and concise rewrite. Before the year was out, Bradbury had written an entirely new version that no longer tried to incorporate every scene from the original novel.

But the following year's departure of David Picker from the studio, along with opposition from CEO Barry Diller, soon ended all preproduction preparations at Paramount; by January 1977, the project was all but officially canceled.[8] This was a learning experience for the younger Douglas, but he went ahead and continued with the project, trying to finance the Paramount option payoff with another studio deal. He came close at Twentieth Century Fox, but it was an uphill battle all the way; the major studios liked the book but not its chances for success at the box office.

Peter Douglas soon found a safe haven for *Something Wicked* until circumstances might change. He knew that his father preferred to have a studio take on the financing up front, but Kirk Douglas soon agreed to buy the property and simply keep it off the market for a while; that way, Bradbury and Peter could let offers come in for evaluation over time. In January 1977, the elder Douglas sent a copy to Charles Bronson, who had starred in Bradbury's haunting 1955 *Alfred Hitchcock Presents* television episode, "Riabouchinska," noting that the decades-long travels of *Something Wicked* was beginning to resemble the odyssey of *One Flew Over the Cuckoo's Nest*, which was rejected by a number of studios before achieving its Oscar-winning success.[9]

Still more time passed without a deal, and Jack Clayton became anxious. In April 1977, the Academy Award–winning director wrote to Peter and Kirk Douglas to summarize his concerns. Clayton felt that the discussions of independent funding after the Paramount deal collapsed would involve a complicated arrangement of executive producers that could distract him from directing once production started. He was already deeply involved in evaluating the Bradbury script, and he wanted to know who all the players would be before he could go on. He was also hesitant about a possible contractual change that would have Kirk Douglas play the role of Will's father, Charles Halloway, whose inward-turning and deeply reflective personality had long ago generated distance between himself and his wife and son. For Clayton, this was "the point of the story. For the beauty of Halloway is that this mild, gentle character develops under the strain of terror and through his love for his son, into a man of bravery and action."[10]

Clayton had great respect for both Douglases, and during his nine months of work on the project he had grown to trust them as filmmakers. He was convinced, however, that the role of Charles Halloway ran against the grain of all the dynamic and wide-ranging acting qualities of Kirk Douglas; Clayton admitted, though, that his view might reflect his own lack of imagination, and a broader review of Douglas's career would show that he was quite capable of playing such a role of inner conflict during the course of solving a dark mystery of great consequence—as he had for *Seven Days in May*. But perception was reality for the truthful Jack Clayton, and he noted deep and honest regret in leaving the project.

As it turned out, Kirk Douglas was quite willing to give way on playing the Halloway role, but Clayton's main concern was becoming more and more clear; as he told Bradbury in an exchange of letters that same month, he was still completely committed to the project, but he could not delay other offers indefinitely. He cited two offers he had passed up while *Something Wicked* was stalled at Paramount and revealed his decision to accept an offer from Twentieth Century Fox. In reality, Clayton's next film would be a 1987 British production (*The Lonely Passion of Judith Hearne*) and that venture was still a decade beyond the horizon.

Clayton was an important director who had sparked British New Wave cinema and made at least one successful and award-winning film in each decade from the 1950s through the 1970s. But there would always be long intervals between his films—his indecision was legendary, as was his constant quest for perfection in the way that he thought the story should be told. Clayton would come back to the project in 1980, as the actual Disney-Bryna production began to take shape, but Bradbury eventually came to realize that his old friend's vision of the story would be at odds, for different reasons, with both author and studio.

If one door had, for the moment, closed in Hollywood, other doors were still open to him. In 1974, Bradbury had received the prestigious Valentine Davies Award from the Writers Guild of America for his public service and contributions to the entertainment world. That same year, he played an important behind-the-scenes role in preparing the American Film Institute's tribute to acting legend

James Cagney, a documentary film aired on CBS and produced by his friend George Stevens Jr. "Where does one begin," Cagney wrote to Bradbury in June 1974. "I've been hard at it trying to find the words to say in appreciation . . . your contribution was truly a startler for which warm thanks."

In March 1977, as work on *Something Wicked* temporarily ground to a halt, Bradbury became one of the principal writers for the 49th annual Academy Awards Ceremony. Academy president Walter Mirisch's relationship with Bradbury went all the way back to the Warner Brothers 1956 production of *Moby Dick*, but Bradbury also knew many of the distinguished presenters and nominees; not surprisingly, his style is present in the scripted remarks of Jane Fonda, cohost Ellen Burstyn, and in William Holden's presentation of the Oscar for best film editing. Yet this renewal of his connections to Hollywood history also served as a prelude to a very special personal moment—for the ceremony itself, he was able to bring his daughter Bettina, who was just embarking on her own award-winning career as a television writer.

Part II

Beyond Eden

How could you survive on Mars? The loneliness that occurs on distant planets, how do you compensate? When people moved west from Ohio and Indiana, they took their architecture with them. And there are buildings here, there are streets in Redlands and San Bernardino that are right out of Muncie, Indiana. So they brought the architecture with them. And up in Sacramento. You can shoot *Dandelion Wine* up there. Every street is my home street, where I grew up.

—RB, March 14, 2002

10 The God in Science Fiction

Bradbury's 1977 impasse with *Something Wicked* was counterbalanced by producer/director Terrence Shank's stage success with *The Martian Chronicles*. Initially, Shank wanted to revive the problematic *Leviathan 99* at the Colony, where he was founding artistic director. Bradbury was not yet ready to revisit *Leviathan*'s production challenges on stage; he was impressed with Shank's recent productions, however, and gave him a script for *The Martian Chronicles*, which Shank worked into what he called "staged stories; a theatre piece." Bradbury's modified script focused on the four stories of first contact with the Martians in the first act, and staged stories from the rest of the *Chronicles* for the second act, performed with 52 actors on a translucent Plexiglas stage.[1]

The June 1977 run-through performances led to full staging in July by the Colony acting company, with performances at Studio Theatre Playhouse near Dodger Stadium. The large cast included Colony cofounders Kathryn Kates and John Larroquette; subsequent productions (with Kates and Ed Harris) played in the 1978 season at the El Rey Theatre with the net costs under $10,000. The El Rey's lobby entrance and ticket window were framed within a large Egyptian mask, a structural feature that complemented the work of Shank's designers Patrick Duffy Whitbeck and Conrad Wolff—golden skin, costumes, and masks that became a hallmark for this production wherever it was staged.

Bradbury's old friend Paul Gregory coproduced and developed a touring production that took Bradbury's golden Martians around the country as well. Bradbury's first lessons in stage adaptation had come at the hands of Paul Gregory and Charles Laughton in the mid-1950s; Gregory had always had a good working relationship with Bradbury and Don Congdon, who appreciated the producer's business sense. During the *Chronicles* productions, both men visited the Desert Hot Springs home of Gregory and his wife, retired actress Janet Gaynor, who had won the very first Academy Award for Best Actress in 1929.

Bradbury knew many key figures who started out in the silent film era, including Gaynor, Patsy Ruth Miller, Fay Wray, Loretta Young, Karla Laemmle, Fritz Lang, James Wong Howe, and King Vidor. The full list is unknown, but undoubtedly longer. These were Time Machines as well as friends, for they collectively reconnected him with the Silent Screen of his childhood memories.

: : :

In early August, 1977, Bradbury experienced Shakespeare's *Hamlet* as he had never experienced it before. Initially, he was just as interested in experiencing the magic of San Diego's Old Globe Theater as he was in seeing the play itself. It was built for the California Pacific International Exposition in 1935; Bradbury had actually seen its exterior the following year, when his family took him down to visit the Exposition's replication of Spanish colonial architecture. The Globe had been remodeled since then, and Jack O'Brien's production of *Hamlet* would forever change the way that Bradbury viewed a play that he had known in its broader outlines since high school.

He had never quite connected with Hamlet's absolute conviction that his father's ghost was manifest and speaking truth. "I cared not only for the poetry," he wrote to Congdon the next week, "but for the characters, the moral dilemmas, the people, for the first time in my life that I can remember."[2] Bradbury had grown up in a woman's world, especially during his early years with extended family in Waukegan, and Hamlet's relationships were suddenly crystal clear to him. "I saw it again and again," he would recall years later, "it dominates the whole play, and explains why he treats his mother that way, because his mother went to bed with his murderous uncle. And why he treats Ophelia that way, because she's a woman, and a woman helped kill his father. So women were all of his life, and he rejected his mother and Ophelia. I never truly understood his relationship to those women until Hamlet convinced me his father was really dead and it killed his heart."[3]

Bradbury had finally fully absorbed Hamlet's tragedy, channeled through nearly four hundred years of time in San Diego's Old Globe. Seven years later, he was devastated when teenagers destroyed the Old Globe by fire. He would later join Christopher Reeve and other actors in San Diego to raise funds for the rebuild.

One last performance event awaited Bradbury in 1977, and this time he would be a participant. The Allegro Ball was an annual presentation of the Chamber Symphony Society of California, and Bradbury would join British actress Jean Marsh in honoring *Masterpiece Theatre*'s host, Alistair Cooke, in the Grand Ball Room of the Beverly Wilshire Hotel.

Over a fifteen-year span the honorees had included Isaac Stern, the legendary Gregor Piatigorsky, Victor Borge, Zubin Mehta, Arthur Fiedler, Jack Benny, and Aaron Copland. Bradbury had been the fifth of the Symphony Society's seven presidents, and he remained on the board. The current president, Efrem Zimbalist Jr., convened the ball on the evening of November 1, 1977. Following Jean

Marsh's presentation, Bradbury spoke under the title "Ray Bradbury, Martian Chronicler of the Future, pays tribute to Alistair Cooke, Masterpiece Chronicler of the Past."[4]

The 1977 Allegro Ball placed him in the midst of British culture on American soil, another reminder that British writers and intellectuals had been early encouragers during his mid-century breakout into the literary mainstream.[5] His broader relationship with the California Chamber Symphony Society also opened national and international friendships and opportunities that a regional performing arts enterprise would not normally provide. In so many ways, the music and cinema of Southern California had been his gateway to the world since his arrival in Los Angeles as a young teenager in 1934, at the height of the Great Depression.

: : :

As 1977 drew to a close, Bradbury published his provocative essay "The God in Science Fiction" in the December 10th issue of *Saturday Review*. In its basic structure, the essay was little more than a series of well-written synoptic retellings of the stories that expressed his evolving sense of God, writ large across the Cosmos. Here was "The Man," "The Fire Balloons," "The Messiah," *Leviathan 99*, and his Bernard Shaw homage, "GBS Mark V," with internal bridges formed of retellings of his screenwriting adventures with John Huston (*Moby Dick*) and MGM (*King of Kings*). This was an entertaining but recursive exercise, yet it was offered with purpose. The spiritual intersection of science and science fiction that he had suggested in his 1974 *Day at Night* television interview was now out in the arena for debate:

> Somewhere farther along in time, Christ moves in Space, cargoed on missions that, for Now anyway, take the name of Apollo. So old myth and new circumnavigate the stars, rebuild old dreams, re-promise better destinies on far worlds we cannot now imagine. . . .
>
> Are we ourselves in some miraculous fashion the Holy Ghost that will haunt the cosmic dusts and call them alive? Will we conjure dead matter on Martian thresholds and Christ-like summon it up into intelligence and immortal life as we pass?

Through most of the essay he was fitting bits and pieces together from his story examples, weaving in his conviction that humanity would take God back out into the universe, and find humanity in the terrifying Otherness of alien worlds: "If a creature knows the difference between good and evil, light and dark, can choose love instead of murder, can withhold violence, can extend peace, can judge, can value, that creature is human, regardless of its outer appearance, be it flesh or fire." This last observation echoed all the way back to his first screen story, Universal's 1953 3-D feature experiment, *It Came from Outer Space*.

"The God in Science Fiction," like some of his other article-length musings of the 1970s, was still a work-in-progress. His explosion of Shavian wisdom, for example, was still ragged and somewhat untempered; refinement would come nine years later, in his 1986 *Planetary Report* essay, "There Is Life on Mars, and It Is Us!" But his view of the place of science fiction, forming an ever-tightening nexus between science and religion, was now fully set out in print: "Doctors and saints, meanwhile, will give great argument. Science fiction writers will lean more and more into theology, forced by NASA's blasphemous intrusion on the Lord's territorial imperatives to question where we have come from and just where in Heaven or Hell we are going."

The implicit prologue for "The God in Science Fiction" was his cathartic review of *Close Encounters of the Third Kind*, published in the *Los Angeles Times* on November 20, 1977, less than a month earlier. He proclaimed *Close Encounters* as the first film to fully lay out—from the perspective of everyday people—how humanity could be finally united if evidence of other intelligent life in the cosmos ever became manifest. His film review title—"Opening the Beautiful Door of True Immortality"—suggested that *Close Encounters* represented the culmination of the new faith in humanism that he had been proclaiming and refining for decades:[6]

> We feel ourselves being born truly for the first time. *Close Encounters* is, in all probability, the most important film of our time. For this is a religious film in all the great, good senses, the right senses of that much battered word. Spielberg has made a film that can open in New Delhi, Tokyo, Berlin, Moscow, Johannesburg, Paris, London, New York and Rio de Janeiro on the same day to mobs and throngs and crowds that will never stop coming, because for the first time someone has treated all of us as if we really did belong to one race.
>
> I dare predict that in every way aesthetically or commercially it will be the most successful film ever produced, released or seen. It will be the first film in history to gross one billion all by itself. Every priest, minister, rabbi in the world should preach this film, show this film to their congregation. Every Moslem, every Buddhist, Zen or otherwise in the world can sit down at this moveable feast and leave well fed. That is how big this film is. That is why it will be around the rest of our lives making us want to live more fully, packing us with its hope and energy.[7]

But Bradbury's review, as well as "The God in Science Fiction" itself, presented a darker set of unaddressed possibilities: If one of the best-known visionary writers of our time gives godlike attributes to Hollywood, does moral responsibility fall by the wayside? One could argue that this had already happened in the international world of high finance. Had the unseen forces of Hollywood gone the same way, under divine license? When David McClintick published *Indecent Exposure*, his best-selling 1982 exploration of the systematic financial predation of Hollywood executive David Begelman and others, McClintick offered the core passage from Bradbury's review as a well-intentioned celebration that held a wide range of cultural consequences—a marvelous gateway between heaven and hell, one that could swing both ways.[8]

:　:　:

The November 20th issue of the *Los Angeles Times* also contained Bradbury's review of Loren Eiseley's last book, *Another Kind of Autumn*. As the deep space Voyagers that both men celebrated moved through the outer solar system, Eiseley was slipping into his final illness. Ray's good friend passed away on July 9, 1977, with cause of death indicated in the media as a heart attack. Eiseley's wife, Mabel, responding to Bradbury's condolences, offered a glimpse of the long and painful bout with pancreatic cancer and three major surgeries that had led up to the merciful heart attack. Her description of Eiseley's fortitude was prophetic in a way, for her words unknowingly characterized how Bradbury himself would respond to his own final hospitalizations: "But he was courageous—uncomplaining—philosophical and a model patient. The surgeons and nurses grew very fond of him."

Mabel Eiseley also offered Bradbury her celebrated husband's final verdict on his own writing: "In his opinion . . . you were the best in your field." Both Eiseley and Bradbury ranged well beyond any one field of writing, but there was no mystery in what bonded the master storyteller and the distinguished anthropologist. For nearly three decades, Eiseley's engaging prose offered that rare combination of scientific insight and a fine literary style, and he had earned Bradbury's abiding admiration from the start. Bradbury had initiated their long correspondence in 1948, writing to confess how much Eiseley's "The Fire Apes" had enriched his understanding of Mankind's place in the intricate weave of time and evolving life on Planet Earth. Bradbury found a kind of magic in Eiseley's prose; looking back from the 1990s, he would observe that Eiseley conveyed "a sense of the mysterious without being mystical. That's not an easy thing to do. We are surrounded by people who tell us they know what life is all about, and he doesn't tell you that at all."[9]

They read each other's works, and Bradbury always urged his older friend to develop speaking skills to match his genius for the printed word. But Eiseley always anticipated the frailties of mind and body inherited from his ancestors, and physical ailments took their toll through much of the 1970s. When he died, Bradbury immediately wrote a reflection, noting that we should feel "the time and the force and the running of the universe to have suddenly fallen into error." In the face of death, Bradbury would often turn to the immortality of books, and for him Eiseley's books contained more than a glimpse of human destiny: "Mankind in its mystery had no greater friend than this duster of bones and keeper of truths. He haunted the dustbins of the past, the elephants' graveyards of all time to sift out our incredible prehistories."

Bradbury took great stock in the meaning of graveyards and gravestones, and as he grieved for his friend, he appropriated the words of a favorite poet, Stephen Vincent Benét, and his poem of the pioneering Daniel Boone:

> When Loren Eiseley walks our night
> The phantom deer arise
> And all lost time and life and blood
> Is burning in their eyes.

Bradbury never published the poem or the reflection, and never even revised this late-night roughly typed draft. He turned, instead, to his own bookshelf to conclude: "Loren Eiseley is not dead. For I have just opened one of his books, and I am *reading* him."

∴ ∴ ∴

A deeper grieving came to Bradbury a few months later. In March, 1978, his great friend and onetime mentor Leigh Brackett Hamilton passed away after a long battle with cancer. During her final months, Bradbury was involved in the last great drama of her life—would she be able to complete her first draft screenplay for the *Star Wars* sequel, *The Empire Strikes Back?* George Lucas had selected Brackett because of her early prominence in the space opera tradition, and her subsequent success as a screenwriter for a number of Howard Hawks films, beginning with *The Big Sleep* in 1944–45. She was a master of situational dialog, and a great creator of interplanetary worlds where solitary men and women faced long odds for survival in the face of natural as well as man-made dangers. She was just as good with noir situations, and Hawkes hired her based on her writing; it was said that he didn't know she was a woman until he saw the spelling of her first name on paper. The writing side of filmmaking was not a woman's world at the time, but he put her to work on what would become a Bogart and Bacall classic film, teamed with veteran screenwriter Jules Furthman and the reclusive William Faulkner.

This unexpected opportunity initiated the thirty-year trajectory that would bring her to Lucas and the *Star Wars* universe, but at the time it broke up a fascinating working relationship with her younger pal Ray Bradbury. During the war years, Brackett spent Sundays on the Santa Monica beach playing volleyball and reading with Bradbury, who would bicycle north from Venice to meet her. She critiqued his stories while he read her more polished work in draft and finished form. They loved the same films (they formed a two-member "Bogey and Bergman" club after *Casablanca* was released), and she refined his reading of noir and related aspects of criminology. She was "Muscles," he was "Genius," and Bradbury learned a great deal from studying her multi-genre fictions.[10]

The call from Hawks came while she was halfway through a contracted 20,000-word novella for *Planet Stories*, tentatively titled "Red Sea of Venus." Without hesitation she handed the work over to Bradbury, offering a single sentence of advice on how to write the second half. Brackett shared more than the payment with him—while he finished up his half of the novella, Brackett brought Bradbury onto the set of *The Big Sleep* to meet Hawks, Humphrey Bogart, Lauren Bacall, and even William Faulkner.[11] As "Lorelei of the Red Mist," the cover story in the Spring 1946 issue of *Planet Stories*, their collaboration became a seamless indicator of how well they knew each other's work. By the end of 1945, Brackett married Edmond Hamilton, another Bradbury mentor who greatly improved Bradbury's range of reading in English literature. He stood as best man at their wedding, and they remained among the closest of his friends.

Hamilton's passing in 1977 had been a blow, but Bradbury was encouraged that Brackett had the *Star Wars* work to sustain her as she began to decline. Knowing of their close early association as genre writers, the studio asked if Bradbury would complete her work if she didn't live to finish the screenplay. He agreed to do so anonymously, but only if her name remained with full credit for the initial submission. In the end, his intervention was not needed; Leigh Brackett turned in the script in February 1978 and passed away less than a month later.

Bradbury' final memories of his friend were good ones. Brackett spent the 1978 New Year's holiday with the Bradburys, clearly weak but renewed by the memories they shared one last time. In mid-March, she phoned Bradbury from a hospital in the high desert, where she was lucid but heavily medicated. Far from despondent, Brackett told him from her hospital room that working on *The Empire Strikes Back* had given great meaning to her final days; she was grateful to be "going out" shaping the cinematic culmination of her early interplanetary romances. Leigh Brackett died on March 18th, before Bradbury could see her again. Ten days later producer Gary Kurtz reached out to Bradbury to confer about a suitable donation in her name. He relayed her final words to studio executives and eventually to Irvin Kershner, who subsequently came on to direct *The Empire Strikes Back*.[12]

The initial Brackett script strayed from the course laid out in George Lucas's outlines and his initial discussion with her, prompting Lucas to work with Lawrence Kasdan on several heavily revised drafts through the spring of 1978. Eventually the fourth draft, still carrying Brackett's name along with Kasdan's as coauthors, arrived at Bradbury's house, where he preserved it as a memento for the rest of his life. Although the script had evolved in a number of different directions, some of Brackett's ideas and exotic aliens were carried into later episodes, seen most notably in the tall, slender-necked creatures of a remote star cluster, the genetic creators of the Dark Side's clone armies.[13] Judging by his later conversations with Kurtz and Kershner, it appears that Bradbury never read his copy of the revised script before he actually saw the film; perhaps it was tied too closely to the loss of a great friend.

11 Infinite Worlds

"In Mexico, the pilgrims rub fireflies on their flesh in the shape of a cross. The phosphorescence, thus grained in, shines in the dark."[1] This note for a possible poem was written in 1978, more than three decades after the experience. Bradbury's memories of Mexico in 1945, and his chance meeting at Lake Janitzio with Madame Man'Ha Garreau-Dombasle, wife of the French ambassador to Mexico, were periodically revived in his fiction and constantly renewed in correspondence; indeed, Man'Ha was his most faithful correspondent until she passed away forty-four years later at the age of 101. They had met in the dark as fellow travelers by canoe across the famous lake to the tiny island village of Janitzio to witness the midnight observances of El Dia De La Muerte.

Their relationship continued on the thinnest of threads. The next day, crossing a street near his lodgings in Patzcuaro, he was hailed by a lady in a dark limousine. It was Man'Ha, with her teenage daughter Francione, who had also ventured out on the previous night's water adventure. Here, in the light of day, Man'Ha revealed her identity, gave him her card, and then recommended that he and his traveling companion, Grant Beach, should head north to tour the catacomb mummies of Guanajuato. That underworld tour would represent one of the grand terrors of his life; as Bradbury reached the end of this dark gallery, he turned and felt the eyes of the dead gazing from both walls, as if blocking his return to the stairs and the world above.

Writing was his way of coming to terms with the traumatic moments of his early life, and Guanajuato would inevitably resurface in stories of the late 1940s, his unfinished Mexican novel of the early 1950s, and in the moment of final redemption for Pip, hero of *The Halloween Tree* in his final 1972 revisions. But Man'Ha would become the real-life redemption to this abiding dark; her long letters, written in nearly flawless English in a hand that was almost indecipherable, wove a lifetime friendship that was instrumental in his literary prominence in postwar French culture.

Even before her important partnership in the distinguished diplomatic career of her husband Maurice, Man'Ha was already an influence within the world of French art, literature, and cultural criticism. She was a part of the Surrealist movement and had helped French writers and artists find wartime sanctuary in America and Mexico. Late in the summer of 1957, after finishing his script for the unproduced film *And the Rock Cried Out* in London for Sir Carol Reed, Bradbury came through Paris, where Man'Ha had helped to orchestrate the significant French media and literary reception that Bradbury encountered. Now, more than twenty years later, Man'Ha would once again facilitate a critical moment in Bradbury's international career.

The year 1978 marked the 150th anniversary of the birth of Jules Verne, and the French observances were monumental. Bradbury received an invitation from the French government for an international seminar on Verne, where he was featured prominently. He was not universally favored by critics, but his role as an inspiration for fantasy in the Surrealist tradition made him perennially popular in France. Inevitably, the intense theoretical exchanges between the critics left him at a loss. His appearance on the French television program *L'Apostrophe*, where he was caught within an intensely speculative exchange of views, triggered a typical common-sensical Bradbury remonstrance: "You speak only of ants; I wish to describe the elephant!"[2]

One aspect of the Paris celebrations spoke to the young boy who remained a very active part of his adult personality—Bradbury's childhood love of fireworks was awakened on a grand scale during the July 14th celebrations of Bastille Day. That evening, he was allowed to join the bombardiers on the Troccadaro, just beyond the Eiffel Tower, as they lit off the nation's annual fireworks extravaganza. Earlier that week, his editors at Denoel arranged a cocktail party for the press and a number of French authors who wanted to meet him.[3] The following week concluded with a private tour of Versailles and a performance of Puccini's *Madame Butterfly*. During the final week of July, he and Maggie were also able to honor personal invitations to see the singer Charles Aznavour and Jean-Louis Barrault, a distinguished stage actor-director whose production of *The Martian Chronicles* had been destroyed before opening during the 1966 student riots in Paris.

: : :

Bradbury's command performance in France was actually prelude to an even more meaningful personal adventure. He would now be able to travel on to Rome, where Italian director Federico Fellini had invited him to visit. Bradbury and Maggie were now joined by their youngest daughter Alexandra, who flew to Rome for her birthday.[4] She was not yet born when her three older sisters accompanied their parents on the 1957 trip to see her father's aging mentor,

Bernard Berenson. Now she would make her trip as well, and the three would be entertained by a film director whose career had exploded in international cinema during the intervening decades—a director who already considered Ray Bradbury to be a kindred spirit.

The two first crossed paths, if only briefly, in 1970. Bradbury's many years as cofounder of the Writer's Guild Film Society had expanded his already broad experience with foreign films; he had a great deal of freedom in coordinating the large-screen viewing schedule during the 1960s, and he was able to reprise his sense of Fellini's earlier successes, La Strada and Nights of Cabiria, both of which had won Best Foreign Film Oscars in the mid-1950s. In the 1960s, La Dolce Vita and 8½ earned two more Oscar nominations, and Bob Fosse had adapted Nights of Cabiria into Sweet Charity in America. Bradbury made his opinion of Fellini more widely known in 1966, through a review of Fellini's Juliet of the Spirits in a regional newspaper.[5] He closely followed Fellini's trajectory, as well as Fellini's growing influence on American directors. When Fellini came to the West Coast in 1970, Bradbury attended his lectures.

From that moment, it took seven years and two tokens of Bradbury Magic to form an enduring bond with Fellini. There was no spark of recognition when Bradbury introduced himself after Fellini's 1970 lecture, but he approached Fellini again with an Italian edition of The Martian Chronicles in hand. Fellini's face lit up with recognition (the Chronicles had been a popular Mondadori edition in Italy since 1954). He undoubtedly knew Truffaut's adaptation of Fahrenheit 451 as well, but there was no time on this whirlwind tour to make a real connection.

Christian Strich's landmark edition of Fellini's Films was published in America in 1977, and Bradbury's unusual review of this book in the Los Angeles Times emerged as the second and decisive magical token.[6] All of Bradbury's book reviews were unusual, in one way or another; he had published reviews for the Times at intervals since 1969 (this would be his twenty-seventh in the Times Book Review and Calendar sections), and like many others it presented a mix of metaphorical mega-praise and incisive analysis. Bradbury declared Fellini to be the heir to Chaplin and Lon Chaney's vision of the sublime and the lonely:

> When Fellini walks at night and calls, the gargoyles on Notre Dame waken to play parts. Quasimodo comes down and in new shapes speaks lines in La Strada and Satyricon, or lies a nameless monster on the beach in La Dolce Vita, surrounded by bored sophisticates who, momentarily touched by repulsion and sadness, wander off to their dooms.

Bradbury drew delightfully accurate parallels between Fellini and the great era of Chaplin, but in response to the more recent Fellini films, he offered the cautionary tale of the later Chaplin grown too old and too serious:

> Can Fellini run back on his own time track, regain that lost innocence, to some degree at least, and keep it? Or is he doomed to wander the earth like the Mastroianni character in 8½, haunted by ghosts and guilts, which will not be exorcised by trapping them on film and rerunning their terrors again and again? . . . Fellini seems almost to have doubted himself out of existence, helped by those false friends we all find surrounding us, using up the air we need to breathe.

The review clearly revealed that these two men shared much more than a birth year; Bradbury admired Fellini's love of the fantastic, as well as his disdain for authoritarianism. Most of all, he loved Fellini's impulse to go his own way, as Bradbury had always tried to do, free from "friends who are the enemy of the true self." Bradbury did not care for some of the other new European directors (Jean-Luc Godard left him cold), but he loved Fellini's approach to life with a passion. It would only be a matter of time before Bradbury's review found its way into the director's hands, by way of Fellini's Swiss editor Daniel Keel at Diogenes, who was also Bradbury's editor and had worked on the German-Swiss edition of The Illustrated Man.[7]

Fellini's January 1978 response offered heartfelt gratitude, and a genuine urge for a meeting. "Will you ever come to Rome? I don't know when I'll come to America." Fellini slipped immediately into a candid summary of his current professional and personal uncertainties: how the many American offers to direct were counterbalanced by his anxieties about making films in another land and language. Yet he was nonetheless tempted, given the growing expense of making films in his native Italy. Fellini also shared with Bradbury his sense of the lengthening shadow of time: "And there is the ghost of an unhappy, resigned aging. Each day I hope the next week will bring changes and that life may once more have all its charms, surprise and the delight of days gone by."[8]

Now, more than ever, Bradbury wanted to spend time in Fellini's kindred world of magic, and the Jules Verne Sesquicentennial invitation from the French government suddenly offered the opportunity. Before these plans took shape, Bradbury was already trying to pull Fellini into his dreams, as he had done with John Huston and, less insistently, with other American and British directors that he had admired. He sent Fellini a copy of his stage version of The Wonderful Ice Cream Suit, and wasted no time urging Fellini to consider adapting it to film: "I believe that its Latin temperament would travel. I sense that there is little difference between the dreams of six young Latins trying to own one suit in California, and six young Latins in Italy trying to do the same." Fellini was not sure of his own English, and had Bradbury's letter translated, but not before a quick note saying, "You're really sympatico, Ray."[9]

The real chance to speak of film ventures came soon enough, as Bradbury's official July 1978 engagements in France were quickly followed by an August week in Rome with Fellini. The journey from Paris to Rome was an adventure in itself, for the French government's hospitality continued all the way to the Italian frontier.[10] The journey took Bradbury and Maggie south into Provence and San Tropez for the dinner with Charles Aznavour. Jean-Louis Barrault met them on the Mediterranean island of Port-Cros in the island's remote Maritime National Park.

Next, they visited Arles, Nimes, Avignon, and Carcassonne before finally meeting a train in Marseilles for Rome. Their stay in Avignon triggered Bradbury's abiding fascination with the Avignon Papacy of the High Middle Ages; the result was a new poem drafted on his portable typewriter, "A Miracle of Popes, All with One face. Poem written on perambulating the Papal Palace at Avignon and discovering that one artist, enraptured with his mirror, had cloned each Holy Father as spitting-image of himself." Bradbury then began another poem intended to capture the deadly undertones of this unstable period in Papal history: "Only the Pope, at Dinner, Had a Knife."

They joined Alexandra in Rome and began a week in Fellini's company. As it turned out, Fellini would be in Rome for most of August, working in the sprawling Cinecittá film studio, known as "The Dream Factory." Bradbury posed with Fellini in front of the head of a colossal Venetian carnival bust built on set for Fellini's recent Academy Award–winning film, *Casanova*. A wonderful luncheon that included Fellini's composer, Nino Rota, was a high point of the week. Here Bradbury observed a creative relationship similar in scale—but not in formality—to what he had observed between Alfred Hitchcock and Bernard Herrmann in the early 1960s; here, instead, was a spontaneous Mediterranean warmth that expanded the conversation outward in many unexpected directions.

Bradbury's discussion with Fellini and Rota suddenly turned to the legendary Italian "prince of laughter," Antonio De Curtis, known around the world simply as "Toto." Fellini had first worked with him while standing in for Roberto Rosselini to direct a scene in the 1954 Italian film *What Is Freedom?* Two years later the celebrated Toto lost most of his eyesight, but his subsequent films never betrayed this handicap. Fellini told of the way that the nearly blind Toto would come alive at the director's word "Begin!" and play his scenes flawlessly, in full command of his stage presence and movements, only to lapse back into a world of darkness at the word "Cut!" Bradbury was enthralled by this "true" fantasy, and would eventually compose a poem titled "Fellini's 'Toto'":

Tell me of Toto
Tell of Toto the clown,
Time out of mind, gone blind,
But waiting patiently
On set for film to start, his art inside him waiting,
Not debating how it comes or goes
It knows.
Director says: "Begin!"
Within blind Toto, lost to night,
Quick sight,
He walks, he runs, he gestures:
Sees!
With ease the blind man does his part,
His heart gives light to him, his mind pure day,
His feet and face and hands know what to say,
And do.
"Now that's it! Cut!"
All actions freeze.
"Please . . . ? says Toto, turning, round,
His face now swiftly blank, his eyes blind stare.
"Will someone find and bring to me . . .
. . . my chair?"

The poem was never published, but Bradbury's rapidly scribbled notes from that luncheon survive, jotted in a small notepad with a playful cover by Jean-Michel Folon, the Surrealist Belgian artist who would soon illustrate an edition of *The Martian Chronicles*. Folon's "Eyeglasses" notepad contained a rare moment of Bradbury self-analysis, a fleeting glance beneath the surface of the man who wrote about other people's masks, triggered by Fellini's story of Toto's hidden life:

You do not meet R.B. when you meet me—you see only the prison. I am the keeper. The prisoner is within & he is splendid! He is the real R.B.! I only pretend to be him![11]

The week with Fellini, punctuated by great conversations over lunch and dinner, became one of the happiest memories of his life. From this point on, whenever he recalled the unexpected lucky encounters that changed his life or renewed his creativity, the story now included three: John Huston, Bernard

Berenson, and Federico Fellini. Yet talk of *The Wonderful Ice Cream Suit* soon fell by the wayside. The two men earnestly discussed collaboration on filming *The Martian Chronicles* all week, but these exchanges would be as close as it would come to reality. Fellini, like Bradbury, left a trail of unrealized collaborations; there would never be time to lay the complex groundwork of financial backing, and more immediate projects beckoned Fellini into the final phase of his career.

Yet Bradbury had found a kindred spirit in Fellini's inherent avoidance of revision or rational reflection in the midst of creation, and his habitual resistance to reviewing each day's filming results. Fellini's admonition, "Don't tell me what I'm doing, I don't want to know," became a Bradbury catchphrase as well. On the last day in Rome, Fellini drove Bradbury back to his hotel, embraced him, and cried, "My twin, my twin!"[12] Like Fellini, Bradbury's kind of creativity depended on originality and the need to write his own perceived truths without interference from critics or publishers.

But as a screenwriter, Bradbury's beloved cinema had, more often than not, strangled his own way of doing things. In Fellini he had discovered a twin who was able to navigate his own way in that world of cinema, sustaining Bradbury's hope that he might yet succeed as well. He now had a sense that an international collaboration might be the way to go with his own stories-into-film. This had worked for Truffaut in the filming of *Fahrenheit 451*; perhaps his long-deferred dream of a Ray Bradbury Theater would open out in the same way. Only time would tell.

: : :

Such film and television possibilities weighed heavily on him in Paris and Rome, especially when he measured the gradually diminishing engagement he had from his own media representatives at the Zigler-Ross Agency back home. He was a hard client to handle in Hollywood, for his expectations always surpassed the probabilities of success in that complex world. So much of his success there had come from lucky breaks and a few long-shot contacts that he had made himself, and over the years he had spun through successive relationships with various agencies. He had always liked the energy and savvy of Zig Zigler, but during the decade of their relationship, he was more and more often handed over to other agents in the firm. The excessive enthusiasm and attention he was receiving in Paris offered a contrast to what he might receive when he returned home. Of course, the French had the relatively easy task of celebrating his past, not negotiating his future, but this experience nevertheless became the tipping point.

On July 15, 1978, the morning after his participation in the Bastille Day fireworks on the Troccadero, Bradbury wrote to Ziglar from Paris to say that he was leaving the agency. He cited a lack of contact in a year where science fiction had been as prominent in America as it was in France for the Jules Verne festivities: "This, in the face of the two biggest films, *Star Wars* and *Close Encounters* raking in half a billion dollars between them. In sum, it has been an s-f year, and yet no one has called me with Great Plans for R.B.'s participation in same."

On one level, he knew he was a handful. "You have seen my clay feet. I acknowledge the clay and hope that when we meet over the years we can manage some sort of cheer." This was the saving grace in many of his broken professional relationships. He would remain friends with Ziglar, even as he changed over to representation through Margaret Field at the Writers & Artists Agency.[13] He would soon drop media representation completely; Don Congdon had essentially been working many of the media negotiations from New York anyway, and Los Angeles–based Ruth Alben continued to handle his ever-increasing speaking engagements, as she had for nearly a decade.

The Paris celebrations and the Roman holiday had been a wonderful experience; the three Bradburys visited Florence and Venice before Alexandra flew back home. Bradbury and Maggie continued on by rail to Vienna before returning to Paris. This had been their first trip to Florence since the death of Bradbury's mentor Bernard Berenson; his devoted companion and guardian, their friend Nicky Mariano, was also gone. They traveled home by ocean liner and transcontinental train, completing, yet again, the time-honored process of flightless Bradbury travels abroad.

It was now a quarter-century since his first voyage with Maggie and the two older girls, Susan and Ramona. Each voyage offered a microcosm of the broader world, from royalty (the Duke of Windsor, once King Edward VIII, had occupied the cabin next to the Bradburys during the 1957 trip) to writers, academics, and figures of state. Each voyage brought new acquaintances, including economist Milton Friedman, a Nobel Laureate, and the distinguished stage and film actress Geraldine Fitzgerald. During the 1984 voyage, stage producer Joseph Papp, founder of New York's Public Theater and Shakespeare in the Park, introduced himself and asked Bradbury to send him some plays to consider.[14]

Other voyages sometimes renewed old friendships. During one crossing in the late 1970s, astronomer Carl Sagan reminded Bradbury that birds, like humans, navigate by the heavens, immediately prompting Bradbury to rewrite his poem-in-progress, "They Have Not Seen the Stars." The August 1978 voyage home from Europe would yield a similar surprise—Bradbury received a shipboard note from Herman Wouk, whom he had not seen since a Beverly Hills lunch many years earlier. The author of *The Caine Mutiny* and other best sellers explained his long silence: "I hear you're aboard. . . . I've just completed a war novel that took me seven years." And another enduring friendship was rekindled over cocktails.[15]

After the voyage and yet another transcontinental train journey home to Los Angeles, Bradbury turned again to the events that had held his interest before the summer trip began: the NBC *Martian Chronicles* miniseries, where he had no control at all, and his new project with the Smithsonian, where he truly hoped he did. He had expressed his concerns about these ventures to Don Congdon just before setting out for the summer of travel: "I gather that *The Martian Chronicles* moves apace with shooting to begin in Spain in August. They owe us a large piece of change now, don't they? And, of course, we must ride herd on the Smithsonian people who seem as organized as a kindergarten pajama party."[16]

12 Abandon in Place

Bradbury returned home from Europe in August 1978 to discover that his control of the Smithsonian project was indeed slipping away, and quickly. The project had begun the previous year as a film fantasy outline progressing through the exhibits of various older Smithsonian museums en route to a magical celebration of the new Air and Space Museum's treasures. Joe Mugnaini, Bradbury's good friend and longtime illustrator, gave vision to Bradbury's fantasy through half a hundred paintings. The project, "The Ghosts of Forever," had the feel of *The Halloween Tree*, as costumed trick-or-treaters storm through the Capitol Mall. Only Timothy, in his astronaut costume, sees the animated robot that lures him into the Smithsonian's old red brick castle near the foot of the mall. He then leads the other children to discover the Air and Space marvels, even launching and then safely recovering the museum's legendary aircraft and rockets with the aid of his mysterious robotic interlocutor.

It was a beautiful concept, but an incomplete one. In April 1978, he had conceded that the art and outline text provided only "a skin for ourselves which gives us an opening and a closing . . . the middle portion is fairly open."[1] The Smithsonian team would have to sell the concept to an underwriter, and even Bradbury realized that changes were inevitable. By early December 1978, "The Ghosts of Forever" had been reshaped by the Smithsonian sponsors into a more sequential narrative, and both Bradbury and Mugnaini would be expected to react to a series of further changes.

At the end of the year, Bradbury returned the advance money and parted ways amicably but with no small feeling of regret. The decade had begun with Monsanto's rejection of his "Great Shout of the Universe" history of mankind, illustrated by Disney's legendary Marc Davis; now, eight years later, he and Mugnaini reached a similar impasse with the Smithsonian. But the museum's key players in the project, especially telecommunications chief Naz Cherkezian, and Karen Loveland of the Exhibits Central office, were still hopeful that another project would emerge. As it turned out, Bradbury already had another idea in the works, one that would involve, he hoped, one of the gems of the new Air and Space Museum—the Albert Einstein Spacearium.

: : :

Each new interplanetary probe had served to reassure Bradbury that the space program was not completely mired in low-Earth orbital missions. He held a deep-seated fascination with mankind's "robotic children," and he saw each of the deep-space missions as a covenant renewal, of sorts, for the greater human destiny of interplanetary and interstellar colonization. The Voyager missions offered a doubled gratification for him, as the JPL commemorated Voyager 1's close encounter with the Jupiter system—the first trans-asteroid belt planetary flyby—with a reenactment of the "Mars and the Mind of Man" panel where he had been able to celebrate the Mariner 9 orbital insertion and the groundbreaking photos of Mars that followed.

On March 4, 1979, his friends from that earlier celebration gathered again for "Jupiter and the Mind of Man." Walter Sullivan, science editor of the *New York Times*, returned as moderator. Carl Sagan, now the Pulitzer Prize–winning author of *The Dragons of Eden* and the prime mover behind the interstellar messages placed aboard Voyager 1 and Voyager 2, teamed up once again with Bruce Murray, now director of the JPL, on the scientific side of the panel. This time Bradbury was alone on his side of the stage, but Arthur C. Clarke was able to complete the reunion by telephone.

The setting was, once again, Beckman Auditorium on the Cal Tech campus in Pasadena, a campus where Bradbury had often lectured to large audiences since his first visit to a single class in 1956. The following day, he was able to witness the actual Voyager 1 encounter from the JPL control center, as the images of closest approach were received from the craft. Photos of the Jovian moons were just as striking and would soon show a volcanic plume along the terminator line of the innermost large moon, Io.

As the exploratory decade of Mariner, Viking, and Voyager drew to a close, Bradbury's own Mars "landing" was itself in jeopardy. The 1976 contract with Charles Fries productions had now evolved into a *Martian Chronicles* television miniseries with a good screenplay by Richard Matheson, who had been inspired and encouraged by Bradbury for many years. Bradbury's successive motion picture scripts of 1961 and 1964 remained unproduced, but as they evolved he had added more continuity by bringing Captain Wilder, commander of the fourth and ultimately successful mission to Mars, into the progressive stages of Martian colonization. Bradbury's 1977 script was not purchased for the project, but Matheson followed a similar yet distinctly different progression of bringing Wilder through all of the six episodes that were emerging as final structure.

Along the way, there was interest from PBS to acquire the project as part of a proposed series of feature-length television movies that would begin with an adaptation of Ursula Le Guin's *The Lathe of Heaven*. PBS eventually found that NBC had already acquired the *Chronicles*; as it turned out, the PBS *Lathe of Heaven* feature and the NBC *Martian Chronicles* miniseries would both air in January 1980. That was not the original plan for NBC's *Chronicles*, however. Broadcast was initially scheduled for September 1979, but postproduction editing took longer than expected.

Bradbury was very critical of the screening he saw in mid-July 1979. The film was slightly recut, and Bradbury attended a September press conference where the new release timetable was announced. He had signed on to the usual contractual agreement requiring that any public comments be cleared with Charles Fries in advance, but Bradbury characterized the first screening as "boring"—a summary verdict he would often cite in years to come. He offered more positive comments to Fries and his associates after seeing a new cut in early October, but he still urged adjustments to several episodes. "You've plenty of time. Let's work together to smooth out the final blips."

But there were no further meetings of substance, and the "blips," as Bradbury saw them, remained as the late January 1980 broadcast dates approached. When he was interviewed by phone for Steve Ditlea's January 6th *New York Times* preview article, he simply let it all out in print. "They cut corners in production. I believe they started with good intentions that got lost along the way."[2] Bradbury also said that the special effects were shoddy. In his article, Ditlea noted that $2 million of the $8 million in production costs were committed to special effects, and he agreed with Bradbury that the "simple animation" effects (the "globular, disembodied Martians" of "The Fire Balloons") were the best effects in the series. But Ditlea also cataloged the first-night effects that worked against any sense of reality in the three-night broadcast: "The miniseries opens with the shot of a Viking lander wobbling toward the surface of Mars in a rather unconvincing manner. This is followed by model work intercut with Saturn moon rocket footage that does little to establish the reality of a Mars expedition at the turn of the 21st century."

On January 17th, the formidable law firm representing Charles Fries (there were 33 attorneys listed on the letterhead) wrote to Bradbury notifying him that he was in violation of the agreement provision to clear all media statements with Fries ahead of time; without written approval, Bradbury was clearly in violation.[3] The letter was a reminder that Bradbury really had no say in the production itself, but he knew that he cast a very long shadow when the Martian dreams that were now shared by millions of potential viewers were about to be realized on film. He knew that as long as he said no more for now, attention would return to the upcoming broadcast. He was playing the long game, as he always did in Hollywood; he saw the dynamics between writer and studio as a process of education, and he had said as much at the conclusion of Ditlea's article: "I think this will get viewers to read the book. In the future, I hope the producers will get into people's imaginations."

The series was broadcast in three two-hour segments on the evenings of January 27, 28, and 29, 1980 (on the first night, *Chronicles* ran against the first half of ABC's attempt to resurrect the canceled *Battlestar Galactica* series as a made-for-TV film, *Galactica 1980*). First reaction to the *Chronicles* reached Bradbury by Mailgram from *Omni* editor Ben Bova in New York: "Despite NBC's interference enough Bradbury got through to make it all worthwhile."[4] The fact that Bradbury came through at all on screen was the result of a good teleplay by Richard Matheson. Matheson was frustrated that the director lost the intensity of the opening "Ylla" story and cut the powerful "Usher II" and "There Will Come Soft Rains" episodes entirely.[5]

Bradbury would always blame the directing of Michael Anderson for the uninspired interludes that he continued to call "boring." But he never faulted the actors, a strong ensemble cast that included Rock Hudson, Maria Schell, Roddy McDowall, Fritz Weaver, Bernadette Peters, Barry Morse, Darren McGavin, and Bernie Casey. It was a sign of things to come—his *Ray Bradbury Theater*, produced by a far smaller consortium than NBC could command, would attract an even larger pantheon of established film and television stars.

∷ ∷ ∷

The disappointing July 1979 *Martian Chronicles* screening was counterbalanced by the nationwide ABC primetime broadcast of "Infinite Horizons: Space Beyond Apollo," which Bradbury had cowritten with rising documentary producer-director Malcolm Clarke. The program aired Thursday, July 19th, on the eve of Apollo 11's tenth anniversary. The 60-minute show opened with Bradbury's solitary reflections on and around the tower complex of Cape Canaveral's Launch Pad 19, the site of Gemini program manned orbital launches in the mid-1960s. But the focus was on the slow decade-long transition from the Apollo missions to the emerging Space Shuttle era, projected to bring a new wave of communication, energy, habitat, and telescopic achievements into low-Earth orbit.

He worked through two preliminary drafts on his own, one given the Proustian title "Remembrance of Things Future," and the other "Beyond 1984," a title that would float around in several forms before reaching print in other works. For Bradbury, "Space Beyond Apollo" offered an opportunity to bring an extended arc of his metaphors into focus. His angry 1972 *Time* magazine response to the end of Apollo had been framed around the final debate scene of the H. G. Wells 1930s science fiction film, *Things to Come*: "All the universe . . . or nothingness. Which shall it be?" Bradbury and Malcolm Clarke embedded a short montage of this famous footage in the opening of "Space Beyond Apollo" before Bradbury himself answered the question on screen and proclaimed the Space Shuttle as the new liberator of mankind from the "gravity that has held us down since the beginning of time."

Bradbury metaphors emerged at key points throughout; the second segment opened with an allusion to his 1972 essay, "From Stonehenge to Tranquility Base." This portion of text is clearly Bradbury's and opens with a scene of the ancient monoliths: "Stonehenge, in England. Thousands of years ago, man feared darkness and desired the sun. These stones that they cut and set in circles, may have trapped and measured the way of the sun in their sky." The scene shifts to aging launch pads: "Cape Canaveral, thousands of years later. Man built and abandoned these structures in order to put their own fires in the sky."

Bradbury is never far behind the scene, surfacing with Dick Tracy newspaper comics and a prototype of the two-way wrist radio that Tracy wears. With it, Bradbury "communicates" with ABC science editor Jules Bergman, who takes on the more technical aspects of the discussion. At intervals throughout the film, Bradbury facilitates a three-way telescreen discussion between Bergman, Isaac Asimov, and *Future Shock* author Alvin Toffler. Bradbury's distinct phrasing and ideas surface constantly in the coauthored script, including references to Leonardo DaVinci and Herman Melville, a sound bite from his friend David Bowie's "Space Oddity," and a reference to what he always believed to be "the scientific miscalculations and short-sighted budgetary decisions" that led to the orbital decay and destruction of Skylab.

But the real payoff for Bradbury came through the opportunity to voice his final existential caution, yet again, in the closing words of the show:

> One day, if the sun should die, we would all die with it, and so, we would have to find another sun, another Earth. Right now, on the Moon, those first great footprints wait to be filled again and again and we must fill them . . . otherwise time itself will wear those prints away. For Earth is only our birthplace after all. It needn't be our home forever.

Seeing the Cape again had been great fun, but he could never feel comfortable with the challenge of delivering scripted dialog—even when he wrote it himself. The limited special effects and launch simulations reflected a tight budget, and the *New York Times* review noted the overuse of Aaron Copland's

Fanfare for the Common Man, which had become a Space-Age cliché. Yet Bradbury's efforts, along with those of his cowriter and director Malcolm Clarke and cinematographer Gregory Andracke, garnered two Emmy Awards for News and Documentary Programming.[6] Bradbury and Clarke shared the writing Emmy, the first of two Emmys and several Cable ACE awards that Bradbury would win in his career.

But his chance to return to the Cape and the excitement of these subsequent honors came with a new and unexpected heartbreak that he would have to work out in another form of writing. Nothing had launched from the giant rocket pads and gantries at Cape Canaveral in years, and the actual Shuttle launches were still two years off in the future. Bradbury was stunned as he walked around within the inconceivably large and visibly deteriorating structures of the launch facilities and was pierced to the heart by the signs that read "Abandon in Place: No Further Maintenance Authorized."

He dealt with the immensity of that possibility the only way he could, by writing through it. He was preparing his third and final volume of poetry for Knopf, and his morning exercises in verse soon produced a poem in three elegies that carried the sign's edict as an overarching title. Bradbury arranged publication in the May 20, 1979, issue of the *Los Angeles Times*, fully two months before the ABC broadcast of the documentary. He was perhaps too close to the emotions, and the resulting verse is derivative and heavy-handed in places, but the repeating imperatives of the first elegy's final lines offer a simple and powerful lament:

Cut off the stars. Slam shut the teeming skies.
Abandon in Place.
Burn out your eyes.

"Infinite Horizons: Space Beyond Apollo" was made in the interval between the air-launched trial flights of *Enterprise*, a prototype that was not capable of launch into space at all, and the first true launch missions of *Columbia* in 1981–82. With this ABC documentary, Bradbury began what would be a series of dutiful homages to a program that, in spite of its subsequent achievements, constantly reminded him that, since Apollo 17, the human heartbeat remained imprisoned in low-Earth orbit, navigating the boundaries of the thermosphere—achieving near-full vacuum conditions, but still technically within the far boundary of Earth's atmosphere.

Bradbury's role in this award-winning network documentary is very elusive today; the abridged half-hour version widely circulated for use online and in schools eliminated most of Bradbury's presence and metaphors, retaining only the bare bones of the projected Shuttle missions. During this pre-Shuttle interval in the Great Tale, Bradbury's hopes would be compressed into the final florid but heartfelt lines of "Abandon in Place":

Old ghosts of rocketmen, arise. Fling up your ships, your souls, your flesh, your blood
Your blinding dreams
To fill, refill, and fill again
Tomorrow and tomorrow and tomorrow's
Promised and repromised skies.

13 | Beyond Eden

"The Space Shuttle! This will not be an article about it. I mention its name as I once mentioned Zen Buddhism in a crowded editorial office, merely to attract attention." His new article in the April 1980 issue of *Omni*, "Beyond Eden," was intended and timed to provide a rationale for NASA's first Shuttle mission and its successors, but there was wry truth in his opening paragraph. Most of "Beyond Eden" was devoted to articulating an underlying Trinity for his well-developed belief that humanity's God-given mission was to reach the stars.

First, however, he did his duty for NASA, realizing that the biggest hurdle would be to convince Americans that the odd composite Shuttle spacecraft they would see through the highly reductive medium of a television screen was indeed worth the investment. He had often preached the disadvantage experienced by generations who had only seen the majesty of *King Kong* diminished to small-screen television, or the grand wall-size art of Titian and Tintoretto confined to the dimensions of a book. Assuming that only a small percentage of Americans would ever actually see and hear the otherwise unimaginable Earth-shaking power of a Shuttle launch in person, Bradbury decided to play devil's advocate: "As we remember the triumphant ascensions of Apollo, with their thunderous blossomings of fire, we glance half-sideways at the Shuttle. Have we given up our grand Roman biremes for some smaller Viking open boat? Have we leapt off the Queen Mary onto some dumb life raft?"

Writing before the nation experienced the succession of tangible triumphs and high drama that would follow, Bradbury had to pass over the imagined spectacle of launch and emphasize instead the full transition to research that the last three extended Apollo missions had previewed and the subsequent explosion of machine technology that would enable the Shuttle crews to perform such wonders as the construction of space station islands, the placement of satellites and telescopes in orbit, and the ability to repair or upgrade them as needed. "The Space Shuttle, if less dramatic, less romantic, less beautiful to contemplate than Apollo, could be a greater cornucopia of miracles once it reaches Space." In presenting these things to come, he was aided by his friends at JPL and NASA, who provided details of projected missions for him to preview.

Through his preparations, Bradbury was learning about the wondrous machines that would augment and extend the reach of the Shuttle's human crews, and for the first time he fully explored how machines fit into his long-established Cosmic view. He had generated much fascination—as well as some terror—with machines in his fiction, endowing spaceships with sentience and personality ("I, Rocket," 1944), and even resurrecting George Bernard Shaw as a spacefaring android ("GBS Mark V," 1976). Now, Bradbury's layman's sense of space-age machinery became part of a larger whole—a Trinity: "God clones Himself in Man. Man clones himself in machines. Machines, if properly built, can carry our most fragile dreams through a million light-years of travel without breakage. Such machines, and the Shuttle with them, are the armor of our Life Force."

For "Beyond Eden," Bradbury presented the new Space Shuttle as a metaphor, no more, no less; he was not numerate in either his education or inclinations, but he realized that the Shuttle itself was only the first of many building and repairing and experimenting concepts to come. The American Shuttle era would not survive him—STS-135, the final mission, returned to Earth in July 2011, almost a year before his passing—but in this 1980 article he had once more done his best to popularize the first journeys of the Space Age: "Tossed out of Eden, we now go to replant our Garden on God's own front lawn."

∴ ∴ ∴

As his Space-Age trinity was coming into full focus in the pages of *Omni*, Bradbury was preparing an article surveying recent achievements in science fiction filmmaking and speculating about where these achievements would lead Hollywood in the years to come. Essay writing did not come naturally to him; he preferred to shoot from the hip and emphasize his own vision of present-into-future, thereby minimizing the research component—he loved reading and learning history, but he hated homework. An East Coast magazine had commissioned the film article, and the opportunity would allow him to move on from the personal frictions and mixed reception of NBC's recent *Martian Chronicles* miniseries.

He already knew where to go for perspective. In March and April 1980, Bradbury arranged a series of very informal one-on-one interviews with the friends who were largely responsible for the major science fiction film productions of recent years. These included Gene Roddenberry and director Robert Wise, who had recently made Paramount's first *Star Trek* feature film; Lucas Films producer Gary Kurtz and director Irvin Kershner, who were finishing up *The Empire Strikes Back*; producer Steven Spielberg; and special effects production artists Douglas Trumbull and John Dykstra.

It's not clear if Bradbury was able to schedule all of these discussions, but long portions of his tabletop recordings of his sessions with Roddenberry, Kershner, Kurtz, and Dykstra survive. He had prepared for these private visits by looking for the impact of recent science fiction films on the broader worlds of visual art and music, for he was, above all, a writer who absorbed storytelling through all of his senses. In his April 9, 1980, discussion with Gary Kurtz, Bradbury noted how the latest generation of science fiction films had brought Hollywood's long association with symphonic music into a new level of engagement.[1] Kurtz had a deep knowledge of musical traditions, and he discussed the importance of bringing John Williams into the Star Wars universe. Kurtz felt that Williams had created the perfect Wagnerian romantic score, with motifs composed to fit the characters in the first film, and he revealed that the second would introduce new themes; the point was to have a complete symphonic composition by the conclusion of the third film, sometime in the future.

Kurtz's point was indeed serendipitous, for Bradbury was also in the midst of writing a long liner note for the forthcoming Star Wars soundtrack release on the Sarabande recording label. Bradbury's concurrent research into Hollywood symphonic composition had led him to film editor George Korngold, son of Erich Korngold, one of the founding symphonic composers of Hollywood. Both Kurtz and Bradbury loved such early Korngold scores as The Adventures of Robin Hood, The Sea Wolf, and King's Row, and Bradbury's converging research on both the film essay and the Star Wars recording liner note had already helped him to understand the new level of symphonic score found in the initial Star Trek and Star Wars films.

Bradbury had also given a lot of thought to the impact of science fiction and fantasy films on visual art, especially in galleries, where he had long been in conflict with most postwar abstract impressionists and minimalists. Bradbury maintained that the evolution of science fiction and graphic art had initiated what he called a "neo-Pre-Raphaelite revolution" in illustration, impacting not only film-associated art but spreading into the galleries, book illustrations, and phonograph record album covers. His view was generalized and impressionistic, but it had shaped his research for his interviews. Before the year was out, Bradbury would, rather predictably, ask John Williams to collaborate on a musical theater version of his Melvillesque space opera, Leviathan 99. Williams, well acquainted with Bradbury's work, found the stage text interesting, but he could not commit the time that this ambitious project would demand.[2]

Bradbury had launched his interview odyssey by meeting separately with Gene Roddenberry and Irv Kershner on March 4, 1980. His afternoon with Roddenberry was grounded in a long friendship that went back fifteen years or more. Roddenberry was just three months past the release of Star Trek: The Motion Picture, and he was only just beginning to see that his long struggle with Paramount over budget and cutting decisions had established groundwork for a sequel. Only later would the two men realize that their discussion occurred in the strange interlude between the release of a troubled film and the production of the defining film in the series, *Star Trek II: The Wrath of Khan*.

Ironically, they were also reflecting on the merits of *Star Wars* before the release of the defining film of that franchise, *The Empire Strikes Back*. Both men had enjoyed the first film, although Bradbury felt that *Star Wars* had not yet completed its core metaphor: "The Force is pure Zen, but they don't *really* work the metaphor so that you come out learning something about creativity. That's what you need to get out of it. What applies to warfare, running a ship, also applies to painting, acting, being a mechanic—you train your body so well it disappears."

For that insight, Bradbury would have to wait until dinner that evening with Irv Kershner, who was just finishing his work as director of *The Empire Strikes Back*. Bradbury had an idea of what might develop in this episode, for the Force had in some ways been hovering about him since the beginning of 1978, when he had guaranteed completion of Leigh Brackett's initial script if she did not live to finish it. She was able to hand in her draft and, after her passing, Bradbury had received a copy of the fourth revised script.

But Brackett's passing had hit him hard, and he really never studied the product as heavily revised by George Lucas and Lawrence Kasdan. Kershner assured Bradbury that all of the implications of the Force would play out in the new film, manifest in the pivotal training interlude that would introduce Master Yoda to film lore. Bradbury saw the connection with his own loose adaptation of mysticism in *Zen in the Art of Writing*, telling Kershner—as he would many others—"I get out of my way, and let me happen."

Kershner agreed with Bradbury's version of the disappearing artist, that is, the way that Bradbury could, when the Muse allowed, subordinate self-consciousness and wait for the inevitable subconscious idea to arise. But Kershner had made a study of Zen and the cross-cultural traditions of the fairy tale, and he took Bradbury's point one step further: "When self-consciousness leaves, and you lose the sense of time passing, you merge with the environment. But *don't* lose track of your own importance and value. Zen has opposites built into every concept."

What future projects interested his distinguished friends? Kurtz was intrigued by the risks of attempting to film Frank Herbert's *Dune* and saw the more contemporary world settings of Asimov's *I, Robot* as a project of great potential. Irv Kershner wanted to explore the fairy tale tradition more fully and perhaps film Madeleine L'Engle's *A Wrinkle in Time*. John Dykstra was interested in Alfred

Bester's *The Stars My Destination*; Gene Roddenberry, not yet aware that Paramount would become a better partner in four more *Star Trek* films and a *Next Generation* television series, wanted to write novels, where he could have full responsibility for the work. He even quoted Bradbury back to himself, reminding his friend that he had once said, "Science fiction just happens to be one form in which we can say something with sometimes more power and excitement than you can say it in any other way."

This series of private interviews, an engagement in turn with various friends approaching the best years of their respective careers, was rich in meaning and insight—too rich, perhaps; Bradbury was never able to boil it all down into a publishable article. Only his comments on the return of beauty and form to art in galleries and books made it into his next article, tucked away in the spring 1980 issue of the Canadian academic journal *Mosaic* as "Dusk in the Robot Museums: The Rebirth of Imagination."

Yet the entire exercise was well worth the effort—and in unexpected ways. The watershed moment in these interviews came with Irv Kershner, when he observed that the fundamental power of a machine is that it can repeat or replicate. "Repetition is trapping time, it does something that is inhuman, unnatural." In response, Bradbury fell back on his usual consolation in the face of this argument: "The computer is a book, but it doesn't look like a book. The more ways we can find to trap time, so we can learn from it, we can grow. So that we'll never lose the basic truths we need to grow with."

At this point, Kershner asked the fateful question: "What do you mean by growth?" This simple question prompted Bradbury to walk through an unexpected rehearsal of his fully formed response to human insecurity in the modern world:

> We grow when we begin to believe in our own capacity to perform, and we allow ourselves to perform so that we get over that initial insecurity we grow up with, regardless of background. We have two insecurities at the age of twenty. We feel ineffective maybe because we lack education in certain fields and we fight that by doing things. Then the other thing that hasn't anything to do with education itself, it is just that we feel that we fail at everything. I remember when I was twenty, I was afraid of everything—I'm afraid of the world. No matter what I do, I'm not going to do it very well. And by doing, I begin to get more secure with myself, and then I begin to grow.
>
> Now, I guess what's true for the individual would be true for society, and when they test things, and remember things, and test themselves against what they remember, then growth can occur. And then the day comes when you

finally don't think—just do it. And then out of that comes growth. You don't even feel yourself growing. You turn around and ten years have gone by, and you have three hundred short stories. You compare the ideas you have today with the ideas you had thirty years ago, and you see the growth. You are able to look at the clichés, to consider what the machine embodies.

For Bradbury, this formulation began in the mid-1940s with "The Creatures That Time Forgot," set on a planet where everyone had the terrifying knowledge that *there is no future* for anyone. This 1944 story, better known by the title "Frost and Fire," began as his reaction to a thought experiment proposed by Henri Bergson: if you lived in a world where people were born, matured, had families, grew old, and died, all in eight days, how would anyone know that this was not the natural order of things? The answer is that nothing would ever progress; there would be no time to develop science and pass it on for fuller development by subsequent eight-day generations.[3]

Now, nearly four decades later, Bradbury was living and writing at the height of the Cold War, four decades into a world defined largely by nuclear brinksmanship. Necessity had led to his concept of growth as an act of self-willed confidence in facing the future. But there was no guarantee; only hope. Bradbury was on the verge of articulating a metaphor for that hope, and it would be a short story with a strange name: "The Toynbee Convector." This story would represent everything he had hoped to convey in his stories of the future, and in his lectures, and in his interviews. That story was just over the horizon.

Given Bradbury's long years as a public speaker, it's easy to forget that his insights were not created at the podium. For Bradbury, the rare moment of significant concept articulation happened, usually in the form of short or extended metaphors, through those brief creative blazes when he wrote his most significant stories—moments when he was, essentially, in conversation with himself. On very rare occasions, the insights surfaced in conversations with others, but very few of these were ever captured in time. In his evening talk with Irv Kirshner, the forty-year path from "The Creatures That Time Forgot" to "The Toynbee Convector" came fully into his mind.

14 | Robot Museums

Bradbury's deepest journey—so far—into the culture and politics of Washington, D.C., actually began in Canada in the spring of 1980, when the academic magazine *Mosaic* published a Bradbury article titled "Dusk in the Robot Museum: The Rebirth of Imagination." His celebration of science fiction as "the history of ideas" had evolved years earlier, but now he was using this definition as the trigger point in a dual revolution—the growing acceptance of science fiction and fantasy in the teaching of literature across the nation, and a parallel revolution in pictorial art and illustration that promised to extinguish the abstract and minimalist art that he abhorred. For Bradbury, the dual revolution was already finding traction in libraries, galleries, and museums, and it was only a small step to imagine a museum curated by robotic re-creations of the world's great thinkers.

One could always take issue with his Bernard Berenson–bred views on modern art, but there were people in Washington who fondly remembered the sources of Bradbury's broader dreams. The Smithsonian's senior editor, Don Moser, had worked at Time-Life in the 1960s, and he had seen Bradbury's ability to wed technology and imagination in a series of *Life* magazine articles celebrating Space Age achievements. Communications director Naz Cherkezian, who had overseen Bradbury's ill-fated 1978 attempt to explore the Smithsonian buildings through the eyes of young Halloween visitors in "The Ghosts of Forever," was eager to see if the new "Dusk in the Robot Cities" essay could lead to a more marketable variation that focused more fully on the Air and Space treasures and their new facility. Plans for a summer 1980 return visit to the Smithsonian quickly took shape.

A late-1970s trip to Washington had included a tour of the National Air and Space Museum; Bradbury maintained that he had first seen the impressive new building very late at night, illuminated by the momentary flashes of an approaching thunderstorm. That visit led him to write an enthusiastic book review of C. D. B. Bryan's *The National Air and Space Museum* in a November 1979 issue of the *Los Angeles Times*. The review was a hit in the halls of the Smithsonian administrative offices, and it may have been the first time that Bradbury presented what became one of his most often quoted metaphors for inspired invention: "the long march from the rim of the cave to the edge of the cliff where we flung ourselves off and built our wings on the way down."[1] For his summer 1980 visit, Bradbury was interested in pitching an expanded article on robot museums and developing a new planetarium show, tentatively titled "The Great Shout of the Universe," for the Air and Space "Spacearium."

July 31st, Bradbury's first day in Washington, was exceptionally hot, but he was able to spend most of the day in the halls of Congress. His escort fell ill, and Bradbury was escorted through much of the day by Senator Claiborne Pell of Rhode Island. The senator led Bradbury through a floor vote, a short lunch break, a Postimpressionist art show tour, then back to the senator's office to meet with official visitors and reporters; he even shadowed Senator Pell through a session of the Senate investigation of the president's brother, Billy Carter.

Bradbury was back in the care of his Smithsonian hosts for dinner, and he would spend the morning of August 1st in discussions with the editorial staff; they agreed to buy a visual adaptation based on his "Robot Museums" article, and for the moment Bradbury believed that his last three years of work on Smithsonian projects were finally about to yield results. He took lunch in the venerable Arts and Industry Building, the second oldest building of the Smithsonian complex on the Capitol Mall. The A&I retained the typically Victorian multicultural design features of its 1880s origins; Bradbury noted with some interest that he dined in an area of the sprawling building that reminded him "of San Chapelle in Paris, with its blue, constellated ceilings."

Here, as with his mid-1960s Disney Studio vault tours with Walt Disney himself, Bradbury's Smithsonian hosts wanted him to see the potential for future collaborations. His travel notes—recorded in the anecdotal present tense—reveal that his afternoon tour behind the exhibits of the Natural History Museum did not disappoint:

> Then after lunch we go over and visit the gentleman who freeze dries animals, you name it, crocodiles, snakes, birds, all perfectly preserved . . . also: germs and viruses . . . new medical uses for slices of specimens frozen-dried, then re-activated with waters . . . then on down to visit the young men who are putting together a false "reef" in a tank, with mechanical tides, waves, and daylight rising, fading with sunlike illumination, to study growth, life factors, nutrient factors, aereation factors in such tanks . . . fascinating. [ellipses Bradbury's]

A large audience of resident associates attended Bradbury's Baird Auditorium lecture that evening,[2] but plans for a planetarium show remained his prime objective. The national museum complex, especially the new Air & Space Museum, held potential to extend the celebration of Past-Present-Future that he had created for the 1964–65 New York World's Fair and refined during his decade of work on Disney EPCOT's Spaceship Earth ride, at last nearing completion near Orlando. Bradbury left Washington in the summer of 1980 with a strong hope that "The Great Shout of the Universe" would eventually materialize as a "Spacearium" program. Progress on the Bradbury narration was the key element, however, and the entire project would hang on his ability to accommodate the Smithsonian's desire to privilege scientific fact over the inspirational truths of the imagination. Within a year, he would discover that his optimism was premature.[3]

Bradbury still did not fly, but rather than negotiating the crowded East Coast corridor train, he traveled to the Plaza Hotel in New York City by limousine on Saturday, August 2nd. Late that afternoon, he met with actor-producer Cliff Robertson at the Plaza to discuss "The Kilimanjaro Device," a teleplay that Bradbury had retitled and adapted from his own 1965 *Life* magazine story of a time machine that returns Ernest Hemingway to the 1954 plane crash in East Africa that should have killed him, thus saving Hemingway from enduring the final pain-filled years of his life in our timeline.

Robertson saw potential in extending Bradbury's short story into a full-length film on Hemingway's late life, but Bradbury wanted to retain the short teleplay form; he remembered all too well how the expansion of "In a Season of Calm Weather" into the feature-length film *Picasso Summer* had spiraled down from plans for a widely distributed theatrical release to a late-night television movie with no future at all. They would, nevertheless, remain friends. He admired Robertson and his proven record in Hollywood, but Bradbury just didn't want to put yet another good story in harm's way.

Bradbury was joined in New York by his wife (who had no fear of flying), and together they made the usual ocean liner voyage to France, where Maggie's fluency in French helped them form a quiet island of relaxation. Bradbury never really stopped working, but Paris allowed for a more or less one-way cycle; he could write and communicate, but he could be somewhat selective in choosing to answer business matters. He had, as usual, conferred with Don Congdon before departing New York, and the day-to-day publishing matters were well in hand. In all, Bradbury would be away from home for nine weeks, returning to Los Angeles in early October.

But they would return to an America in transition; as the Iranian hostage crisis dragged on, it was now more and more likely that the elections would bring Ronald Reagan to the White House, and the campaign to unseat longtime Democrats in Congress might bring down several prominent targets, including Frank Church of Idaho and Senator Warren Magnuson of Washington. Hope for a philosophically sound and broad-based Republican administration had attracted

Bradbury's friend Russell Kirk, who had helped to establish a compassionate conservatism that was wary of the materialist appropriation of traditional values by the Far Right. Bradbury was also coming into the Reagan fold, largely for the same independent reasons that had resonated for Kirk. Both Russell and his wife Annette Kirk visited the Bradbury home the following year, after Reagan's inauguration had set the stage for the tax cuts that Bradbury considered essential for economic recovery.

: : :

Personally, his greatest joy in 1980 came through the October release of *The Stories of Ray Bradbury*. The one hundred stories showcased in Knopf's retrospective collection came in at nearly 900 pages. The opportunity lined up almost like a conjunction of planets; this was a period in time when Knopf and Bradbury could command hardbound rights to almost all of his previously collected stories. Bantam and Ballantine held the mass-market paperback rights, and kept most of his earlier work in print, but almost all of the earlier Doubleday, Ballantine, and Simon & Schuster hardbound editions were out of print. More recent hardbound editions of *I Sing the Body Electric!* and *Long After Midnight*, along with new 1970s hardbound editions of the ever-popular titles *The October Country* and *Dandelion Wine*, were all Knopf books.

Over the previous year, Bradbury had worked with Don Congdon, his Knopf editor Nancy Nicholas, and Knopf's editor-in-chief and president Bob Gottlieb to round up the hundred best, presented in the order in which the stories first appeared in his earlier collections or novelized story cycles. For stories with an earlier publication history—and there were many—he used the versions he had revised for his books rather than the original magazine publications. Bradbury's lifelong tendency to further revise his stories *between* collections caused some trouble, for he had revised many of his 1947 *Dark Carnival* stories for *The October Country* in 1955. In the new retrospective, Nancy Nicholas convinced him to open with nine stories from the *Dark Carnival* versions, and at the proper point he placed seven more in the forms he had revised for *The October Country*.

Bradbury had the advantage of a long history of inclusion in textbooks and commercial anthologies, a record that provided a pretty good idea of which particular stories in his perennially popular collections had become canonical Bradbury titles. Nevertheless, some well-known stories, as well as lesser-known tales that stand as significant markers during the best years of his career, would have to be omitted. These deferred tales included "I See You Never," a 1947 *New Yorker* story reprinted in the *Best American Short Stories* annual; "—And the Moon Be Still as Bright," the central thematic story folded into *The Martian Chronicles*;

"The Whole Town's Sleeping," perhaps his best-known suspense shocker; and such ever-popular weirds as "Zero Hour" and "The Dwarf."

The twenty-six-story *Vintage Bradbury* compilation of 1965 represented a fairly successful trial of the retrospective concept, and it remained in print. Even so, Bradbury was not always the best judge of his own stories, and as the years passed he had come to favor some tales that lacked the tight, emotionally powerful plots of his best work. The distinct edginess, the trademark Bradbury twist, did not inhabit every supernatural tale, and some of the fantasies and tales of magical realism dissolved into sentiment. It would be hard to disappoint his broad readership, but *The Stories of Ray Bradbury* was a rather expensive hardbound edition only; book review commentary, as well as the places these reviews appeared, would have an impact on the giant collection's longevity in print.

One of the most unsettling major reviews Bradbury would ever receive came from New Wave science fiction writer-reviewer Thomas M. Disch. It appeared in the October 26, 1980 issue of the *New York Times Book Review* and took a tone in direct opposition to the critically insightful introduction that Gilbert Highet had provided for *The Vintage Bradbury* retrospective fifteen years earlier.[4] Bradbury wrote his own introduction for Knopf's hundred-story compilation and unintentionally provided a very personal and off-trail focus for Disch to follow through the words of this isolated passage:

> I was in love, then, with monsters and skeletons and circuses and carnivals . . . I was *not* embarrassed at circuses. Some people are. Circuses are loud, vulgar, and smell in the sun. By the time many people are fourteen or fifteen, they have been divested of their loves, their ancient and intuitive tastes, one by one, until when they reach maturity there is no fun left, no zest, no gusto, no flavor. Others have criticized, and they have criticized themselves, into embarrassment.

This brief excerpt from Bradbury's introduction echoed his celebration of popular culture, and his conviction that the popular loves of early reading and life experiences don't have to be left behind in the adult world. Disch opened up a personal attack from this passage: "There's the choice—love Ray Bradbury, out there beyond embarrassment, or be enrolled among those loveless, zestless critics who never go to the circus." He labeled Bradbury's stories "meretricious more often than not . . . because his imagination so regularly becomes mired in genteel gush and self-pity, because his environing clichés have made him nearly oblivious to new data from any source."[5]

By contrast, other leading New Wave writers and editors, including Judith Merril, Brian W. Aldiss, J. G. Ballard, and Michael Moorcock, had an appreciation for Bradbury that could be contextualized without being destructive or insulting. As writers they all grew past what he could offer, but early in their careers they had learned from his style, and his emotional focus, and his sense of humanity. Science fiction was an armature for Bradbury to place his explorations of the human heart, and his desire to see humanity properly launched into the larger cosmos. He came into the early lives of young readers on their way to becoming writers or astronauts, teachers or librarians. Ironically, Disch conceded this point, but removed it from the final published version of his review: "In SF circles there is a truism that the Golden Age of Science Fiction is twelve, and Bradbury is incomparably the poet laureate of that Golden Age."

There were other ironies in Disch's attitude, including the fact that both Bradbury and Disch valued Poe, Verne, and Wells over almost any other science fiction authors.[6] But the greatest irony of all centered on Disch's decision to discuss only two stories of Bradbury's hundred, "The Night" (1946) and "The Black Ferris" (1948). Disch conceded that these were early stories, but he argued firmly that "the vein of schmaltz evident in 'The Night' recurs in Mr. Bradbury's work as regularly as he reaches for the unattainable. Early and late are meaningless distinctions in his output." Yet neither of these stories, as reprinted in the new retrospective, represented finished work at all.

For this Bradbury was partly to blame, as he had decided to open the volume with an early version of "The Night" that was actually a transitional experiment in second-person storytelling from a young child's point of view. Somerset Maugham, an early Bradbury influence, had inspired the attempt, but very shortly Bradbury would completely transform the story into a third-person narrative that became a seminal moment in *Dandelion Wine*. Similarly, "The Black Ferris" had been held out of all of his collections as it grew into the incident that generates all of the pursuits and dark entrapments of *Something Wicked This Way Comes*. The story progenitors that Disch used to bludgeon Bradbury no longer existed anywhere else in the Bradbury canon, and hadn't for more than three decades.

The Disch review demands analysis largely because it was the most prominent review, magnified in critical circles by the absence of other major reviews. This situation was largely the result of Bradbury's near-absence from the major market magazines for more than a decade, but the limited reviews of *Long After Midnight*, his only story collection of the 1970s, had not helped. The other major American review came from *Time* magazine's Peter Stoler, who noted that Bradbury's reputation, as showcased in *The Stories of Ray Bradbury*, rested on the dark fantasy tales, those "chillingly understated stories about a familiar world where it is always a few minutes before midnight on Halloween, and where the unspeakable and unthinkable become commonplace." Other reviews appeared in library journals, a regional edition of the *Wall Street Journal*, and Canada's *Globe and Mail*.

In the end, the diminished critical attention had less impact on this career-spanning volume than it would have on a newer and smaller collection of unproven tales. The year had begun with the rather uneven *Martian Chronicles* miniseries, and it would end with one of the larger single-author story volumes to make it past a first printing. Yet, *The Stories of Ray Bradbury* has endured for four decades, approaching the shelf life of undisputed canonical writers of the twentieth century, writers such as Maugham, Steinbeck, Hemingway, Welty, Porter, and Cather—all writers who inspired him throughout the formative years of his career.

15 | The Great Shout of the Universe

In February 1981, Bradbury finally completed the planetarium show scenario that he had promised the Smithsonian Institution's Air & Space "Spacearium" staff during the previous year's visit to Washington. As usual for his programs and film treatments, he essentially submitted a full script of what, in this case, amounted to a history of the universe. He didn't really believe in the Big Bang, and he certainly never believed that it was a mystery that scientists would ever be able to accurately date, but he nevertheless began his show with it, as requested. Predictably, even the Big Bang grew into a Bradbury title metaphor, "The Great Shout of the Universe." He also loved "The Ghosts of Forever," left over from his unsuccessful Smithsonian fantasy-film submission of 1978. As a stand-alone, that 1978 title had since been bestowed upon the art book he had recently coauthored with the prominent Argentine artist and photographer, Aldo Sessa; thus, the planetarium show went to the Smithsonian editors as "The Ghosts of Forever: The Great Shout of the Universe."

"The Great Shout" offers perhaps the best explanation for why so few of his major project commissions were ever mounted in their intended venues. With the exception of his 1964 World's Fair narrative and his Spaceship Earth program for Disney's EPCOT, there was often an insurmountable divide between the dream he created and the grounding in reality that his sponsor desired. His cover letter for "Great Shout" indicates that he was aware of this potential problem: "I have been not informational but inspirational. . . . I don't think a planetarium is a place to teach, per se. It is after all, a theatre. And just as I was inspired by museums when I was a child . . . so I feel that you and I and everyone connected with your planetarium, are in the business of shaking people up and rousing their blood so they go out of the show half-mad with love and stunned with the beauties of space. If we do that, the rest will follow."[1]

The Smithsonian was not a venue where his argument would have traction; what would be acceptable in any of his inspirational lectures at Caltech or NASA or the Library of Congress did not pass muster with Air & Space, where expertise and technical accuracy understandably represented a major component of museum practice. But as David Romanowski (later writer-editor for exhibits at Air & Space) has noted, Bradbury's brand of visionary prose was a known quality going into the venture.[2] The detailed criticisms of administrators, astronomers, and Spacearium staff at the museum established, from Bradbury's perspective, an unbridgeable gulf between his cosmology and the established science of the day.

The nine-page compilation of comments that Bradbury received from Air & Space had been condensed and tastefully redacted to remove some of the most blunt comments of the various experts ("crude and devoid of meaning," "reeks with misunderstanding").[3] What Bradbury actually received was a paragraph-by-paragraph breakdown of the cuts, rewording, and conceptual modifications that would be required for the Spacearium to mount "The Great Shout of the Universe." Terminology was a big issue for the experts.[4] Bradbury's use of the term "light-years" was far too careless and did not reflect distances of "6 times 10 to the twelfth power miles across"; planetary formation did not involve "the antiquated notion of fire, flame, or forging of the planets"; in short, "modern theory is desired" throughout Bradbury's journey down through time and across the galaxies.

Perhaps Bradbury could have worked with "modern theory" to some extent, but his metaphor-rich style was something that the Spacearium staff should have reckoned with ahead of time. When discussing matters of the cosmos and existence, he did so in the style that came naturally to him, a style that represented the core "truth" of his writing. He wrote about the cosmos just as he had adapted *Moby Dick* for the screen in the 1950s—Bradbury by way of Melville, the Old Testament by way of Shakespeare. But Air & Space was a public institution, and he would need to find another way. His attempts to describe a great "night" before the Big Bang would have to go by the wayside, as would his beloved ghosts of forever:

> The ghosts of possible worlds, possible light, possible flesh. Suns that must birth themselves. Light that must birth matter, matter that must ghost itself to flesh.

The Air & Space response was simple: "Please delete any references to objects birthing themselves, both here and elsewhere, because this is something which the uninformed public can easily misinterpret." The same held true for any references that were "too animistic for good science," or that might imply "a living, breathing entity which contained what was to become the Big Bang." From a mission standpoint, Air & Space administrators were correct, of course; the Spacearium was there to teach, not to preach—what would play well in a private sector museum or planetarium had its limitations in a public institution of the late twentieth century.

Bradbury took payment only for work done on the project, in return for release from the Smithsonian contract. This venture was not all for naught, however. Three years later, in July 1984, the Aerospace Museum at Exposition Park opened in Los Angeles, and within a few years annual attendance was reportedly second only to the Air & Space itself among American museums of this kind.[5] It was a state-operated venture, but the funding sources were private sector. Bradbury's wayward planetarium show was reborn here, with narration by his good friend, distinguished actor James Whitmore. The final thirteen-minute show, retitled "The Windows of the Universe," retained its original dual focus on the birth of the universe and the prospects of human exploration.

Bradbury's many subsequent retellings of his Air & Space museum adventure reflected his own point of view. In describing the experience to a bookstore audience in 2002, he compared it to some of his Hollywood studio disappointments of the past.[6] But the Smithsonian misadventure had also sparked his final full rejection of Big Bang cosmology. "I got to brooding over the Big Bang Theory. . . . Why wouldn't it be possible that the universe has been here forever? Isn't that a better idea? Is it impossible? Everything's impossible! We are impossible!" His 1981 showdown over "The Great Shout of the Universe" also helped him begin to articulate the next logical question, one that he would further refine in several essays of the 1980s:

> The next thought was, why are we here? What is the purpose of life? A lot of people say it's meaningless. Nonsense. There's no use having a cosmos, no use having a universe, if you don't have an audience. The universe, needing an audience, created us. We are the meaning of life. We're the gift the universe gives back to itself.

: : :

Bradbury's Smithsonian disappointment over "The Great Shout of the Universe" played out as another exhibition opened back home in Los Angeles. In 1980, almost four years before "The Windows of the Universe" opened at Exposition Park's Aerospace Museum, the Park's adjacent Museum of Science and Industry prepared for a major exhibition by artist Tony Duquette, well-known for decades of set and costume designs for stage and screen. "Our Lady Queen of the Angels" was an immense installation inspired by Duquette's study of world religions. He believed that eight archangels identified in a number of Judeo-Christian sources had parallels across the world's religious traditions, and he conceived a work of environmental art centered on a twenty-one-foot-tall Madonna flanked by twenty-eight-foot metal armature representations of his eight archangels.

Jewels, tapestries, and wooden altars created by Duquette completed the visual effect, but in 1980 he partnered with Ray Bradbury and composer Garth Hudson to enhance the visual impact with sound.

This was just the kind of transcendent concept of overarching human faith and destiny that Bradbury could get excited about, and he wrote original verse in the form of the *saeta*, a tradition of religious song and lyric composition with roots in the mixed Christian and Jewish pre-Renaissance history of Spain. He had no training, of course, in any form of music, but his 1950s experience in composing Restoration operetta verse for Charles Laughton had given him a passion for experimentation. In the late 1960s and '70s he had attracted major composers to orchestrate his space-age verse in cantata and madrigal form, and he had no reservations about exploring yet another historical form of music in verse, and soon wrote "A Walk in the Garden of the Queen of the Angels."

Charlton Heston, who had narrated Bradbury's *Christus Apollo* cantata for its Royce Hall premier in 1968, recorded his friend's *saeta*-inspired verse. Unlike the earlier work, there was to be no choral accompaniment; Heston's narration was backed solely through an electronic score composed by Garth Hudson, a founding member of the popular rock group "The Band" and an innovator in orchestral music. This time, Bradbury's verse did not have to stretch for choral interpretation, and the magisterial tones of voice and music merged well with Duquette's awe-inspiring installation. The full experience remained on display in the Museum of Science and Industry from 1980 until 1983, when major expansion work began at Exposition Park for the 1984 Olympic Games.

The remarkable blend of image and voice caught the attention of David Boss, a trained photographer and National Football League executive who had published Bradbury poems in the NFL's *Pro Magazine* years earlier. "I was truly excited by the visual richness it provided," he wrote to Bradbury. "Seldom have light, textures, color, and atmosphere been so beautifully handled. A true theatre for the senses."[7] The exhibition and the text of Bradbury's *saeta* (along with a rare Bradbury self-portrait) were documented in Duquette's limited edition illustrated book, *Our Lady Queen of the Angels*. This proved to be a providential move; in 1989, an extensive fire in San Francisco's Duquette Pavilion destroyed the entire relocated installation, including its extensive jeweled tapestries and armatures.[8]

: : :

As Tony Duquette's collaborative installation began its long run at Exposition Park, Bradbury was already preparing for a return to lecture in the teaching conservatory environment of the American Film Institute. Two months after founding AFI in 1969, George Stevens Jr. had Bradbury lecture to the first class of fellows—including emerging director David Lynch—enrolled in AFI's Center for Advanced Film Studies. During his decade as director of AFI, Stevens generally brought in directors to speak, since many of the students were on a directorial track of studies. But he also brought in writers like Bradbury and Oscar-winning cinematographers, like Bradbury's friend James Wong Howe. Bradbury's next seminar lecture occurred on April 15, 1981, following a screening of the two films he was most associated with at this time in his career, *Moby Dick* and *Fahrenheit 451*.[9]

He arrived at AFI's Greystone campus in Beverly Hills for his April session, and delivered the kind of unconventional remarks on Hollywood and screenwriting that had won his earlier lectures a place in the AFI compendium of sessions. Despite his frequent studio contract writing assignments in the 1950s and early 1960s, Bradbury always regarded himself as a Hollywood outsider; his comments in April 1981, as well as his return to Greystone in June 1982, provided AFI students with a perspective they would not get elsewhere.

Bradbury offered the animated give-and-take spark that energized the AFI seminars, and Stevens found his three appearances significant enough in the history of the seminar program to include excerpts in his 2006 AFI anthology. Bradbury was one of only two writers included among the thirty selections, but he had either worked for or been friends with many of the legends of filmmaking in these pages, including King Vidor, Fritz Lang, Rouben Mamoulian, William Wyler, George Stevens Sr., Alfred Hitchcock, George Cukor, John Huston, Robert Wise, Gene Kelly, Richard Brooks, Jean Renoir, Federico Fellini, and James Wong Howe.

In all three of his seminars, Bradbury's deep-seated desire to protect his creations from directorial interference constantly simmered beneath the surface of his comments. Occasionally, he would erupt, as he had during his first seminar in 1969:

> People come to you and they say, "Boy, we love your work. We love this and we want to buy it." Then, as soon as they buy it, the teeth come out. You become not the father of the work, but the stepfather. All of a sudden, you're the outsider, a villain. I have often said to these people, "Look, I'll do the script for free for you if you'll shoot my mistakes instead of yours. My mistakes are better.[10]

Stevens selected this passage as the epigraph for Bradbury's chapter in the AFI anthology. Portions of the two 1980s seminars were silently blended into the 1969 seminar text, but one passage clearly postdates Bradbury's 1976 breakthrough in understanding Shakespeare's *Hamlet* on the stage of the Old Globe in San Diego. In one of his 1980s AFI seminars, he used this new awareness as he underscored the vital importance of character in cinema:

> You have to give us the moments of truth and take enough time with each of the characters so they become ricochet boards off which things happen. A really good production of *Hamlet* sets up the all-important mechanism in the first scenes for the whole play. . . . It's a death-play, the darkest play ever written, and the character of Hamlet is written so that if it's played right, you see him destroyed in front of you.[11]

This was a lesson that he had learned in scripting *Moby Dick* for John Huston three decades earlier and then applied to his own creations for his unproduced 1961 *Martian Chronicles* screenplay for MGM.[12] Now, two decades further into his career, he would pass this lesson on to the AFI classes of 1981 and 1982.

At the same time that he was preparing for the 1981 AFI seminar, he was also deeply involved with securing the foundation for a relatively new motion picture memorial award dedicated to George Pal, a pioneering director of mid-century science fiction films. Bradbury knew Pal and cherished his own memento photograph astride Pal's version of the Time Machine on the set of Pal's 1960 adaptation of H. G. Wells's novel. Four of Pal's films, including *Destination Moon* (1950), *When Worlds Collide* (1951), *The War of the Worlds* (1953), and *The Time Machine* all won Academy Awards for Special Effects.

In the early 1970s, prominent genre filmmakers were able to spin off the Academy of Science Fiction, Fantasy, and Horror Films as a showcase for the work of Pal and other influential names working in these genres. The Golden Scroll awards became ASFFHF's equivalent of the Oscars, and on January 31, 1976, Ray Bradbury presented the Best Fantasy Film Award to George Pal for *Doc Savage: Man of Bronze*, his final feature film.[13]

After Pal's passing in 1980, the Academy Foundation created the George Pal Memorial Award, an open category prize "for any achievement deemed worthy of recognition." To further distinguish the Pal Memorial Award from the annual slate of Golden Scrolls (later Saturn Awards), the awards ceremony honoring 1980 achievements featured the first annual George Pal Memorial Lecture on Fantasy in Film. Bradbury inaugurated this series and presented his lecture at the Academy's Samuel Goldwyn Theater on February 19, 1981.[14]

With his return to the AFI seminars and his inaugural George Pal Memorial Lecture, Bradbury was becoming a chronicler and celebrant of the films in the genres with which he had, in spite of his unconventional wanderings beyond traditional genre forms, been most closely associated throughout his career. He would soon win a Saturn Award for Best Writing—his 1983 nomination for

Something Wicked This Way Comes won over the George Lucas–Lawrence Kasdan nomination for *Star Wars Episode VI: Return of the Jedi.*

Three months after his memorial lecture for George Pal, Bradbury was himself honored by distinguished Hollywood friends who shared his passion for understanding mental illness and fighting the exclusion of the disabled from mainstream culture. On May 26, 1981, Bradbury received the first annual Mental Health Association Performance Award at the Ambassador Hotel in Los Angeles. The honorary chair was Alan Arkin, who had just starred in *The Other Side of Hell,* a biographical film on Mental Health Association president Bill Thomas. Bob Newhart, then at the height of his television career, was the master of ceremonies. Gene Roddenberry chaired the event and secured participation from two special Bradbury friends. Charlton Heston read excerpts from Bradbury stories, and Gene Kelly, who had encouraged Bradbury's work in fantasy and science fiction since the early 1950s, presented the actual award.[15]

: : :

One of Bradbury's more intriguing metaphors of life remains buried in the radio archives of the *CBS Radio Workshop*'s 1956 season—his brief introduction to an Antony Ellis adaptation of his Greentown story, "Season of Disbelief": "Life, to all of us, is an endless coil of rope playing through our hands every moment of every day. The long line of the rope goes back to the time we were born and extends on out ahead to the time of our death. In between lies the eternal 'Now,' the flickering moments when each of us must play the rope as best we can, without burning our fingers, snarling the coils, or breaking the line."

With the passion of an independent visionary prone to challenge audiences and interviewers, it was inevitable that he would, at times, burn his fingers on his life cord. In 1957, he may have been one of the first writers to say, on a New York television show, that he was glad that Senator Joe McCarthy was dead.[16] He would occasionally stand up to Hollywood executives and producers that he felt had crossed the line with his rights as a writer, and occasionally he would be wrong. One of the few times that he truly "snarled the coils" of his lifeline occurred in the very first days of 1982, when he was the featured speaker in "The Mind and Supermind" adult education series at Santa Barbara City College.[17]

Bradbury was at his best speaking on a focused topic, where he could bring up stories from childhood, from his evolution as a storyteller, or from the space-age achievements he often witnessed and celebrated. There was never a script, but appropriate inspirational examples usually slotted into place as he moved through a presentation. There was always the risk of distraction, however, and the distractions multiplied as he arrived in Santa Barbara to speak on the required topic, which had no readily apparent Bradbury anchor at all: "The Invisible Revolutions in Our Society."

He came to the stage distracted by poor travel directions, a rushed dinner hosted with more drink than food, and an introduction by the moderator that encouraged him to be devilish and controversial. Writer Nils Hardin attended, later observing privately that Bradbury made the mistake of "trying to force the emotion he usually evokes, without much problem, and it showed, and he became loud and really didn't make much sense in context at times."[18] He got off on politics, which almost always made him confrontational in a public forum; on this particular evening, Bradbury was sharply critical of the widespread despair and disengagement in society, blaming filmmakers, television hosts, and former presidents. There was far more criticism, laced with profanity, than inspiration, and some of his audience left early.

It was a rare thing, and he immediately regretted the effect of his rage-tinged spontaneity. He apologized appropriately and asked to return to speak gratis and "with all gentility and good manners."[19] Bradbury accepted full responsibility, as well as the judgment of the Santa Barbara News-Press column on the incident, which mercifully cited a far worse performance by gonzo journalist Hunter S. Thompson a few years earlier.[20] For Bradbury, as always, the assigned topic was really an invitation to extemporaneous storytelling. When asked if his featured speaker had digressed, moderator Dr. Edward Crowther was firm: "The subject is whatever Ray Bradbury wants to talk about." Most of the time, the storyteller's emotions ran true, no matter what the topic.

16 A Eureka Year

If 1981 had its high and low points, 1982 proved to be a year of unexpected discovery. It began with an unanticipated opportunity to repay a debt to the memory of old friends. Bradbury's relationship with the *Magazine of Fantasy & Science Fiction* (F&SF) went back to the late 1940s and the very first issues of this groundbreaking, digest-size quality genre magazine. It was still hard for Bradbury to accept the loss of founding editors Tony Boucher and Mick McComas, who encouraged and advised him as he rapidly made the full transition into the literary mainstream. F&SF was perhaps the most significant way that Bradbury had kept his ties with the genre magazines while living in the major market world, and Boucher's passing in 1968 had deeply saddened him. McComas had died in 1978, and now his widow, Annette Peltz McComas, needed Bradbury's help in memorializing both men.

She wrote in early 1982 to see if Bradbury could somehow help her promote *The Eureka Years*, an unusual homage anthology scheduled for publication by Bantam.[1] It contained many of the best stories from the early years of the magazine (including Bradbury's "The Exiles"), as well as letters from Bradbury and other writers who corresponded with the founding editors. Bantam provided no advertising budget, so Bradbury wrote to Ben Bova, founding editor of *Omni*, to suggest a review-article.[2] The high standard of literary quality established by Boucher and McComas in the pages of F&SF had paved the way for *Omni*'s sophisticated interdisciplinary blend of science, fiction, and mainstream culture, and Bradbury's review appeared in the October 1982 issue. Slowly, through introductions, reviews, and interviews, Bradbury was paying his debt to the memory of writers and editors who had played crucial roles in his early career.

There were eureka moments for Bradbury as well in 1982. The year began with a major break into children's programming through NBC's January 17th broadcast of "The Electric Grandmother," a full hour *Project Peacock* special. Veteran director Noel Black worked with a screenplay cowritten by Bradbury and Jeff Kindley, who would have further successes on his own with children's television programming. The show included a masterful performance by Maureen Stapleton and received an Emmy nomination for Outstanding Children's

Program along with other critical recognition. Bradbury's greatest satisfaction came from receiving a Peabody Award for this show, which paved the way for significant circulation in schools and libraries following the initial broadcast and distribution. The show was widely enjoyed by Gen-Xers, and more than made up for the problems he encountered with the 1962 version he had scripted for *The Twilight Zone*'s third season, which was not cut to his specifications.[3]

The award-winning success of "The Electric Grandmother" was soon followed by another well-made television adaptation of a well-known Bradbury tale. During the spring of 1982, the Learning Corporation of America produced "All Summer in a Day," one of the most often anthologized Bradbury tales. This 1954 story dated from a time before interplanetary probes, when it was still possible to imagine Venus as a world of unbroken clouds and constant rain. Every nine years, Earth's colonists find that the sun emerges for a brief two hours that brings out the true beauty of this strange world and renews the colonists.

But the children cannot remember this miracle, and they dislike a more recent arrival in the colony's school—a shy young girl who can actually remember sunlight on Earth. They simply don't believe her, or their parents; as the predicted day and hour approach, the story becomes one of Bradbury's best explorations of the darker side of childhood. "All Summer in a Day" was broadcast on a cable channel in the summer of 1982 and three years later would reprise to excellent reviews on the new PBS series "Wonderworks."[4] If "The Electric Grandmother" explored what it means to be human, the televised adaptation of "All Summer in a Day" offered a reminder of Bradbury's early ability to blend beauty and edginess in a tightly focused short story.

March 1982 brought yet another journey into Bradbury's past—this time, biographical rather than literary. Two decades of work championing an elevated monorail to replace his beloved Yellow Car and Red Car trolley lines had led nowhere, but he had managed to become deeply involved with the city and regional rapid transit agencies created in 1976. Bradbury spent much of March 1982 trying to inject at least a glimmer of his dreams into the planning efforts of the Rapid Transit District Los Angeles City Transportation Commission. On March 6th, Bradbury and the *Today* show's Tom Brokaw headlined "Los Angeles in the 80s: An Urban Feast," a four-hour symposium spread across the Grand Hall of the Dorothy Chandler Pavilion. Bradbury, lecturing as an "optimistic futurist," also spoke at the 1982 Mass Transit Show and Conference, held in the Los Angeles Convention Center in early April.

His reward would be a day spent out in Riverside County's historic trolley museum, which had grown into the Orange Empire Railway Museum in the old

Santa Fe rail-stop town of Perris, by this time a burgeoning suburb. But he wasn't here to see the new growth; on March 16th, he had a chance to climb aboard and briefly ride one of the old interurban Red Cars of the Pacific Electric Company, retired in 1961; during the war years, the old P-cars had taken him home from his day-office in downtown Los Angeles all the way out to his parents' home in Venice, stepping off before the old cars turned south on down the coast. He also saw the old inner-city yellow car narrow-gauge trolleys; during the Great Depression, he had often shared a friend's trolley pass, handed out the window so that he could then jump aboard at the rear of the car. The conductor and the motorman always looked the other way.[5]

: : :

The scripted cue cards he had endured for his 1979 role as host of ABC's "Space Beyond Apollo" had been unnerving, especially for a writer who loved to speak extemporaneously; but the Emmy that Bradbury won had only added to the interest that NASA and the Smithsonian had in engaging him for further activities. But it was an engagement to speak at the Library of Congress that provided the opportunity for his summer 1982 trip back to the nation's capital.

Bradbury had supported the Reagan campaign's proposed tax cuts and strong opposition to Soviet expansion, and another Washington visit would provide an opportunity to at least approach the White House staff and to rejoin his preelection conversations with congressional leaders, some of whom had long admired his vision.[6] Bradbury was not a big fan of the defense side of the Space program, but he knew that any of these initiatives might offer at least a chance to get more money for NASA's true mission as well. When it came to the Space program, Bradbury had never shied away from dealing with the devil.

On the evening of April 6, 1982, the Bradburys had dinner with Bruce Murray and his wife, and Murray outlined a list of contacts that could help Bradbury make the most out of his Washington trip. Murray was still director of the Jet Propulsion Laboratory and a senior planetary scientist at Caltech, and he arranged for Bradbury to have a tour of the National Air and Space Museum before opening hours, courtesy of the Museum director. Murray's cousin, Congressman Tom Foley, future Speaker of the House, was the Majority Whip at that time, and could provide a Congressional perspective for Bradbury;[7] it's not clear if he actually met with Foley, but he was able to interact with the Senate, where he met Senator Bob Packwood for the first time; Packwood—and eventually Senator Alan Cranston—would form friendships with Bradbury that helped him see the inside challenges that NASA encountered year in and year out in the halls of Congress.

As always, Bradbury set out on his long transcontinental journey by rail from Los Angeles. His first stop, at Bowling Green State University in northern Ohio, was a personal one; longtime friend Bill Nolan had sold his own Bradbury archives to the university, and Bradbury stopped in to dedicate the collection on April 19th. The crown jewel of Nolan's collection had been a gift from Bradbury many years earlier—the typescript used as setting copy by Ballantine Books for the 1953 first edition of *Fahrenheit 451*, complete with pre-galley revisions in Bradbury's hand.[8]

By the time he reached Washington on the evening of April 21st, Bradbury's focus was completely on the future. After taping an interview for a new documentary on Herman Melville on the morning of the 22nd, he spent several days consulting with Smithsonian administrators, primarily in the National Air and Space Museum. He was critical of the placement of exhibits (and said so), but he also tried to make headway with the narration he had prepared for a film display of flight and space history. He also toured the national Gallery of Art and other major museums, both public and private, including the Hirschorn.

Most of his explorations of the way things happen in Washington occurred on April 26th, 1982, when he had lunch with Senator Bob Packwood. The Senator brought in all of his Bradbury books for signing, and that quickly broke the ice; the two established a lasting long-distance friendship. Bradbury had now broadened his contacts in Congress, and that evening he would lecture at the Library of Congress as planned. But he had done nothing in advance to follow through on his idea of a visit to President Reagan's White House. Bradbury's hotel was close by, and after his Congressional lunch, he simply walked over to the White House and asked if he could go in. "I've never done anything like that in my life," he would later recall in a private interview.[9] After giving his name at the security perimeter, he had the presence of mind to ask security to tell the White House press office who he was. With no prior knowledge of his intentions, the press staff recognized him and brought him right in.

Bradbury's White House tour was overseen by Larry Speakes, at the time President Reagan's assistant press secretary, and discussion soon turned to Bradbury's offer of assistance in support of the administration's economic policies and the future of NASA, which seemed to be approaching an historic crossroads—the interplanetary missions that Bradbury favored were overshadowed by Shuttle missions, the space station, and antiballistic missile research and development. Predictably, his views had no immediate impact, but his support was noted; three years later, he would find himself presenting his critiques and visions in front of the National Commission on Space.

Bradbury's potential value as a public speaker in a wide range of audience venues was well-known, and the encouragement in the follow-up letters to Bradbury was hard to mistake, even couched in the usual indirect style of bureaucracy. "I know you will serve as an articulate spokesman for our point of view," Speakes wrote, "and certainly a welcome addition to those of influence who are willing to step forward and take a stand."[10] Speakes briefed White House Chief of Staff James Baker on the Bradbury visit, as well as political advisor Ed Rollins and Republican Party chair Richard Richards.

Bradbury's support of Reagan's leadership and certain administration policies was not simply an example of another prominent democrat flipping to the Republican Party. Like his good friend Russell Kirk, architect of the compassionate conservatism of postwar America, Bradbury stood openly against any form of authoritarian intolerance, either from the left or the right. A generation earlier, Bradbury had openly resisted McCarthy and the intolerance of McCarthy's climate of fear while also publicly calling out naive liberal intellectuals who remained blind to the nightmare horrors that continued within Stalin's postwar Russia. In much the same way, Russell Kirk could stand against those on the left who condemned traditional western values while at the same time actively condemning conservative champions of conspicuous consumption who used western values for their own purposes. Bradbury and Kirk were known first and foremost as independent visionaries, and this was a distinction that gave them credibility with a large sector of the population no matter which presidential candidate they might each vote for.[11]

That evening, Bradbury was guest speaker at the Library of Congress. The spring issue of the Library's *Quarterly Journal* contained his recent poem, "Of What Is Past, or Passing, or to Come," and during the evening he was put to work signing 500 copies for his hosts. This poem would soon anchor his refined justification for science fiction and his settled vision of human creativity in the space age, and it no doubt emerged in the presentation for his Library of Congress audience; as always, he would punctuate his comments with retellings of a Bradbury story or two (this time, his humorous Hemingway homage, "The Parrot Who Knew Papa," was a highlight). "Fascinating, hilarious, and inspiring" seemed to sum up his talk, as conveyed to Bradbury later by the *Quarterly Journal*'s associate editor; here was the reaction he hoped for, almost everywhere he spoke. Trouble came only if he got too political or argumentative, but on this particular evening he was at his visionary best.[12]

Bradbury continued on to New York for consultations with Don Congdon and a few editors. The return rail trip home, with a changeover in Chicago between

Amtrak trains, still followed the ghosts of the Santa Fe, Union Pacific, and Southern Pacific passenger trains that had carried him across America for decades. His mind was full of the larger experiences of this long trip, but he never forgot the people who read his books and were inspired by his stories. On the way home to Los Angeles, as Amtrak's *Southwest Chief* negotiated the relatively smooth BNSF rail tracks through New Mexico, he was finally able to type a long critique of a promising story he carried along with him throughout the trip—a story by a teenage writer who sought out Bradbury's judgment and would someday grow up to become the prominent mystery and horror writer Dan Chaon.[13]

17 One-Way Ticket Man

After returning to Los Angeles from his April cross-country train journey, Bradbury spent much of the rest of 1982 involved in the increasingly complex dynamics of filming *Something Wicked This Way Comes* at Disney. He was also trying to pull together a new story and other previously published tales for Byron Preiss's concept of an illustrated collection centered on Bradbury's ever-popular dinosaur tales. But in October, he would take to the rails yet again for another Disney project that he had worked on, at intervals, for more than a decade—the opening of Disney World and EPCOT's Spaceship Earth venue outside of Orlando, Florida. He had no way of knowing that this adventure would be one of his last transcontinental journeys by rail—and a one-way journey, at that.

At the Los Angeles Union Station, he realized that there was no direct Amtrak link between New Orleans and Orlando, and it was too late to navigate the time-consuming alternative from New Orleans up to Washington to catch the East Coast train back down to Florida. After a scheduled lecture at Tulane University, he was unable to find student volunteers who could drive him from New Orleans to the Disney World opening and the interviews that had already been scheduled for him there. In his mind, there was *always* a work-around; after all, this was the author who could not fly to Florida to receive the Aviation Space Writers Association's Robert Ball Memorial Award for his 1967 *Life* magazine article on the Apollo program. He had been represented at that ceremony by a photo of himself riding a bicycle, and his *Life* editor couriered the award cross-country to his Los Angeles home.[1]

Bradbury ended up renting a private limousine for the rest of his journey. A flat tire en route led to the discovery that there was no adequate spare aboard the car; when the tire was finally replaced, the engine blew more than a hundred miles out. Bradbury spent yet another night on the road, his only companion a television broadcast of the World Series. He completed his journey by hired cab, convinced that higher powers were reminding him of the gentle hint that astronaut Walt Cunningham had given him a decade earlier, after narrating Bradbury's *Madrigals for the Space Age*: "Up, up the long delirious burning blue . . . | Where never lark or even eagle flew."

Nevertheless, Bradbury could put that decision off, at least for a few more days. For now, he would live out a dream of the new theme park—a dream first placed in his mind by Walt Disney himself as they discussed their separate interactions with the 1964–65 New York World's Fair planners. Bradbury had prepared the voice narration for the United States Pavilion, and Disney had tried out many of the ideas that would evolve into the EPCOT Future World and World Showcase concepts in Florida. In a very real sense, Disney had taken Bradbury's lament for the ephemeral legacy of many of the most famous and magical World's Fairs, and wiped it away by saying, "Nothing has to die." Bradbury often spoke and wrote about that 1963 admonition from Disney, who maintained that a well-conceived entertainment park with deep roots in the past and present would endure into the future.

After Disney's passing in 1966, Bradbury's long involvement with WED (later Walt Disney Imagineers) began in 1970 and accelerated in the mid-1970s, when he was brought into the planning forums. It was during these years that he established enduring working relationships with Marty Sklar and John Hench, who were carrying on the Disney vision for the Florida park complex. Subsequent Bradbury addresses to the Imagineers (including his December 1976 "You are Renaissance People" talk) and the Disney World Conference on Agriculture and Energy brought him deeper into the project.[2] In 1981, Disney executives celebrated the 1971–81 "Tencennial" of the Magic Kingdom at Disney World and secured an essay from Bradbury for the special Sunday supplement published in the principal Florida newspapers.

In that seldom-seen essay, Bradbury recounted his early conversations with Walt Disney, conversations that had, with the passage of time, shifted Walt's actual words into Bradbury dialog without diminishing the essence of the conversations.[3] But he spoke his own latter-day reflections without distortion, revealing implicitly how closely Bradbury felt that his own secret loves paralleled those of Disney himself:

> I listened to him talking about his childhood much like my own, comfortable with candy butchers and horse-drawn milk wagons, beginning to fall in love with the newly invented movies. . . . There lay Walt's greatest strength. He displayed constant proofs of his childhood. He wasn't childish in any way. He didn't let his memories get in his path. But he did use them and grow with them. He didn't let anyone talk him out of his loves, as most of us do by the time we are 17 and our so-called friends and well-meaning but ignorant relatives have brainwashed us into insignificance. Walt spoke of his past with immense affection, but the Future, now! Well, that was really something!

After days of travel by train, limousine, and taxi, Bradbury would at last see the culmination of his history of mankind saga that he had worked through various iterations with Disney animation and ride design legend Marc Davis. The concept had evolved significantly; Bradbury's original "crash" back through time, inspired by his reading of books on the successive layers of cities on the site of ancient Troy, was eliminated. The ride would instead rise up into the lower regions of the sphere and move forward in time through the advances in communication and art from prehistory to the beginning of the information age. At the end of the radial journey up the interior shell of the great geodesic sphere, the inner dome formed a planetarium surface for projection of future advances into the cosmos.

From Bradbury's perspective, the October 2nd opening of EPCOT's combined Future World and World Showcase centered on Spaceship Earth. The great sphere housed a fully enclosed ride that had grown, through the hands of many artists and designers, from his initial "Yestermorrow Time Machine" of 1970 and the "EPCOT Theatre" concepts of 1976 into the fully articulated wonders of EPCOT's Spaceship Earth. The festivities included singer-dancers in futuristic dress and flights of doves symbolizing the hope for humanity that Bradbury had tried so hard to inspire within the sphere's dark interior.

Just two years before his death, Bradbury revisited his opening day thoughts for Disney's *Twenty-Three* magazine: "Through the crowd came John Hench, and when he held me and hugged me, I thought, *Oh, my God. This is the greatest moment in my life, in my world, to be part of the birth of EPCOT.* . . . We can keep growing with it. We can change parts of it. We can even rebuild parts of it. But it will continue to influence us." This evolution was inevitable; the communication technologies displayed in the upper portions of the ride itself changed through several iterations to reflect advances in fiber-optics and the internet; the carriage seats were eventually equipped with interactive screens for the riders.

These technological updates made it easier for Bradbury to accept successive transformations of his own narrative script. Bradbury's poetic and metaphor-rich descriptions, spoken by character actor Lawrence Dobkin, played out too slowly for a ride in motion; Bradbury himself had experienced a similar challenge at the 1933 Chicago World's Fair, when he encountered the moving radial track around the dinosaur exhibit (he was removed for walking backward against traffic to extend his experience).

Imagineer Tom Fitzgerald was tasked with the first revision in 1986: "People couldn't process the poetic narration and still process the movement and what they were seeing. I rewrote it for Walter Cronkite, who recorded the new narration in the Magic Kingdom with a cold, at a fifth-grade level so that it was slow enough that kids understood, but not offensive or boring for parents." Further script revisions, due more to the changing technologies of the images than to issues of style, occurred as the narration was rerecorded for Jeremy Irons and finally Dame Judi Dench. But Bradbury had been at the creative nexus of Spaceship Earth for a long, long time; his influence on the basic concept and choices of historical moments, as well as his inspirational narrative tone, remain.

As the EPCOT opening wound down, and as he finished his prescheduled interviews for next year's release of Disney's *Something Wicked This Way Comes* film adaptation, Bradbury faced the inevitability of another one-way ticket trip—this time, and for the first time ever, by air. The time-consuming detour by rail through Washington, with no direct route west at all, was simply not feasible; there was too much work to do back home. He would have to travel by air, and he soon realized that the best way to overcome his lifelong fear of flying would be to make it essentially an out-of-body experience. His antidote to terror turned out to be preflight drinks and the company of a number of Disney executives and staffers who were also making the trip back to the West Coast.

Bradbury managed to emerge from his reverie long enough to observe the Mississippi River, but he later refused Roy Disney's invitation to look out at the Grand Canyon. Yet he was fascinated by the way that time seemed to slow down to a crawl; it had been sunset when he crossed the Mississippi, and only a little deeper into sunset when his flight began the long hundred-mile descent into Los Angeles airspace.[4] He would always work through the various traumas of life by revisiting those moments and encounters recursively, through his writing. But flying was a fear that had only existed in his imagination, made large by his deep-seated susceptibility to the power of suggestion. What he really feared was himself, and the possibility that he might literally lose control of himself in a plane full of passengers and crew. But he now knew that he could stare down this specter, and so did the American public; the November 8, 1982, issue of *Time* magazine ran a color photo of Bradbury secured in his seat, offering a gritty smile, captioned "Bradbury: one giant step for man."

Part III

1984 Will Not Arrive

So I ran over to the studio, and there was Orson Welles, sitting with his dog, recording *Something Wicked This Way Comes.* . . . And then in 1984, . . . we did a broadcast together, New Year's Eve 1984 on CBS. I did a full hour with Orson. He read from the book and I interpreted it. . . . It was CBS TV, celebrating New Years. We were there to wish people a happy New Year and I was to say that 1984 is never coming. I'm not a pessimist. I believe in the future.

—RB, October 22, 2007

18 "My Name Is Dark"

The fate of Ray Bradbury's far-traveling hopes for his next feature film would be determined during 1982. Several years earlier, the quarter-century odyssey of Bradbury's various *Dark Carnival* and (eventually) *Something Wicked This Way Comes* screenplay *nachlass* had found sanctuary under Kirk Douglas, who held the property while his son, Peter, evaluated various offers with Bradbury. Chances of making the film under the 1976 Paramount contract ended when David Picker left the studio, but Paramount's $50,000 option on the latest Bradbury script would eventually have to be paid off by someone if the film was to be made elsewhere. Peter Douglas and his father were now carrying the option on their own shoulders, looking for a studio to take on production costs.[1] In 1978, Steven Spielberg expressed interest in optioning the script, but once again that was no guarantee of production.[2] Disney had twice offered to buy the film without financing it, but it was not until David Irman became director of creative affairs that Disney fully committed to the film and the paramount option was finally paid off.

Irman had previously been with Twentieth Century Fox, where Peter Douglas had almost negotiated a multisource financial package after the Paramount deal was canceled. Irman was already a strong supporter of *Something Wicked's* potential for film, and he soon convinced newly arrived Thomas Wilhite, Disney's vice president for production.[3] Kirk Douglas provided a copy of the script, which was soon approved, and preproduction began just as the summer of 1981 came to an end.

Peter Douglas would produce, and Jack Clayton would direct, although initially there was trouble with Clayton over studio publicity access to the set. This was reminiscent of Clayton's dynamics during the Paramount option period; he was not Disney's choice for director, but Peter Douglas backed him. Bradbury continued to back his old friend as well, but events would soon change their thirty-year relationship in significant ways.

The source of the problem originated back in 1976, when Clayton worked closely with Bradbury to deal with the many cinematic difficulties of the 1974 script that Bradbury had fashioned on his own during the earlier Chartoff-Winkler option period. Bradbury's old "film the book" instinct, which had been reinforced by his early 1970s preliminary conversations with Sam Peckinpah, had resulted in an impossibly long 262-page screenplay by 1974. During September 1976, Clayton provided Bradbury with a written critique and a 34-page screen treatment that Bradbury followed closely that fall, as he prepared a much more manageable 113-page script.

Bradbury's 1976 script became, essentially, the working script of 1981. As British media scholar Phil Nichols has observed, this tighter, more textured script also introduced problems that would come back to haunt writer, director, and studio later on.[4] Nichols traces the main difficulty to the loss of some of the recursive scenes at the carnival, through which Bradbury had originally built up the terrors of the mirror maze and the centrality of the carousel's ability to advance or regress age. Clayton had hoped to eliminate the carousel completely, just as he had cut Halloway's "bullet trick" destruction of the Dust Witch, but these economies had consequences. The final destruction of the three principal evil characters—Dark, his partner Cooger, and the Dust Witch—was completely reworked in the 1976 script and remained that way as shooting began in late September 1981.

Or, *almost* the same. During the summer, while Hollywood was immersed in a writer's strike, Clayton brought in John Mortimer from England, an accomplished writer who had previously worked with Clayton on two films. Mortimer's work was not deeply invasive (Bradbury's 113-page screenplay grew by only ten pages), and Mortimer succeeded in bringing the townspeople more fully into the predatory net of the Carnival. Clayton had wanted the horror to rise from the experiences of these everyday lives, believing that horror arising from fantasy alone is not really horror at all. Mortimer's changes came at a price, however, as he cut dialog elsewhere that continued to diminish the central characters for the sake of accelerating the tempo of events.

Bradbury's reflections on these script dynamics changed greatly over time. In late August 1981, just four weeks before shooting began, he approved the changes with only one reservation. That concerned the elimination of the second scene at the carousel, where Jim and Will cause Dark's partner, the brutish Mr. Cooger, to accelerate far into old age and the skeletal horrors of a living death. Instead, Mortimer's revisions simply drop Cooger from the story, a move influenced by Clayton's aversion to playing the same trick twice in a horror film. Bradbury was right in anticipating that this significant cut would cause problems for the final resolution of the film, but at the time he simply agreed to disagree.[5] The great sense of betrayal that he would later express in countless interviews was probably prompted by what happened after the initial filming was completed the following spring.

If there was disappointment and some degree of anxiety after the final Clayton-Mortimer revisions, Disney's expensive and richly detailed exterior set for the film provided a significant emotional lift. Bradbury always thought and wrote from a deeply visual mix of imagination and memory, sparked by many pre-literate trips to the movie theaters of 1920s Waukegan with his mother. In 1952, when he went to work at Universal-International on his original screen story *It Came from Outer Space*, he would sometimes eat a solitary lunch on Universal's timeworn set for *The Phantom of the Opera*—the first silent film that his mother had taken him to see at the age of three. As the exterior set for *Something Wicked* went up on the Disney backlots, Bradbury walked over to find the Waukegan of his youth meticulously fashioned out of Disney magic.

He was frankly not prepared for this, or for what he saw when he entered the center of the re-created town: "I turned the corner in the lot and there, sitting in the middle of the plaza, was my Buick, my old Buick from 1928. Well, I ran over and I opened the door and I put my hand in, and I burst into tears; it was like an old friend. We traveled back and forth to Arizona once, and we came out again and stayed in L.A. So that car was part of our lives." Bradbury's father Leo had no money when he brought his family to Los Angeles in 1934—just that 1928 Buick, nicknamed "Effie." Leo saved the gas in the tank for a month as he walked all over Los Angeles looking for work. In 1939, they were finally able to buy a Plymouth, and his father sold the Buick for ten dollars.

Here, on a Disney back lot, was the same make and model as Effie, right down to the upholstery, and this simulacrum symbolized the greatest transition of Ray Bradbury's life. His screenplay had bridged time and distance, and he would find that the largely veteran cast could bring nostalgia and terror together in a number of well-made scenes. Jason Robards portrayed Charles Halloway, an aging man who finds purpose and renewal as the protector of two boys targeted by the masters of a strange, predatory carnival that has come to Green Town out of season, at Halloween. Jonathan Pryce, in his first major American screen role as the combined Illustrated Man and co-owner of the carnival, offers a masterful counterpoint to the Charles Halloway of Robards; in his first scene, Pryce will quietly introduce himself to the young Will Halloway and his best friend Jim Nightshade through the terrifying understatement, "My name is Dark."

Bradbury was excited to have Jason Robards in the pivotal role of Will Halloway's father, a role that had interested Robards ever since Sam Peckinpah had introduced him to Bradbury a decade earlier. Jonathan Pryce was a very pleasant surprise; Bradbury had long wanted his friend Christopher Lee to play the role of Mr. Dark, but Clayton's choice of Pryce resulted in a masterful performance.[6]

Filming kept close to schedule and Bradbury was able to view a rough cut in March 1982.

After the screening, Bradbury had some worries about the agency of the final lightning storm that destroys the carnival, but he told Peter Douglas that he enjoyed most of the film, especially the pivotal library scene, where Charles Halloway tells the boys what he has discovered about the true history of the carnival and tries to protect them when Mr. Dark finally tracks them down. The Halloway-Dark confrontation is one of the more memorable terror scenes in genre films of that era. Together, Bradbury and Clayton had greatly heightened the power of this confrontation for the 1976 script. That had been a high point of their on-and-off seven years of collaboration, but events would now test their ability to work together under deep stress.

Disney's early July 1982 screening changed everything. The audience surveys were troubling enough that Disney executives pulled the film from release pending additional writing and shooting.[7] Bradbury's version of this adventure eventually became that of a parent saving a child from a near-death experience and varied little from this form, offered in private interview many years later:

> The next day, the head of the studio, Ron Miller, called me, and said, "Will you come in?" I said, "I will." I went to the studio, I looked in the door, and he said, "I hope you're not going to say, 'I told you so.'" I said, "There's no time for that. Rehire the actors, re-build the set. Make me the director. I'll fix the film for you." So I did the whole thing over, including editing the film. I fired the composer, and got a new composer to come in. . . . And I wrote the narration, and I re-edited the last reel to make it work, and there you go.[8]

Archival reconstruction of these events by Nichols reveals the actual dynamics. It's clear that Bradbury's opinion was valued; as the shooting schedule was laid out in October 1982, Bradbury was perhaps less marginalized than Clayton, who had never been favored by the studio. But neither played a major role; as Nichols notes, Bradbury's voice "was just one of many contributing to the reshaping of the film. Far from being the director, Bradbury was frequently ignored. Except in the final phase, when Bradbury's and Clayton's dissatisfaction led them to threaten to withdraw their names from the film, both writer and director were just cogs in the Disney machine."

Although Bradbury would always maintain that he did not work with Clayton during the remaking of the film, the archival record shows that they joined forces—both in writing and in person—to urge retention or reinstatement of scenes with Disney executives, including Ron Miller and Tom Wilhite. Their original writer-director working relationship remained viable, and Bradbury's subsequent revisionist memory may have been due in large part to his almost visceral desire to downplay any friction in his relationship with Disney.

Scenes were reshot to resolve problems with the Dust Witch's hunt for the boys in their homes, the mirror maze sequence, and the destruction of the carnival. To replace the Dust Witch pursuit, Clayton's alternate idea for an invasion of spiders was filmed with the same actors, now distinctly older in appearance. Bradbury won a battle for control of his opening narration. In most other respects, the reediting and reshooting of Something Wicked This Way Comes was, first and last, controlled by Disney, and in particular, Tom Wilhite.

The special effects expertise of Lee Dyer was prominent in the reshot sequences, and in planning these shots Bradbury's very visual imagination and deep understanding of his characters proved most useful. Bradbury worked closely with Dyer in person and through written descriptions of how the revised scenes might play out; intense work, but in June 1983, shortly after release, Dyer thanked Bradbury for his "honesty and sincerity in working with me and my unit." Clayton also worked closely with Dyer on the special effects storyboards, indicating yet another point where, contrary to Bradbury's subsequent commentaries, he and Clayton almost surely worked together during the reshooting and reediting stage.

The substitution of a new score by James Horner for the original Georges Delerue score, along with an evocative film poster by David Grove, completed the reworking of the film. The up-and-down drama of production and the subsequent reshooting and editing of the revised film had taken more than a year. For better or worse, the film was heading toward its actual release on April 29, 1983. Jack Clayton would be back in Europe by that time, but he arranged for Bradbury and some of the remaining cast and crew to have a private screening on April 13th in the Animation Building at Disney Studios.[9] Since the studio's decision to reshoot, the two men had focused on the modifications to the film and did not revisit the disputes of the previous year.

In one sense, both Clayton and Bradbury were dissatisfied with the lessening of darkness and the touches of commercialism that the studio brought to the final production stage; Clayton resented the former element, Bradbury more the latter. His thirty-year friendship with Clayton had survived Moby Dick and John Huston at the beginning, and long delays before Something Wicked even reached the production stage. There were irreparable strains on their relationship, especially from Bradbury's authorial perspective, but they parted with civility. He would not see Clayton again before the director's death in 1995.

Bradbury still maintained strong ties to the Writers Guild Film Society he had cofounded in the early 1960s and with the parallel societies that it inspired. On

May 13th and 14th, the Screen Actors Guild Film Society held two screenings at the Doheny Plaza Theater in Beverly Hills, sponsored by Disney Productions. But by far the best event from Bradbury's perspective preceded the premier and screenings. Disney arranged for an 86-minute radio preview of the film, using selected dialog cuts from the film bridged by passages adapted from the novel read by Orson Welles.

During the second week of March, 1983, Bradbury attended the narration taping session, but he arrived near the middle of the live take. He was immediately concerned with the prepared script given to Welles—some passages were written in the anecdotal present, others lapsed into the past tense. This was a synopsis prepared from the film script, originally Bradbury's but heavily altered by John Mortimer and Jack Clayton; in retrospect, the relatively few present-tense passages—apparently pulled forward from scene descriptions embedded in the script—blended well with the overall mix of Welles's narration and the actual soundtrack excerpts. Bradbury was, of course, too close to both novel and film to realize this during the isolated audio recording session, and he wanted time to rewrite and have the Welles narration retaped.

On March 14th, he sent a photocopy of Welles's reading text to Howard Greene, head of publicity at Disney, marked up to show the variations in verb tense. "Why didn't someone call me and show me this before it was too late? Did anyone there read it beforehand? Why weren't these errors caught? And— finally—why wasn't I asked to write the script for Welles? I would have been delighted to have done so!"[10] Bradbury's compulsion to orchestrate any variation of this wayward film, now so close to release after so many years of delay and crisis, prevented any sense of objectivity. His letter to Greene betrayed this understandable lack of perspective, but Greene had handled more complicated characters than Ray Bradbury (a long list that included Jack Clayton).

Greene couldn't bring Bradbury to agree with the framing technique of the original narrative—he would always grumble about it, to the end of his days—but Greene helped him realize that Welles's magisterial delivery and the mixed-in soundtrack cuts, featuring Jason Robards and Jonathan Pryce, would completely overshadow any stylistic inconsistencies; besides, the cost of rerecording on a Wellesian scale was clearly out of proportion to the benefit. Bradbury was able to regain his sense of participation on March 31st, when he recorded a brief introduction for the entire 86-minute radio recording.[11] He was eventually rewarded with photos of himself with Welles and his dog, but the true memento came from Welles himself, who handed Bradbury the reading script with a hand-drawn flying saucer inscribed, "For Ray from his admiring friend, Orson."

Critical reactions to the film were mixed. *New York Times* reviewer Janet Maslin found the opening lumbered by "an overworked Norman Rockwell note" until the unfolding horror element, underscored by Jack Clayton's direction, evened out the "gee whiz" nature of Bradbury's dialogue and provided a tension superior to the original novel. Roger Ebert found it "a horror movie with elegance" that broke free of the genre boundaries, a quality he credited to Bradbury's script without knowing Clayton's significant influence on the tightness of the action.

Alan Dean Foster, whose science fiction credits included the novelization of *Alien*, wrote a very comprehensive review that found merit in the sustained suspense of the pivotal moment in both film and novel—the library confrontation between Jason Robards's Halloway and Jonathan Pryce's Dark. For Foster, the power of suggestion melts away in the unimpressive tarantula scene and the very predictable disintegration of Dark in the final moments of the film. Fundamentally, Foster found Bradbury's acknowledged power as a prose poet had become a liability in this film, where horror must be delivered: "If you are going to give them poetry, it had better draw on Edgar Alan Poe and H. P. Lovecraft, not Robert Frost."[12]

In spite of the residual elements of unevenness in the final release, there would be awards that underscored the high points of the collaborative effort that went into the project. The 11th annual Saturn Awards, given by the Academy of Science Fiction, Fantasy, and Horror Films for productions released in 1983, took place on March 23, 1984. The tandem Best Film winners by genre were *Something Wicked This Way Comes* in Fantasy, and *The Return of the Jedi* in Science Fiction. For a time, at least, winning the Best Writing Award (over the *Jedi* script of Lawrence Kasdan and George Lucas) diminished his anger with the early screenplay revisions of John Mortimer.

Categories other than Best Picture were combined for all genres, and *Return of the Jedi* dominated a strong field of nominations; nevertheless, *Something Wicked* received nominations for Best Supporting Actor (Jonathan Pryce), Best Special Effects (Lee Dyer), Best Costume (Ruth Myer), and Best Music (James Horner). Horner was actually up for three films—*Brainstorm*, *Something Wicked*, and *Krull*—and he eventually won for *Brainstorm*. The meticulous, brilliant, but unpredictable Jack Clayton would also have his day in the sun, nominated for the Grand Prize at the Avoriaz Fantastic Film Festival in France.

19 A Most Favorite Subject

As 1983 opened, Bradbury published a celebration of science fiction art in the Los Angeles *Herald Examiner*. He had sold the afternoon edition weekdays on a downtown street corner for nearly four years after graduating from high school, and he never let his long-term relationship with the *Los Angeles Times* interfere with occasional articles and reviews for the *Examiner*, the paper that had once paid him a penny for every three-cent newspaper he sold.

"1982: A Helicon Year for the Artists of Science Fiction" appeared in the January 2nd issue, and it served as a reminder that, since the early 1940s, Bradbury had followed science fiction art more closely than he had followed science fiction itself. The visual image of King Tut had led him into the pages of his father's newspaper at the age of five, and the daily comics had jump-started his reading that same year. By 1928, he was hooked on the *Amazing Stories* and *Wonder Stories* cover art of Frank R. Paul. The science fiction he continued to read after the mid-1940s was mostly that of his friends and former mentors, writers who were outnumbered by the science fiction artists, new and old, who had successively caught his interest as storytellers of a different kind. He reveled in standing some of these artists up against any number of painters enshrined in the Museum of Modern Art, and often did so in print.

In a very real way, "A Helicon Year" offered a fanfare for *Dinosaur Tales*, a Byron Preiss concept book that gave a new and very visual life to Bradbury's presentation of dinosaurs in his fiction. For his introduction, Bradbury turned back to the very earliest loves of his life: "At dinner one night, some years ago, someone asked each of us to name, in order of importance, our Most Favorite Subjects in All the History of the World. 'Dinosaurs!' I cried. Followed swiftly by, 'Egypt, Tutankhamen, Mummies!'"

These "Most Favorite Subjects" were, of course, the foundational loves of a young child's reading and moviegoing life in the 1920s and 1930s, and in Bradbury's case these loves inspired and periodically recharged his creativity as a writer; as time went on, the metaphors that these magic subjects invoked also served to safeguard him from the disappointments that came with age and the slow ebbing of fresh ideas welling up from his subconscious. *Dinosaur Tales* was never meant to be a significant book for anyone but the new generation of young readers who were now exploring his stories in textbooks and perhaps in Bantam editions. Yet this short collection of his dinosaur tales and poems contained two early 1950s classics that had found widespread acceptance among adult readers in the major market magazines—"A Sound of Thunder" (*Collier's*) and "The Beast from 20,000 Fathoms" (*The Saturday Evening Post*), known better as "The Fog Horn."

The original magazine illustrations have a recurring internet popularity, but Preiss, whose book designs and concepts were well-known in popular literature and graphic arts publishing, took this legacy one step forward. There was no scarcity of Bradbury admirers among magazine and book illustrators, and Preiss lined up seven to provide interior art for *Dinosaur Tales*: the long-established cartoonist/illustrator Gahan Wilson, graphic artist Jim Steranko, French science fiction artist Moebius (Jean Henri Giraud), children's book illustrator David Wiesner, and artist/designer Overton Loyd.

Kenneth Smith's frontispiece illustrations framed up a rare chance by Ray Harryhausen to comment on the intersections of his friend's "path of the written word" and his own "path of the moving visual image." One of Harryhausen's early encounters with a difficult Hollywood producer was witnessed by Bradbury and featured in *Dinosaur Tales* as "Tyrannosaurus Rex." This tale and most of the others were reprints from earlier times, but the volume included one new story, "Besides a Dinosaur, Whatta Ya Wanna Be When You Grow Up?"

"Besides a Dinosaur" was another variation of life in Waukegan with a stubborn boy and a wise grandfather, written specifically for the targeted age group of *Dinosaur Tales*—a strong contrast with the tone and terror of the next story, the classic Bradbury time travel adventure "A Sound of Thunder." But such thunders had been part of the tradition since Willis O'Brien animated *The Lost World* and *King Kong*; in fact, Bradbury dedicated *Dinosaur Tales* to O'Brien, who "so changed my life, forever."

Dinosaur Tales also contained a playful and seemingly insignificant poem that offers the only clue to a creative path not taken. "Lo, the Dear Daft Dinosaurs!" offers a *Fantasia*-like sequence of dancing dinosaurs, finally slipping down into ancient tar pits along with the tiny fleas that feed from their blood. Dr. Bruce Murray, Jet Propulsion Laboratory director at Caltech, had told him of recent research into the preservation of megafauna DNA through insects recovered from amber and other solidifying media. Bradbury made a note of it, touched on the concept in his 1983 poem, but never found time to write the story or novel that he planned.[1] Nearly a decade later, Michael Crichton's *Jurassic Park* led Bradbury to close the door on that plot line; he would never write another tale about the majestic creatures that first fired his imagination as a young boy.

: : :

As Bradbury collected his dinosaurs, he continued collecting his poems as well. The 1981 publication of his third and final Knopf poetry volume in a decade was by no means the end of his verse explorations of life, death, family, the need for love, and the human compulsion to explore and discover. He published another dozen poems in 1982 and 1983 and showed no signs of slowing. For some time, his inspiration had traveled beyond the nineteenth- and early-twentieth-century poets he had read—often with suggestions from his wife Maggie and friend and mentor Edmond Hamilton—in the 1940s. During the 1960s and 1970s he had gravitated to contemporary poets who wrote light verse with more insight than the critics sometimes credited. This was especially true of Phyllis McGinley and Helen Bevington, two mid-century writers whose poetry greatly encouraged Bradbury.

McGinley's subtle light verse revolved around home and family and was not favored by feminist critics or devotees of confessional poetry, yet her imagination and verse structures were respected by W. H. Auden, who provided a foreword to her Pulitzer Prize–winning 1961 volume, *Times Three*[2] (Auden had enigmatically revealed an unspecified respect for Bradbury's fiction a decade earlier, perhaps for similar formal and imaginative qualities).[3] Bradbury intended to write McGinley for years and felt great guilt over the lost opportunity when he read of her passing in 1978. If she was out of date, so was Bradbury, and he felt a kinship with her independent vision.[4]

He had also followed Helen Bevington's rise as a poet, and, in July 1983, having learned his lesson from McGinley's death, he began a correspondence with Bevington. He began by saying, "I think it is important for a writer to tell another of their love." And, indeed, he had loved the older woman's poetry for many years. In the 1960s, Bradbury's Aunt Tilita gave him a copy of Bevington's *When Found, Make a Verse Of*, and this gift was a major factor in his return to poetry in middle age. He continued to follow her career as a Pulitzer Prize finalist and frequent contributor of light verse to *The New Yorker* and *The Atlantic*.

She was an explorer of the mysteries of faith across all religions and cultures, a path that Bradbury had also followed. Like Bradbury, Bevington had learned to read by way of the newspaper comics, beginning with one of Bradbury's abiding favorites, "Little Nemo." He sent her a copy of *Dinosaur Tales*, and she reciprocated with her new book, *The Journey Is Everything*. Bevington called Bradbury's imagination "a fanciful world strange and new to me." She felt, from his letters, "as if we had been related at birth but somehow lost touch till now." As their correspondence continued, it was clear that Bradbury felt the same way, even though she was fourteen years his senior.

Bevington's childhood allusion to "Little Nemo" proved ironic, for Bradbury was involved in his own grown-up adventure-nightmare with an animated film project based on Winsor McCay's early-twentieth-century comic strip, *Little Nemo in Slumberland*. Japanese producer Yutaka Fujioka, head of Tokyo Movie Shinsha studio, wanted to produce a feature-length animated film around McCay's Nemo that would be true to the original comic character. He intended to explore the American practice of recording dialog and then animating the characters, and he first approached American animation legend Chuck Jones in 1979.

The underlying problem was that Nemo's dream fantasies were stand-alone newspaper strips that never had an overarching storyline or extended adventure. Fujioka needed a sustainable story, so Jones asked his then-publicist Steven Paul Leiva to introduce Fujioka to Bradbury. There were script discussions, but nothing came of this initial meeting. Meanwhile Jones declined the project, as did George Lucas. In 1982, Gary Kurtz, producer of *Star Wars*, asked Bradbury to script the project in consultation with Steven Paul Leiva, who was now Kurtz's director of animation development; Leiva assembled a team of supervising animators that included Chris Lane, Roger Allers (who later codirected *The Lion King*), and Andy Gaskell, as well as Canadian animator Robin Budd.[5]

Bradbury admired the inspirational art of Chris Lane, especially his images of airplanes. Initially, Kurtz wanted Bradbury to develop a visually descriptive treatment rather than a script, resulting in the concept of Nemo sailing off to slumberland in a flying bed inspired by Lane's images.[6] Bradbury also came up with the concept of "Omennemo," later shortened to "Omen," a darker alter ego who took control of Nemo's dreams in ways that promised to open out into suspenseful adventures. For a year, Bradbury came in periodically with descriptive scenes that responded to the inspirational art that the Japanese were producing in collaboration with Leiva's artists but was unable to form a sustained story line.

But there would be no Omen, and no suspenseful entrapment of Nemo in the dark dream world. This was simply not what was wanted by Fujioka or his animation team; they were used to the Japanese method of preparing animation before recording dialog, and they rejected the entire duality of Bradbury's Omen-Nemo. Kurtz released Bradbury and left the production team himself in 1984, but by this time Bradbury had actually written a script on his own. It continued his development of the Omen-Nemo duality, a concept he had worked to good effect in both the novel and screenplay forms of Will and Jim in *Something Wicked This Way Comes*. This characterization was simply a nonstarter for the Japanese team, and Leiva was not even given Bradbury's script before his team disbanded and left the production. The entire project moved on in other directions that no longer resembled Bradbury's ideas at all.

Bradbury and Leiva had hoped that the Japanese producers and their artists would approach a comic-into-animation film as Disney had, with an eye toward broad audience appeal. But the Japanese studio team wanted an animated feature aimed at the very young. Bradbury's valuable name power led the studio to bill the final film as "based on a concept by Ray Bradbury," but even that credit was an exaggeration. "I worked on *Little Nemo*, of course, for the Japanese, but they didn't understand what I was doing. It could have been fabulous. They made a film, but it's for three-year-olds. And Disney's films were for all ages."[7]

Bradbury was compensated for these animation frustrations by the continuing popularity of his illustrated *Dinosaur Tales*, as the Bantam trade paperback eventually became available in hardbound and mass-market paperback formats. In collaborating with Preiss and his cavalcade of artists on this book, Bradbury had successfully come home to a safe harbor from his past. *Dinosaur Tales* was simply a very pleasant exercise in connecting with a new generation of readers, an exercise that also allowed him to renew and recalibrate his own creativity, and to do so on his own terms. But his next return to old harbors was not destined to be enjoyable, and was not of his own making at all.

20 Memories of Murder

Periodically, Bradbury had revisited his preliminary 1940s work toward a detective fiction novel, inspired to some degree by his reading of post-Chandler and Hammett talents like his friends John D. MacDonald and Kenneth Millar. Millar was a colleague from the Santa Barbara Writer's conference series, better known as Ross Macdonald, creator of the Lew Archer novels. The 1978 publication of James Crumley's *The Last Good Kiss* also recharged Bradbury's interest in the off-trail aspects of the genre that he had pursued during the mid-1940s, and it would only be a matter of time before he would turn again to the risky novel-length fiction form that had always given him so much trouble. What he didn't know was that his first return to that long-lost period of his career would be forced upon him by the rules of the publishing game.

During the mid-1940s, Bradbury's oddball detective mysteries and off-trail weirds far overshadowed anything he had so far placed in the science fiction pulps, where he had not yet developed an ability to tell his own truths and develop his own situations. Here again, as he had done with the science fiction and weird stories, Julius Schwartz circulated Bradbury's crime yarns and negotiated sales, primarily with the genre pulps owned by the Popular Publications syndicate. Senior editor Alden Norton and his sub-editors, Mike Tilden and Ryerson Johnson, eventually accepted sixteen of Bradbury's submissions for the pages of *Dime Mystery*, *Detective Tales*, *Flynn's Detective*, and *New Detective*. Schwartz knew all the editors, and his Manhattan office was just blocks from most of the pulp syndicates, but he failed to limit the rights to first North American serialization.[1]

Down through the years, problems would occasionally surface when various pulp editors refused Bradbury-initiated options for second serial or anthology rights of his science fiction and fantasy stories; Don Congdon, who became his agent in September 1947, was often able to handle these situations and arrange releases from the original pulp houses. Bradbury left most of his early crime stories out of his collections; only "The Coffin" and the ever-popular "The Small Assassin" reached the pages of *Dark Carnival*, and only "The Small Assassin" carried through into *The October Country*. In the early 1950s, Bradbury had considered allowing adaptations of these stories by the talented illustrators at EC and found that Alden Norton would not release rights. Rather than allow Norton's proposed 25 percent fee share with Popular Publications, Bradbury steered EC toward his weird tales instead. Norton had no interest in reprinting the stories for Popular's surviving pulps, and that's where the situation rested for another three decades.

But everything changed in the early 1980s, when Joel Silverstein discovered that pulp historian, collector, and anthologist Robert Weinberg had purchased all of the Popular Publications story rights. Silverstein found an eager publishing partner in paperback giant Dell Publishing, and he approached Bradbury and Congdon with a proposal for a collection of these early crime tales. Congdon confirmed that Bradbury would have to accept the inevitable, but they nevertheless had some leverage with Dell editors who wanted to keep Bradbury's good will and secure a Bradbury introduction.

With this leverage, Congdon was able to gain the rights through one-time publication of the collection, limited to a single paperback print run, no hardback or subsequent options, and no overseas publication whatsoever. By the spring of 1982, Bradbury had drafted an introduction for the as-yet untitled collection and provided Dell editors with copies of the original pulp versions for fifteen of the stories. He had been able to keep the sixteenth story out of the collection—"Killer, Come Back to Me!" In 1946, he had arranged a release for radio adaptation of this tale, and Norton had allowed it. But the other fifteen went in, leaving only the title story undecided.

Initially, Dell editor Robert Mecoy made the worst possible suggestion for a volume title: *Ray Bradbury's Corpse Carnival*.[2] Of all of the publication titles that Popular's editors had forced on him during the 1940s, this was one of the worst in Bradbury's mind, and he was not amused by the irony. His submitted title for this story had been "One Minus One," a too clever allusion, perhaps, to the story of a conjoined Siamese twin survivor who searches out the murderer of his brother. But that wasn't really the point; Bradbury considered all of the better titles, either his own or those imposed by editors, and wrote possible choices all over the letter from Mecoy—"The Long Night," "The Long Way Home," "Wake for the Living," and "The Trunk Lady." Exclamation marks penned after these titles indicates his irritation at the whole process.

Mecoy, actually a long-standing admirer of Bradbury's work, followed up his unintended gaffe with another sensitive question, asking if Dell should "turn our copy editors loose on your manuscript."[3] This was an offer, not a directive, and Bradbury apparently allowed house styling of spelling, punctuation, and very limited word usage. He always maintained that he lightly revised the stories for the collection, yet comparisons between the new versions and the original serial versions show very little revision or word choice variation at all.

In his first letter, Mecoy had given a word-picture of the proposed wrapper illustration, designed to "reproduce the feeling of the pulps. The menaced female and the menacing skeleton will be rendered in the dark, stylized manner of the old magazines. The background will be a circus / carnival midway. It's night, and there are hundreds of colored lights, a Ferris wheel and a background of midway banners." In an odd way, this description was very close to Bradbury's 1945 description of a dust jacket for his first book, *Dark Carnival*.[4] It may have struck a chord, and this cover design carried through without major opposition from Bradbury. *A Memory of Murder*, the final generic title decision, avoided privileging any of the individual story titles.

Bradbury's introduction, and his decision to lead off the collection with "The Small Assassin," his finest story in the group, was about all he could do to frame up the inevitable comparisons that the critics would make to his work in other so-called genres. *A Memory of Murder* was, indeed, a wide-ranging survey of the ways he had explored very odd premises for crime story plots. His "what-ifs" were typical of Bradbury's early years: What if a baby, born well beyond term, was mature enough to secretly plot revenge against both parents for inflicting the trauma of birth ("The Small Assassin")? What if a wise-cracking private detective could bait four mob bosses into killing each other ("Four-Way Funeral")? What if a murderess could make her rich hemophiliac lover bleed out without knowing he was even in danger ("A Careful Man Dies")?

He was convinced that, once imagined, his characters would have to work their own solutions, without the benefit of any traditional form of ratiocination. He never knew the answer to these mysteries when he started, and that sometimes frustrated the magazine editors who greatly admired the young man's style but sometimes despaired at the way his tales resolved. Even with his new introduction for context, there was no way of telling how reviewers would judge the new collection—if they judged it at all.

: : :

Throughout his complicated and wide-ranging creative career, Bradbury usually found that a bad publishing or film adventure was often counterbalanced by an uplifting one. Such was the case in 1983, as the frustrations of *A Memory of Murder* gave way to a wonderful experience reviving one of his best early science fiction stories of the mid-1940s. Its pulp origins as "The Creatures That Time Forgot" (*Planet Stories*, Fall 1946) masked the quality of this tale until Bradbury finally pulled it into his 1962 Doubleday collection, *R Is for Rocket*, as "Frost and Fire."

The story had quite a pedigree, in fact; the self-imposed wartime reading regimen that substituted for college had led him to Henri Bergson by way of Bertrand

Russell, where he found one of Bergson's subtly expressed thought experiments about time. As Bradbury understood it, the question was: If humans lived on a world where they were born, matured, and died within a span of eight days, how would they know that this was not the natural order of Time? Bergson sensed how the people would become aware of this unnatural tragedy—there would be no time to pass on and extend knowledge, no time to advance a civilization. Bradbury imagined such a world, gave it a surprisingly plausible explanation, and focused on one character who was able to find the way out for his people within the few short days of his prime.

By 1983, this story had caught the interest of Bradbury's good friend, Saul Bass, one of the most highly regarded film title artists in Hollywood history. His animated title art framed many of the great feature films of the 1950s and 1960s, but by the 1980s he and his wife Elaine had turned to making award-winning documentaries and experimental short films. Bass envisioned a world of deep darkness, relieved only by a distant and mysterious faint light that means nothing to these people other than a possible means of escape. Where the light leads, no one can even imagine. Any adult they send has never returned during the tragically short eight-day lifespan, so they teach what little wisdom they have to a young child and send him off on the unknown journey.

Bradbury and Bass titled it *Quest*; Bass built a miniature set for background shots while Bradbury modified his original tale for a half-hour film. What remained was almost completely visual description, a writing challenge that Bradbury welcomed, and Bass would use music and sound effects for the long journey of his live-action actor. The child grows to manhood during these adventures and experiences wonderment as he finally passes into the light and discovers an external world that his people had never seen before. He's able to open this path to the others, and a new world is born.

Bass offered the film in 16mm and videotape format for libraries and colleges through Pyramid Films, but the real market destination was overseas. The film was financed jointly by an anonymous Japanese philanthropist (Bradbury would never know his name) and The Church of World Messianity. *Quest* was commissioned to show at intervals every day in the philanthropist's M.O.A. Museum of Art in Atami, Japan, a planetarium-temple east of Tokyo.

In a review for *Fantasy & Science Fiction*, Harlan Ellison maintained that Bass had done "what studios spending millions have not been able to do: he has conveyed the ephemeral magic of Bradbury without awkwardness in translation, without stilted dialogue or precious pomposity." The film never went into commercial distribution, but the irascible Ellison made this shaming plea to film programmers everywhere: "In their lemming-like rush to saturate film programs with dross, scheduling officials would be ennobled by a sober shake of the head and the presentation of an important little film that is *about something meaningful*."

These were not idle thoughts, for the global Saul Bass reputation parlayed carefully placed screening copies into sixteen national and international film competitions and garnered numerous awards, including Gold Medals from the Moscow Film Festival, the Chicago International Film Festival, and the New York International Film & TV Festival, First Prize from the Aspen Film Festival, and invitations to show from the London Film Festival and the Cannes Film Festival.

The painful editorial teasers inflicted on the covers of *A Memory of Murder* ("Revealed—for the first time! The Skeletons in Ray Bradbury's Closet!") had wrenched an entire phase of his early career completely out of context. In his sixty-fourth year, the long transformative journey of "Frost and Fire" from the science fiction pulps to *Quest* restored continuity to Bradbury's complex and mysterious sense of authorship and creativity.

21 1984 Will Not Arrive

On New Year's Eve, 1984, Bradbury was brought together with Orson Welles one last time for an hour-long program at a local CBS television affiliate. Earlier in the year, Welles had read paraphrased passages from the text of *Something Wicked This Way Comes* that were subsequently intercut with soundtrack excerpts from the Disney movie, to be broadcast as a half-hour radio show "trailer" prior to the 1983 release of the film. Now, on the final day of 1983, Welles read passages from Orwell's *1984*, and Bradbury offered commentary during the intervals to proclaim that 1984, as Orwell envisioned it, would not arrive. After the show, Bradbury asked for his recording of the program, but the producers told him this was a live television broadcast and was not filmed for archive. He was stunned, and truly saddened that the magical evening would be lost in time.

Welles died less than two years later, and the memory of Bradbury's final meeting with Welles, like his first meeting in 1948, would pass away with Bradbury himself, undocumented in any public way. Yet that very first meeting offered a hint of the way their paths would cross later in life. It occurred by accident; Bradbury had gone to the office of his CBS radio producer, Bill Spier, to give him a copy of his new story collection, *Dark Carnival*. He was told that Spier was in a nearby bar, and when Bradbury followed him there, Spier was seated with Orson Welles and actress Ava Gardner. Bradbury was still young enough to be stunned by the presence of the director of *Citizen Kane* and creator of the H. G. Wells *War of the Worlds* radio program, and he watched in amazement as Spier handed *Dark Carnival* to Welles. After studying it for a few moments, Welles turned to Bradbury and said, "I too have these dreams."[1]

: : :

The 1984 that Ray Bradbury experienced was more Wellsian than Orwellian, but with a difference. Bradbury's new world of science did not center on the H. G. Wells vision of an elite world of scientists, isolated from the broader population. Bradbury saw science, and especially the related disciplines of the Space Age, as all-inclusive. Everyone should share in the dream, and he had made no bones about sharing that dream with newcomers as well as the physically and economically disadvantaged.

Even as he drifted into the economic and space program initiatives of the Reagan years, he remained proud of the nation's role as a beacon of hope for the less fortunate of other lands. His poem "America," published in the August 13, 1984, issue of the *Los Angeles Times*, displayed his irritation with those critics who saw late-century America as a failing and polarized culture, lacking dreams of the future. Bradbury saw the dream most intensely reflected in the faces of those who would come from afar:

> Sit down, stare in their faces, see!
> You be the hoped-for thing a hopeless world would be.
> In tides of immigrants that this year flow
> You still remain the beckoning hearth they'd know.
> In midnight beds with blueprint, plan and scheme
> You are the dream that other people dream.

By 1984, Bradbury also found himself the Chair of a new visionary nonprofit organization, The World Interdependence Fund. With actress-turned-business-woman Polly Bergen as honorary chair, Bradbury and others hoped to leverage funding to harness the new technologies to fully free the disabled and the disadvantaged by bringing inspiration and culture to them. It was a typical Bradbury vision, in concert with his vision of efficient urban transportation and malls that doubled as stimulating works of art. He could not know that his was a concept in transition, and that the next thirty years would enable many disabled youths through the internet and related advances.

But if the initial plans for "the finest museum of learning for those with disabilities," as he described it in his first call for support, would be overtaken by technology itself, his leadership would have tangible results early on. In late April 1985, his World Interdependence Fund cohosted NASA's 22nd Space Congress in Cocoa Beach, Florida. Bradbury read nine of his Space Age poems in a special session staged on behalf of the Fund and had a small chapbook of the poems privately published for Interdependence Fund distribution. Most had been published between 1973 and 1981, including the Yeats-inspired "Of What Is Past, or Passing, or To Come," which was coming to represent his overarching view of human potential—past, present, and future.

In later years, Bradbury would move into the role of honorary chair, as others carried the WIF into significant advocacy initiatives under federal and private-sector funds and the public support of such individual sponsors as Nobel Laureate

Linus Pauling, Itzhak Perlman, athlete Wilma Rudolph, entertainer Stevie Wonder, and Hollywood's Goldie Hawn, Emilio Estevez, and Edward James Olmos, who would play a leading role in the 1996 Disney adaptation of Bradbury's *The Wonderful Ice Cream Suit*. But his most direct act of creativity growing out of the 22nd Space Congress was in advancing the possibilities of including disabled children in the exploration of space. In January 1987, less than two years after the Space Congress, Bradbury's "Walking on Air" was first broadcast nationally on the PBS show, "Wonderworks." Bradbury's original story was turned into an Emmy-nominated teleplay by Ed Kaplan, who had directed Bradbury's 1982 PBS special, "All Summer in a Day."

Bradbury's "Walking on Air" took its central metaphor directly from his dreams for the WIF, as the wheelchair-bound protagonist is encouraged by his science teacher (Lynn Redgrave) to work for a chance to go to space, even when his parents and NASA have significant doubts. The ending has the feel of a classic Bradbury reverie, completely uninhibited by the realities of life, but it nonetheless inspired a young audience. Along with "The Electric Grandmother" and "All Summer in a Day," "Walking on Air" signaled Bradbury's reentry into the world of wonder for an entirely new generation of children influenced by "after school" programming in the 1980s.

: : :

The same child's-eye view of life that led Bradbury to develop these three award-winning programs for young viewers finally led him across the great untraveled bridge to his own childhood. In October 1984, he made his first official trip home to Waukegan. This was a long time coming, and many residents of Waukegan wondered why it had taken so long. Former mayor Robert Sabonjian, who had served as mayor for thirty years, noted that Bradbury's absence contrasted with the activities of Waukegan's older native son, entertainer and actor Jack Benny. Benny passed away in the mid-1970s, but he visited regularly and had a history of referencing Waukegan in his radio and television show broadcasts.

Bradbury had visited Waukegan a number of times, but always privately, well out of the public eye. Fifty years had now passed since he had last lived there; his childhood years in Waukegan ended in the spring of 1934, when the Great Depression forced the family west to find work in California. Occasional bus or train trips through Chicago to New York allowed brief family visits in 1939 and 1946, and subsequent rail stops in the mid- and late-1970s provided other opportunities. He could have had a public reception during any of these stops, but he deliberately remained out of the spotlight.

Time was his excuse, as public engagements across the county had to be negotiated by rail travel; he was usually only in Chicago long enough to change trains, as he described to a reporter on the eve of his 1984 official visit. "I was last there about five years ago. I go and hire a taxi or a limo and I don't tell anyone I'm coming. I just love to prowl around downtown and look at things. I visit my old home and my grandma's house, go down into the ravine for a moment, go by the Genesee Theatre and all the places I knew as a kid and then I just leave town without saying anything. I only have an hour so there's no time to see anyone."[2]

The reporter, *Waukegan News-Sun* staff reporter Maryann Dadisman, had met Bradbury's train four hours out in Galesburg, the first stop on the Illinois side of the Mississippi River. This was a route Bradbury knew well; he had taken the *Super Chief* in the old days, before Amtrak's *Southwest Chief* offered a pale ghost of the old-time Santa Fe Railroad's passenger service. East of Galesburg, Bradbury's reflections to Dadisman hinted at an unspoken anxiety about meeting the past: "But I really didn't have as many friends as I suppose I should have had. Maybe because I was, ah, too much for them. Maybe I overloaded their circuits. Maybe that drives you, too—if you don't have as much love as you'd like to have. I suppose a lot of that goes into writing."

Over time, as he became a popular lecturer and one of the best-known writers in American culture, it was easy to forget how solitary he had been as a child. Writing protected him from competition in the real world of school and sports. "I could be excellent all to myself."[3] He was no shut-in, of course; the young Bradbury was, at times, a storyteller and a talker at Central School, but he had never "mixed," in the normal sense, beyond the footpaths and wild shadows of the nearby Powell Park ravine. It was only during his final eighth grade year of 1933–34, in a chapter of the Little Orphan Annie society, where he began to reach out and attend social events in the homes of other children his age.

Even then, however, he was becoming a stranger; his father's first attempt at finding work had taken the family all the way to Tucson for most of the boy's seventh grade year, and they would leave again before the end of the eighth grade for Los Angeles. That was a home he had learned how to negotiate as an adult; Waukegan, though, was frozen in the time of his youth, and Bradbury was now 64 years old. He really didn't know how to return home at all.

He would find, with great relief, that Waukegan would make his first formal return a happy time. The trip had been in the works for almost a year and a half, allowing time for the city to plan a Ray Bradbury Festival that coincided with the 125th anniversary of Waukegan itself. And the atmosphere was perfect; Dadisman drove him into town on the evening of October 25th, as rain and fog brought back memories of the Autumn People he had created in 1940s issues of *Weird Tales*.

The recently renovated Genesee Theatre, a grand vaudeville stage built when Bradbury was seven years old, hosted a Bradbury film festival in the days leading up to his visit. During his weekend stay, the Community Players performed a trio of Bradbury stories at the Genesee for three days running. Bradbury introduced the plays all weekend, and answered questions after the final performances of Sunday, October 28th. As a final unintended homage, the city's unrelated decision to move Halloween Trick or Treat observances to the 28th gave Bradbury his first Halloween in Waukegan since 1933. A teacher's strike ended in time for Bradbury to spend much of the weekend in events with students.

On Saturday, he was also able to have lunch with his art teacher and two classmates, including his old friend Abraham Davis, one of the very few Black students in the Central School population of that era. His classmates recollected that he never wrote in cursive script at school—a habit he often followed throughout his life, in those rare instances where he wasn't at his typewriter. His immediate family members had all passed away or moved elsewhere over the years, with one exception—he was joined by his younger first cousin, Patricia Bradbury Larsen, characterized in three of Bradbury's *Saturday Evening Post* stories, who came up from Bourbonnais to see him.

If one event allowed him to come to terms with his past, it was the Friday afternoon tour that festival organizers asked him to host: from the Courthouse, through the Powell Park ravine, and south across Washington Street to the two neighboring houses where he lived in Waukegan. A large audience followed him through the tour and surrounded him on the porch of his grandparents' house, where he used a bullhorn to witness and attest to years gone by. The apple trees were no longer in the yard, but the old maple was still living, impressively large even with most of its autumn leaves fallen to the ground.

He stepped next door to 11 South St. James, also owned in those days by his Bradbury grandparents, where he had lived with his parents from birth. Both homes were rentals now, and the surprised families invited him to step inside.[4] His grandparents' home still had the feel of the rooming house that his grandmother Bradbury had managed after his grandfather's death in 1925. But his own childhood home next door was now very different. The front porch was gone, as was the upper story dormer window. The large side porch, where his family had watched Uncle Bion fire his toy canon on the fourth of July, was now an extension of the house, which had been converted into a duplex rental.

Bradbury was able to maintain order in his audience and good will of the rental families, orchestrating the whole scene just as his character Douglas Spaulding does in the magical opening scene of *Dandelion Wine*. This was quite a spectacle for a Friday afternoon in Waukegan. The policeman assigned to safeguard the tour participants crossing Washington Street had not been briefed on the cause of it all. He reportedly asked, "What's going on? These people are following him around like he was Jesus."

His interactions were actually more patriarchal, though, as he promised to return more often. In later years, the city would rename lower Powell Park in his honor, and he would attend those ceremonies as well. By the time he left Waukegan on October 29th, he had met with city leaders and seniors to envision how the renewal of Waukegan's downtown might be accomplished. Bradbury echoed his recent essays on urban planning, making his case for putting people back in proper scale and eliminating the large outlying malls. This was quixotic, for the most part, but it nonetheless echoed the renewal of traditional values he saw in the Reagan Era vision—turning the clock backward is the way forward. Bradbury was speaking in the midst of what became known as the decade of nostalgia, a time he had come to represent in his own work and legacy even as he also looked forward into the Space Age.

22 | *Death Is a Lonely Business*

Bradbury had been fascinated with the young writer he once was for decades, and in 1985 he published that writer's story in an experimental form of fictionalized autobiography, reminiscent in some ways of James Agee's posthumously published *A Death in the Family*, a memory of Agee's father so cleverly mimicking fiction that his heirs had it published as a novel. Agee's final work subsequently won the National Book Award. Bradbury had no illusions of honors with this new project, however. A detective novel had been forming around his 1944 unpublished story "Where Everything Ends" for many years; now he had finally figured out how to shave it a bit closer to real memory than he had ever done with his life before.

He had, in fact, already taken a step toward an experiment in autobiography by exploring the young boy *beneath* the young writer in his 1960s stage adaptation of *Dandelion Wine*; his onstage narrator, a forty-something Bradbury, re-created the dandelion-flavored world of that young boy to try and fully remember the crisis of that summer of 1928, the events through which the boy began to discover the mysteries of life and death, stepping across the threshold of mortality that would lead him eventually into the adult world. In the final scene of that play, the older Bradbury speaks with his imaginary twelve-year-old self, and the full memory of that Waukegan transition resurfaces in the older man's mind.

This was a kind of Bradburyian form of psychoanalysis, and it had satisfied the autobiographical impulses of the forty-six-year-old writer in the mid-1960s. Now, at sixty-five, he would revisit the young Los Angeles writer of the early 1940s as well. This time, however, Bradbury would have to fully merge with that young writer he had once been. It was time for the Teller of Tales to tell his own story, but it would be risky—every instinct rebelled at the prospect of self-conscious, rational thinking that formal autobiography required. He had found his own way as a unique and often masterful writer of short fiction by suppressing rational, judgmental thought, relying on an idea or a memory to create characters that would tell *their own* tales. When it worked, a powerful story would transfer from his mind through his fingertips to typed pages in a matter of hours. Revision, an unwelcome but necessary invasion from the rational mind, would come later.

He could tell parts of his story in the form of loosely connected anecdotes punctuated with moments of insightful reflection, as he had done in his un-published 1970 summer interviews with his agent, Don Congdon. He could tell even shorter fragments of his story in media interviews or in public lectures and had done so for decades. Yet these were only glimpses, filtered through an older man's impulse in the "now" to entertain or inspire. It was time to capture the essence of how he *became* a storyteller, and he could only do this by entering the mind of a much younger man.

But why mystery and murder? There had been times, as he aged, that he felt the urge to write a long work of detective fiction. The off-trail stories he had placed in the 1940s detective pulps had played out quickly, and his better ideas soon pulled him into more mature forms of fantasy and science fiction. He would produce very successful suspense stories—most notably "The Small Assassin," "Touch and Go" (better known as "The Fruit at the Bottom of the Bowl"), "The Screaming Woman," and "The Whole Town's Sleeping"—but by the late 1970s only one of his early detective tales still interested him. In his mind, the intriguing 1943–44 Venice Beach crime story, "Where Everything Ends," had the potential for novel-length suspense—an invisible murderer, moving from crime to crime in impossible ways, until Bradbury's detective realizes that the old oil- and algae-slicked canals of this fading ocean-side community provide the means for the murderer to move unseen.

He had known from the start that "Where Everything Ends" needed expan-sion; the murderer was never developed as a character, and there were really no suspects to consider at all.[1] Yet the original story was well-written and showcased Bradbury's talent as a keen observer of life. He had known that world well; the twenty-four-year-old Bradbury was living in Venice at the time and witnessed its decline into the perfect setting for noir. This was the best of the stories turned down by Standard Publications, home syndicate for the crime magazines where Bradbury published his off-trail murder tales of the mid-1940s; the typescript remained inactive for decades.

Sometime in 1977, as Bill Nolan and Donn Albright urged him to return to his old unpublished stories, Bradbury began to see "Where Everything Ends" as the trigger point for his experiment in autobiographical long fiction. His creative warm-up exercise was a short July 1977 screenplay titled "The Cinema of Lost Films," an enchanted version of the Venice Cinema at the foot of the old Amusement Pier, where lost souls could wander in and find themselves starring in fantasy projections of the many Hollywood films that had been contracted but never made. This project was never produced, but it provides a marker for the beginning of Bradbury's earnest work on the expansion of "Where Everything Ends."

He still needed a detective to serve as a roughhouse muse for the young writer he had been, living and observing life's adventures and tragedies in 1940s Venice Beach. At that time, his short-story detectives had little or no personality—the situations, not the sleuths, were what counted for Bradbury. At best, they had been parodies of a Chandler or Hammett detective. Steve Michaels, the private investigator of the unpublished "Where Everything Ends," represented Bradbury's only attempt to shape a believable noir protagonist, but that path could only open out into imitation. The original plot of "Where Everything Ends" was already headed in that direction, as Michaels investigates extortion turned to murder in the patchwork of oil fields slowly merging with the dying recreational canal system of the town.

The first victim is found at the end of one of the canals, near a remarkable image that would propel the seeds of this story into the anchor point for Bradbury's suspenseful novel-length story of a writer—old circus wagons beneath the surface, dumped into the canal before anyone's living memory. Michaels would disappear from the evolving novel, and the story line itself would fade away, but the eerie circus wagons would become the implicit time machine metaphor that would take Bradbury back to the Young Writer of another era:

"Where Everything Ends" (1943–44)	Death Is a Lonely Business (1985)
In the old days a circus had dumped its ancient red wagons and yellow-painted cages into the canal. It looked as if a long parade had rolled and rumbled off the rim to pile up and rust brown under the grey motionless waters. There were about ten cages, wheels turned up, the paint of old years flaking like leaves from a calendar.	At the end of one long canal you could find old circus wagons that had been rolled and dumped, and in the cages, at midnight, if you looked, things lived—fish and crayfish moving with the tide; and it was all the circuses of time somehow gone to doom and rusting away.

Discarding the genre strictures of the original plot left Bradbury free to fashion his own detective companion, and his model would be C. W. Sughrue, novelist James Crumley's irreverent protagonist from the 1978 novel *The Last Good Kiss*, a book that Bradbury greatly admired for its infusion of a pragmatic touch of humor into the world of violent crime. Bradbury's new detective would be named Elmo Crumley, who was able to negotiate the life of a 1940s Venice Beach homicide detective through bad beer and a secret fiction writing habit of his own.[2] As with Bradbury, the real-life Crumley's genre influences included both Raymond Chandler and Ross Macdonald. Bill Nolan soon reawakened the final element of this noir trinity in Bradbury's mind; in the early 1980s, Nolan was writing a biography of Dashiell Hammett, and he would pass the chapters to Bradbury for reading just as *Death Is a Lonely Business* began to come together in its final form.[3]

This trail of inspiration was interrupted for a time by the unexpected resurrection of his earliest published crime stories in *A Memory of Murder*. This 1984 collection brought the Young Writer of detective fiction back into the public spotlight in a way that the Older Writer didn't like at all, refueling his desire to evolve "Where Everything Ends" into a novel that better represented his mature talents. The logic was circular, however, and brought him back to the central problem of his career—how to successfully expand the action, conflict, and suspense of a fine short story into a fully sustained novel? He had managed it with *Fahrenheit 451*, and far more extensively with *Something Wicked This Way Comes*, but now he was returning to a genre where he had never followed the rules at all.

As he developed the novel, a familiar pattern began to emerge in the form of threats to the eccentric, isolated, and lonely characters who populate so many of Bradbury's works of magical or supernatural realism. He would once again recall all the Lonelies and Isolatos from his years as a young writer in Venice Beach and in downtown Los Angeles. But the highly autobiographical *Death Is a Lonely Business* is more than just a parade of down-and-out victims in a town that has seen better days. It is also a walk through Bradbury's living memories, offering a full view of a time when he would either find his way into the literary mainstream or fail in his attempt to make his living solely as a writer. In such a tale, the murderer is always found within.

The phrase "death is a lonely business" becomes the first clue left by the murderer; when the young writer hears it spoken by an unseen passenger on the old Red Car trolley line late at night, fear keeps him from turning to look at the speaker. A few minutes after leaving the trolley, the writer comes across the speaker's first victim, an old man stuffed into one of the submerged circus wagons in the canal. He will be shadowed by the killer throughout the novel, made all the more terrifying as the writer begins to sense the widening circle of victims even before each murder occurs.

The young writer is never named; he's simply known as a young pulp writer with a grand and eccentric imagination, affectionately called "The Crazy" or "The Martian" by his old friends in the downtown Los Angeles tenement where he had lived during the war years. His steady girlfriend is studying in Mexico; her name is Peg, one of Bradbury's early nicknames for his wife Maggie. While she's away, his typewriter provides the basic frame of reference; it's now early October 1949, and the dated title page of the young writer's "Untitled Novel" has been languishing on the platen for three months.

Once the writer hears the mysterious phrase "death is a lonely business" on the midnight trolley, he places it on his title page and his typewriter soon begins to produce the very novel we are reading. The first murder throws him into the company of Homicide Detective Lieutenant Elmo Crumley, who has also started to write a crime novel, with little success. To encourage Crumley, the writer gives him *Death Is a Lonely Business* as a title, but the growing number of murders and disappearances distract them both. The killer seems to be stalking the down-and-outs that the young writer knows in Venice, and soon his old friends in the Los Angeles Barrio tenement find themselves under surveillance as well. Both Crumley and the young writer find spots of dampness and algae from the canals outside of their homes, evidence that the killer is still moving through the canals and watching their every move.

The entire unraveling mystery is sustained through the keyboard of the young writer's typewriter; each evening, he places the newly typed pages in his Talking Box: "That's the box," he narrates, "I kept by my typewriter where my ideas lay and spoke to me early mornings to tell me where they wanted to go and what they wanted to do." For most of his career, Bradbury would refer to this morning ritual as the hidden theater of the mind; the new novel revealed the origins of this magic, a metaphor made literal as Bradbury re-created the period when he could finally believe that he was going to make it as a writer.[4]

The murder mystery at the center of *Death Is a Lonely Business* had provided a framework for Bradbury to reveal his state of mind as various novel-length projects wound down into despair or stalemate in the late 1940s. The failed novel-length projects of this period—*Masks* (1946–47, 1949) and *Where Ignorant Armies Clash by Night* (1947–1948)—would not play directly into the plot at all;[5] they were instead personified in the Venice Pier bookshop owner A. L. Shrank, a reclusive intellectual who purports to be a "Tarot card reader, phrenologist, dime-store psychiatrist, day- and nighttime psychologist, astrologer, Zen/Freudian/Jungian numerologist," and, as the young writer discovers, a "full Life Failure" of monumentally evil intent.

The grand old Venice Amusement Pier is not only the hidden lair of Shrank, whose collection of the most pessimistic and hateful books of the Western World finally tips off the writer that Shrank hates everything and everyone, without exception. The pier is also home to a number of the Lonelies of Venice Beach, and they all must scramble for a new life as the pier and its old wooden roller coaster are slowly demolished (as indeed they actually were in 1946). The young writer has become an amateur sleuth himself, fumbling along in ways that are ultimately effective. Bradbury projected him as "the fool who knows," a carnivalesque compliment to the unorthodox and highly emotional methods of some of his early crime protagonists.

He finally flushes out Shrank on the abandoned Amusement Pier and learns the terrifying truth—the monster has been trailing the young writer for months, using him as an unwitting guide to his prey. He turns on Shrank, naming many of the victims and near-victims—his friends: "You were looking for Lonelies. And damn fool stupid dumb me, blinder than Henry, helped you find them. Fanny was right. Constance was right! I was the death goat after all. Christ, I was typhoid Mary. I carried the disease, you, everywhere. Or at least you followed. To find Lonelies."

Shrank is, of course, the epitome of all the things that can destroy a young writer: competition, an overcrowded market, heartless publishers, the temptation of slanting his work for money, diminishing creativity, the fear of waking up one day and not being able to write at all—and above all loneliness, and a life without love. Shrank fed on all of these fears, killing the people who inspire a writer's creativity: "You were my good dog of death," Shrank boasts, "for more times than you guess. Over a year. You showed me the people you were collecting for your books. All the gravel on the path, chaff in the wind, empty shells on the shore, dice with no spots, cards with no pips. No past, no present. So I gave them no future."

But Shrank is vulnerable—Crumley's creativity finally kicks in, and then the young writer finally makes his first major market story sale to *The American Mercury*. On those days, Shrank's spectral image was nowhere to be seen. The entire novel builds to the moment when Bradbury, as Young Writer, defines the rest of his life: "I'm not a Lonely. I'm not a failure. I'm not lost. I'm going to make it. I'm going to be happy. I'm going to marry and have a good wife and children. I'm going to write damned fine books and be loved. That doesn't fit your pattern. You can't kill me, you damn stupid jerk, because I'm okay. You see? I'm going to live forever." The novel ends as it began, with a murder victim in an old circus wagon below the slimy surface of a Venice Beach canal. This time, the prey has taken the predator.

: : :

In the end, several ghosts had collaborated in the final process of writing *Death Is a Lonely Business*. The principal ghost emerged in a very personal and unexpected way, as he watched his great friend Kenneth Millar descend into the fog of Alzheimer's and die in 1983. As Ross Macdonald, Millar was a true heir to Hammett and Chandler, and in the years that Bradbury knew him, Millar was generally credited as a genre-breaking mainstream literary talent, perhaps the greatest private-eye writer of the mid- and late twentieth century. They were close in age—Millar was just five years older—and his friend's passing only complicated Bradbury's decision to reenter the world of detective fiction, so late in time, and so late in his own life.

The loss of Millar meant that everyone he felt a debt to in this genre was now gone. His dedication page began with a thanks to Don Congdon, who had encouraged him to stay with this book and provided suggestions to clean up digressions caused in early drafts by too many characters going in too many different directions. He also dedicated *Death Is a Lonely Business* to the masters he had read as that Young Writer, so many years ago—Raymond Chandler, Dashiell Hammett, and James M. Cain.

But now his personal triumvirate of mentors and encouragers was also gone, and his final remembrance was to Ross Macdonald and "my friends and teachers Leigh Brackett and Edmond Hamilton, sorely missed." At least one ghost would eventually acknowledge the honor; in 2002, as Bradbury was completing *Let's All Kill Constance!*, his third and final novel in this process of channeling autobiography through detective fiction, he would receive the first annual Ross Macdonald Literary Award.

He met the mixed reviews with his public mask, but he revealed his inner feelings about his own sense of the novel to a special few. In February 1986, Bradbury sent a copy of the novel to poet Helen Bevington, with whom he had initiated and maintained an active correspondence for the previous three years. She took an unusual approach to reading an unusual novel that defied any preconceived notions of genre. "Contrary to the usual way of reading a suspenseful novel to reach the end at one sitting, I have been living with *Death Is a Lonely Business* in a word-for-word relationship."[6]

She was fascinated by the slightly surreal world of war-time Los Angeles that Bradbury remembered through his dark glass: "I like the young writer (yourself) who has a weird adventure a minute. It is very heady business to accompany him. . . . I like the time of it, the setting, the nostalgia. . . . How is it that a man so obviously in love with life, living it so aware, happy, should be concerned with death? Well, I guess we have to be."

Bradbury's answer began with his sense that he was working with a form of fictionalized autobiography quite distinct from the memories of others that had often populated his fictions. "I absolutely love it. It is a special child to me, with a special face and flavor. . . . This affair, lying in bed with me, started long ago. Out of bedding myself, and listening to voices, all my good stuff has arrived. I am sure much of your work has arrived the same way, through that peculiar thing called intuition." The full answer, however, was where it always was—locked in the visual memories that shaped his overarching connection to high and popular culture:

> You ask how I do what I do. I have answered it partly overleaf, but the great thing is I have a list of loves, started when I was 3, and I have stayed in love with all of them for a lifetime. Out of this fabulous trash, I have built my life. Quasimodo, dinosaurs, Buck Rogers, Tarzan, the Chicago World's Fair, the New York World's Fair, the history of architecture, H. G. Wells, Jules Verne, ten thousand motion pictures . . . Prince Valiant (I corresponded with Hal Foster who drew it, for 30 years!) oldtime radio, Burns and Allen, Fred Allen, Jack Benny, Bernard Shaw, Shakespeare, Melville, The Bible, Alexander Pope, and . . . Helen Bevington . . . you all go with me everywhere. I have left none behind on the road. [ellipses Bradbury's]

Here he offered Bevington one of the best recaps of the eternal Bradbury catalog that, in its various forms, would madden literary and intellectual critics throughout his career. But he also offered her a tantalizing glimpse of the inner writer in an unpublished poem that he had written shortly before beginning his correspondence with her three years earlier. Eventually, he would publish "The Other Me" in a limited edition of new poems, but it didn't reach a wide audience until 1990; in 1986, he sent a revised draft to Bevington to explain "how I live with myself":

> There's nothing for it but I join his ruse, his game,
> And let him run at will and make my fame.
> On which I put my name and steal his stuff,
> And all because I sneezed him forth
> With sweet creation's snuff.
> Did R. B. write that poem, that line, that speech?
> No, inner-ape, invisible, did teach.
> His reach, clothed in my flesh, stays mystery;
> Say not my name.
> Praise other me.[7]

23 | A Poet's Heart

In 1985, President Reagan and the United States Congress created the National Commission on Space and tasked it with predicting and describing what a civilian space program would look like fifty years in the future. The final report, "Pioneering the Space Frontier," offered a technological preview of the most stable orbital station coordinates, or Lagrange points, of the inner solar system, the essential elements of a lunar base for interplanetary mission staging, and the requirements for a viable Mars base supporting travel and colonization. A blend of technology and imagination was called for in this study; many technical and visionary sources were consulted, including Ray Bradbury.

He shouldn't have been surprised. Former NASA director Thomas O. Paine, the Commission's chairman, knew Bradbury, as did Senator John Glenn, who was one of the Congressional advisors to the Commission. But Bradbury's perennial fear of losing his way in a scientific discussion flared up when he was asked to testify before the commission in the late summer of 1985. "I'll be up there amongst a goodly mob of scientists, technicians, super experts," he reflected a year later, "men and women whose knowledge outruns mine by several thousand light years. How dare I speak, and speak only with a poet's heart?"[1]

He soon discovered that the commission's charge was based, in large part, on the dreams and speculations of science fiction. There would be sections on applied science, technology, and enterprise, but the overarching mission was to "support human settlements beyond Earth orbit, from the Highlands of the Moon to the Plains of Mars." Themes emphasized throughout the commission's report included "opening the space frontier for personal fulfillment, enterprise, and for human settlement," and "the relevance of these hopes and dreams to America's pioneer heritage." The former could be a one-line synopsis of The Martian Chronicles, the latter a fitting subtitle to his 1964 World's Fair American Pavilion narration.

The flavor of his 1985 Space Commission testimony emerges in his more focused reflections for an issue of The Planetary Society's Planetary Report: "But go I would, and speak I did. Even as I must speak now for that very special planet Mars." Here he cited some old friends, Ahab and Nemo, from his often-reprinted Bantam introduction to 20,000 Leagues Under the Sea. He also cited his old spiritual pal George Bernard Shaw, but he did so in a more comprehensive way than he had done in earlier commentaries on why we must go to Mars:

> What Shaw said in essence was: "What are we in the long night of time? What is this thinking, idea beast? Why, we are matter and force, making itself over into imagination and will."
>
> There you have it. It describes for all time, for me anyway, what we are up to with our astronautics and our vacations in space.
>
> No use having pure matter and brute force, if it knows not itself. We know ourselves. But no use knowing unless there is doing. And in the doing, no use has will power if you have no power to imagine, and no use imagining if you have not the will power to engine it along.
>
> We are the composite thing, then, come alive out of blind matter and dumb force.
>
> And we will ourselves to dream, to blueprint, to build, to move, and finally, to fly.
>
> And the object of our will is Mars.
>
> In the beginning, anyway.[2]

Bradbury's quarter-century progression from Bergson's *élan vital*, refined through Kazantzakis's *The Saviors of God*, now had the voice of Shaw as well to show how the life force and intelligent purpose combine, at least in Bradbury's mind, to take humanity through the fifty-year plan outlined by the National Commission on Space, all the way to Mars. There was no need here to invoke his ace card, the great debate at the end of H. G. Well's *Things to Come*, because there was no opposition to face down—both the President and Congress sanctioned the commission, and the task was to find the reality to realize the dream. By the time that Bradbury passed away in 2012, the timetable for human missions to Mars was settling into the fifty-year projection of the commission's report.

: : :

The Ray Bradbury Theater, a dream that had almost become reality under several title concepts spun out over thirty years, gained unexpected traction in the early 1980s through the interest of actor/producer Larry Wilcox, and his business partner Martin Leeds. For Wilcox the interest was really a passion, and he began to circulate the concept under the working title *The Martian Chronicles*. The *Chronicles* had indeed formed the core of Bradbury's 1950s attempts to launch a television series, but at the moment that title for TV was still tied up with Charles Fries Productions, who held rights by virtue of the 1980 NBC miniseries.

Many of these Martian stories were indeed gems with perpetual adaptation potential, but Wilcox was thinking of "Chronicles" in the far broader sense of Bradbury's entire storytelling history. It was no great leap to the title *Ray Bradbury Theater*, and initially Wilcox did what he did best, forming a partnership with the international Canadian production company Atlantis. The final part of the puzzle was filled by HBO, a prime player in the rapidly expanding cable television industry. HBO signed on to broadcast an initial three-episode season in May, June, and July 1985, subsequently expanded to include an additional three episodes to be broadcast in February 1986.

This split first season began with James Coco and Leslie Nielsen in "Marionettes, Inc.," William Shatner in "The Playground," and Frank Mancuso in "The Crowd." Each was a vintage tale with the trademark Bradbury "twist" ending. The winter 1986 trio included "Banshee," a later Irish tale with an effective rendering of John Huston that attracted Peter O'Toole to the role. HBO did not renew the series, but the prominent star power and award nominations led to a second season contract with the USA network for a full twelve-episode package.

Atlantis's Peter Sussman depended on international partners to make the productions viable, with locations principally in France and New Zealand, and a few each season filmed in Canada. Each show generally involved completely different production crews with very little continuity, and the episodes were all different in look, acting, and direction. Later seasons would develop more continuity through the show-running talents of Tom Cotter, who was brought on for the final four seasons of the series. Nothing was certain, but continuing award recognition led to one of the longest-running single-author dramatic series in television history.

Bradbury had a great deal of control as co–executive producer with Wilcox and as sole author of the story adaptations. Cotter would bring more consistency and effective script revisions to the series, all done quietly behind the scenes. He also honored all of Bradbury's suggestions and revisions by giving him full attention whenever required, and that interaction led to mutual respect and trust.

It was clear from the start that Bradbury wanted everyone in the game; the wide-ranging demands he made included having representatives on location, and his desire to control script revisions seemed at times like a faint echo of John Huston's controlling hand on a much younger Ray Bradbury. The pressure fell mostly on Larry Wilcox, who Bradbury eventually perceived as having too many distractions from other production ventures. The arrival of the talented and dependable Tom Cotter for the third season eased many of these challenges but only added complexity to the original production relationships between these strong-willed partners.

: : :

In August 1985, Bradbury sent a birthday card to Malcolm Cowley, one of the last living members of the Lost Generation of 1920s American literary expatriates. The card accompanied a presentation copy of *Something Wicked This Way Comes*, which Cowley knew but had not read. They were not well acquainted, but Bradbury had been impressed by Cowley's postwar revival of Hemingway, Faulkner, and Fitzgerald through his editorship of the Viking Portable editions and in various influential essays. Bradbury did not share Cowley's leftist political heritage, but he appreciated any critic or author who, like himself, had survived FBI scrutiny and the mid-century Climate of Fear.

Bradbury also sensed a kindred spirit in the old Modernist who distrusted the increasing darkness of realism in American fiction, and he was not disappointed by Cowley's October 1985 reply: "The imaginations of American readers have been methodically starved by realistic fiction, which tells them how things were but not how the writer feels they will be day after tomorrow." Cowley was now 87 years old, and he reflected on the path not taken: "If I were 20 again I should try my hand at rapidly written sci-fi as an exercise in releasing the imagination. It wouldn't be as powerful as yours has proved to be."[3]

Bradbury could appreciate this sentiment, for he was equal parts storyteller and truth seeker. His various literary masks, from his exotic and inscrutable Martians to the adventuresome boys of his Illinois youth, were designed to make the truth bearable, not to hide from it. He expected—and welcomed—tragedy in literature that renewed, that offered insights in how to live—and he often said so publicly. What he did not expect was the cruel imitation of art that reality brought to Los Angeles the following spring of 1986, when a swiftly moving fire created an unimaginable inferno in the massive cylindrical stacks of the Los Angeles Public Library.

The library was in many ways a model operation for the core facility of a large urban public library system, but the very design of the building would prove its undoing—most likely at the hands of an arsonist. The sensational prosecution of the suspected arsonist ended without conviction, but in the early aftermath of the tragedy it was the horror of the fire itself that held public attention in Los Angeles and all across the nation. The building's architecture was dominated by massive stack towers that housed most of the library's circulating collections, along with certain irreplaceable special collections. Once the fire started in the literature collections, the structural design sent the flames into an inferno of fury that consumed the books of the gigantic northeast and northwest stacks.

Here was Ray Bradbury's worst nightmare, created not by the legion of totalitarian fire starters he envisioned in the dark future of *Fahrenheit 451*, but by a single individual. The *New Yorker*'s Susan Orlean would eventually provide a detailed accounting of the horror in her best seller, *The Library Book*. Flames reached temperatures above 2,000 degrees Fahrenheit, at times taking on the colorless look of perfect combustion that few firemen will ever see. Destroyed were 400,000 books, and another 700,000 books were damaged.

This kind of intense and consuming cultural loss had rarely been felt in America (the destruction of the great European library of Louvain in the early days of World War I comes to mind), and it touched the root convictions of Bradbury's entire purpose in life as a preserver of libraries and freedom of the imagination. This loss of past treasures was intensified in his mind by the way it followed so closely on the heels of the *Challenger* disaster, a national and global tragedy that jeopardized his hopes for the future of Mankind. *Fahrenheit 451* gave an added perspective to Orlean's account of the fire. A library card signed out to Ray Bradbury and others graces the back endpapers of *The Library Book*, and the opening epigraph includes a line from *Fahrenheit*'s Book People: "And when they ask us what we're doing, you can say, 'We're remembering.'"

Just days before the Los Angeles Library fire, events in Europe had also jolted Bradbury's sense of security and international stability. A massive terrorist attack in a popular West Berlin discotheque was traced to Libyan agents, and on April 15, 1986, the United States launched a retaliatory bombing of Tripoli. As it happened, Ray and Maggie Bradbury were arriving in New York for events prior to continuing on aboard the Q.E. 2 for France and England. The trip was to be part vacation, and part promotional tour for *Death Is a Lonely Business*, his first novel in nearly a quarter-century.

For the moment, terrorism and high-stakes retaliation cast a long shadow over these plans, and, at the last minute, Bradbury canceled the trip and more than twenty media interviews in London. "I simply did not want to travel with the situation as it is with Libya," he wrote to his retired British publisher and good friend, Sir Rupert Hart-Davis. "And it seemed inevitable that the news people would ask me more about politics and less about my book. Perhaps I am wrong."[4] As his closing "perhaps" suggests, Bradbury knew that at times like this, his own vivid imagination could exaggerate the vulnerabilities of any public situation; he was, after all, never very far from the public eye.

: : :

Bradbury's selection as Guest of Honor for Atlanta's CONfederation, the 1986 Science Fiction WorldCon, provided a chance to renew old friendships just as the first two seasons of *The Ray Bradbury Theater* were winning television industry recognition through multiple ACE Award nominations. Bradbury's speech was preceded by Bradbury poems set to music and performed (somewhat forte) by other talents; Mike Glyer, reporting on the Con, noted that "Ray presumably loved it. Not unlike God, Ray loves everything." This was not a cynical observation. The audience had already heard most of the Bradbury mythology recounted once again in his GOH speech, but Glyer conceded the effect of the dream retold. "As always, by the end of Ray's speech the audience was ready to get up, go out in the street and *do something* to get us closer to the stars."

As it happened, this honor came in a year that had started with the *Challenger* tragedy, and that evening Bradbury recognized the crew's sacrifice in a way that actually added a new dimension to a speech that otherwise revisited many of the hallmark Bradbury stories heard in a range of lectures for decades. All of the hallmarks were still motivational, of course, because each autobiographical memory-tale dramatized a crucial moment in the overall progression of luck and initiative that influenced the course of Bradbury's improbable career; but in speaking of the loss of *Challenger* and its crew, a newer metaphor emerged.

This metaphor would form the final evolution of his thoughts on the purpose of the Human race in the universe. These thoughts had their origins in his early 1940s reading of Henri Bergson on the nature of time and his discovery of Bergson's notion of *elán vital* through Nikos Kazantzakis's *The Saviors of God*. By the mid-1960s, he had absorbed the Kazantzakian notion of Bergson's universal life force—a microbiological reflex perfected in humanity's subconscious preservation of the essence of God—and projected it on out into the Cosmos as the instinctive purpose of future Mankind, a Bradburyesque purpose centered on taking God's legacy back out into the universe. In considering the *Challenger*, the largest single loss of human life so far in this cosmic endeavor, Bradbury was prompted to add a newer insight to his vision, one that he had observed on an episode of Carl Sagan's *Cosmos* television series. His first articulation of this final phase of his vision had come during an appearance on Ted Koppel's television show, the evening after the *Challenger* loss, and was reprised at the Con:

> I remember one night [Sagan] did a thing where he had a mock-up of a DNA molecule in one hand and a giant enzyme model in his other hand. He had these two models that he displayed to the audience, and describing the process whereby the enzyme calls out to the DNA molecule, and then, from that, all of the building blocks for all of the creatures of the world are created.
>
> I look upon the universe as a giant enzyme calling upon Earth, and we, the DNA molecules of earth, must respond to the call. That's what this is all

about. It is a larger thing. If you want to call God an enzyme, he's an enzyme. Call it what you will, but the enzymes of the universe call; we rouse out, and we must move. . . . We go because we are inheritors of the gift.

We have a responsibility. We only live once, each of us, and we must give back something for this gift. So space travel is the gift we give to ourselves, to ensure our children's children's children immortality. That's what it's all about. If it isn't that, it's not worth doing. . . . So this is the way I'm going to talk from now to the end of my life.[5]

This was indeed his fullest articulation of Humanity as "inheritors of the gift." He saw this as the saving grace for the *Challenger* crew, the justification of the risk taken by all who will ever lift off from this planet. For Bradbury, this full realization had been a forty-seven-year journey, beginning with "Thought and Space," a poem in the very first issue of his fanzine, *Futuria Fantasia*, in the summer of 1939. Even if Bradbury really didn't fully understand the science of the metaphor he had created from Carl Sagan's words, it still compelled.

His speeches of the mid-1980s also document his most mature justification for science fiction, and his sense of its evolution in the creative drive of humans since prehistoric times. The path was marked out in his May 1953 article for the *Nation*, "The Day After Tomorrow: Why Science Fiction?" Further versions surfaced in various speaking engagements, including NASA's 1976 panel, "Why Man Explores," and many interviews. But he now firmly believed that the complex process of science fiction moving into the literary mainstream was not solely the province of the future. This settled view had peeked out in his presentations from time to time, but it was now codified thanks to his rediscovery of Nobel Laureate William Butler Yeats's influential poem, "Sailing to Byzantium," in the early 1980s. Characteristically, his first instinct was to work out his response in writing; this time his response was a poem taking as its focus the final lines of Yeats: "Of what is past, or passing, or to come."

Bradbury saw the origins of science fiction in the earliest evidence of human thought and expression, and in "Of What Is Past, or Passing, Or to Come" he traced Neolithic cave painting life-and-death problem-solving projected into the future:

The tiger, mammoth, fire, the one, the all.
So these first science fictions circled thought
And then strode forth and all the real facts sought,
And then on wall new science fictions drew,
That run through history and end with . . . *you.*

His full articulation of science fiction, and why we are drawn to it, came at a time when he was once again hardly writing any science fiction at all; nearly all of his writing focused on composing new stage and screen adaptations. He wrote a great deal to that purpose, but he published no new stories at all in the magazines during the final four years of the 1980s. The new stories he did write were different, a bit more self-indulgent, and not really selling; these stories would form the contents of his next story collection, *The Toynbee Convector*, in 1988. For the most part, these years were taken up with the great joy of adapting more and more of his stories to television and producing them for subsequent seasons of *The Ray Bradbury Theater*.

24 Forms of Things Unknown

In the summer of 1986, Bradbury's Guest of Honor comments at the Atlanta World Science Fiction CONfederation coincided with the federal government's first substantive responses to the *Challenger* tragedy of the previous winter. The June publication of the final report from the Presidential Commission on the Space Shuttle *Challenger* Accident was followed in August by congressional and presidential approval for the commissioning of *Discovery*, a new shuttle that would take on the lost *Challenger*'s role in the construction of the international space station.

Bradbury's place in the Great Tale was now, more than ever, a crucial element of the public perception that program continuity would remain central to NASA's adjusted timetable. He was asked to be the keynote speaker at the Thirtieth Annual Goddard Memorial Dinner in Washington, D.C., where the most prestigious space program awards were presented under the sponsorship of the National Space Club. This organization was chartered in the 1950s to reach far beyond the annual celebration of Dr. Robert H. Goddard, father of American rocketry through the first half of the twentieth century; it also brought together the combined leadership of industrial, governmental, media, and educational components of American astronautics.

As the dinner and awards ceremony convened in Washington on the evening of March 20, 1987, Bradbury's longstanding role as a visionary at Caltech, the Jet Propulsion Laboratory, and NASA itself was now extended, at least for the evening, across the aerospace arm of the nation's military-industrial complex. Bradbury admired many in the audience and many past winners, including a number of astronauts he knew personally; but he had been, and remained, a vocal critic of the yawning gap between the Department of Defense budget and the NASA budget ever since the Nixon administration began the gradual slide downward in NASA's budget allocation in the early 1970s.

He honestly believed, and often made this point in his lectures, that the aerospace industry could be a source of economic recovery and stability unlike any other arm of the private sector. In his mind, this was the best way to wage war on poverty and inequality as well. His visionary perspective was often unassailable, but his unvarying reliance on basic common sense in addressing the complex challenges and stresses in American society was often overly simplified. Bradbury's critiques were almost always motivational, but they rarely contained workable solutions.

However, his broader reflections on why we explore, and why we have to find a meaningful place in the cosmos over time, would always have far more impact than his systemic critiques. It compelled, and it continued to compel into the next century as science revealed more and more evidence of the global catastrophes of deep time past and the inevitable asteroid encounters and solar events of deep time future.

Bradbury's presentation that evening sought a balance between criticism and motivation that he didn't always maintain on other nights, and his criticisms were, for once, tactfully offered within the larger context of national grief and reassessment. National Space Club President T. Bland Norris expressed thanks for "the upbeat nature of the talk. Your enthusiasm is infectious and very much what this group needed to hear after a most difficult year." Norris, former head of NASA's entire astrophysics division, also expressed the sentiments of many: "A number of those involved in the program have experienced a twinge of self doubt and some recrimination as a result of the *Challenger* failure and ensuing public reaction. Your perspective on what we are really about and why was a lift to us all."[1]

In July 1987, just four months after Bradbury's keynote address, NASA submitted its plan for addressing the *Challenger* Commission's recommendations. The announced major adjustments to managerial and technical aspects of the Space Shuttle program represented the first major reconfigurations at the agency since the Nixon administration's shift away from plans for a moon base and human expeditions to Mars. The objective now was to save and extend the Shuttle program, and Bradbury continued to play a supportive role; there was a cost, however, for the objective that he held most dear—Mars would remain a dream deferred, and more than twenty years would pass between the *Viking* 1 and 2 landings of 1976 and the 1997 landing of *Pathfinder*. The surface of Mars had been silent since communications were lost with *Viking* 2 in 1982 and would remain so until the final years of the twentieth century.

: : :

The optimism Bradbury envisioned for the distinguished guests and honorees at the 1987 Goddard memorial dinner was focused on the delicate balance between the demands of war and peace, the demands of economic prosperity, and the potential for the space program to unite all of these efforts globally. But as that evening came and passed, Bradbury was also immersed in bringing out his first story collection in more than a decade, and the eventual title story explored the underlying mindset required to secure the future of humanity in a far broader context. His sense of the interconnectedness of past, present, and future had resulted in some of his best time-travel stories, and one of his most recent was also one of his most visionary. "The Toynbee Convector" might also be said to represent the true essence of his beliefs about mankind, now fully matured in the fifth decade of his storytelling career.

He had published this story in the January 1984 issue of Playboy, and now he would privilege it in his new collection. But once again, there would be many old tales in this new book of stories, and the selection process was not easy. In February 1987, he sent a "hunk of manuscript" to Bob Gottlieb at Knopf, who continued to broadly oversee Bradbury's submissions during his two decades as editor-in-chief and eventually president of the publishing house. "The Toynbee Convector" was part of the "hunk," and Gottlieb suggested that the new collection include more of the "time travel" tales without tipping the volume into the "science fiction" category that Bradbury had tried to transcend since his earliest major market successes with Doubleday: "I don't think people consider you primarily a Sci-Fi writer any longer," Gottlieb pointed out, "and haven't for a long time, but you're so wonderful at it (as in Toynbee), I miss you in that vein."[2]

Gottlieb would soon be leaving Knopf to assume William Shawn's well-worn editor's chair at The New Yorker, and Bradbury would now be working with managing editor Kathy Hourigan. They would get along well, and by the fall of 1987 she made a preliminary selection from the stories that Bradbury continued to send in. At this point, "The Thing at the Top of the Stairs" was her preferred title story and was the choice of others at Knopf as well: "This title speaks Bradbury more than any other in the collection might and does not (others tell me) indicate (as I feared it would) a collection weighted heavily on the scary."[3]

There were nowhere near enough recently published stories to fill a collection, and Bradbury faced the same challenge he had faced in pulling together Long After Midnight a decade earlier. Bill Nolan had helped him navigate that process, and now his principal bibliographer Donn Albright would advise.[4] Bradbury had come to depend on Albright to evaluate the earlier range of uncollected stories, but he resisted Albright's sense that some of the Greentown stories that had fallen out of Dandelion Wine were serious contenders.[5] Instead, he sent Hourigan a group of weirds from his 1947 Dark Carnival collection that had not been strong enough to pull into The October Country. She dropped all save one of these from consideration, but the final selection of twenty-three stories still included eight older tales.

Of these eight, the strongest was "At Midnight, in the Month of June," a near-masterpiece sequel to his most famous tale of suspense, "The Whole Town's Sleeping." The prequel described the slowly rising terror of a woman returning home alone after an evening at the cinema, braving the depths of the town ravine on the very evening that another woman had been murdered by the Lonely One. At last, in the familiar darkness of her home, safely locked in, she hears the voice of a man softly clearing his throat behind her. The sequel, written and published in 1954 at the request of *Ellery Queen* publisher Frederic Dannay, offers the murderer's twisted point of view.

"At Midnight, in the Month of June," with a title and mood inspired by the first line of Poe's "The Sleeper," frames the unforgettable internalized consciousness of a serial killer acting out a continuous cycle of revenge on the hated mother who had slowly killed his father "with her temper and her tongue." Slowly, the reader comes to realize that he *wants* to be caught, that he is deliberately setting up crime scene evidence, finally arriving at an all-night diner where he waits, eating graham crackers and drinking milk.

In the early 1980s, Albright had persuaded Bradbury to publish five old mid-century typescripts (they represented the only Bradbury stories published in 1981 and 1982 at all), and he managed to get four of these into *The Toynbee Convector* as well. "A Touch of Petulance" was the best, a time-travel terror that stood in perfect opposition to the inspiring time-travel lie of "The Toynbee Convector." Jonathan Hughes doesn't believe the middle-aged doppelganger who has come from his future to warn him that he will someday murder his beautiful new wife—until, now sensitized to clues, he notices just the tiniest touch of petulance in her voice.

Albright also conjured up an older Martian tale ("The Love Affair"), a beautiful fantasy of love under the stars ("One Night in Your Life"), the lost enchantments of childhood ("The Last Circus"), the revisited terrors of childhood ("The Thing at the Top of the Stairs"), and two unpublished stories of Bradbury's supernatural Elliott family, one old, one new. But Bradbury was still the storyteller, and he used some of these resurrected older stories to anchor more recent explorations of love and loneliness: the love and alienation between parents and children ("I Suppose You Are Wondering Why We Are Here?," "By the Numbers!"); loves lost ("Promises, Promises," "The Laurel and Hardy Love Affair," "Long Division,"); loves betrayed ("Banshee"); loves parodied ("Junior," "Come, and Bring Constance!"); and a remembered childhood confessional ("Bless Me Father, for I Have Sinned").

In the end, however, the catalog of contents overreached. The best tales gathered in *The Toynbee Convector* were obscured by lesser ones; the conversational wit and descriptive humor wasn't always successful, especially in the newer stories. The collection was released on May 24, 1988, and selected as a Book-of-the-Month Club alternate, but there were few major reviews. *Publishers' Weekly* found the collection "a very mixed bag," acknowledging the charm and emotional power of a few stories but condemning "some of the author's weakest frail conceits feebly decked out in the same stylistic knickknacks Bradbury has been pulling from his well-used trunk for the past 35 years." Most significantly, however, these dispassionate verdicts gave credibility to the reviewer's high regard for "The Toynbee Convector":

> The title story concerns a man who claims to have traveled into the future and declares that there the world's problems have been resolved. He produces documentation of his claims and lives to see the realization of his vision, even though a vision is all it is. The documentation turns out to be fabrications, but the hope it had inspired allows mankind to bring about its own salvation. The fiction creates the truth in this lovely exercise in utopian dreaming.

Bradbury's humanistic view of salvation went all the way back to "No Man Is an Island," his 1953 celebration of books for the new Brandeis University library: "Books are fairly new things in the history of man. I do not for an instant claim they are the cure-all or that they can save us. Man, after all, is his own salvation." For Bradbury, books were tools, remarkable extensions of the human mind, as Professor Faber describes them in *Fahrenheit 451*: "Books were only one type of receptacle where we stored a lot of things we were afraid we might forget. There is nothing magical in them, at all. The magic is only in what books say, how they stitched patches of the universe together into one garment for us."

With "The Toynbee Convector," Bradbury completed a forty-year arc from the origins of *Fahrenheit*, where knowledge must rise from memory, phoenix-like, to Toynbee's famous "Challenge and Response" formulation, projected through Bradbury's settled conviction that the destructive potential of the modern age can only be overcome if mankind truly *believes* that it will be overcome. Bradbury's Time Traveler, Craig Bennett Stiles, establishes the most convincing lie in human history, lives to see the lie become profound truth in the next century, and then climbs into his machine a second time. As Stiles anticipated a century earlier, his time machine finally becomes reality as it euthanizes him; Stiles becomes a true time traveler, falling farther behind in time every moment as the world moves ever further into an even brighter new future up ahead.

"The Toynbee Convector" gave definition to all the tantalizing dream-world uncertainties that Shakespeare's Theseus called "forms of things unknown."

Bradbury's utopian dream represented the culmination of everything that he had been trying to convey—in fiction, in essays, in interviews—throughout his entire career. Here was the full blossoming of his individualized "Optimal Behaviorism" into a planetwide achievement for the Human race. This late in life, an uneasy balance between science, religion, and human values was no longer good enough for Bradbury; one had, above all, to *believe* in humanity, and thereby, like his own Time Traveler, "seize the future and shape it."

"Age has done nothing to dim your genius." Sir Rupert Hart-Davis, his former British publisher, offered this opinion in response to reading *The Toynbee Convector*.[6] For Hart-Davis, the best story was "Lafayette, Farewell," the heartbreaking true story of Academy Award–winning cinematographer Bill Skall, Bradbury's next-door neighbor. Skall had flown for the Lafayette Escadrille in the Great War, and Bradbury captured in fiction his friend's lament for those he had killed in fair fight over France so many years earlier, relieved only by a slow and sad descent into dementia. Fiction, through this story and others, helped Bradbury face the possibility of this slow death of the mind, but he would be fortunate enough to remain lucid to the very end of his life. Perhaps Skall's Academy Award statuette was a talisman; it was given to Bradbury, and stood sentinel on his mantle, always.

: : :

After the spring 1988 release of *The Toynbee Convector*, Bradbury and Maggie made their usual working vacation pilgrimage to Paris. Once again, Bradbury hoped to lure Federico Fellini away from his beloved Cinecittà studio in Rome. The previous fall, he had almost succeeded, as Fellini considered coming to Paris to work on the French translation of his new film, *Intervista*. But the great director found this kind of work both time-consuming and ultimately frustrating—Fellini had not visited the Bradburys during their fall 1987 visit to Paris, and he would not be able to come as they returned for the summer of 1988.[7]

This time, however, the Bradburys did not stay in their usual accommodation, the Hotel Normandy. Lawrence Gordon, their Los Angeles attorney and primary representative for the family's Ray Bradbury Enterprises, owned an apartment on the Avenue de la Bourdonnais in the Gros-Caillou Quarter, near the Eiffel Tower. The Bradburys were given the apartment part of the summer of 1988, and they found the deeper seclusion of Parisian apartment life delightful. With *Toynbee* out and *A Graveyard for Lunatics* nearly complete, Bradbury could think of such deferred major projects as his planned collection of Irish stories and his earliest Illinois book project, eventually titled *Farewell Summer*.

For the most part, Bradbury and Maggie would stay there during every subsequent vacation as well, insisting on paying the Gordons, who lived there at other times of the year.[8] Bradbury was, appropriately, not far from the Champ de Mars, but this extensive park was not named for Bradbury's Red Planet alone; the name had a deeper derivative—the Campus Martius in Rome, honoring Mars, the classical god of war. The Eiffel Tower shared this urban greenspace with France's Ecole Militaire, and when Bradbury returned to the Avenue de la Bourdonnais apartment in 1989, his thoughts turned to memories of a more deeply felt military heritage of his own.

Few, if any, readers or reviewers of The Toynbee Convector ever knew that "Lafayette Farewell" was second only to the collection's title story in Bradbury's heart at that time. In the late summer of 1989, the story of Bill Skall's haunting memories of the Great War would lead Bradbury to come to terms with his own family's deep sacrifice in France during the final weeks of World War I. He began the process during his usual summer Paris vacation with Maggie, when he wrote to the European Office of the American Battle Monuments Commission.

The response identified the final resting place of his uncle, Samuel Hinkston Bradbury, who had been taken down by the terrifying unseen killer that haunted the world at the end of the Great War—the global Influenza Pandemic of 1918–19. "Captain Samuel H. Bradbury is interred in the Oise-Aisne American Military Cemetery. . . . At the time of his death on October 17, 1918, he was a member of the 49th Regt." The letter heading identified the location of one small area of American soil in northeastern France: "Plot C Row 12 Grave 18 | Oise-Aisne AMC." Ray Bradbury would not be the first of his family to pay homage over Grave 18; incredibly, his paternal grandmother, never one to travel far from Waukegan, made the trip in 1934 with her daughter, Bradbury's beloved Aunt Neva.

He journeyed deep into the countryside northeast of Paris, arriving at the cemetery by way of a network of rural roads west of the famous cathedral town of Reims. Bradbury met his escort in the Visitors building at Oise-Aisne and placed his floral decoration by the gravestone of the uncle he had never met. But Uncle Samuel's widow, Tilita, was one of his favorite aunts, and her love formed a more tangible bridge of memories for many years. In his mid-twenties, Bradbury had taken time from a New York publishing visit to spend a weekend with her on Long Island. After that visit, with tears in his eyes, he said, "Oh God, I hate to go; everything's ending." The captain's widow replied, "Oh no, my dear, everything's beginning. You go home and begin." He had gone on to live most of his career by constantly renewing that admonition.

At long last, Bradbury stood graveside, in the memorial presence of the oldest and most distinguished Bradbury of his father's generation, a graduate of West

Point; the cemetery held the remains of more than 6,000 American troops killed in action, as well as early pandemic victims like Captain Sam Bradbury. Back in America, influenza would also claim his namesake, Ray Bradbury's older brother Sam, Skip's twin. Bradbury's mother, Esther, nearly died as well; her last child, Ray's baby sister, Betty Jane, would later become the family's third influenza victim. In the 1920s and early 1930s, Ray Bradbury's childhood Saturdays were sometimes spent at the cemeteries in Waukegan. At the age of 69, he was finally able to honor his uncle in the same way.

25 | Time Flies

Bradbury's August 1989 working vacation in Paris was bracketed by June and October performances of a new musical version of *Dandelion Wine*. This was not the much-troubled Billy Goldenberg and Larry Alexander musical of the late 1960s and early 1970s; he had never been able to resist the impulse to extend his stage adaptation into song lyrics that invariably caused trouble with his lyricists, and *Dandelion Wine*'s history on the musical stage was a prime example. But this new venture would be different; Bradbury would offer his draft verses to one of the best-known popular music composers of the day—Jimmy Webb.

At this point in his career, Bradbury had spun out almost five hundred pages of lyrics for *Dandelion Wine*. Some dated to the early 1970s and his last effort to revive the 1960s Lincoln Center success of the Goldenberg-Alexander songs. Many new lyrics had been written in the early 1980s, as he continued his decades-long attempt to master lyrical composition. Bradbury even drafted an offer for schools to use his script and his lyrics to craft their own performance music.[1] He wrote new lyrics for such episodes as his grandfather's bottling memories in vintages of dandelion wine, young Douglas's blueberry-picking discovery that he is alive with the electricity of youth, Leo Auffman's attempts to generate happiness through machine-made sights and sounds, and above all, the growing awareness of the passage of time that pervades the entire novel.

There were natural connections between Bradbury and Webb; both were largely self-taught in their respective fields, and were mistrustful of corporate consumerism; furthermore, both had spent decades navigating the consequences of a rapid rise to fame. Webb had exploded on the pop music scene at the age of 21, as his 1967 hits "Up, Up, and Away" (Fifth Dimension) and "By the Time I Get to Phoenix" (Glen Campbell) earned two Grammy nominations and one Grammy Award. The next year his meteoric rise continued with "MacArthur Park" (Richard Harris), "Wichita Lineman," and "Galveston" (Glen Campbell), and "The Worst That Could Happen" (Brooklyn Bridge). Yet Webb had dropped out of college before any of this success began, and his deep immersion in the pop-rock culture through the 1970s never attracted the fan base of peers that he had hoped for. In the 1980s, Webb found new success in projects and songs for a wider range of singers, and at this point he accepted an offer to work with Bradbury on *Dandelion Wine*.

A love of science fiction was a constant presence in Jimmy Webb's reading life, and the chance to work with Bradbury interested him from the start. Bradbury and Webb met for lunch in Los Angeles at the Bistro Garden (a Bradbury favorite) on January 18, 1987.[2] By springtime, the poetic and lyric nature of Bradbury's prose encouraged Webb, who was "nothing less than awe struck about the possibility of working with him."[3] However, as Bradbury revised lyrics that summer, Webb wisely told Don Congdon that they needed to go slowly; Bradbury's notion of lyrics had evolved from the comic operetta style he first learned writing *Happy Anniversary 2116* for Elsa Lanchester in the 1950s, with an echo of the radio comedy he had learned as a teenager. The slow evolution of their working relationship gave Webb more control of the lyrics, and by early 1989 a well-developed musical was ready for performance.

Ten performances of the musical were staged at the University of Tulsa Theatre in early June 1989, followed by five more performances in late October. During the summer, Bradbury provided requested revisions to certain lyrics, and that process triggered familiar tensions over control. For the October 25th performance, Bradbury flew to Tulsa to confer with Webb and the resident director, Nancy Vunovich, only to find that Professor Vunovich had further revised Bradbury's changes without consultation. Webb was not present, and by the time he had explained the travel misunderstanding to Bradbury, it was too late to avoid a dispute over control of the final form of the musical and Webb's well-intended desire to promote the musical by performing songs from the score in his own stage shows.[4]

In the past, similar disputes with other stage collaborators usually meant the end of the road, but this time Bradbury and Webb were able to continue working together as the play evolved. This was achieved largely through the efforts of Webb himself, who had skipped the October 25th performance so that he could meet with Kennedy Center officials and potential New York production backers at a subsequent Tulsa performance on October 28th. The entire Tulsa venture was in fact a workshop concept, and the lukewarm reactions of these East Coast representatives convinced Webb that another series of workshop performances was in order.[5] It would also take time to rethink the score and other aspects of the production, but Webb's perseverance eventually paid off.

In 1993, Kermit Christman, founding producer of the annual Palm Beach Shakespeare Festival in Florida and a longtime friend of Bradbury's, convinced Webb and Bradbury to stage a new version of the *Dandelion Wine* musical. The six performances in early March 1993 represented the first non-Shakespearean production at the Palm Beach Festival;[6] for these performances, Webb had composed "Time Flies," a haunting new ballad that evoked orchestral echoes of his earliest popular hits.

In retrospect, Jimmy Webb observed that, as both a reader and a collaborator, he had learned a great deal about "writing beautiful prose, choosing words" from Ray Bradbury.[7] "Time Flies" builds effectively on Bradbury's sense of time manifest through the progression of seasons in the world around us and the parallel internal progression of memories that mark the seasons of life. The lyrics of the original Bradbury-Webb collaboration all focused on the "Now" of summer 1928; for the Palm Beach Festival performances, Webb's new song set out the mixed joy and sadness of remembrance—life becomes memory, recalled again and again through dreams and the waking dreams that Bradbury knew as reverie. Yet beneath the seemingly timeless experience of our dreams, time flies.

This final moment of collaboration with Ray Bradbury would go on to become one of Jimmy Webb's best-known concert and nightclub ballads. It would be performed in concert and recorded by Linda Ronstadt, Rosemary Clooney, and Michael Feinstein. Throughout his career Bradbury had many rewarding collaborations with visual artists and symphonic composers, but in terms of the demanding work involved in musical stage adaptation, he may have learned the most from working with Jimmy Webb.

: : :

In November 1989, just after Bradbury returned home from the second run of the *Dandelion Wine* musical in Tulsa, the third season of *Ray Bradbury Theater* completed its broadcast schedule on the USA Network. This was the second twelve-episode season broadcast of RBT under USA sponsorship; together with the original six-episode season with HBO (1985–1986) and the twelve USA Network episodes of the second season (1988), the third season brought the total number of Bradbury-scripted broadcasts to thirty episodes by the end of November 1989.

What had been a pioneering anthology series in the early days of pay TV cable on HBO continued to evolve on the USA Network as subscription lists increased and a wider range of Bradbury's stories aired. The strong casting evident in the six early HBO episodes continued through seasons two and three on USA, but there was little continuity of production and almost no continuity in direction at the various international locations. The uneven production values were further eroded by tight budgets limiting the series to minimal, pre-digital special effects.

Of the twenty-four USA episodes broadcast in 1988 and 1989, the better ones all benefit from strong cast performances by veteran stars combined, for the most part, with the effective storytelling values of Bradbury's original tales. His trademark alienation, paranoia, suspense, and sense of an eerie "otherness" comes through effectively in Bradbury's adaptations of "Skeleton," "On the Orient, North," "The Coffin," and "There Was an Old Woman." For "And So Died Riabouchinska," "The Small Assassin," and "A Sound of Thunder," strong acting performances make up for the compressions and omissions demanded by the 23-minute limitations of 30-minute time slots. By the end of season three, Bradbury's sense of nostalgia and the need to be loved broke through production limitations very effectively in such episodes as "The Lake," "To the Chicago Abyss," and "Hail and Farewell."

The Ray Bradbury Theater continued to receive recognition from the rapidly emerging cable TV broadcasting industry—the third season would net another five CableACE nominations—but there were also changes coming for the series. It was time to confirm the stories for season four and prepare contracts in advance of USA's decision to extend or cancel the series for 1990. This was a complicated process involving three distinct production entities: Ray Bradbury Enterprises, Inc. (essentially Bradbury as author, script writer, and coproducer); Bradbury's producer-partner, Wilcox Productions (Larry Wilcox and Martin Leeds); and the actual production company, RBT Productions, Inc. (Peter Sussman of the Canadian-based production company Atlantis).

There were issues to settle before the season four contracts could be prepared and signed.[8] As co–executive producer, Bradbury wanted to review and approve production locations, directors and, as much as possible, actors. For the 1990 season, Bradbury wanted at least half of the episodes shot in Canada, but the Atlantis plan was to film nine episodes in New Zealand and only three in Canada to minimize production costs. Bradbury compromised here, while Atlantis continued to consult with Bradbury on director selection and casting.

Producer Tom Cotter would be in charge of the Canadian and New Zealand locations. Since joining the production team for season three, Cotter had effectively functioned as the series "runner" for continuity of production and script revision, working closely with Bradbury by mail and fax.[9] In spite of the distance challenges of global production, which had taken the series to England, France, and New Zealand in earlier seasons, Bradbury insisted on working up revisions whenever Cotter or his directors needed script modifications. Cotter engaged actively with Bradbury at every turn, but in reality, there were script and shooting modifications by directors and probably light interventions by Cotter in the filming of most episodes, regardless of location.

Friction slowly emerged in the interactions between Bradbury and Wilcox, who was a dynamic producer with obligations outside of the Ray Bradbury Theater venture. He had provided useful but limited script suggestions when requested, but Bradbury dominated writing and focused more and more on revisions requested or suggested by Tom Cotter. Wilcox had been the main catalyst behind the initial 1985 venture and was instrumental in negotiating Bradbury's control of the series, but after 1990 his participation would be diminished.

By November 1989 Bradbury, was at work on season four's story adaptations. Cotter's shooting schedule for the nine New Zealand episodes was set for February through early April, with the three Canadian episodes set for filming in Alberta during May 1990 to meet the fall broadcast season.[10] The USA network renewed the series on that timetable. The last piece of the puzzle also fell into place in November, solving a long-standing problem: In all of these first thirty episodes, there had not been a single *Martian Chronicles* adaptation, or even a glimmer of the night terrors of *Something Wicked This Way Comes*.

Both of those works had required rights negotiations. In early November 1989 Sussman was able to negotiate a *Martian Chronicles* release from Fries Entertainment, which had produced the 1980 NBC miniseries. Three days earlier, Disney CEO Michael Eisner personally telephoned Bradbury with the approval for Atlantis to use "The Black Ferris," the root story behind the 1983 Disney feature film *Something Wicked This Way Comes*.[11] Season four would include Bradbury's adaptation of "The Black Ferris," along with four *Martian Chronicles* episodes: "Mars Is Heaven!," "Usher II," "—And the Moon Be Still as Bright," and "The Long Years." Three more *Chronicles* tales would follow in seasons five and six.

Season four yielded some pleasant Martian surprises. The suspenseful shape-changing premise underlying "Mars Is Heaven!" and Hal Linden's strong lead performance combined to yield a memorable episode. Robert Culp's lead in "The Long Years" added impact to Bradbury's more hopeful re-working of the conclusion for Culp's robotic family—they now have the ability to resurrect the image of their creator. There were some structural problems with this episode, but on balance, all seven Martian episodes of the final three seasons added richness to the entire range of stories.

26 Beyond the Iron Curtain

Ray and Maggie arrived in Paris in early January 1990 for a three-week stay sponsored in part by the French publisher Denoël; Jacques Chambon, Bradbury's Denoel editor, had arranged a series of media events around the new fortieth anniversary edition of *The Martian Chronicles*. Shortly after arriving in France, Bradbury used these events to lead his own trans-Atlantic assault on Doubleday, which so far had no serious plans to bring out a fortieth anniversary edition of a book that had made them a considerable sum since 1950. For most of that time, Doubleday had shared Bradbury's income from the ever-present Bantam paperback editions of the *Chronicles*, with no hardbound editions under the Doubleday imprint since the 1970s.

"It has made a good deal of money for Doubleday over those 40 years," he wrote, "hundreds of thousands in fact, and deserves a bit of champagne and confetti. It is being studied in almost every high school and college in America now, as you also know, and similar readings occur in all the European nations."[1] This was hyperbolic, of course, but his next reference hit home. "I hope you will be in touch and that we can work together in this special year for my Martians. Have you seen the cover for the new edition Bantam plans? . . . A true beauty. You might wish to use it on the hardcover." Bantam's new cover illustration was indeed a stunner—golden skinned Martians languidly looking out over a vast landscape of rust-colored hills and canal-graced valleys, the creation of noted science fiction and fantasy artist Michael Whelan. Doubleday would in fact bring out a fortieth anniversary edition late in 1990, graced with a wrap-around enlargement of the Whelan painting.

Bradbury's letter also contained news about the larger drama unfolding on the other side of Europe, as the Iron Curtain began to collapse in uneven bursts of political activity from the Baltic to the Black Sea. "While I am in France I will go to Prague to visit the new president, who is a *Chronicles* buff." Exactly one week earlier Czechoslovakia's Federal Assembly had elected Vaclav Havel president of the nation.

One might suspect that Havel, a former political prisoner and one of the best-known international dissident literary figures of the day, would have preferred *Fahrenheit 451*, but the entire communist-era arc of Bradbury books in Czechoslovakia had been remarkable. For four decades, Prague had been dominated by one of the most rigorous of the Warsaw Pact regimes and one of the most pervasive secret police systems in the entire Communist Bloc; yet the Czech government had followed the Soviet lead in allowing Bradbury's works to enter the culture, beginning with a 1957 edition of *Fahrenheit 451* translated and published by Josef Skvorecky, who also published banned works by Havel and Milan Kundera and smuggled them into the country.

Yet by 1959, Czech editions of *The Martian Chronicles* and *Fahrenheit 451* were circulating freely, along with a Slovak edition of *The Golden Apples of the Sun*. Czech editions of *The Illustrated Man* and two other remixed Bradbury story collections would follow over the years. Skvorecky also translated Hemingway, Evelyn Waugh, and Raymond Chandler; Bradbury was now in the vanguard of new Western models for rising Czechoslovakian writers. "I suddenly saw that you could write dialogue as people spoke it," Skvorecky would later observe. "It opened my eyes."[2] By then, Skvorecky was in exile, but Bradbury's cultural impact was tangible for those who remained behind. Latter-day Czech anthologist Radek Dojiva maintained that Bradbury was perhaps more widely read under the Czech communist regime than all other American science fiction writers combined. Dojiva and others would eventually compile an anthology of Czech science fiction under the title *Bradbury's Shadow*.

Czechoslovakia was caught up in fast-moving transitions, however, and Havel was only just beginning to negotiate his nation's disentanglement from the complex economic and military structures of the Warsaw Pact. Bradbury apparently deferred the Prague trip to his planned summer 1990 return to Paris, but it remains unclear if he was ever able to visit his Prague publishers or meet with Havel.[3] Yet his popularity in Eastern Europe had endured one of the harshest regimes of the Cold War and would continue to expand there. By 1992, *Fahrenheit 451* would be staged as a rock opera in Prague—an unthinkable venture just a few years earlier.[4]

Bradbury's winter 1990 stay in Paris coincided with what would be the twentieth (and final) annual Avoriaz Fantastic Film Festival in the French Alps. Jack Clayton had been nominated for the Grand Prize at the 1984 Avoriaz festival for his direction of *Something Wicked This Way Comes*, and, in mid-January 1990, Bradbury made his own visit as well. On January 15th, he enjoyed a screening of *Dial Code Santa Claus*, a European forerunner to the Chris Columbus film *Home Alone* that remains underappreciated today; he was seated in an audience that included Wes Craven and Roman Polanski.[5] That same day Bradbury was interviewed by the press as arranged by his Paris editors and literary agents, who also wanted him to return to Avoriaz for the third and final week of the film festival. Bradbury was coming down with the flu, however, and headed home early to Los Angeles with Maggie.[6]

An important postscript to their winter's stay in France arrived in Los Angeles a couple of months later. In April 1990, John Phillips, sportswriter for the *International Herald Tribune* and one of their expatriate friends in Paris, sent Bradbury a small fragment of the Berlin Wall. "I think of displaying it under my middle finger's fingernail," he wrote to Phillips, "so that I can tell some Soviet politician, when next I meet one, where to put it."[7] He was unaware that in little more than a month, he would be shaking hands with the leader of the communist world.

: : :

In early 1990, shortly after returning home from Paris, Bradbury had the opportunity to host a very special award ceremony. Los Angeles Mayor Tom Bradley had declared February 24th to be "Gene Roddenberry Day," and that evening The March of Dimes Birth Defects Foundation honored Roddenberry at the Foundation's annual Jack Benny Memorial Award Dinner. Bradbury enthusiastically accepted the role of master of ceremonies for a distinguished audience in the Sheraton Grand Hotel.

The two men had known each other a long time. In the mid-1960s, Roddenberry had shown his friend the *Star Trek* pilot episode and asked him to consider writing original teleplays for the new series. With regret, Bradbury declined.[8] It wasn't a question of adapting the work of others; in 1960 he had scripted a well-received *Alfred Hitchcock Presents* episode based on Stanley Ellin's "The Faith of Aaron Menafee," and his earlier cinematic adaptation of *Moby Dick* for John Huston had opened many doors in Hollywood. But those were stand-alone challenges, with no recurring evolution of characters crafted by other hands over the course of an entire season or more.

They often joked about the public's propensity for confusing (and even conflating) their names and careers, especially in the frenzy of genre conventions and autograph lines. That confusion spread all the way to the National Space Institute as Viking I approached the Red Planet—the June 1976 issue of the Institute's *Newsletter* cited the Martian tales of "Gene Bradbury." Roddenberry sent a copy of the gaffe to his friend with a note: "Here's one for the scrapbook. . . . Two for the price of one. No wonder Viking is on budget!"

He admired Roddenberry's ability to bring out important cultural issues in his early 1960s television series *The Lieutenant*, with casts that included actors he would bring into the *Star Trek* universe as well. He also identified with the studio battles that Roddenberry had endured to sustain and eventually syndicate his television shows and establish a franchise beachhead in science fiction film;

indirectly, these achievements provided a climate that aided the cable TV rise of *The Ray Bradbury Theater* in the mid-1980s.

For the ceremony, Bradbury teamed with longtime friend Jane Wyatt, one of Hollywood's most prominent March of Dimes volunteers, and introduced as well original *Star Trek* stars and the primary cast of *Star Trek: The Next Generation.* Bradbury's annotated script indicates that at one point in his remarks, he offered Roddenberry's daily work ethic as the epitome of the Bradburyian philosophy "Optimal Behaviorism"—do something every day, and get your work done. In what had become his favorite compliment for another Space Age visionary like Roddenberry, Bradbury invoked Yeats and the ability to know "what is past, or passing, or to come."

: : :

"The President of the Union of Soviet Socialist Republics and Mrs. Gorbachev request the pleasure of the company of Mr. Ray Bradbury at luncheon on Thursday, May 31, 1990, at 1.00 p.m."[9] The event was held in the Gold Room of the Soviet Embassy on Sixteenth Street, just four blocks from the White House. The invitation came as a surprise to Bradbury, but the event itself (and analysis of the guest list in the media) explained the surprise. Gorbachev wanted to address a broadly defined intellectual audience during what would be his final state visit to America. His wife Raisa further broadened the audience with a request for Hollywood representation, and invitations were extended to American writers Ray Bradbury and Isaac Asimov because they were favorite authors of the family, and especially of Gorbachev's daughter.

Bradbury knew a few of the guests already, including Asimov, Gregory Peck, and Douglas Fairbanks Jr., whose lineage and long career represented nearly a century of Hollywood history. Gorbachev's remarks were free-wheeling, at times very informal, but also expressive of Gorbachev's hope that the two nations would continue to find avenues of trust in the rapidly changing times. He alluded to the range of guests as well; the *Washington Post* quoted from the official translation of his remarks: "Gregory Peck, Jane Fonda and others that bring us together . . . Isaac Asimov and Ray Bradbury, who write science fiction. . . . All my favorite writers are here, and what's published in the Soviet Union, I was able to read. So, we have known each other for quite some time."[10] Douglas Fairbanks gave Bradbury a wink and a thumbs-up when Gorbachev mentioned him by name.

There was unintended irony here, as Gorbachev may not have known that *Fahrenheit 451*, initially well received in the Soviet Union, had become one of the most coveted black market titles by the end of the 1950s.[11] Bradbury, in spite of persistent efforts by Don Congdon through publishing contacts and even political go-betweens, had never really broken through the Soviet Union's complicated system of buying magazine rights that somehow transformed into book publication without equitable royalty payments (the ownership of magazines by the major government-controlled book publishers had something to do with it). But the ever-increasing Soviet publication of Bradbury novels and story collections, often repackaged in different combinations than found in the West, had touched younger generations in Russia; Bradbury reading clubs, informal but widespread, were common.[12]

Bradbury kept his luncheon seating place card as a favored memento, and his engraved invitation soon filled up with the autographs that he sought out and was sought out to reciprocate, during the eventful afternoon. There were a lot of guests to choose from, including some who wielded power largely behind the scenes. Beside one of the most prominent autographs, Bradbury noted "Arbatov!"—the exclamation revealing Bradbury's awareness of the abiding influence that Georgy Arbatov had exerted over Soviet-American policy for decades. Arbatov was known to the public of both nations and was deeply involved with planning a soft landing for his country as the Soviet system of rule gave way to what he considered inevitable changes. Others signing Bradbury's card included Peck and Fairbanks;[13] economist John Kenneth Galbraith; Henry Kissinger; Jesse Jackson; pianist Van Cliburn, whose successful performances in Russia during the 1950s and 1960s had won countless admirers there; and former Senator Eugene McCarthy, who might have taken Bradbury's vote in the 1968 presidential election if he had not withdrawn from the race. Ted Turner escorted Jane Fonda; he would soon recruit Bradbury to judge a new literary prize that, like all things in Turner's world of enterprise, would prove to be a high-stakes game indeed.

Bradbury had two direct interactions with the Soviet president that afternoon. In the receiving line, Raisa Gorbachev beamed at Bradbury, turned to her husband, and said, "This is our daughter's favorite writer!" Gorbachev smiled and said, "I know, I know." But the more significant dialog came later in the afternoon, when he had a chance to ask about President Bush's predecessor: "At the end of lunch I said to him, 'Mr. Gorbachev, what do you think of President Reagan?' He said, 'Your greatest president.' I said, 'Why do you say that?' He said, 'None of your other presidents ever said, "Tear down the Wall".'"[14] The candor was apparently genuine—there were no diplomatic points to be won, and the cameras were not rolling.

Federico Fellini (l) with Ray Bradbury, August 1978, in front of a carnival bust from Fellini's film *Casanova* at the Cinecittà film studio in Rome. Fellini's invitation led to a long friendship based on their mutual love of the fantastic and disdain for authoritarianism. Personal photo courtesy of Ray Bradbury Literary Works, LLC; used by permission.

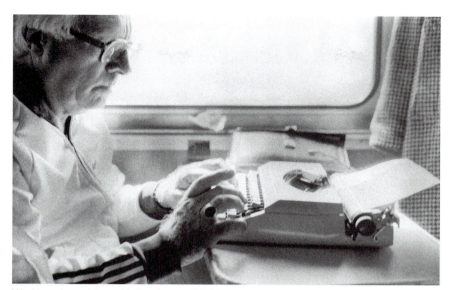

Working aboard Amtrak's Southwest Chief between Los Angeles and Chicago, 1980. Bradbury's deep-seated fear of flying lasted until 1982, but rail travel always "provided time to weigh, in the balance, myself and my life, my past, my present, and my future." Photo © Lisl Steiner, All Rights Reserved. Courtesy of Ray Bradbury Literary Works, LLC; used by permission.

In his sixtieth year, Bradbury reprises the hands-in-pocket pose of the family photo taken when he was three years old, displayed on the wall behind him in his Wilshire Boulevard office in 1980. He always felt that the boy he had once been remained a force in his creativity throughout his life. Photo © Lisl Steiner, All Rights Reserved. Courtesy of Ray Bradbury Literary Works, LLC; used by permission.

Prominent Argentine photographer and artist Aldo Sessa (l), discussing final proofs of *The Ghosts of Forever* with Bradbury in New York, 1980. Their collaborations on *The Ghosts of Forever* and a second book, *Séances and Ghosts* (2000), centered on Bradbury's conviction that the mysteries of science and religion would continue to merge through science fiction and the art it inspires. Photo © Lisl Steiner, All Rights Reserved. Courtesy of Ray Bradbury Literary Works, LLC; used by permission.

Bradbury always thought and wrote from a deeply visual mix of imagination and memory. Disney's exterior set for *Something Wicked This Way Comes* included many touches of his childhood Waukegan world. He often walked the set on his own, as seen here in a personal photo taken in 1982. Courtesy of Ray Bradbury Literary Works, LLC; used by permission.

This 1981 image of Bradbury at work in his Wilshire Boulevard office features one of his IBM Selectric typewriters, a favorite desktop model. The many mementos, including gifts from NASA and Disney, were moved to his home basement office and the lower basement area by the late 1980s. Photo © Lisl Steiner, All Rights Reserved. Courtesy of Ray Bradbury Literary Works, LLC; used by permission.

Ray and Maggie Bradbury with their beloved Man'Ha Garreau-Dombasle (center) in the mid-1990s. Their 44-year friendship advanced his early acceptance among French literary critics. Bradbury's verso note to his daughter Alexandra reads "Le Crazee Americains with Man'Ha at Beaumont, on the French coast, in front of the church where William the Conqueror celebrated his last Mass before crossing to invade England in 1066." Personal photo courtesy of Ray Bradbury Literary Works, LLC; used by permission.

A page from Bradbury's final unproduced screenplay for *The Martian Chronicles*. This script was the culmination of earlier versions dating back to 1961; it was completed in January 1997 in Paris. The revised page is from "Night Meeting," where the Earth colonist Tomas encounters a spectral Martian from the distant past. Bradbury's holograph revisions replace Tomas with Cherokee, a Native American crew member of an early expedition. As revised, the ghostly encounter involves the displaced indigenous peoples of both worlds. From the Bradbury Center. Image courtesy of Ray Bradbury Literary Works, LLC; used by permission.

"I dare not go—that land has ghosts | And haunted rains along the coasts." The first draft of "To Ireland," written in one sitting on six small memorandum sheets. It was privately printed in 1982 but remained uncollected until 2002. From the late 1960s on, Bradbury's verse often surfaced, almost fully formed, through his early morning reveries. Very few of the heartfelt lines of "To Ireland" were ever altered in revision. From the Bradbury Center. Image courtesy of Ray Bradbury Literary Works, LLC; used by permission.

Bradbury speaks to the 2004 Presidential Commission on Moon,, Mars, and Beyond. His April 15th interview was conducted by live video feed from Los Angeles to the public hearing session in San Francisco. The objective of this session was to gather testimony from cultural figures closely involved with the Space Age. In all, more than 180 witnesses were called to the various open sessions; Bradbury was the only writer chosen to appear. NASA photo by Greg Knott.

Part IV

Graveyard for Lunatics

I'd go over the graveyard when I was a kid. I couldn't get into the [Paramount] studio any other way—we'd go over the wall, and climb down the other side, and walk around like I belonged to the studio. That's the great secret—don't look as if you're a fugitive, look like you belong there.

—RB, March 14, 2002

27 | *A Graveyard for Lunatics*

On July 3, 1990, little more than a month after his luncheon with President and Mrs. Gorbachev in Washington, Bradbury's sequel to his heavily autobiographical *Death Is a Lonely Business* was released under the intriguing title *A Graveyard for Lunatics*. In the first novel, he had presented his life at the moment of his first great crisis of authorship—his very private failures in the late 1940s with the novel form. For *Graveyard*, he would compress more than a decade of episodic encounters with Hollywood (1952–65) into a single imagined season of 1954, where Bradbury could finally examine his next great crisis point as a writer—the temptation to descend into the financially secure anonymity of a screenwriter's life, or even worse, the twilight world of a Hollywood executive, no longer able to write at all.

The elusive and horrifying murderer of *Death Is a Lonely Business* had propelled the journey through Bradbury's memories of real-life noir characters and mysterious Hollywood personalities. He would once again need such a figure for *Graveyard*, a character mysterious and terrifying in other ways, more suitable to the Hollywood memories he intended to reveal. The horror effect would have to be visual rather than literary, the character more rememberable than the bizarre Poesque parody A. L. Shrank of the earlier novel. *Graveyard*'s monster would also have to evoke both fear and pity in equal proportions.

The solution came to him in the middle of the Atlantic Ocean in early July 1985, as Bradbury and Maggie were en route to Europe by liner. He had finally accepted air travel three years earlier, and they would soon cross the ocean mostly aboard the supersonic Concorde. But they still crossed by liner occasionally, and this particular trip would have far-reaching creative consequences:

> I went down to my stateroom, and on the way there, I passed a man who walked by with some people, and he had this horribly destroyed face. It looked like he had shoved his face into a furnace and been burnt, that his face was wax, so it all melted. His face was so horrible that a few seconds after I passed him, I burst into tears. I didn't know who he was, but I couldn't imagine how a man could live with that face, you know, terrible, terrible, terrible.[1]

Bradbury's reaction was conditioned by a lifetime of memories, beginning with his early childhood silent film encounters with *The Hunchback of Notre Dame* and *The Phantom of the Opera*. Even before encountering death or the small-town terrors of the dark, he learned—on some preliterate, preschool level—the hopeless sadness of unrequited love portrayed by Lon Chaney. As he learned to read, his first book—the 1925 edition of *Once Upon a Time*—opened with the story of "Beauty and the Beast," accompanied by the striking Art Nouveau illustrations of Margaret Evans Price.

The despair and loneliness of Hunchback and Phantom, and the great rage manifest in Beauty's captor, came back to Bradbury in those rare moments when he encountered disfigurement in his adult life. But his mid-Atlantic encounter had a completely unexpected second act: "That night, at dinner, down below in the dining room, I saw the man seated at a table about forty feet away, with his wife and his daughter, and they were laughing and enjoying themselves and drinking champagne. And it struck me like a blow, you know, now here's a man that should have killed himself years ago, out of despair, and here he is with his wife and his daughter who made him forget that he was ugly. So, the gifts of love right in front of you, a metaphor you put on the screen if you had a way of doing it."

After debarking and continuing on to Paris, just months before his prequel *Death Is a Lonely Business* would be published in America, the image of this man's tortured but loving face opened out a pathway from his earliest movie house memories of Phantom and Hunchback in 1920s Waukegan, to his 1930s teenage adventures caging autographs in front of the L.A. studios and the restaurants that the stars and movie moguls frequented, and on through his legitimate entry to the studios as a writer in the 1950s. A studio murder mystery quickly unfolded in his mind, a mystery where, like his shipboard encounter with the faceless man, nothing is what it seems to be. Bradbury's portable typewriter was a silent battery-operated model, and it was not unusual for him to type through the night during their Paris sojourns. He was a touch typist and while Maggie slept he composed a hundred pages or more in darkness during much of their two-week stay.

The search for a title proved to be a true odyssey, highlighting his trouble finding the central autobiographical moment around which the novel would turn. In typical Bradbury fashion, the quest for the right title emerged from a cascading series of word associations, in this case triggered by what had been his secret teenage access route into the fabled world of Paramount—the shared wall between the studio and Hollywood Cemetery, soon known as Hollywood Memorial Park. On just one of his working title pages, prepared on bright orange paper, the stream included *Over the Wall Is Out*, *The Dead Ride Fast*, *In the Midst of Life*, *The Time of Your Death*, *Occupation: Dead*, *Death's Occupations: Another Tale of Two Cities*, *Occupied Country*, *Corpse with Tinsel*, *The Tinsel Cadaver*, *Night of the Tinsel Cadaver*, and *Cadaver in Tinsel*.

For most of the three years that the novel evolved, however, the working title was *Falling Upward*, one of Bradbury's favorite creative placeholders that eventually stuck, instead, to one of his Irish plays. Yet in all of these wanderings he never strayed far from his notion that the cemetery and the studio were simply different aspects of the same largely artificial threshold between life and death, illusion and reality. Finally, he settled on *A Graveyard for Lunatics*, ironically subtitled *A Tale of Two Cities*. The connection between these cities was also a literal one; Paramount was built on land originally purchased from Hollywood Cemetery.

The autobiographical threads of the *Graveyard for Lunatics* tapestry were spun principally from his 1961 time at MGM. This adventure began with a screenplay treatment for *The Martian Chronicles*, but as studio support slowly unraveled Bradbury was redirected to write the voice-over narration that Orson Welles would read for the New Testament epic *King of Kings*. Another memory for the new book came in from Bradbury's brief 1952 stint as a contract writer at Twentieth Century Fox, where he ran afoul of studio executive Sol Siegel, who had not forgotten his mistrust of science fiction projects when their paths crossed again later at MGM on the *Martian Chronicles* project.[2]

A major character thread evolved into the no-nonsense director Fritz Wong, a combination of two of Bradbury's oldest Hollywood friends in real life—German director Fritz Lang and Chinese American cinematographer James Wong Howe. Both men fought uphill battles to Hollywood prominence, and Bradbury combined their go-it-alone legacies to form a character who could work within and around the studio system to protect the "Young Writer" as *A Graveyard for Lunatics* unfolds.[3] Lang's film-making genius emerges more strongly, for Bradbury needed at least a hint of Lang's eerie Weimar-era lost souls (*Dr. Mabuse*, *Metropolis*, and *M*) to help fashion the complex nature of his own monster.

The final significant character thread came from his early studio adventures with Ray Harryhausen at the beginning of his friend's legendary career in stop-action animation. By bringing Harryhausen into the novel as special effects artist Roy Holdstrom, Bradbury was able to present the two sides of his own Hollywood inner passions—his love of professionalism and craftsmanship and his hatred of dictatorial producers and studio executives who seemed to erode creativity at every turn.[4] Bradbury needed to keep the Young Writer balanced as the crime-solving central consciousness of the novel, and thus transferred most of the go-it-alone drama to Holdstrom.

As the novel opens, they have been called in to Maximus Films to write a science fiction script, *Meteor Crater*, around the most horrifying creature that Holdstrom can devise. But someone is trying to blackmail the studio over events long forgotten; an anonymous note sends the Young Writer into the cemetery adjacent to Maximus Films, where a mannequin with the face of J. C. Arbuthnot, the long-dead studio founder, is balanced precariously on a ladder placed against the wall between the city of the living and the city of the dead. The unfortunate founder has been gone for twenty years, the victim of a multiple fatality head-on automobile collision; yet the studio executives are terrified and angry at this mysterious prank, and both the Young Writer and Roy Holdstrom are caught in the middle.

Another note sends Holdstrom to a late-night dinner at the Brown Derby. The Young Writer accompanies his friend and together they see a privacy screen slip, just for a moment, to reveal a woman dining in seclusion with a well-dressed man whose face is horribly disfigured, no longer human in any way. Holdstrom immediately realizes that the anonymous note has given him the gift of the monster that he has not yet been able to imagine for their film, and he immediately begins to craft it on paper as the terrified Young Writer watches:

> Roy drew and the face was there. It was a face that was in an entire stage of collapse; as if the occupant, the mind behind the apparition, had run and swum a thousand miles and was now sinking to die. If there was bone behind the flesh, it had been shattered and reassembled in insect forms, alien facades masked in ruin. If there was a mind behind the bone, lurking in caverns of retina and tympanum, it signaled madly from out the swiveling eyes.

In this description, Bradbury focused an entire lifetime of encounters with the sadly malformed and tortured characters of film, literature, and lived experience, right up to the tenacious and courageous will to live epitomized by the tragic figure he had seen in mid-Atlantic just weeks earlier: "Roy and I sat riven by the bursts of incredible laughter that ricocheted off the walls behind the screen . . . his laughter at last sounded true as a bell."

Everything in the novel radiates out from these first two "gifts" given by the mysterious notes. The mercurial studio head, Manny Leiber, a survivor from the days of the dead founder, sees Holdstrom's life-size clay model of the film's new monster, and goes into an unexpected rage. Holdstrom is fired, banned from the studio, his name never to be mentioned, his priceless sets of miniatures for the science fiction movie destroyed. *Meteor Crater* is canceled, and the Young Writer is immediately reassigned to the troubled Bible movie, *Christ and Galilee*, to work with legendary director Fritz Wong.

Holdstrom turns suicidal and disappears within the back lots of the huge studio, a prime target for the hidden keepers of the studio's secrets. The Young Writer will need mentors to solve the mystery of the Maximus Films founder and save Roy Holdstrom from insanity, or worse. Near mid-novel, the Young Writer brings in his father figure from *Death Is a Lonely Business*, Homicide Lieutenant Elmo Crumley, who immediately sees the hidden blackmail motivation behind the anonymous notes.

Eventually the Young Writer discovers that the supposedly dead studio founder of Maximus Films, J. C. Arbuthnot, is one and the same with the disfigured man, leading a secret life of the living dead. A hidden passage from Arbuthnot's mausoleum in the cemetery connects to the labyrinth of tunnels and storage rooms beneath the studio, allowing him to secretly run the studio for decades from behind the mirror in his former office, where Manny Leiber presides only as a figurehead. Someone from the original inner circle has turned blackmailer, however, leading the Beast to murder within his own studio.

Bradbury was not capable of keeping his nostalgic sensibility and his addiction to vintage film humor from deflecting the novel from true noir to, at times, harsh satire. There can be no willing suspension of disbelief, but Bradbury used a valuable lesson he learned from Val Lewton's 1940s horror films to good effect—make every plot twist, no matter how digressive, lead relentlessly to the point that reveals the existential moment at the heart of the tale. In this case, it is the moment when the Young Writer must decide his own destiny, as Bradbury himself had done far less dramatically but no less emotionally in his own life story.

Almost too late, the Young Writer realizes that, during his rampage of revenge, the Arbuthnot/Beast has been stalking him, not as a victim, but as a potential heir to the empire he can no longer control. He is dying of cancer, and he makes a fateful offer: "It's yours if you want it. The studio." The Young Writer resists, still not understanding, but the Beast persists:

> "You don't understand. You're the only son I have."
> "I'm sorry that's true. Why me?
> "Because you are a real honest-to-God idiot savant. A real fool, not a fake one. Someone who talks too much but then you look at the words and they're right. You can't help yourself. The good things come out of your hands into words."

In these 46 words, Bradbury has Arbuthnot, the dying Beast, articulate the simple truth of his own creative life. For decades he would only say that characters welled up from his subconscious and simply told their own stories, and that he was born with a mysterious gift for metaphors. He would allude to creative bursts, but what was the process? *Was* there a process? Bradbury never really knew; now, in his odd storytelling form of autobiography, he simply told his readers, as honestly and frankly as he could, and more openly than he ever would again: "You look at the words and they're right. You can't help yourself. The good things come out of your hands into words."

It was also time to reveal the second major decision point in Bradbury's writing life, and to do so in fearful symmetry:

> "Last chance? Last offer?" His voice was fading.
> "And give up my wife and my writing and my life?"
> "Ah," whispered the voice. And a final "Yess . . ."

In reality, Bradbury had never felt the lure of executive power in Hollywood; he simply hated the way it all worked, and always would. The Beast's offer really symbolizes a choice between what is easy and what is right. The Young Writer forgives the Beast his sins, but he will not accept the offer—the studio would have become his life, to the exclusion of his unwritten novels and unborn children.

The remembered moment of decision has magnitude, for it documents—through fiction—Bradbury's real-life decision to limit his stints as a studio contract writer during the 1950s, thereby preserving a degree of creative independence during the most significant decade of his writing career. He would, however, spend much of the rest of his life negotiating options on his stories and novels with many producers and studios, writing screenplays and teleplays with mixed success. The story of those adventures was a novel he would never write.

The personal revelations of *A Graveyard for Lunatics* allowed Bradbury to merge the surface revelations of conventional autobiographical fiction with a deeper form of subjective self-exploration, a unique blend of confessional and memorial storytelling that proved very difficult to fulfill. He began in Paris on July 9, 1985, continued for a time after returning home to Los Angeles, but the full novel evolved through fits and bursts of development across another three years of composition. Bradbury completed a 450-page incomplete second draft at the end of July 1987, but his characters had taken him as far as they could. In January 1988, he bogged down near the end of the 550-page third draft as he tried to resolve the fate of Roy Holdstrom, who represented the chance-taking go-it-alone half of his own personality.

If Donn Albright was instrumental in shaping the later story collections, Sid Stebel would prove just as important to working through the unexplored possibilities of all three of Bradbury's late-life detective mysteries. Between January

1988 and the actual completion of the finished novel in early March of that year, Stebel helped Bradbury find resolution to the Roy Holdstrom character and bring him back from the edge of insanity. Don Congdon and Kathy Hourigan, his new editor at Knopf, also wrote detailed critiques that helped Bradbury smooth out the novel. In fact, all three of the autobiographical novels—*Death Is a Lonely Business*, *A Graveyard for Lunatics*, and *Let's All Kill Constance!*—would require significant critique prior to publication. He was, in the final analysis, a master of the short story form who never fully made the transition to novel-length fiction.

Graveyard was published in early July 1990. In spite of the structural complexities, reviewers were drawn to Bradbury's handling of his Hollywood memories.[5] The *Publisher's Weekly* review labeled it "a loopy funhouse of a novel," noting that Bradbury "toes the fine line between reality and illusion." British reviewers had been guarded whenever Bradbury strayed from science fiction, but Patrick Catling's review in the *Standard* offered a more accurate sense of the novel's form as "a sort of Phantom of the Studio, presented, or so it seems, as *comic* horror. . . . Bradbury uses realistic fantasy as the foundation for a ferociously critical satire of the studio system in the 1950s." Catling felt that the British dust jacket illustration, featuring "a detail of Goya's 1794 painting of 'The Madhouse at Saragossa,'" was spot on.

But in Bradbury's mind, the best review took the form of a postcard from Robert Bloch, who knew a thing or two about psychosis. Bradbury and Bloch had been friends since the 1946 WorldCon in San Francisco, and they had often corresponded. Like Bradbury, Bloch had known Fritz Lang and was influenced by the early Lang films in Germany. "You got it all together, didn't you?" wrote Bloch. "I only wish Fritz was here to read and appreciate it as much as I did!"[6]

28 | Disputed Passage

The July 1990 release of *A Graveyard for Lunatics* was bracketed by a busy travel schedule. In April, he had given the Poudre Lecture at The Johns Hopkins University in Baltimore; met in Washington, D.C., with Senator Alan Simpson and political satirist William Safire; and somehow managed to tape a televised *Worldnet* Dialog Program discussion on "Contemporary World Literature" for the United States Information Agency for broadcast in three participating Latin American capitals—Buenos Aires, Santiago, and Lima.[1] His unexpected trip back to Washington in late May for the Gorbachev luncheon was soon followed by a planned trip east yet again to Illinois and the July dedication of Bradbury Park in his home town of Waukegan, which was just beginning to grow a local theater and arts culture on the roots of its historic past.[2]

But this was only the beginning of a far longer journey that summer. On July 16th Bradbury appeared on the *Today Show* in New York, and he and Maggie were soon on their way via Concorde to London and a longer stay in Paris, their now-familiar base for European travel. While in London during August, his British publisher, Grafton Books, arranged for him to sign books at London's Forbidden Planet bookstore, the principal hub for science fiction and fantasy books in Britain. He was scheduled to sign for an hour, but he arrived early and signed well past his time slot, departing only to meet the plane that would make the short hop to Paris.

Long lines waited for Bradbury, who was able to sign books, old and new, for readers old and new. "It is certainly rare," wrote Grafton's paperback publishing director, who attended the signing, "for an author to command such affection over such a wide age range."[3] But this kind of devotion to readers who loved what he loved was a hallmark of his behavior. Book dealers and more commercial autograph seekers were beginning to remark that Bradbury signatures did not command high values, since there were so many of them. But it was a function of passion rather than profit, as his British publisher concluded: "I guess that Ray Bradbury inspires a greater than usual degree of loyalty in his readers; once hooked on his work, it would seem they remain so for life."

As they made their way from London to Paris, the 1990 Science Fiction World Con was only a short trip away in The Hague, but he did not attend; Paris had become a place to relax.⁴ They might visit his publishers at Denoel, or the artist Jean-Michel Folon (Bradbury had just prefaced Folon's new art book for the Metropolitan Museum of Art), or consult with his Euro Disney contacts, but otherwise it was a way to invoke some distance from outside demands. It was a special summer in other ways, for Bradbury had convinced Don and Sally Congdon to come stay, along with his longtime writing friend and advisor Sid Stebel and his wife Jan.⁵ These were friendships that went back to the 1940s, and each morning in the normally quiet apartment began with memories voiced over toast and fried eggs.

When the Muse spoke, however, his quotidian impulse to write would begin, and he would turn to his portable typewriter, always at hand. Long-deferred projects often surfaced in his mind during these Parisian interludes, and in August he wrote a very visual opening scene for a film or television version of *Fahrenheit 451*:

> A DARK SCREEN. We hear a ripping sound, PAN down to a man's hands ripping a small page out of a small Bible. We can see the heading Matthew or Mark. The fingers drop the small Bible and begin to roll the small printed page into a half cylinder. The CAMERA pulls back to see the man, dark-helmeted, has a small bag of BULL DURHAM tobacco held by its yellow string in his teeth. He now opens the Bull Durham sack and taps tobacco into the half-rolled MATTHEW or MARK paper. Then he rolls the tobacco and the biblical text into a cigarette.
>
> CLOSEUP he strikes a match which he applies to a larger printed page on which we see MOBY DICK or THE WHALE. Chapter One. Call me Ishmael!
> . . .
> He lights this page, throws away the match and uses the burning page to light the Biblical-text cigarette.
>
> CLOSEUP we can see "Call me Ishmael" curling into chars as he puffs once and then: Whoosh! Blows out the flaming page. Instant darkness and a musical chord. Words burn upward: FAHRENHEIT 451, the temperature at which book paper catches fire.
>
> This blows away in chars.

Truffaut had chosen to avoid any such title text in his 1966 adaptation, opting for spoken titles instead, but the visual image of these three numbers now identified Bradbury around the planet. Unfortunately, typing in a Paris vacation apartment drew him no closer to the film project that he wanted now, more than ever: to move forward in a new Hollywood-based production. He knew from long experience that even if he could secure an option, there was no guarantee that the film would ever be made.

In mid-August 1990, Bradbury and Maggie returned stateside in time to prepare for a long-anticipated event—the first production of *The Wonderful Ice Cream Suit* as a musical. A decade of periodic options by Harry Belafonte never got as far as production; the two men remained friends, but the idea was deferred for a decade until popular composer and singer José Feliciano became interested in the late 1980s. Bradbury's story of five young Hispanic men who throw in their last dollars for a beautiful white suit appealed to Feliciano, whose 40 gold albums included Spanish language recordings. Feliciano received his fifth Grammy Award while he and his wife Susan prepared the music and lyrics to accompany Bradbury's stage treatment.

From the time that Bradbury arrived in Los Angeles the summer he turned 14, he began to interact with the city's Hispanic culture. That contact became immersion during the war years, as he kept a day office in a downtown tenement at Temple and Figueroa. "The poverty of the area caused many people to band together," Bradbury reflected in his liner notes for the performance program. "Men and women would share their nice suits and dresses with other residents who needed those clothes. By sharing what was most precious, these people were able to share their dreams for the future."

Feliciano's score ranged from ballads to Latin Rock to a ballet suite. Bradbury and his longtime director, Charles Rome Smith, managed to secure the Pasadena Playhouse for the August 1990 rehearsals and the ambitious September–October performance schedule. *The Wonderful Ice Cream Suit* was coming to symbolize Bradbury's commitment to producing smaller venue alternative theater for Southern California. The early 1964 performances at the Coronet and the 1970s Chicago-based Organic Theatre Company performances of *The Wonderful Ice Cream Suit* with Joe Mantegna formed a natural progression to the very successful Feliciano musical. The musical itself would lead Disney executives even closer to approving a feature film version; by the late 1990s, the film would finally become reality.

: : :

The richly rewarding 1990 Feliciano musical collaboration represented the kind of life-renewing activity that reminded Bradbury what writing was all about. Returning to such early memories as *The Wonderful Ice Cream Suit* provided also reminded him of where it all began:

My first stories, at age twelve, were written on a toy. One of those tin dial typewriters with a circular, rotating alphabet that you turn and press down, taking roughly half an hour to do one or two paragraphs. But rotate, press, rotate, press I did, and writer I became. . . . How come this madness, early and late, for toys? Because I early-on sensed that they, like poetry, were essences of things, compacted symbols of possible or impossible lives. In sum, I absolutely knew that metaphor was all and everything! . . . [W]ithout metaphor we cannot understand, we cannot comprehend, we cannot know ourselves, or others.[6]

This observation prefaced his next collection, but it was not to be a story collection at all. Over the next year, Bradbury pulled together a collection of his essays, publishing it in December 1991 as *Yestermorrow*. The vital importance of knowing one's identity as a writer and a commitment to emotional truth-telling in the art of storytelling, often expressed through metaphor, provided the underlayment for his entire concept of authorship. But before this collection of essays was published, Bradbury's long-standing dispute with intellectual notions of authorship would suddenly erupt in a very public way.

For the most part, he had avoided direct disputes with critics and other writers, limiting his reactions to occasional panels and interviews, rarely citing other authors by name. But all this changed when Ted Turner brought him into the highly publicized world of the Turner Tomorrow Award in 1991. Turner conceived the project as an award for a never-before-published novel, length 50,000 to 100,000 words, with a prize of $500,000.00 for the single winner.

The range of judges was impressive and international. Bradbury was joined by Rodney Hall (Australia); Carlos Fuentes (Mexico); Nadine Gordimer (South Africa); Bradbury's old friends Ian and Betty Ballantine, founders of Ballantine Books and publishers of *Fahrenheit 451*; and three other American author-judges: William Styron, Peter Matthiessen, and Wallace Stegner. Within this jury were two Pulitzer winners (Styron and Stegner), a future lifetime Pulitzer winner (Bradbury), that year's Nobel Laureate (Gordimer), and a Cervantes Prize winner (Fuentes).[7] Each juror accepted a $10,000 honorarium.[8]

During May 1991, as the judges gathered in New York, the consensus centered on four submissions, of which Daniel Quinn's *Ishmael* was seen as clearly "first among equals"—but that was where agreement swiftly and dramatically ended. Styron, Matthiessen, and Stegner felt strongly that none of the finalists deserved a half-million-dollar prize. Michael Reagan, head of Turner Publishing, intervened on the basis of the award parameters, which asked for a jury-based full-award decision for one author, or none. The June 3, 1991 press release announced Quinn as winner of the $500,000.00 prize, describing *Ishmael* as "a poignant novel that ultimately asks the question: does the Earth belong to man or does man belong to the Earth?"

Most of the judges had nothing to say publicly; Bradbury would have had nothing to say as well, if Styron, Matthiessen, and Stegner had not started a media firestorm two days later.[9] Styron and Matthiessen accused the award administrators of deceit, with Styron leading the charge: "We were unable to circumvent the giving of this awkwardly prodigious amount of money to one single contestant. We feel tainted very much by the whole thing." Matthiessen added, "It makes us uncomfortable to see this much granted for what we see as a publicity stunt." Stegner took the veil off the real issue by invoking the pedigree of established authorship: "All of us felt that not even a book of our own would deserve that much. We were agreed that there was not a worthy prize winner."

That was about all that Bradbury could stand, and he started in by calling his two most vocal fellow judges "professionally literary," and suggested that they return the $10,000.00 judges fee that they each had accepted: "William Styron thinks he's William Styron. Peter Matthiessen thinks he's Peter Matthiessen. That's very dangerous. They're muddying the waters worrying about their reputations. I believe in this book enough to put my name in a quote on the jacket flap."

Years later, in private conversation, Bradbury still saw this incident as central to his abiding views on the darker side of authorship: "They wanted to be 'Authors,' they're acting 'Authors.' Come on, that's wrong. You're going to distort your fiction acting a role. I don't want to act a role, I don't want to become 'RAY BRADBURY' in capitals, I don't want to live my reputation. I want it to come as a result of getting something done. But don't hand me that 'Author' crud. I'm a writer who has a hell of a lot of fun and as a result of it, you have fun."[10] He had, of course, already become 'RAY BRADBURY' long ago. Usually, his public presence mirrored these sentiments; but he was also an unreserved individualist with controversial views on many subjects (usually informed views, but not always), and sometimes the forceful way he expressed these views, rather than the ego he was usually able to control, would get the upper hand.

: : :

The highly publicized tensions surrounding the Turner Prize soon eased into another long summer working-vacation in Paris. Traveling several weeks ahead of Maggie, Bradbury arrived at their regular apartment on Avenue de la Bourdonnais in mid-June 1991, where he worked very productively. In late June, he flew to Rome and traveled on to Spoleto for a speaking engagement that had been in the works for months. Fondazione Sigma-Tau, a rapidly rising Italian institution promoting the links between science and interdisciplinary creativity, invited Bradbury to keynote the opening session of the foundation's annual

Spoletoscienza within Spoleto's broader *Festival dei Due Mondi*. He agreed to speak on "Imagination in Science."

Bradbury traveled to the conference via Rome in late June so that he could visit Federico Fellini and recall the memories of his earlier 1978 trip, when Fellini's filmmaking career was still in full swing. Fellini was unable to make it to lunch on June 28th, but he arranged to have Bradbury come to his home in early July, after Bradbury returned to Rome from the *Spoletoscienza* conference.[11] That summer of 1991 both men were beyond seventy, but the years had told on Fellini more markedly than they had on Bradbury. In their last photo together, Bradbury's usual white tennis jacket and travel outfit contrasted with Fellini, sitting in the shade with a heavy orange jacket draped over his shoulders.

Fellini's final films lacked the zest for life and sense of wonderment that Bradbury had loved so dearly in his friend's early work. Through his close ties to the Writer's Guild of America and the Guild's Film Society, he had discovered a new force in Italian cinema—the young Academy Award–winning director Giuseppe Tornatore. In fact, Bradbury had already asked Don Congdon to reach out: "He is the natural successor to Fellini, and all of his work has overtones of my own stories and novels, which is why I want to contact him."[12]

He was especially taken with Tornatore's *Cinema Paradiso* (Best Foreign Film Academy Award, 1985) and *Everybody's Fine* (1990). It was admiration, far more than ambition, that led Bradbury to reach out in this way time and time again, hoping as always that the realities of film production would not stand between two kindred spirits. He intended to send some of his books, but there is no evidence that the connection with Tornatore was ever made. Only one thing was certain—time was on no one's side. Bradbury left Rome not knowing, but perhaps suspecting, that this would be his final meeting with Fellini.

He returned to Paris before making a brief four-day trip to Madrid and the Prado Museum and arrived back at the apartment on July 11th. Maggie had arrived on the 9th, and together they settled into their normal routines for the rest of July and into early August.[13] Here Bradbury could rejoin the creative rhythm of work and leisure that he enjoyed best—day trips in and around Paris alternating with his regular late-night writing. His work consulting on the development of Euro Disney was done, but he could not resist making a trip out to the site, fully a year before the scheduled grand opening. "It's enormous," he told Sir Rupert Hart-Davis, "and will cost, when finished, almost three billion dollars."

On some level he knew that this might be the last major project he would work on with Marty Sklar and the Disney Imagineers, and he reflected on the unexpected ease with which he worked with such technologically focused professionals: "I love working with the Disney people. They are all golfers. Which means like my Dad used to bring home weekends when I was a kid. Hard-working linemen for the electric power company during the week, gentlemen on Saturdays and Sundays: nice guys, good fellows like my Pa. I've worked off-and-on for the Disney people for 21 years and have yet to have a fight with any of them."[14]

Sir Rupert, who had published Bradbury's most enduring work in Britain for more than two decades, had hoped to see his friends before they returned home, but it was not to be; Bradbury was working on the penultimate season of story adaptations for *Ray Bradbury Theater*, episodes that would be filmed in Canada and New Zealand, and had managed to send off five scripts while in France. Paris always represented a most reliable incarnation of the Jamesian "great good place," where creativity could be spontaneous, as it had been one night in early July: "The great thing is to have a night like the one I experienced here a month ago. I couldn't sleep. My Muse kept seizing me by the nape and dunking me into the typewriter. Write this, do that, go here, jump there, it cried. I wrote the beginnings and endings of six short stories plus the start of a new novel between midnight and dawn." And with that news, the Parisian summer came to an end.

His next book, published in the final days of 1991, would actually be the nonfiction collection he compiled before his summer adventures, dutifully reported to Hart-Davis as a "book of essays on future cities, malls, museums, titled *Yestermorrow: Obvious Answers to Impossible Futures*, all written as if I truly knew what to solve next." These essays recounted his sense of "The Aesthetics of Lostness" in the design of San Diego's Horton Plaza shopping mall; the notion of art and science fiction; "The Aesthetics of Size" in museums, art, and architecture; and snapshot memoirs of his friendships with Bernard Berenson and Federico Fellini.

Overarching all of these essays, however, was the idea he had put forth in the preface, that toys and poetry were both built on metaphors that taught the values of life. He would close his preface to *Yestermorrow* as he began it, with a hint of the value of toys in the preservation of the imagination:

> I end . . . with the memory of a Sausalito toy shop where I lingered a few summers ago. On the way out a gang of boys ran by. One boy lingered, staring in longingly at the bright objects.
>
> "Go in," I urged, "now, run in, stay."
>
> "Aw, come on!" the boys urged. "that's kid stuff! C'mon!"
>
> "No!" I whispered, my head turned away. The boy hesitated, then ran off with his friends. It broke my heart.[15]

29 | *Green Shadows, White Whale*

As the summer of 1991 wound down, Bradbury was contacted by Dr. Sallie Baliunas, the recently appointed deputy director of the Mount Wilson Institute. She wrote to invite Bradbury for a "behind-the-telescopes" tour of the famed Mount Wilson Observatory, which was in the midst of dramatic changes.[1] The 100-inch Hooker telescope at Mount Wilson, the instrument that Edwin Hubble had used to begin mapping the cosmos beyond our galaxy, had been dark for two years. It was simply too close to the lights of Los Angeles for the kind of deep space astronomy of the day, but Baliunas and the new director, noted author and astronomer Dr. Robert Jastrow, were leading the transition to an adaptive optics technology at Mount Wilson that would bring the 100-inch refractor back to life within the year. They both knew that Bradbury represented the eyes of the broader American public; this was the beginning of a time when Ray Bradbury, late in life, would be sought out to have hands-on experiences with the technology of the stars.

He knew far less about certain earthbound matters, however. Late in the summer of 1991, Bradbury's long-standing impasse with the Soviet Union over royalties was about to become even more complicated. He had been given an opening the previous summer, when he received a joint invitation from the rapidly fading Soviet Union and the United States government to visit Russia. He also received an entrepreneurial offer to endorse a Moscow-based creative project called Cosmopolis and a request to help young students there. In August 1991, Bradbury replied to all three with one letter that opened up the royalty issue. "Until such a time," he wrote Congdon, "as the Soviets cough up with lists, dates, etc., etc., and carload a few rubles into our coffers, I am playing Elusive Pimpernel to them all. . . . Quite a week, you must admit, for a Worm That Has More than Turned."[2]

Bradbury agreed to the visit, and to endorse the projects, if he could in return receive a full list of all of his books published in the Soviet Union, a list of all Soviet films adapted from his works in recent decades, and "an accounting of the rubles placed in a Russian bank under my name, the profits accruing to me as a percentage of the profits from my books."[3] That last condition was just a shot in the dark, but he had some fairly solid anecdotal evidence from various

Russian reporters interviewing him that there was an account holding rubles that he could spend only in the Soviet Union. Furthermore, during his last trip to Disney World the previous year, he had learned from a Russian director that his fiction had been the basis for at least fifteen films.

Within months the Soviet Union ceased to exist, and Bradbury's trip to Moscow never materialized. On the first day of 1992, the Gorbachev Era ended, and Russia became sovereign in Moscow. Now Bradbury and Congdon could deal directly with the new Russian Federation; over time, full representation and an accounting, of sorts, led to a publishing relationship with Eksmo. A wide variety of documented editions and impressive cover art would give Bradbury a glimpse of his popularity in Russia for the rest of his life, and beyond.

:   :   :

As he began to weave his Irish tales into another autobiographical experiment, Bradbury found himself, once again, on treacherous ground. Initially, he had conceived them as stage plays and found occasional success with these memories of Ireland in small stage venues close to home. There was occasionally earnest interest from New York stage producers, and in 1970 he even received high marks from Hilton Edwards, chairman of the Dublin Gate Theatre production company in Ireland: "Speaking as a non-Irishman, who has lived here for many years, you certainly seemed to have sucked the juice out of the situation during your brief stay here, and have hit many nails neatly on the head." Bradbury wrote them in the spirit of Sean O'Casey's light-hearted *A Pound on Demand*, but the stereotypes of mid–twentieth century village public houses found in his plays were sometimes taken as an implied criticism.

Bradbury had spent the entire fall and winter of 1953–54 based in Dublin as he wrote and rewrote his *Moby Dick* screenplay for John Huston's film adaptation. It was a commuter's life; three or four days a week, Bradbury would leave his wife, daughters, and their governess at the Royal Hibernian Hotel in Dublin and travel by Mike's hired car west to Courtown House, where the director principally lived and worked during these years. Late at night, Nick's taxicab would arrive from the local pub in nearby Kilcock to ferry Bradbury back to his family in Dublin.

On the fringes of his focused and increasingly stressful script work under Huston's direction, two overlapping chronotopes slowly emerged in his imagination. One was populated by the voices and faces of the city—the poverty-veined but robust characters of the shopkeepers, workers, families, street vendors, buskers, and occasional beggars he encountered in his daily walks through Dublin—and the other, a more concentrated locale haunted by the larger-than-life afternoon and evening patrons of tiny Kilcock's principal pub.

For years, Bradbury's efforts to produce work-intensive stage adaptations of these dozen tales diverted him from revising and compiling them for a specialized story collection. The fact that there were only a dozen was also problematic; his collections usually rounded out at 18 to 22 stories, and that's what his readers expected. Furthermore, there was nothing new here; all of the Irish tales had already appeared in earlier collections, and they didn't have the trademark Bradbury cachet of his science fiction, which had anchored such specialty young reader collections as R Is for Rocket and S Is for Space.

Nevertheless, two significant media adaptations provided the motivation to take up the story collection concept yet again. The first was the February 1986 debut broadcast of "Banshee," part of the trio of episodes that launched Ray Bradbury Theater on the HBO network. "Banshee," based on one of the more harmless pranks that John Huston played on Bradbury in Ireland, offered a dramatic fictional reversal of the prank accomplished through a masterful portrayal of John Huston by Peter O'Toole. Two years later, Bradbury's successful March–April 1988 stage production of Falling Upward, combining his two Irish stories "The Great Collision of Monday Last" and "The Cold Wind and the Warm," opened up the possibility of bringing the full range of his Irish stories together in some kind of a bridged story collection.

Bradbury intended to keep his more ambivalent and complicated personal reflections on John Huston for a separate volume, but he began to waver when Katharine Hepburn chronicled her own experiences working for Huston in her 1987 memoir, The Making of the African Queen. Hers was a completely different story that focused as much on the challenges of the primitive sets as it did on Huston himself, but Bradbury felt upstaged in a way that was out of proportion to the situation.[4] In Hollywood, though, timing is everything, and he began to feel a need to follow the Irish story cycle with the Huston volume as soon as possible.

It helped that his Knopf editor, Kathy Hourigan, had also edited Hepburn's African Queen memoir. She encouraged the balanced treatment that Bradbury hoped to strive for in his planned but as yet largely unformed Huston book, but he knew only too well that his own over-sensitized and somewhat naive disillusionment with his once-worshiped mentor-director might make it impossible to achieve any level of objectivity.

By 1991, however, he found that many of the bridges he was writing into the story collection were also bringing Huston deeper into the margins of these separate tales. Bradbury's inner conflict was manifested in several ways, the most obvious being his inability to settle on a title. "Under separate cover," he wrote in an October 1991 letter to Don Congdon, "I've just sent on another copy of *Green* or *Green Shadows, White Whale* or *The Great Green Whale* or *The Same Only Different* or. . . . . but why go on . . . [ellipses Bradbury's].

This version included 50 or 60 pages of bridging inserts about his work with Huston on the *Moby Dick* screenplay, which had essentially formed the skeleton that supported his various story-length Irish experiences. He was still working with Kathy Hourigan to place these new inserts, but he had clearly reached a watershed moment: "All of them are pulled out of my other book, the Huston book, which I have decided I probably will never publish. These honest and truthful (as far as possible) pastiches will more than establish the Huston character, light and dark. There'll be no need, I think at this time, for me to ever publish the rest."[5]

From this point on, the current book came together rapidly. The twelve Irish story-chapters, along with his anecdotal essay, "Hunt Wedding," a memory of a combined foxhunt-and-wedding day in Huston's Courtown House, formed the brícolage basis for the collection, novelized through twenty additional bridge-chapters linking Dublin streets and Kilcock lanes with the overarching drama of Bradbury's quest to interpret *Moby Dick* successfully for film adaptation. Huston's very masculine games of control were also a challenge for Bradbury to navigate, but there was really no space in the book to fully explore the ambivalence of his own feelings toward Huston and his methods.

The actual events, historically separated in both time and place, now merged into the fictionalized climax of his adventures in Ireland. He would make his peace, at least for a time, with John Huston; the future dispute over screen credit remained a memory, part of the book he had decided never to write. In another departure from chronology, Bradbury would end *Green Shadows, White Whale* not with Huston in London, but with an imagined farewell visit to the lads and the proprietor of his beloved Heber Finn's pub. Only then, no longer distracted by his formidable screenwriting task, does he really see Ireland: "I did not look back as Finn's vanished in the past. I saw with wet eyes that, God, the hills were green. Oh, yes, the hills were *green*."

Knopf published *Green Shadows, White Whale* in May 1992 to mixed reviews. In part, this was a consequence of the fact that Ireland no longer resembled the land he had left forty years earlier. Some were not pleased with novelized stories reflecting mid-century echoes of the poverty, social strictures, and violence of a troubled past, even when presented as a celebration of the Irish spirit and imagination. Bradbury touched on this history obliquely by bringing in a chapter based on his stage play *Stop Think Consider Do*. It was a quintessential Bradbury "what-if" extrapolation: what if Heber Finn tells a story of long ago, when a touring car pulled up outside of the pub and Bernard Shaw stepped out? This fiction within a fiction allowed Bradbury to capture the defining spirit of these people, in Shavian language but without the bite of Shavian satire. Bradbury's Shaw knows the history of imposed authority, poverty, and exile, but he also knows the great treasure trait of the Irish mind:

> The Irish. From so little they glean so much: squeeze the last ounce of joy from a flower with no petals, a night with no stars, a day with no sun. One seed and you lift a beanstalk forest to shake down giants of converse. The Irish? You step off a cliff and . . . fall up!" [ellipses Bradbury's]

It is significant that Bradbury pulled his stories together in the form of a novel without ever returning to that green land—even after his acceptance of air travel made it far easier to negotiate his frequent trips to England and continental Europe. He had been saddened by the poverty and limited opportunities he saw in a corner of Europe that had escaped the destruction of the Second World War, and from time to time he would say that such sadness had kept him from returning. But as the years passed, he knew that what he experienced no longer existed. In the lines of "To Ireland . . ." (1983), written thirty years after the fact, he worked through the true reason in verse form, revealing that his sadness was really caused by the passage of time.

In its middle verses, "To Ireland . . ." builds a somber catalog of the Dubliners he had once known and described in life-affirming, Whitmanesque language through his letters home. Three decades later, in verse, his mournful words form a memorial to the "book clerks . . . hotel staff . . . candy butchers, beggars, maids, . . . harpists" and others long gone. But the deepest lament opens and closes the poem with his growing sense of mortality, and his deepening kinship with these ghosts from his past:

> I dare not go—that isle has ghosts
> And spectral rains along the coasts
> Such rains as weep their loss in tears
> Till I am drowned in sunken years.
> When last I walked a Dublin street,
> My gaze was clear, my pulses fleet,
> Now half a life or more is gone
> I cannot face sad Dublin's dawn.

Green Shadows, White Whale was also an implicit companion to the autobiographical fictions of *Death Is a Lonely Business* and *A Graveyard for Lunatics*, recounting a fire and water baptism in film through John Huston—an event that would open many doors in Hollywood. This further experiment in autobiography was also an indicator of things to come in his final years; it was not the oldest tale he had deferred, but in telling it he had paved the way for weaving his far earlier vampire family tales (*From the Dust Returned*), his cannibalized first try at a novel of his Illinois youth (*Farewell Summer*), his late 1950s novella of a small town with an immortal secret (*Somewhere a Band Is Playing*), and his space-age analogue to *Moby Dick* (*Leviathan 99*) into sustained and publishable works of book-length fiction.

: : :

Ray Bradbury was no longer a stranger to death; the losses began to accelerate among his wide circle of friends and fellow writers as he moved past the age of seventy. The unexpected deaths were the ones that saddened him the most, and in October 1991—normally his favorite month of any year—his good friend Gene Roddenberry passed away suddenly, leaving a vast empty quadrant in the imaginary cosmos of Hollywood television and film production. As he spoke at the memorial service, Bradbury observed that Roddenberry's Hollywood cosmos represented family on many levels.

Roddenberry was, almost to the day, one year younger than Bradbury, and their individualized paths of creativity had met many times. Bradbury would sometimes have to redirect mail about *Star Trek* to its creator, just as Roddenberry would occasionally redirect mail about *The Martian Chronicles* to his friend, the author. Similarities in name, looks, and vision sometimes led to humorous confusion in public as well, and it was more often than not Bradbury who had to explain to well-intentioned fans that he was not Gene Roddenberry. But for the most part, Bradbury let the mistake lie: "I learned not to disappoint, because to tell them the truth would be terrible. Their faces would have been destroyed. I let them go away happy. It made me happy too."[6]

By this time in his life, there was more and more of a predictable sameness in his many articles, interviews, and introductions, in part a function of the demand on his time and the growing number of requests to respond to anything and everything about the Human Condition. The vision was always sincere, clouded only at the infrequent times when he was riled to anger by audiences or circumstances, but the predictability of delivery was also becoming detectable when he spoke or wrote for memorials. He didn't always have a "take" on the life's work of the subject, and he would have to fall back on a single critical observation, usually right on target, or the accumulated memories of association and friendship to shape his remarks. But for Roddenberry, he knew the man and his work, and these reflections on a respected and loved friend were perhaps the best of this kind that he would ever offer.

For Bradbury, Roddenberry's understated work ethic echoed the wisdom of Albert Schweitzer, one of the great humanitarians of the age: "Do excellent work: someone may imitate it." Bradbury felt echoes of Roddenberry every time he lectured at Caltech over the years: "I saw all these young science students dealing with the morality that he taught, and taught in a very quiet way—he didn't pontificate with his stories in his show—but he showed by example." And, harking back to quiet discussions with his friend in years gone past, Bradbury put his finger on the central point of the *Star Trek* concept that had flat out eluded most of the studio executives and producers that Roddenberry had had to contend with throughout his career: a really good science fiction film has to have "something to do with the universe. . . . Once we see the stars, we want the stars. So at the center of *Star Trek* for me, time and again, was the whole problem of the universe itself—the mystery of life. Very mysterious. The mystery of life and the mystery of death. . . . Gene's show time and again dealt with these two miracles."

His comments say as much about Bradbury as they do about the legacy of his departed friend. Bradbury's lifelong desire was to plumb the interrelated mysteries of life and death, and what he believed to be the eternal continuity of the universe as seen in his *Dandelion Wine* story of the great grandmother, awakened from the great sleep of eternity ninety years earlier and now passing back into that timeless dream once again. Bradbury often used this tale in memorial services, and he could not help but bring it in again to send off his old friend. It was not out of place, and neither was his return to the humor of their often mistaken identities in his final words of farewell: "Maybe even in the years ahead, strangers will come up to me and will have lost track of time. And they will look at me and say, 'Mr. Roddenberry, I thought you were dead!' And you know what my answer will be? 'Not as long as I'm alive.'"

30 | The ABCs of Science Fiction

The completion and critical reception of *Green Shadows, White Whale* ran a course through much of 1992, but even the publication of two books in three years could not distract him away from his part in the Great Tale slowly expanding outward above the atmosphere of Earth. Two years earlier, the Hubble Space Telescope had begun the task of extending our views of interstellar and intergalactic space; unfortunately, a crippling aberration in Hubble's mirror would not be corrected for another year. This was worrisome, but Bradbury was far more concerned with the extended hiatus in the Mars exploration program.

It was now sixteen years since Earth had probed the surface of the Red Planet. NASA's *Mars Orbiter* launched in September 1992, but contact was lost late in the following summer, just prior to orbital insertion around Mars.[1] The cause of this heartbreaking failure was never determined, and the resulting lack of high-resolution survey mapping would inevitably delay an American return to the surface of Mars. The next phase of surface exploration, employing a lander that would deliver the first Martian rover, was still at least five years in the future.

How would NASA prepare the public for this long-awaited new phase of Martian exploration? In 1976, the *Viking* missions to the surface of Mars had simply been too successful. Like the lunar landing of Apollo 11, a great milestone had been reached, and the public (as well as Congress) had turned back to more immediate issues on Earth. But Bradbury's good friend Bruce Murray was already addressing this challenge, even though he no longer directed the Jet Propulsion Laboratory in Pasadena. In late April 1992, Murray came over to Bradbury's home and asked for permission to send *The Martian Chronicles* to the surface of Mars.

Murray, along with his Planetary Society cofounders Carl Sagan and Lou Friedman, had devised the ABC project to get a library to Mars, beginning with the Society's principal advisors—Isaac Asimov, Ray Bradbury, and Arthur C. Clarke. The late Robert Heinlein had not been an advisor, but his representation among the vanguard titles of the library was considered essential. Lou Friedman had originated the idea and coordinated the outreach, which remained confidential for the moment. Each writer would be asked to buy into the underlying concept: "to honor the legacy of the fiction which led to fact—putting robots and humans on Mars and to inspire the human exploration of Mars by publicizing the library's emplacement there."[2]

The first installment would include Asimov's I Robot, Bradbury's The Martian Chronicles, Clarke's Sands of Mars, and a work to be determined from Heinlein's early novels of Martian settlement. The library would be sent on a spaceworthy CD, and arrangements would need to be made with the authors for a commercial release to help regenerate interest in the next phase of Martian exploration. Asimov had actually been approached more than a year earlier, for he was quite ill; he passed away in early April 1992, but not before endorsing the ABC project. Bradbury was faxed a copy of Asimov's blessing just before Murray's visit, scrawled in a weak but clearly-worded note—"Do whatever you want. It's okay by me."[3] It had been only two years since Bradbury had last seen his old friend at the Gorbachev reception in Washington, D.C., but his sadness was tempered by the exciting joint venture now at hand. He gave his consent to Murray, even though there was a catch—the library would have to be transported to Mars aboard a Russian lander.

Russian support for the ABC project was not really a surprise. Bradbury and Asimov (along with writers such as Hemingway and Salinger) were ranked among the favorite American literary figures during the final decades of the Soviet Union. "The big Soviet cities boasted dozens of Ray Bradbury fan clubs," Mikhail Iossel would later observe in his 2012 New Yorker reflections on Bradbury. "It was impossible, as well as extremely uncool, for any au courant Soviet teenager or intelligentsia-bound young engineer not to have read and be able to discuss, at a party or in a dentist's chair, Fahrenheit 451, Martian Chronicles, or Dandelion Wine, and the iconic stories 'A Sound of Thunder' and 'There Will Come Soft Rains.'" But Bradbury's constant and sizable Russian language print runs weren't all about love, of course. "Science fiction, in the Soviet Union, was an ideologically intensive literary genre, whose ultimate, overriding agenda lay in claiming the future for a unified, beautifully homogenized, meaningfully sterile, stateless, and classless world—patterned in its development, supposedly, on the Soviet model of society."[4] Here, in the early post-Soviet years of the Russian Federation, the aesthetic and ideological views of science fiction remained essentially unchanged. Bradbury and Asimov were both loved and needed.

The American planners of ABC were playing the long game. Russia's Mars 94/96 lander would provide the means to transport America's science fiction library to Mars as a prelude to the projected American Pathfinder mission. The publicity, and the development potential for The Planetary Society's Mars Exploration Fund, would be extended through sales of CDs and a book. Bradbury was fiercely protective of the American lead in planetary exploration, but he felt the end justified the means. "I thought the idea was okay," he wrote to Congdon, "if the proper details can be worked out. I'd like to support our endeavors to at last get the Space Program going again. I gather the Russians will be moving before we do, with their Mars project. I would be flattered and thrilled to think that The Martian Chronicles, along with a few other Martian books, would be the first library to land on the Red Planet."[5]

Bradbury's sense that NASA needed to "at last get the Space Program going again" reflected his deep-seated priorities. The Space Program, was of course, a going concern, with Endeavor about to be added to the Space Shuttle fleet, and Bradbury always supported low-Earth orbital programs when asked. But his heart was firmly centered on Mars and the occasional deeper planetary flybys, and he was counting on NASA's new Advisory Committee to follow through on new mission priorities for the future. As it turned out, the science fiction library would not reach Mars before the end of the century; shortly after launch, Russia's Mars 96 lander missed its post-orbital Martian trajectory boost and fell back to Earth in scattered fragments, strewn across the South Pacific and South America.[6]

: : :

Although his publishing debut on Mars would be delayed, other surprises fundamentally changed his publishing relationships back on Earth. In 1992, Bradbury witnessed a significant change in the way his enduring titles were reprinted in America. The time-honored practice of auctioning off mass-market paperback rights was generally controlled by the trade house that published the first hardbound edition; that house would then take 50 percent of the author's paperback royalties.

Doubleday had done well with Bradbury's ever-popular Bantam paperbacks of the 1950s, and each five-year contract renewal that Doubleday negotiated with Bantam had extended the arrangement. Consequently, it proved difficult for Congdon and Bradbury to persuade Doubleday to keep hardbound editions in print, or even to spend money marketing the stock that remained. In the early 1960s, Bradbury and Congdon had left Doubleday, but the shared paperback royalties remained in force.

Fortunately, the passage of time gave rise to new corporate relationships in the book trade. After two years of negotiation, Congdon was able to secure a five-year renewal with Bantam at a slightly reduced royalty rate of 10 percent, but with all royalties accruing to the author alone. Bradbury's perennially strong sales history probably turned the trick, and now most of the works that had initially made him famous were secured under terms that many authors could not achieve. *The Martian Chronicles*, *The Illustrated Man*, *Dandelion Wine*, *The Golden Apples of the Sun*, *A Medicine for Melancholy*, and the two derivative collections, *R Is for Rocket* and *S Is for Space*, were now securely his for the future. It didn't really matter that the last four titles were now combined in Bantam's two-volume *Classic Stories*; his new Bantam contracts, like the original agreements he had signed with Ballantine for *Fahrenheit 451* and *The October Country* in the 1950s, reflected the full earning power of a long-established mainstream author.

As his books continued to maintain pride of place in bookstore windows, his face and trademark black-rimmed glasses became even more prominent in Hollywood events. Long ago, Bradbury had received an Academy Award nomination in 1962 for his short animated film *Icarus Montgolfier Wright*, but now he would be able to present the Oscar for lifetime achievement in animation, the Gordon E. Sawyer Award, at the Academy's March 1992 Scientific and Technical Awards ceremony. He was the natural choice to present the Oscar to his friend Ray Harryhausen, and excerpts from the presentation aired on Oscar night later that week.

Bradbury was, by now, likely to be a featured guest at almost any Hollywood event, even if he had little or nothing to do with the cause for celebration; often, it was his love of the subject that was being celebrated as much as the subject itself. In 1992, he was the most recognized guest of honor at a special cast screening of what had become a classic Disney film, *20,000 Leagues Under the Sea*. There were few surviving cast members from this 1954 production; Kirk Douglas was the only surviving principal actor, and he was away and unable to attend. Bradbury's involvement with Disney did not begin until the mid-1960s, but in 1960 he had written "The Ardent Blasphemers," the most popular and widely read introduction to the mass-market Bantam edition of Verne's novel.

There were no recognizable film stars present, but Bradbury was well aware of the legendary figures from the other side of the camera lens who joined him that night. Bradbury's longtime friend, producer Elmo Williams, had been the Academy Award–nominated film editor on *20,000 Leagues*. The film's director, Richard Fleischer, was also present (as a boy Bradbury had enjoyed the *Popeye* cartoons that Fleischer's father had animated). Harper Goff, designer of the iconic *Nautilus* and its interiors, attended the screening, as did Peter Ellenshaw, the special effects artist who pioneered the backlighting technique used to film the *Nautilus* underwater exterior shots.[7] Bradbury's deep understanding of the work of all these artists provided far more than a personal joy for him that evening; his collective understanding also informed the best of his comments on cinema and explains why his often controversial views on the cinema led to multiple American Film Institute seminars and magazine articles throughout the last half of his career.

It was a significant year in America for Bradbury, but his favorite 1992 event actually occurred overseas. On April 2, 1992, Bradbury arrived in Paris to promote the new French Denoel edition of A Graveyard for Lunatics, aptly titled Le Fantome D'Hollywood, since the gravely disfigured studio head at the center of the novel, living on secretly beneath the studio and its adjacent graveyard, was in part an homage to Gaston Laroux's Phantom of the Opera. Bradbury's love of the early film versions of Phantom and Victor Hugo's Hunchback of Notre Dame was well-known in France, and his event schedule included television and radio station stops as well as newspaper interviews with La Monde, L'Express, and Liberation.

In spite of the fanfare, book promotion was not the primary purpose of his Paris trip. Roy Disney had personally invited and arranged travel for Bradbury and Maggie to attend the grand opening of Euro Disney Resort and the resort's original theme venue, Disneyland Park, on Saturday, April 12th. "How rare it is," he told Disney, "that one looks forward to a truly splendid and exciting time."[8] Bradbury had consulted for Marty Sklar and his Imagineers at various points during Euro Disney's twenty-year development history, and he had worked with Tim Delaney on the final design of the space-age Orbitron ride.

Orbitron offered the perfect example of the intuitive way he had always con-tributed to Imagineer projects, completely devoid of any semblance of scientific or technical understanding. What he did understand as well or better than anyone was the feel of a ride, the experiential impact on passengers, regardless of the sophistication of the machine itself. Delaney's team was having trouble getting Orbitron to give the sensation of speed as the passenger cars orbited in concert with the celestial bodies representing the solar system. Bradbury suggested that the passenger cars orbit in one direction, the planetary bodies in the opposite direction, thus doubling the relative speed observed by the passengers.

As he prepared to attend the "Premier," as he called it, of Euro Disney, his thoughts turned back to the late 1920s. He anticipated "a few joys left over from my tenth year," he wrote to his Knopf editor Kathy Hourigan. That was when he had seen Mickey's "Steamboat Willie" debut in one of Waukegan's two movie houses; two years later, he became a card-carrying supporter of Mickey himself. "I was a member of the Mickey Mouse Club that year, 1932, in Waukegan. Most people don't remember that the MM Club started long before TV, in the movie houses of America."[9] Neither Mickey nor Ray Bradbury would ever really grow up; sixty years later, Bradbury still had his original Mickey Mouse Club card back home in Los Angeles.

They would stay on in Paris until April 23rd before returning to Los Angeles.[10] On April 10th, just before the Euro Disney celebrations, Bradbury completed his teleplay for "The Handler"; this old 1940s horror tale was his final adaptation for *The Ray Bradbury Theater*, and it would be one of the last four to air during the sixth and final season. He had now managed to sustain his great enthusiasm and energy into his early '70s, largely through the immense satisfaction he drew from finally being in control of a major media production series of his own tales. This came through in his April 10th Paris update to Don Congdon: "Praise God, our actors, our directors, our various producers and, what the hell, *me*! I waited for fifty years for this power to pass into my typewriter hands. Looks like God, He of the Remington and Underwood, understood my dream and my need."

For its entire 65-episode run, series production had been a long-distance process, with much-needed consistency achieved through the addition of Tom Cotter as a producer for season three. Season four's breakthrough in clearing *Martian Chronicles* tales for production continued with season five's emotionally powerful "The Martian"; Bradbury's masterful suspense came through in season four's "Touched with Fire" and "A Touch of Petulance." The hope of desert mirages and drought-breaking rains came through to great effect in season three's "A Miracle of Rare Device" and season four's "The Day It Rained Forever." The intrinsic storytelling values of the original tales also overcame production challenges in season five's "Zero Hour" and "The Jar."

The final season was broadcast on the USA Network from July through September 1992, earning three CableACE nominations along the way.[11] With the exception of "The Lonely One," based on his most famous suspense story "The Whole Town's Sleeping," and "Great Wide World Over There," the final season's fifteen episodes represented lesser stories adapted with varying degrees of success. Tyne Daley's performance in "Great Wide World Over There" was outstanding in Bradbury's mind.

The significant award legacy of *The Ray Bradbury Theater* indicated how lesser stories could be elevated through good writing, technical craft, and acting. The reverse was also true in some cases, but recognition came to every season through primetime Emmy nominations and the CableACE and Gemini (Canadian) Emmy equivalents. The six seasons netted an aggregate 24 nominations and thirteen wins across many acting and production categories, including Bradbury's 1985 CableACE win for writing. The series itself would earn four CableACE nominations, winning for the 1993 final season. Most of the ten names listed for the 1993 Dramatic Series award had been there from the beginning, including Bradbury's original partner and coproducer, Larry Wilcox, and Peter Sussman of Atlantis, architects of the original production agreements in 1985.

Wilcox had little involvement after production disagreements in the fourth season; these had been sharp disagreements at times, but Bradbury never forgot his importance to the dream. "To think, it is all done," he had written to Don Congdon in April, as he reviewed the final season scripts, "it is all finished, at last. And without the aid, strangely sad, this late in time, for he *began* it all, years ago, of Larry Wilcox. Sad, because it was he and his partner, seven years or so ago, who convinced me I should trust them and start the series!"

31 An American Icon

In early July 1992, the Bradburys returned to Paris for what they always hoped would be a two-month annual summer stay, barring what Bradbury called "bacteria assaults or lightning strikes." They settled into Lawrence Gordon's Avenue de la Bourdonnais apartment, as they had now done since 1988. Gordon still handled legal matters for Ray Bradbury Enterprises; generally literary and media business was overseen by Don Congdon in New York and their daughter Alexandra out West, but trouble with *The Next in Line*, the most recent Pandemonium Players stage play in Los Angeles, required the legal counsel of Lawrence Gordon himself.

Cost overrun was a perennial problem ever since Bradbury had begun to produce his own plays in the 1960s, and the recent production had broken the $50,000 budget (five times the cost of his plays in the 1970s). Maggie wrote the cost claim rebuttal and faxed it to Gordon on July 23rd, but the small-venue alternative theater concept that Bradbury was committed to preserving in Los Angeles rarely made back any significant portion of his investment.

If theatrical financing presented a serious problem, the continuing strong sales and classroom presence of his earlier books and stories reinforced his staying power as a force in literature and American culture. In spite of occasional community and school conflicts over the classroom use of his books (*The Martian Chronicles* alone had been challenged at least three times during the 1980s), Bradbury continued to enjoy widespread adoption of his books and stories in junior high and high school classrooms.[1]

In May 1992, the Society for the Study of Midwestern Literature bestowed the Mark Twain Award on Bradbury for "distinguished contributions to Midwestern literature." He would come to be in good company; subsequent recipients included Poet Laureate and Pulitzer Prize–winning poet Mona Van Duyn and Nobel Laureate Toni Morrison. His awards were more and more national and international in scope, but he was just as gratified to receive the Mark Twain Award as he had been to receive a Society of Midwestern Authors prize for *Dandelion Wine* thirty-five years earlier.

That same year the Science Fiction and Fantasy Writers of America (SFFWA) established the Ray Bradbury Award for excellence in screenwriting, with the winner selected by the SFFWA president at intervals until 2009, when it became the Ray Bradbury Award for Dramatic Presentation under the sponsorship of the Nebula Awards. Many prominent science fiction and fantasy filmmakers would receive the award in one of its two forms, beginning with the inaugural presentation to James Cameron for *Terminator 2: Judgment Day*.

His third honor—an asteroid, actually—was discovered, but not bestowed, in 1992. Bradbury's three published Asteroid Belt stories were written during World War II, and only one ("Asleep in Armageddon") effectively transferred Bradbury's haunting sense of isolation and the terror of unseen menace to these distant worlds. In February 1992, Project Spacewatch team members at the Kitt Peak observatory in Arizona detected and cataloged the trans-Mars asteroid 1992 DZ2; eight years later, Dr. Jeffrey Larson wrote to notify Bradbury that this small asteroid was now Bradbury 9766, transforming science fiction into science fact.

With the 1992 completion of *Ray Bradbury Theater*, Atlantis Films began planning for an hour-long television documentary titled *Ray Bradbury: An American Icon*. Scottish-Canadian producer-director Robert Duncan completed the project three years later, with narration by Bradbury's friend and Academy Award–winning actor, Rod Steiger. It joined several other American and British documentaries made since the early 1960s, and though commercial release was slow the documentary benefited from a wider choice of footage than earlier films. In fact, Duncan had a great deal of unused quality footage (his interview with Roy Disney didn't survive the cuts), but he was never able to expand the film beyond the 46-minute limit of a one-hour documentary.[2] Bradbury liked the film, if not the iconic title, but his great dislike of cultural labels was of no consequence; by this time in his life "American Icon" was not only an apt title, but an inevitable one.

: : :

Sometime in 1992, Bradbury turned once again to Ted Turner as he renewed his quest for a second feature film version of *Fahrenheit 451*. Two days after talking to Turner and Jane Fonda at a Los Angeles event, Bradbury sent them one of the eye-catching Easton Press editions with a brief allusion to Truffaut's 1966 adaptation: "It was made as a film 26 years ago. But much was left out. I would like to do a new version. This time, I would like to write the screenplay." As usual, Bradbury was not shy about presenting his own ideas on casting: Peter O'Toole as Chief Beatty; William Hurt as Montag; and Jane Fonda as Montag's wife, Mildred.[3]

But this proposal soon became an academic exercise; Fonda had retired from films the year before, and Turner opted not to go further with the project. Other options moved ahead, however. The Mettee and Holof opera production had gone far to showcase the possibilities of *Fahrenheit 451*, and Bradbury continued to allow broader adaptations for versions in Czechoslovakia (rock opera), Australia (chamber opera), and a London version he described for Turner as "a musical semi-rock performance" composed by a member of the British House of Parliament. Some were performed, but none would have the impact he was looking for in a feature film adaptation designed to keep the original dynamics of the film in play.

In October 1992, Maggie Bradbury fell downstairs at home and severely broke her ankle, ending plans to return to Paris for a third time that year. The injury was apparently an avulsion fracture to an inner anklebone, requiring two hours of surgery.[4] As a result, she was unable to travel until the following spring at the earliest. A full recovery took longer than expected; as the spring of 1993 approached, Bradbury told Lawrence and Jan Gordon, owners of their Paris lodgings, that they would not be able to make their planned spring 1993 trip to Paris. The Gordons would be home in Los Angeles by springtime, and Bradbury still hoped that he and Maggie could use the Gordons' Paris apartment in July and August, as was their habit.[5] A new portable Canon Typestar typewriter awaited them in Paris, along with new appliances.

Although Paris was deferred that spring, Bradbury made his way alone to Washington, D.C., to experience his first virtual mission to Mars. On April 29, 1993, he toured the Challenger Learning Center in Greenbelt, Maryland, where he copiloted a simulated flight to Mars with Dr. Charles Resnik, husband of the late Challenger 51-L mission astronaut Judith Resnik and co-Founding Director of the Challenger Center for Space Science Education. That evening, Bradbury gave the keynote address to the Challenger Center's annual National Benefit black-tie dinner.

The Challenger Learning Centers were spreading out all over the United States and Canada in tribute to the fallen astronauts of the 1986 Challenger tragedy, and the Challenger Center for Space Science Education depended on the annual fund-raising dinner to maintain the educational initiatives available at the various learning centers and online. Hundreds of thousands of students were already participating each year, and Bradbury's inspirational presentation went over well.[6] NPR and ABC journalist Cokie Roberts was matron of ceremonies in one of the most striking Washington venues—The National Building Museum.

Ever the proponent of preserving rather than replacing historic buildings and transportation systems, Bradbury was right at home in the grand hall and the building's famous Renaissance revival architecture; he had, in fact, visited the great Renaissance structures, such as Rome's Palazo Farnese, that had inspired the building's form. Once the U.S. Pension Office, the building now housed architecture, design, and urban planning exhibits. Through its design and repurposed function, the National Building Museum represented the best in human culture, but in his speech, Bradbury offered a caution about human nature: "Space travel isn't going to improve us. We're still going to be selfish. We're still going to be cruel."[7]

Shortly after his return to Los Angeles, Bradbury was back in the spotlight for the American Film Institute's 7th annual International Film Festival. The Bradbury Film Tribute portion of the three-week festival ran on June 16–17, 1993, at Laemmle Sunset 5.[8] It was the first year for the festival at this venue, but the name had deep Hollywood roots. Carl Laemmle, the founder of Universal Studios, had begun the chain in 1939; the new five-screen complex at Sunset had opened in 1992. The theater provided a double treat for Bradbury, who had twice had feature films produced by Universal and knew the venerable actress-heir to the family legacy, the founder's niece, Carla Laemmle. During the two days dedicated to Bradbury, the AFI Filmfest offered two screenings each of *Moby Dick*, *Fahrenheit 451*, and *Something Wicked This Way Comes*.

Once again, distinguished lectures and Hollywood engagements had bled off the time he needed for writing. In various letters, including his spring 1993 letter to Lawrence Gordon, Bradbury indicated he was finishing a novel; this was probably his old nemesis, "the Illinois novel"—once known as *Summer Morning, Summer Night*, and now slowly shaping up under the title of his 1980 Green Town story, "Farewell Summer." His first decadelong stint on this novel ended with the extraction of fifteen stories, bridged to form *Dandelion Wine* (1957). In 1992 and 1993, he continued to work on the remains of the original plot, but it was slow going.

The usual film projects and heavy speaking schedule affected his story production as well. He received rejections from the *New Yorker* and another major market magazine in 1992, and both of the stories he managed to publish that year appeared in *American Way* magazine. One of these, "The Hunt Wedding," was from *Green Shadows, White Whale*. Two of the three stories he published in 1993 also appeared in *American Way*; the third was sold to a genre anthology.

American Way was one of the more enduring in-flight magazines, and Bradbury's light tales circulated through the seat pouches of millions of American Airlines passengers each year. But this kind of visibility was also problematic; with the exception of *Playboy*, the major magazines were rejecting his more recent stories. To have four of the five stories he published in 1992 and 1993 limited to this single specialty magazine offered a pale reflection of the master storyteller of old.

With Maggie's ankle fully healed, the Bradburys were able to make the hoped-for summer Paris trip in 1993, bringing two granddaughters—Ramona's Claire and Julia—for the first time. The new typewriter in the Gordon's Avenue de la Bourdonnais apartment was the vessel for continuing pages of *Farewell Summer* and a revision of his *Fahrenheit 451* screenplay. An inscribed copy of the new 40th anniversary edition of *Fahrenheit 451* from Bradbury had persuaded Clint Eastwood to review the screenplay when his schedule permitted,[9] and there were rumblings of interest from Mel Gibson as well. There seemed to be little new story writing under way, however, and in fact it was, like the year before, a quiet year for his short fiction.

32 | Harvest Time

By the early 1990s, Bradbury's abiding sense of the ambivalence between life and death had cut a fifty-year arc through his fiction; across all this time, the recurring rituals of Halloween had remained a root metaphor of his creative life. Halloween illuminated the unbroken path through time that linked Aunt Neva's transformation of his Waukegan childhood home into a haunted house with more recent memories of the magic he would create for his own family decades later—the Halloween parties and entertainments (once even a Dixieland band) that took over his Cheviot Hills home each and every October 31st.

His enjoyment was never simplistic; it was firmly grounded in historical awareness rather than the pervasive commercialized celebrations that had come to dominate autumn in America. Ray Bradbury would never say "Happy Halloween," for happiness was not the essence of his favorite holiday. He had written two novels and many stories from this perspective, but his most cogent summing up emerged from a brief reflection about one particular Halloween: "It is not supposed to be happy. We celebrate it with a certain amount of fervor and excitement, but at its core it is about those who have gone on ahead of us; one day for all souls and one day for all saints."[1]

That particular Halloween came just two months after Bradbury's 73rd birthday. His measured response to his favorite holiday was changed forever on October 31, 1993, when television broadcasts announced the death of his friend Federico Fellini in Rome. Bradbury had already carved and placed pumpkins all around the house and had set out the usual decorations in preparation for the evening's inevitable ebb and flow of costumed trick-or-treaters. There were fewer Halloween parties now (Maggie preferred a quiet evening reading), but the Bradbury home was still a favorite stop for neighbors. Young and old enjoyed the spectacle of America's October Man doling out treats and talking with the children on their level, maintaining an illusion that he himself had never abandoned as he aged.

But the loss of Fellini changed everything. The great filmmaker had made a strong impact on Bradbury during the 1960s and 1970s, as Bradbury discovered a kindred spirit in Fellini whose films seemed to parallel his own sense of fantasy and the full range of human emotions. His 1977 *Los Angeles Times* review of a book on Fellini's films became the ticket to an enduring friendship, but this was not the near-worship with which he had entered his earlier working relationship with Hollywood's enigmatic John Huston, or the more nurturing friendship he established with the venerable Bernard Berenson. By this time, Bradbury was himself an iconic cultural figure, and the "twin-ship" that Fellini had bestowed on their creative bond in the late 1970s had encouraged Bradbury to think in terms of possible collaborations during the 1980s.

But Fellini's *Amarcord*, with its rich succession of little miracles, was the last of his films that resonated for Bradbury. By the mid-1980s, he found the increasing melancholy and outré aspects of Fellini's later films to be troubling and paraphrased his pleas to Fellini in a 1984 letter to his old *Fahrenheit 451* editor, film critic Stanley Kauffmann: "Cheer up, I said. I'm in the same boat with you, but I'm bailing, while you're encouraging your dark elephant to pee in the gunnels!" Bradbury's instinctive dislike of dark realism in the literature of the modern world surfaced once again here, as he urged Fellini not to let harsh realities shape his films. Yet Bradbury still held out hope that he could work with the master. "I have always wanted him to do my *The Wonderful Ice Cream Suit*. It could be a wonderful romp through Rome instead of Mexican Los Angeles, and I wouldn't mind if he tucked in a few more sombre [sic] notes like those lovely moments in *Nights of Cabiria* where you are smiling one moment and weeping the next."

He would later tell Don Congdon how Halloween 1993 ended: "I threw away the pumpkins, turned out the front door lights, and went to bed early, remembering that fabulous afternoon in Rome when Federico drove me back to my hotel after a full week of lunches, dinners, and visits to the studio."[2] Bradbury would still go forth and engage publicly with Halloween, for he was now a living symbol of the magic and ritual it embodied. Each year gifts and a few jack o' lanterns would appear around the Bradbury home, but his active engagement remained muted when he was away from the public eye. Fellini and he were born in the same year, and Fellini's death was one of the first markers to signal his own advancing age. Over the final two decades of his life, more and more of these lights would go out.

∴ ∴ ∴

But if Fellini's death diminished his own personal celebrations of Halloween, this sadness was counterbalanced by the 1993 release of his animated film version of *The Halloween Tree*, a Hanna-Barbera production that finally brought his 1972 novel back to its original form as the 1967–68 screenplay he had written for master animator Chuck Jones at MGM.

Bradbury had reservations about any animation company that built its success on television programming rather than studio-based features, but Ted Turner's acquisition of Hanna-Barbera changed everything. Prime-time potential was now paired with the follow-on resources of Turner Home Entertainment, virtually insuring longevity for a seasonal show like *The Halloween Tree*. And there was also the personal factor; Bradbury's very public vocal defense of the Turner Tomorrow Award and his service as a judge during that controversial 1991 award competition had created a bond of trust that would help ensure serious animation development of Bradbury's project.

In late June, he submitted the final revised pages to Hanna-Barbera's David Kirshner, Mario Peluso, and Mark Young, who were already into the storyboarding phase of work for the projected fall 1993 broadcast target.[3] Their detailed storyboard development now gave visualized personalities to Bradbury's trick-or-treat adventurers through time. The earlier 1971–72 process of script-into-book provided a key insight that Bradbury now brought into the revised screenplay—the double-edged mystery of Pipkin's fate. They must not only find him as they spin through time, but they must also give of their own longevity to win him back from death.

Bradbury provided the narrator's voice; he was far more concerned about casting Moundshroud, however. For years he had felt that the perfect voice for Moundshroud would be that of his good friend Christopher Lee, but scheduling circumstances led instead to the selection of Leonard Nimoy for this pivotal role.[4] All in all, *The Halloween Tree* took more than a quarter century to evolve from screenplay to novel to radio play to a well-regarded teleplay. Disney's John Hench, one of the Nine Old Men of Disney Imagineering lore, found the color a bit disappointing but praised the unforgettable qualities of certain scenes.[5] *The Halloween Tree* eventually brought Bradbury an Emmy for best animated feature-length teleplay, but the actual October 1993 airing of the show remained the greater thrill in his mind.

As Turner Broadcasting prepared to premier *The Halloween Tree*, Bradbury was also at work on resurrecting an even older unfulfilled motion picture desire—a remake of the 1956 MGM science fiction classic *Forbidden Planet*. He had been asked to script the original version by MGM producer Nicholas Nayfack, but declined due to a heavy workload; Bradbury later regretted that decision after reading the preproduction screen story, feeling that he would have enjoyed dramatizing the suppressed "Id" energies emerging from the marooned Dr. Morbius's subconscious dreams as he unknowingly attempts to destroy the rescue ship and its crew.[6] In the fall of 1993, Bradbury would have a second chance, as Academy Award–winning screenwriter Stirling Silliphant prepared an updated story line for a possible remake by Bradbury's old friend, *The Empire Strikes Back* director Irvin Kershner.

Bradbury was asked to work with Silliphant's new script, which opened with the backstory of Dr. Morbius's arrival on the mysterious planet Altair 4 twenty years before the action of the original film. This opening frame introduced a new ecological theme, as Morbius's captain and shipmates turn from exploration to a fast-paced exploitation of Altair 4's natural resources. Silliphant's opening was not only in line with late-twentieth-century concerns for Earth; it also echoed one of the very influential core premises of *The Martian Chronicles*. During the first week of October 1993, Bradbury prepared a six-page single-spaced revision to the opening frame.[7]

He gave the rapid exploitation of Altair 4 a more believable head start; Dr. Morbius arrives two years after the mining operations have begun. There is more horror in seeing the delicate architectures of a long-lost alien culture lost within the massive earth-moving mining operation of Earth's invaders. Silliphant had voiced Morbius's thoughts at this contrast, but Bradbury reworked a purely visual and more emotional treatment, conveying his points in directorial notes:

> We make our points here, as you will have noticed, not with VOICE OVERS, but with metaphorical proofs. A minute of archaeological wonders, statues, tombs, mosaics. Plus a minute of the landscape-filled architectures. When we have proven what the planet *was*, we attack it and cut back for CLOSEUPS of MORBIUS growing more and more disturbed and finally enraged at what he sees. He doesn't have to ruminate on this; it is all in his face.
>
> Which means we cut out all of the legends up front in the film, we don't need to speak or read it, it is all in the photography, it is all visual metaphor. Which means we don't need MORBIUS'S spoken philosophy. To see the destruction is to hate it. No words are necessary.

Silliphant had introduced Morbius after he has already penetrated the alien ruins and begun to interact with the ancient and undisturbed Kryll instruments of mind expansion. But Bradbury chose instead to lead Morbius through his initial discovery of the ancient Kryll instruments and the "holy and unholy fire" transmitted by the alien machine whispers: "He looks on all sides and in listening we know he learns, he nods, he shuts his eyes, he listens again." These were echoes of Bradbury's 1968 story, "The Lost City of Mars," a place where all the mysteries of the universe would be given through vast and ancient machines. "Mystery is everything," he observed in his closing note to Silliphant. "I have tried to make *Forbidden Planet* more mysterious and therefore more fun."

Here was a focused example of the best in Bradbury's screenwriting intuition, and also the worst. Bradbury's abiding impulse to employ image over dialog was a major screen asset conceptually, but it often prevented him from developing focused dialog and concise emotional interactions for the characters in many of his screenplays. He would never see where his intriguing new opening for Silliphant's screenplay would go, however; the project eventually moved along to New Line Cinema, where James Cameron continued to work with a version of Silliphant's script. The *Forbidden Planet* project moved on through DreamWorks in 2007 in the experienced hands of Michael Straczynski and producer Joel Silver, but was again abandoned two years later. International interest in producing some version of *Forbidden Planet* has never gone away, but it remains to be seen if any of Bradbury's long-ago contributions might survive.

Bradbury had also been asked to write a treatment for a sequel to *The Day the Earth Stood Still* in 1980. This project never got past the earliest stages of development, but one wonders where Bradbury would have taken that well-known adventure. His surviving materials show not the return of emissary Klaatu, but his daughter, Klataa. In any event, Bradbury may be the only writer to have been actively involved with remake and sequel projects for two of the best science fiction films of mid-century Hollywood.

: : :

In early 1994, Bradbury was able to revisit the search for other worlds in ways that he was not free to do when he wrote his first speculative article for *Life* magazine in 1960. In the earlier article, "A Serious Search for Weird Worlds," he was lumbered by research involving radio telescopes and astronomical measurements that he couldn't even pretend to understand. Now, through the garden and studio legacy of one of his favorite impressionist painters, he could take readers to those worlds without the aid of technology at all:

> The place is Giverny with its floodtides of color year-round. Its creator, Claude Monet, the great Impressionist painter, broadcast its seeds and harvested its colors to last from his creative lifetime in 1899 to ours. . . .
>
> The entire history of leaf, seed, and bright flower experimentation over a billion year cycle lies there. And looking beyond we see that all of our Earth is Giverny, it's just so vast, we never noticed. And if that is true, all unseen worlds beyond our solar system are Giverny squared.

For Bradbury, his beloved Giverny was proof positive "that the Universe is nothing if not fecund, a vast honeycomb of furious re-creative activity, dripping with genes and chromosomes." Bradbury's survey of other worlds was unfettered by scientific assumptions and laws, but his tour of worlds was not so very far from scientific method: "As students we should look to Giverny then as a forecast tasting, a sight-and-sound bite of our travels away from Earth unto ourselves. In that year we will rename our entire planet with the name of Monet's house and garden."

In "Beyond Giverny," Bradbury was able to inspire rather than instruct, free of the institutional restraints that hobbled his *Life* magazine article and the two planetarium shows he was invited to develop for the Smithsonian Air & Space Museum in years past. "Thanks for Giverny!" Arthur C. Clarke wrote from Sri Lanka. "I hope you stretched a few minds."[8] Bradbury had full control of this article, but it would be published only in *American Way* magazine. "Beyond Giverny," with all its insights, would momentarily receive high visibility in the seatback pouches of airliners, but then it would disappear forever from public view.

33 | A Promise of Eternity

Bradbury's frequent sojourns in France came with a promise of eternity, as he would observe to one of their American expatriate friends. The years of the mid-1990s were marked off in increments separated by supersonic flights across the Atlantic to Paris, where the Bradburys mixed occasional literary engagements and visits with French and American friends with quiet time in the Gordons' Paris apartment. His story publishing picked up in 1994 for the first time in years, resulting in six placements. Two were very old stories from the late 1940s, dusted off and revised—"The Very Gentle Murders," one of his early studies of husbands and wives, and "The Enemy in the Wheat," a wry commentary on early Cold War anxieties.

All six were published in what, in effect, were genre magazines, *American Way* (2), *Magazine of Fantasy & Science Fiction* (2), *Playboy* (1), and the only issue of the short-lived British men's magazine *Rave* (1). One of the F&SF pieces, "From the Dust Returned" was the most notable of these; it would prove to be the last tale in the Elliott Family saga, forming the final adventure (and indeed the title story) of what was becoming, after nearly a half century, a novelized story cycle built on several of his best supernatural tales of earlier times.

Yet none of these stories were written during the July–August 1994 summer stay in Paris. Instead, Bradbury was hard at work on a *Fahrenheit 451* screenplay. The project that had failed to draw commitment from Ted Turner two years earlier had caught the eye of Mel Gibson, who had enough interest from Warner Brothers to set Bradbury at work on the new screenplay. Gibson himself was in Scotland on location filming what would become *Braveheart*, but his organization wanted Bradbury home as soon as possible to discuss directors. It was possible that Gibson himself would direct, and Bradbury's favorable opinion of *The Man with No Face* and *Hamlet* made that possibility a very desirable option in his mind. But things would slow down as Gibson's *Braveheart* took off to extraordinary success, and his work on the screenplay slowed as the *Fahrenheit* option shifted to the back burner.

By early 1995, Bradbury was at work on a very different kind of cinematic project, a kind even he had only just come to understand—the challenging three-dimensional worlds of IMAX. The proposed *Journey to the Universe* project represented the high point of Bradbury's five-year association with legendary space artist Robert McCall. Like Bradbury, McCall had been pulled into *Life* magazine's orbit in the early 1960s. His mission was to illustrate spacecraft of the future, and by the end of the decade he had produced some of the most iconic art of the Space Age in his paintings for the Hollywood film, *2001: A Space Odyssey*. Of these, his painting of a sleek space passenger shuttle departing the film's grand space station was one of the most recognized paintings of the day.

McCall took NASA commissions frequently, and his popular series of floating cities explored the possibilities of life beyond the reach of gravity. A major 1984–85 McCall art exhibition at the Smithsonian Air and Space Museum led inevitably to an oversize art book of his space illustrations, and in 1991 Bradbury was commissioned to write the volume's introduction. He enjoyed working with McCall immensely, and this collaboration led to Bradbury's inclusion in the 1994 team assembled by the IMAX Corporation to design a four-minute IMAX Theatre journey through futuristic solar system colonies and on out to the first interstellar explorations.

Besides McCall and Bradbury, the project team formed in September 1994 had included IMAX special effects wizard Douglas Trumbull and Apollo 11 astronaut Buzz Aldrin. McCall soon renamed the project *The City in the Stars*, and Bradbury's narrative included eleven planetary encounters, including a culminating planetfall in the Alpha Centauri multiple star systems. He subtitled his narrative and its brief after-show concept "Lightyear Landfall Eleven," and his second draft was completed in late February 1995.

By April, the storyboards had incorporated his words into pictures, leaving only a few grand voiceover lines sprinkled throughout the journey from Earth to the Lunar colony, the Mars outposts deep in the Valis Marineris "Grand Canyon" of Mars, on through Saturn's rings, and then an unexplained sunward loop back through a close flyover of Jupiter's Red Spot before a hurried journey past the outer planets—no time left to make those landfalls before hibernation and the long journey out to Centauri. Trumbull's storyboard artists had introduced new images that would require additional but brief Bradbury descriptions, using the same magisterial cosmic voice that came so naturally to him.

But Trumbull's directions, passed through Mark Rhodes of the IMAX production subsidiary Ridefilm, wanted Bradbury's additional commentary to accommodate the commercial and technological message that the ride was expected to convey for theatergoers. They wanted to keep the "visionary depiction of space" at the heart of the McCall-Bradbury collaboration, but the storyboard sidebar notes reveal that Trumbull also needed Bradbury "to dramatize that computers represent a wonderful technology which allows us to ride through 3D, digitized paintings."[1] The final corporate objective, at least, was more closely aligned with Bradbury's deep-seated Space-Age convictions: "There is a human 'need' to explore the unknown and to test the limits of the imagination."

Bradbury had found out through similar unproduced projects using earlier technologies that his need to "inspire" often conflicted with the sponsor's need to "explain." His inability to bend to the match had doomed earlier projects for Monsanto at Disney and the Smithsonian Air & Space planetarium show. But there was room to compromise with the IMAX concept, and it's possible that Bradbury could have navigated the need to supply short bursts of metaphors on computer technology. It's not clear if Bob McCall ever finished all of the anchoring paintings spaced out through the show concept, or if budgetary constraints came into play, but after Bradbury's summer 1995 return from Paris, there does not appear to have been any more work done on *The City in the Stars*.

There would, however, be another chance to push the space program forward through the work of the Challenger Center for Space Science Education and its North American network of Challenger Education Centers. He had keynoted the national fund-raiser two years earlier in Washington; now, in early 1995, a new center was established at California State University, Dominguez Hills, and Bradbury gave the "Lift Off" keynote address for this milestone as well. His warm-up speakers included retired Navy Captain Charles "Pete" Conrad Jr., a veteran astronaut and commander of the Apollo 12 mission, where he became the third human to walk on the moon.

Bradbury had first met Conrad during his 1967 visit to the Houston Space Flight Center, where he had dinner with Conrad, Jim Lovell, and John Young. A decade later, Bradbury and Conrad were presenters at the fifth annual Saturn Awards for Science Fiction, Fantasy, and Horror Films, where *Star Wars* dominated in many categories. He knew Conrad's Apollo 12 colleague Alan Bean better, but he liked the rugged Conrad and enjoyed visiting with him at the "Landing party" reception following the Challenger Center dedication. It was always a point of quiet satisfaction that these space pioneers all considered him a spiritual pathfinder as the Great Tale unfolded above the Earth.

: : :

This year, there were no health issues to curtail a spring trip to France. He was home in time to turn around and head to Washington, D.C., to preside at the annual Robert Goddard dinner and awards in June, as he had done almost a decade earlier. In July 1995, Bradbury and Maggie settled into what they hoped would be another extended summer stay in Paris. They lived with the ghosts of the Lost Generation, represented by a copy of what had come to be Bradbury's favorite novel, Fitzgerald's *Tender Is the Night* (he bought a new copy in Paris almost every year), and visited their American friends at the *International Herald Tribune*. Reading the IHT had been a daily ritual for American expatriates for decades, figuring at times in the novels of Hemingway and other writers. Maggie's fluency in French made the IHT a preferred habit rather than a necessity during their long stays in Paris, but the paper had also given them friends far away from the hectic pace back home.

Early in the summer 1995 trip, two of their good friends in Paris, editor Bob McCabe and Susan Webb, were married in an Episcopal service conducted in the American Cathedral of Paris. The Bradburys arrived in France in time to attend the civil marriage ceremony held near the Rue Grenelle in central Paris, presided over by a deputy mayor in a hall that delighted Bradbury for its contrast to a standard church service. "The room in which the troths were spoken had one of those fine golden flower-encrusted ceilings and at each end great murals of mythological marriages two thousand years ago in some Grecian forest where a tall handsome groom in a fine white toga led his fair bride surrounded by celebrants with cymbals, pipes, flutes, and flower-throwing, shadowed and revealed in light, children capering, and the promise of eternity in the clear air."[2] They followed on to the reception, and had their driver bring the newlyweds home in the appropriately Grecian-bronze limousine that Bradbury had chartered for the day. McCabe would eventually become deputy editor of the *International Herald Tribune* Paris headquarters, and they remained close to the Bradburys for years, sometimes coaxing them out to their holiday home in Normandy.

Other expatriate friends in Paris included photographic and art editor Mary-Dawn Earley and her husband John Noaks. There were plans to visit all these friends, but it was not to be. Maggie had not been well, and over the next week she had a recurrence of a vision problem that brought great pain and temporary immobility of one eye. They decided to curtail their stay and flew home on July 18th. It was perhaps just as well. Bradbury had not published a story collection since the 1988 release of *The Toynbee Convector*, and he was slowly pulling together old and new stories for two Avon collections that would appear over the next two years as *Quicker than the Eye* and *Driving Blind*.

His Hollywood schedule was even more ambitious, and far less predictable. He was still working closely with Disney on the film adaptation of *The Wonderful Ice Cream Suit*, and the previous summer's interest from Mel Gibson and possibly Warner Brothers led to periods of work on his new *Fahrenheit 451* script.[3] There were still unfinished novel-length projects remaining, some from four or five decades in the past, and he knew he must return to these projects before too long.

: : :

Bradbury had always been a writer who lived through careful observation of people and places, using all his senses to absorb and then write about the world around him. An abiding fear of losing his vision dated back to elementary school in Waukegan, when a premature diagnosis of degenerating eyesight leading to blindness terrified him at age eleven. Further exams revealed the mistake, finding instead a nearsightedness easily corrected by glasses. Relaxation techniques he discovered through the Bates Method of exercises in the early 1940s seemed to stabilize his nearsightedness.[4] Late in life, Lasik procedures corrected his vision, but his fans could not picture him without his prominent black glasses; he started wearing empty frames to preserve the trademark appearance that everyone expected to see.

Yet the first of his senses to betray him would be his hearing. By the 1990s, chronic problems with pain and loss of hearing in his left ear led to a series of exams. Three months of antibiotics failed to ease the pain, and in the fall of 1995 his specialist, Dr. Ellie Goldstein, confirmed mastoiditis. Soft tissue degeneration continued, but his January 1996 exam indicated no sign of any malignancies.[5] Nevertheless, the prognosis was clear; he would soon lose all hearing in his left ear. Over the next few years, he also began to lose hearing in his right ear from other causes, and during the final decade of his life he came to depend on a single hearing aid in all situations.

Bradbury would soon discover that loss of hearing, rather than blindness, presented the greater nightmare. He had come to live through his public image, partly prompted by an element of fame-driven ego, but largely fueled by his constant lecture and public appearance schedule that provided a vital and ever-renewing connection with his readers and with the growing number of institutions that honored him for his books and visionary commentaries on literacy, libraries, creativity, and the Space Age. He could type in total darkness—and had done so from time to time for years—but without hearing, he could no longer engage with audiences in the way he had come to love. During the last seven years of his life, as the hearing in his right ear became more attenuated, he would sometimes cancel public appearances at the last minute if his hearing aid malfunctioned. It was a tangible and very understandable fear, magnified by the power of his imagination. He remained determined not to become one of Poe's worst nightmares—a prisoner of his own body.

34 Séances and Ghosts

"Artists and writers often forget, if they ever knew it in the first place, that they should on occasion take marriage vows." Bradbury's wide-ranging gift of creativity was predicated on the notion of love; he considered his enduring author-agent relationship with Don Congdon a special kind of marriage, and he felt the same way about his long and rewarding collaborations with the artistic genius of Joseph Mugnaini, who would illustrate many of his books and ventures in stage, film, and exhibitions for nearly forty years. In a more fundamental way, Bradbury loved the stories and ideas that welled up from his own subconscious, often unbidden, or were prompted by word associations and reveries. By extension, he loved the readers who loved the things that he loved in life and who appreciated the stories he wrote for them. And beginning in the late 1970s, he loved to work with the internationally prominent Argentine photographer and artist, Aldo Sessa. Through Sessa, Bradbury also found a bridge to engage his own great popularity in Argentina, culminating in a celebrated spring 1997 visit to Buenos Aires.

Sessa's association with Bradbury began nearly twenty years before the well-publicized events of 1997. His interest in Bradbury may have evolved from Bradbury's long-standing popularity in Argentine culture, reinforced perhaps during Sessa's studies in Los Angeles in the early 1960s.[1] In the mid-1970s, Sessa collaborated with Argentine fiction writer and poet Jorge Luis Borges on *Cosmogonias*, a volume of Borges's poetry interwoven with Sessa's interpretive photographs. In 1978, he secured a commission for a similar collaboration with Bradbury, and the two soon developed a concept centered on Bradbury's conviction that the mysteries of science and religion would continue to merge in science fiction and the art that it inspires. Bradbury's 1977 *Saturday Review* essay, "The God in Science Fiction," anchored this exotic volume, followed by five of his poems celebrating and exploring the cosmos and, finally, his Martian tale "The Messiah," his most recent examination in fiction of how men of God might come to terms with the ineluctable mysteries of alien life.

The Ghosts of Forever became the collaborative title, and the book was published in both countries (the Rizzoli American edition included an English translation of the texts in the back matter). Sessa's companion photographs and illustrations were mesmerizing, startling, and thought-provoking. Bradbury secured an epilogue from Melvin Zisfein, the deputy director of the National Air and Space Museum, who stepped away from his scientific grounding for just a moment to consider how this book might help to "broaden the human brain so that it can begin to grasp the shapes of the myriad possible life forms and their artifacts that may be out there—in the cosmos. . . . Will it look like anything that Sessa draws or Bradbury writes about? Who knows? But we must strive to prepare mentally for that day." The 1980 publication generated very few reviews, but the book was more broadly known in the international art world.

Since the mid-1950s, Bradbury's Argentine and Spanish editions of *The Martian Chronicles* had often included a timeless introduction by Jorge Luis Borges, and Sessa's growing association with Bradbury enhanced the already wide readership in Latin America. In the spring of 1997, both Bradbury and Maggie, whose fluency in Spanish made the trip all the more manageable, became guests of the nation for Argentina's twenty-third National Book Fair, an event that drew 1,100,000 attendees to Buenos Aires in early May. The attention exceeded the grand receptions he had received periodically in Paris, when his travels coincided with French literary and national observances. In Buenos Aires, he was the star of the Fair, and his final presentation was fully open to the public.

Those present ranged from publishers and authors to the media and a large audience of readers, especially young readers and their parents. It was a larger version of many audiences back home, and he ran through some of his usual anecdotes of luck in his life and his love of reading. He was seventy-seven, but he spoke with great clarity and conviction—many of the young attendees abandoned their translation headphones and listened to his voice. This day, his reflections turned particularly to the magic connection he had always felt with the authors of the past, and their literary immortality: "I admire many dead writers such as Bernard Shaw or Charles Dickens. I never envied them, they are my friends! Now they are dead they must think that people have forgotten them. That's why I always talk to them, I show them the new editions of their books, I read some paragraphs from the first page to them. And I say to them: 'Look! Your books are still in print. Can't you see that people don't forget you?'"

This particular passage from his Buenos Aires lecture was an homage that served as a wish-fulfillment dream for his own literary legacy, but it also played well in a nation and continent where magical realism was privileged.[2] Bradbury was prominently photographed discussing his books with Carlos Menem, president of Argentina, together with the distinguished Peruvian-Spanish author and future Nobel Laureate, Mario Vargas Llosa. He also spent time in sessions with Argentine writer and longtime Borges collaborator Adolfo Bioy Casares.[3]

Bradbury was speaking in one of the great cities of the Western Hemisphere, and at times his reception seemed that of a national hero. "My face was on the front page of every newspaper," he wrote to his Knopf editor, Kathy Hourigan, "they put on a Martian show at the planetarium and at the finale, my image came floating down out of the Cosmos!" He received an honorary degree from the University of Buenos Aires and a medallion from the city leaders. Bradbury and even Maggie were constantly recognized in public; one passing couple paid for their lunch near the Rio de la Plata. As they boarded the plane to return home, the aircraft's closed-circuit TV showed his face, to the cheers of passengers and crew.[4]

There had been quiet moments as well. He and Maggie had spent a few hours in Aldo Sessa's magnificent studio. For most of their very public stay in Argentina, Sessa had remained in the background. "I wanted to help you," he later wrote, "to be with you, and at the same time, as you were very busy, I didn't want to interfere with your schedule."[5] Yet he was able to photograph his friends, relaxed in the open spaces of his studio atrium, and Bradbury alone, with no crowds, in the vast spaces of one of Sessa's favorite architectural backdrops, the Teatro Colon. Sessa called them snapshots, but they have the quality of his finest work.

At the end of his keynote lecture, Bradbury had promised to return in two years. Tentative plans for another appearance at the National Book Fair were made, along with plans to premier an opera based on a Bradbury story. These plans, and many others, were altered forever when Bradbury suffered a stroke in the fall of 1999. All of his faculties returned quickly, but he never fully overcame the physical damage of the stroke. International travel became difficult, and he would never return to Argentina again. Yet in 2000, he was able to partially collaborate and write the introduction for Sessa's *Séances and Ghosts*, an intriguing extension of their twenty-year partnership. Bradbury's master metaphor went into his introduction as well as his title, offering a reflection on the darker mysteries of photography:

> It is a séance held in a darkroom where the unseen, found chemistries, is raised from the dead. To watch those ghosts rise in emulsion-filled laboratory pans is a Lazarus procedure. You drown the latent images in progressive baths to summon remembrance of things an hour, a day, or half a lifetime gone. The ectoplasm responds. It was claimed a sharp metaphysician could spin that stuff like gossamer smoke, issuing from the mouths and nostrils of the dead or dying.

For Bradbury, artists—and especially photographers—were time machines. "They must work with what is there in three dimensions, flatten it to two, yet find a fourth beneath the obvious look. It must be flash discovered in that instant of genius discovery and intuitively snapped shut in a box before it can cry out or escape."

In 2002, Sessa sent Bradbury a less metaphorical box of new photographs, inspired by various Bradbury poems, hoping to bring together a volume like the one he had made of the poems of Borges so many years earlier. But other projects had already intervened, as Bradbury worked with waning strength to fully shape the books that had been deferred from long ago. The third Sessa collaboration would remain lost in time.[6]

: : :

Lou Aronica was instrumental in bringing Bradbury to Avon Books, but it would be up to his successor, Jennifer Brehl, to bring him fully into the Avon family. Simon & Schuster still controlled the hardbound edition of *Fahrenheit 451*, but Bradbury soon saw all of his other classic titles placed back in hardbound or trade paperback editions under the Avon imprint. It was time to bring out new collections as well, and the available new stories would once again have to be augmented by a significant number of unpublished or uncollected stories from the early decades.

There were simply too many distractions in his life, and not enough time to focus and concentrate on original ideas. There were too many activities in town, and he frankly enjoyed the social engagement; there were too many road lectures as well. He had to go to the Palm Springs house, purchased in the early 1980s, to concentrate on writing, but his writing time was dominated by rewriting film scripts and book-length projects. Donn Albright recommended older stories that exhibited qualities that the newer anecdotal tales generally lacked—older stories that people could relate to, and older examples of the kind of eerie weird tales and light horror stories that had made his reputation. The resulting collections, *Quicker than the Eye* (1996) and *Driving Blind* (1997), each contained 21 stories. Of these forty-two tales, twenty-three were vintage stories, and only two of the older ones had ever reached print before.

As these story collections were being harvested in the mid-1990s, Bradbury was deeply involved in what, at first, promised to be a real breakthrough in his plans for a second film adaptation of *Fahrenheit 451*. Mel Gibson, who had obtained the first of a series of options on *Fahrenheit 451* in 1993, was still interested in negotiating a Bradbury script. By mid-1994 Gibson was close to a deal backed by Warner Brothers for a *Fahrenheit* film involving his own Icon Productions and Storyline Productions.[7] Once again, however, timing was not on Bradbury's side. As the news broke of the impending *Fahrenheit 451* deal, Gibson was already working on location in Scotland and Ireland on *Braveheart*. The stress of both directing and acting led to the greatest film success of his career and set Gibson on a trajectory of high-budget productions that took him further and further away from Bradbury's novel.

Gibson would hold and renew his option for years, however, and during 1996, Bradbury rewrote his new *Fahrenheit* script as Gibson's production staff steered the project from Warner Brothers over to Universal Studios. Bradbury worked on his screenplay in bursts that even included writing in France during the regular spring and summer vacations in Paris, where he could control his engagement schedule far better than he ever could in Los Angeles. Finally, on Halloween 1997, Bradbury completed his third fully revised version and sent it to his production liaison at Universal, Kevin Misher.[8]

It was a strong script; he had learned the value of rewriting and cutting under the driving direction of John Huston on *Moby Dick* in the early 1950s, and subsequently under the more deliberate but enigmatic direction of Jack Clayton as he and Bradbury guided *Something Wicked This Way Comes* down its long path to production in the 1970s and early 1980s. Over four decades, he had also produced teleplays and four screenplays for *The Martian Chronicles*, all unproduced, but all useful as refinements of method. Even in the face of disappointment, he never considered his creative work as time wasted.

Yet he had always had trouble reducing his beautifully descriptive prose to action, and the concise pacing of conflict and resolution, either on screen or on stage, always remained a challenge for him. Unfortunately, there would be no true test of his success with this screen version of *Fahrenheit*. Gibson moved on from project to project into the early 2000s, and over time Bradbury's choices for the principal roles slowly aged out of consideration.

There were, however, indicators in the surviving screenplay that lessons had been learned from all that came before, including the work of other hands. One prime example was the Mechanical Hound, a creation that Bradbury had added to the novel in his final 1953 expansion, fashioning the name from *The Mechanical Bride*, Marshall McCluhan's commentary on the rise of thinking machines in the postindustrial age. The Hound was the great enforcer of *Fahrenheit*, but Truffaut had discarded this marvelous creature from his 1966 film adaptation. Bradbury had retained the creature in his various stage versions, and he was determined not to abandon it now.

As British media scholar Dr. Phil Nichols has brought out, Bradbury's left-behind 1997 script incorporates the Hound with a new vigor suited to late-century special effects, one of a number of evolutions that led Nichols to believe that this unproduced screenplay offers the best fulfillment of the novel's original potential. The hound is mass-produced and hunts in packs, each one given ter-rifying mobility through the eight flexible spiderlike legs. Book ashes are used to fill fireworks, which sometimes spread readable fragments. Montag himself has more opportunity to develop and seek answers on his own, creating a better balance with the characters that represent his three possible futures—Clarisse, Faber, and Beatty.[9]

A decade later, Frank Darabont's schedule for directing the film was exploded by the 100-day Writer's Guild of America strike, which ran from November 2007 to February 2008, but not before Darabont himself composed an excellent script of his own. The project never cycled through again in this form, however; it would be yet another decade before writer-director Ramin Bahrani took up *Fahrenheit 451* and aired his version for HBO in May 2018. Bradbury would not live to participate in this project—*Fahrenheit 451* would be in the hands of a talented international filmmaker who belonged exclusively to the twenty-first century.

In one sense, the mixed reviews for both the 1966 Truffaut and the 2018 Bah-rani adaptations reflect what might be called the curse of the Mechanical Hound, perhaps the most memorable of all of Bradbury's bizarre mechanical children. Truffaut and Bahrani both opted to forego dealing with the Mechanical Hound at all, leaving it to unrelated films like *Red Planet* (2000) to fashion an effective variation through the robotic canine terror of its autonomous exploratory rover-gone-berserk, AMEE. In both *Fahrenheit* films, the absence of Bradbury's Hound was a symptom of a larger risk for the auteur—the dangers of drifting away from Bradbury's original plot. Any variations should really be logical or emotional evolutions of the original, and Bradbury himself just might have been the most likely screenwriter to bring it home.

: : :

During the mid-1990s, Bradbury had three screenplays in progress, but only one would ever be produced. By 1997, Disney actually had *The Wonderful Ice Cream Suit* in production after years of hopes and dreams. Roy E. Disney, Walt Disney's nephew, had been a fan for years, having seen it twice produced on stage in Los Angeles. Disney first gave serious thought to *The Wonderful Ice Cream Suit* in the mid-1980s, when a change in corporate leadership returned him to the Board of Directors and chairmanship of the animation department. At first, Disney was wary of taking on the entire project; in early 1987, he told Bradbury that he would prefer partnering with an independent production for the film adaptation.[10]

By the mid-1990s, Disney's enthusiasm increased through the growing en-couragement of high-profile actors. Joe Mantegna had brought *The Wonderful Ice Cream Suit* to life as a stage play with Chicago's Organic Theater Company more than twenty years earlier, and he would be instrumental in bringing together the prominent cast for the Disney production, a cast that included longtime Bradbury enthusiast Edward James Olmos, Esai Morales, and Gregory Sierra. Bradbury was thrilled to see the framing roles of the two tailors portrayed by veteran comic actors Sid Caesar and Howard Morris. The prime mover in almost every aspect of the film would be Stuart Gordon, founder of the Organic Theater Company. Gordon had a long history with Bradbury's stage version—he would not only direct the film, but also coproduce with Roy Disney and Laura Medina.

More than fifty years had passed since Bradbury experienced the multicultural life around Temple and Figueroa; traces of the original Spanish plaza of Pueblo Los Angeles still remained if one looked closely, but by the early 1940s, Bradbury could watch many cultures mingle. The men who pool their money for the Ice Cream Suit were based on the personalities of Hispanic friends in the old neighborhood. Bradbury did not speak much Spanish, but he remembered the words, and the nicknames, and he could tell Stuart Gordon how the names should be pronounced in that particular neighborhood, at that particular time.[11]

There were many examples of shared dreams in these neighborhoods, but Bradbury's most direct inspiration rose out of a custom he had observed among the Filipino families downtown. There were formal dances for the young ladies, who would then go home to the tenements to change and drop their beautiful dresses from the rooftops to those younger girls who would wear them for the next season. The tight 25-day shooting schedule began in August 1997, with many of the location shots at the Boyle Hotel. The old downtown intersection at Temple and Figueroa had long been rebuilt into an overpass for through traffic; Boyle Heights was not too far east, and it preserved the look that fit many of Bradbury's memories. Bradbury's copy of the call sheet for September 4th lists him in a pawnbroker cameo role.

Bradbury considered this project to be his best Hollywood experience in the production of a major motion picture film. There was only one moment, late in editing, where Bradbury felt a key scene had been altered to the point that the continuity of the entire film was threatened. It was often difficult to tell when he was perhaps too close to the ideal story to be fair in his criticism, but in the end Michael Eisner, then CEO and Board Chairman, helped Bradbury get the cuts restored.

But Eisner could not give Bradbury what he wanted most, which was a full theatrical distribution release of *The Wonderful Ice Cream Suit*. The die had been cast early on, when the film was brokered as a home video product and made with TV union and actor scale wages. Disney and Gordon had Eisner screen the film, but in the end it was not feasible to pay the significant contractual costs required for theatrical distribution.[12] The film was released to home video in 1998 through Disney's Touchstone subsidiary. For the rest of his life, Bradbury periodically urged Disney Studio executives to arrange international theatrical release in the Spanish-speaking world, without success. On balance, though, the film represented one of his most rewarding Hollywood experiences, and it resulted in enduring friendships with Mantegna and Olmos, who would visit him periodically for the rest of his life.

35 An Evening on Mars

By the 1990s, The Planetary Society had become a powerful private sector proponent for the next phase of the Great Tale. The passing of co-founder Carl Sagan in 1996 did not diminish the institution but actually increased momentum as two important Mars missions signaled a return to Mars after a twenty-year absence—the high-resolution capabilities of the *Mars Global Surveyor* and, finally, the arrival of the *Pathfinder* lander and its precious cargo *Sojourner*, the first roving robotic laboratory on the Martian surface. By 1998, Bradbury was the most publicly prominent Planetary Society advisor, and the surviving founders—Bruce Murray, former director of the Jet Propulsion Laboratory, and Astrophysicist Louis Friedman—turned to Bradbury to conceive and present an evening on Mars.

Bradbury's various abiding visions of Mars would coalesce into a benefit performance for the Thomas O. Paine Memorial Award on the evening of May 18, 1998. Tom Paine's years as administrator of NASA culminated in the triumph of the Apollo lunar missions, but he always saw Martian exploration and colonization as the overarching goal of manned spaceflight in our time. The annual award was presented for "The advancement of human exploration of Mars." Previous winners had included the Apollo-Soyuz Test Mission's American-Soviet crewmembers; eventually, in the next century, Bradbury would receive this award, but his 1998 evening on Mars presentation would honor the earthbound men and women of the Mars Pathfinder and Global Surveyor teams.

The 1998 award ceremony was titled "Witness & Celebrate: An Evening on Mars with Ray Bradbury." Since the 1960s, Bradbury had made "witness and celebrate" his role in the space program, but he was always excited by such moments as this, when he was pulled directly into the Great Tale itself. He was able to call on the combined talents of The Planetary Society, NASA, and Hollywood actors—personal friends, as well as those who simply shared his dreams.

The ten readings he forged into the larger vision of his Evening on Mars included six of his poems; a scene from "Ylla," (the opening chapter of *The Martian Chronicles*); a humorous interlude by his good friend, the perennial comic and advertising innovator Stan Freberg; a powerful reading from his *Leviathan 99* stage play; and a final reading from "The Million Year Picnic," the evocative closing chapter of *The Martian Chronicles*. The evening offered a reflection of his entire career as a spacefaring dreamer—the two *Chronicles* chapters had first appeared in print as stand-alone stories more than a half-century earlier. All his life, Bradbury had written about all peoples, imagined from a wide range of backgrounds, and his distinguished readers that night also reflected the diverse nature of those who had found a pathway to his books. That evening, his readers included veterans of various Star Trek franchise evolutions (Nichelle Nichols, John de Lancie, Tim Russ, Robert Picardo); John Rhys-Davies, destined for the film adaptations of Tolkien's *Lord of the Rings*; and Bradbury's good friend, Charlton Heston.

Bradbury's "Evening on Mars" was a fitting celebration of the nation's dramatic return to the Red Planet. *Pathfinder* had landed on July 4, 1997, a date that rekindled Bradbury's earliest memories of fire balloons launched by his paternal grandfather and rising into the Waukegan evening sky, bound for faraway places in the night. He had always considered the fire balloons an ending, the last happy memory of the grandfather who passed away in 1925, but the fire-born landing of Pathfinder was really a beginning. Like the new wave of settlers arriving on abandoned Mars in the final chapter of his *Martian Chronicles*, this was a second chance, opening a new generation of surface exploration after a long absence of what he would call "our robotic children."

Incredibly, the dual transmissions of data and photographs from *Pathfinder* and *Sojourner* completed the assigned mission parameters in exactly one month. The mission lost contact with Earth in late September 1997, but the Aries Valles touchdown point was permanently designated the Carl Sagan Memorial Station. Sagan was the first widely known major space program scientist to pass away since von Braun's death twenty years earlier. The naming of Mars mission landings after key figures in the Great Tale would gain momentum as the new century dawned, eventually honoring Bradbury himself.

: : :

As the years passed, Bradbury had written several afterword essays for successive editions of *Fahrenheit 451*, and even a defiant coda appended to the restoration of the full text after the substantial but silent publisher's emendations of the 1960s.[1] In 1998, he moved from defiance to an outright jeremiad in "The Affluence of Despair."

This stand-alone essay appeared in the April 3, 1998, issue of the *Wall Street Journal*, but in effect it represented *Fahrenheit 451* revisited. Unlike his friend Huxley's *Brave New World Revisited*, however, Bradbury lashed out with scorn instead of lament at the fulfilled prophecies of *Fahrenheit*'s future. When Fred Pohl asked him to contribute stories for a Grand Masters anthology of science fiction—to accompany tales by Alfred Bester, Isaac Asimov, André Norton, and Arthur C. Clarke—Bradbury pressed the essay on him as well: "It could well be titled F.451 45 years later. Many of the things I outlined in that story have become virtual and more than virtual realities."[2]

Bradbury's attack on television news media and advertising was excessive but not unexpected; after all, this was the man who championed Peter Finch's Academy Award–winning role as a renegade news anchor in the 1976 film *Network*. Yet there were moments in "The Affluence of Despair" when his words rang chillingly true, beginning with his quotation from Melville's Starbuck in conversation with the monomaniacal Captain Ahab:

> "Do not fear me, old man. Beware of thyself, my captain." America should beware of itself. Today we are everywhere loving to be watched. . . . We do not suffer from totalitarian lunatics, but from the astonishing proliferation of our images. We perform for ourselves, not Big Brother. We have fallen in love with mirrors. . . . We do not go to the theater, we *are* the theater.

Above all, he blamed the "theater" of our televised news broadcasts for the nation's affluence of despair. "We must speak to these confessors of our dark souls and tell them that their awful truths in awesome repetition end with the Big Lie. We are not as bad as they say we are, but we feel this despair because they have somehow won us over." His *Wall Street Journal* essay offered a timely backward glance at the origins of *Fahrenheit 451*, a half-century earlier.

:   :   :

Despite the staying power of *Fahrenheit 451* and his other early titles, Bradbury never intended to write the so-called "great American novel"; he profoundly mistrusted that term and felt that the quest was a curse for writers who attempted to attain it. In his heart, Bradbury felt that the staying power of *Fahrenheit* owed everything to his having loved the idea, and to his readers, generation after generation, having loved what he wrote. This core idea of love and truthfulness as a writer, guided by the imagination far more than by conscious thought or objectives, had kept him from the more destructive consequences of fame. The novels he considered great were, regardless of reputation, the novels he loved unconditionally. Throughout the final four decades of his life, the greatest of these loves was F. Scott Fitzgerald's *Tender Is the Night*.

In 1999, his speaking agent Ruth Alben arranged for Bradbury to lecture at a Jewish synagogue in Minneapolis. He had some extra time before his flight home, and his driver asked if he could show Bradbury around Saint Paul. He agreed to the offer and soon found himself in front of a Victorian home on Goodrich Avenue. Bradbury was absolutely amazed to find that this was the early 1920s home of F. Scott Fitzgerald, where he had written one of his novels. The tour continued on to the Commodore Hotel, where the Fitzgeralds had lived when their daughter Scottie was born. It was a great moment of literary renewal for Bradbury, and he wasted no time embellishing the tale for his own wonderment. Fitzgerald had actually written *The Beautiful and the Damned* at Goodrich Avenue, but Bradbury (perhaps encouraged by his well-intentioned driver) would always maintain that this was the home where Fitzgerald had composed *Tender Is the Night* (it was really written later in Baltimore). Here was an epiphany, though, regardless of the facts, and it validated the rituals he had built around *Tender Is the Night* for decades.

Quite simply, he loved the texture of this novel, what he called "the asides, the observations, the richness." It was also the novel that mirrored Fitzgerald's own descent into a living hell, perhaps serving to remind Bradbury that no writer of reputation could be truly safe from a similar fate. If Bradbury himself was a talisman of sorts for many young writers (and indeed for the Space Age in general), *Tender Is the Night* had become his own private inspiration and guardian. By the late 1990s, his house was full of different editions of the book, mostly brought back from the many trips to Paris he made with Maggie over the years. It didn't matter to him that Malcolm Cowley and others had published variant forms of the novel; he preferred editions descended from the 1934 original, published when America's interwar writers could still live and write in the Europe that Fitzgerald chronicled. Each trip to Paris offered Bradbury a special and very private time of renewal, as he later recalled for his expatriate friend Bob McCabe, longtime editor for the *International Herald Tribune*:

> When I would go to Paris each year I would buy a new copy of *Tender Is the Night*; I must have ten of them here at home, signed on Bastille Day, in Paris. It has been my sublime occupation to walk from the Eiffel Tower to Notre Dame, taking a whole day, carrying *Tender Is the Night* under my arm and stopping every fifteen minutes or half an hour to have an espresso or beer and read another chapter of this fabulous book, so that by sunset I had finished reading it for the tenth time and by Notre Dame I had a glass of wine and grabbed a cab and returned to the apartment to take Maggie to dinner.[3]

For McCabe and others, more often in conversation rather than on paper, he would weave this enchanted tale, probably a conflation of more than one walk around Paris, but there is little doubt that he reread a new copy of the novel during each of the many Parisian sojourns. It was not always easy. "Have been reading *Tender Is the Night*, a perfect novel to be reading in Paris," he wrote to Congdon in the summer of 1991, "but it is so beautifully painful I have had to take it in small 30-page doses. He is surely my kind of writer, all of it, or most of it is intuitive, nothing is made up." This was the key to his passion, of course; he sensed, rightly or wrongly, that Fitzgerald at times wrote as Bradbury did, from the unpredictable upwelling of emotion and intuition, without self-conscious detachment.

In his mind it all came down to love, really; Bradbury paid the price of fame as all writers of magnitude must, but the effects were tempered by the simple admonition of literary love, a love that did not distinguish between the popular and the literary: "So I always wanted to be on the shelves, with my loves," he would later reflect in private conversation. "That's different than being famous, isn't it? I wanted to share the library dark with them. I wanted to go look up on the shelf and see the titles with their golden eyes—the numerals, the golden numerals, spelling my name with theirs. But that's not fame, that's love."[4] Fame and love were clearly interwoven in his mind, each working to temper the other in ways that managed to avoid, most of the time, a brush with the destructive elements that either emotion can convey.

Part V

Closing the Book

I'm the beneficiary of a generation of kids who grew up out of high school and college and now are middle-aged, and they wouldn't dream of hurting this old man, you see. So, on top of that, they grew up with a love of my books when they were fourteen and fifteen and eighteen. So *that* love never changes. See, I still love Edgar Rice Burroughs—I can't read him, but I wouldn't dream to insult him, because he made my life worthwhile.

—RB, March 14, 2002

36 "Make Haste to Live"

The Park Hyatt Hotel in Century City was only a few blocks north of Bradbury's Cheviot Hills home. On a Wednesday night in mid-June 1999, he made the short journey there to attend the 25th annual Saturn Awards ceremony, where he received the George Pal Memorial Award for contributions to the motion picture genre fields recognized by the Academy of Science Fiction, Fantasy, and Horror Films. He was no stranger to these ceremonies, having won a 1983 Saturn for his screenplay of *Something Wicked This Way Comes* (the film itself was another Saturn winner for Best Fantasy Film). His connections went even deeper, however; a quarter-century earlier, he had presented the Best Fantasy Film Award to George Pal himself and, after his friend's passing, Bradbury also gave the first George Pal Memorial lecture for the Academy in 1981. It was not unusual for Bradbury to have a history of friendships and interactions with more and more of the various film and literary institutions that were beginning to honor him.

That same year, four authors became the 1999 inductees into the Science Fiction Hall of Fame. Bradbury and Robert Silverberg were inducted along with two posthumous honorees, Abe Merritt and Jules Verne. This companionship with the dead absolutely thrilled him; these were two writers he had wanted to join on the bookshelves of libraries since the early 1930s. He went so far as to assemble little books from successive installments of Abe Merritt novels in the pages of *Argosy*, and meeting Merritt in his New York office the day before the 1939 WorldCon was a high point of the trip. He had read Verne through the various translations found in the family households and libraries of his youth; nearly four decades after writing his popular Bantam Books preface to *20,000 Leagues Under the Sea*, his true payment had finally arrived through the companionship of the Science Fiction Hall of Fame, class of 1999.

By the end of the twentieth century, Bradbury had collected most of the master awards of the genres where he had been inspirational or influential, even though he rarely played by the established rules of those genres. National recognition had come early in his career, but always within the context of the genres that he and others were unconsciously elevating into the literary mainstream. Two O. *Henry Prize* anthology appearances in the 1940s, and four selections for the *Best American Short Story* annuals in the 1940s and 1950s, had showcased some of his best early tales. In his mind, the most significant of these early recognitions was the thousand-dollar grant he received at the June 1954 National Institute of Arts and Letters award ceremony in New York.

Yet even there, he had been celebrated for his accomplishments in "the genre of popular weird tales, especially that new sort known as space fiction." It was indeed hard for the literary establishment to position him at mid-century, but Bradbury took great satisfaction that the 1954 Academy citation was honoring him for endowing these genre traditions with "a complexity and intensity and strange beauty that lift much of his work to a level very close to that of poetry."[1] These words, spoken on an auditorium stage filled with many of the most influential writers and critics of the day, had marked a bright place in the sun very early in his career.

The twentieth century ended just weeks after Bradbury's November 1999 stroke permanently limited his mobility. He was now seventy-nine years old, and he was not yet sure how this trauma would affect the heavy agenda of projects, some dating back to the 1940s and 1950s, that he desperately wanted to complete. But the millennial year brought a lifetime of honor into one evening—Bradbury was to receive a National Book Foundation Medal for Distinguished Contribution to American Letters at the National Book Award ceremonies in New York on November 15, 2000.

During the year he had recovered enough strength to make lecture appearances that required travel, including two days of lectures and discussion in June at Butler University in Indianapolis. But ten days before the National Book Award ceremony, he suddenly and permanently lost all vision in his left eye. Three days later, on November 7th, Bradbury faxed the news to Neil Baldwin, executive director of the National Book Foundation, noting that the cause was a burst blood vessel.[2] His doctors were evaluating the possibility that air travel might lead to further damage in either eye, and he expressed doubts to Baldwin that he would be able to make the trip to the ceremony.

Bradbury began to cancel his flight reservations to New York but suddenly changed his mind. There was no real thought process, just intuition; as he observed to his good friend, film critic Charles Champlin, six months later, "Then I said the magical right thing: 'To Hell with it!' and went to New York anyway." His reflection had been prompted by the news that Champlin had just been diagnosed with macular degeneration, and Bradbury offered encouragement through his own recent example. "I made it through and it was a wonderful time, even though I only saw half of what went on; still, it was glorious."

And glorious it was, prompting Bradbury to compress many of his favorite anecdotes into one somewhat overlong backward glance at the good fortune and opportunities of his creative life. He began with a passing allusion to his loss of vision, his gradual but now complete loss of hearing in his left ear, and the effects of the previous year's stroke. "I have one good eye, one good ear, one good leg, and there's other things missing, but I'm afraid to look." Only his attending friends knew the prognosis of permanent vision loss in his left eye; these included his agent Don Congdon, who looked after Bradbury during his time in New York, his longtime Knopf editor Kathy Hourigan, and his current editor, Jennifer Brehl, who had skillfully navigated Bradbury's transition—along with his Avon and William Morrow publishers—into the HarperCollins publishing universe. Donn Albright, now the primary witness and celebrant of his life, was also a special guest that evening.[3]

It was an overwhelming experience for Bradbury, a chance to give a full and rapid-fire summary of his unexpected life in literature and film. Host-presenter Steve Martin played off of Bradbury's performance with good-natured humorous asides as the evening continued, and there was a general atmosphere of implied respect for the pure emotional honesty of his words. Certain key observations by Bradbury had kept his words from spiraling down into pure sentimental hyperbole; he managed this by framing his comments around the great writers who influenced him. "I wouldn't be here except that they spoke to me in the library." He told the stories of how The Martian Chronicles and Fahrenheit 451 were born and named those who helped him bring these books out to the world.

Predictably, his last story that evening turned to the Great Tale, and the triumph of the Apollo 11 Moon landing. Under the pressure of time (he had long since exceeded his time limit), Bradbury did manage to compress his sense of humanity's purpose into a few words: "There's no use having a universe, a cosmology, if you don't have witnesses. We are the witnesses to the miracle."

This was the first great and undisputable national award he had received, given without any kind of genre reservation whatsoever. For decades, he had been fascinated by that young writer he had once been, early in his career, growing out of that naive young boy who suddenly discovered, in a 1920s Illinois town, what it meant to be alive. Now, finally, through the symbolism of this medallion, he realized who the older man had become. "Along the way, I've located myself. Tonight I can look in the mirror and say to myself, My God, who's that there? Why, that's Ray Bradbury."

: : :

In spite of his traditional values he had always been antiauthoritarian at heart, and the receipt of the National Book Foundation Medal naturally led him to look back at moments when he had criticized or disputed the establishment. Now, with a lifetime literary honor at the turn of the century, he looked back to a moment when he had outright defied the climate of fear that permeated mid-century America. To do so with a sense of objectivity, he needed the help of Leon Uris, one of the few writers who had shared his views and actions the night they had resisted a Writers Guild of America West blacklist vote in 1954.

Bradbury had not seen Uris since, but he knew that his old friend remembered. In the late 1990s, after a lecture, Uris's daughter came up and introduced herself to him. His first words to her were: "Has your father told you?" She knew what he meant, and they had a brief discussion of what had occurred that summer 1954 evening in the Crystal Room of the Beverly Hills Hotel. In the spring of 2001, just months after receiving his medal, he wrote to Uris to see if his oft-told version of that evening was indeed accurate, after all these years.

> That night has burned itself in my memory because I recall on the first vote we writers turned down the producers who wanted us to guarantee our appearance before the Un-American Activities Committee. We rejected the offer, at which time Borden Chase, our president, leapt to his feet and cried, "We must have another vote," even though such a vote was illegal. The first vote was a private ballot and the second vote that he insisted on was an open vote with cards held up. When they took the vote, our membership reversed themselves and voted to give away their rights to the producers, at which time I leapt to my feet and cried "Cowards, where is your vote now?" You were on your feet with me and perhaps another dozen other people among the hundreds of writers there that evening that gave away their rights. Borden Chase pointed at me and shouted, "Throw that man out!" I said, "Don't bother, I'll throw myself out." I went outside, sick at heart, and didn't go to another meeting for quite a while. . . .

In gathering his memories for Uris, Bradbury wrote what may have been the longest and most detailed version he had ever given, in spoken or written form. In its main points, his recollection agrees with the very brief side note published in the Hollywood Reporter shortly after the vote.[4] But a response from Uris has never been found; Uris died two years later.

More echoes from Bradbury's encounters with mid-century America's climate of fear surfaced later that same year, in the bridges between the novelized stories of his next book. The long-deferred gathering of his supernatural Elliott family stories finally reached print in the fall of 2001 under the title From the Dust Returned. The five core stories of the Elliott saga were written from 1946 to 1952, and four reached print during that period of his career. This short series of tales had exploded onto the literary scene in the October 1946 issue of Mademoiselle magazine with "Homecoming," subsequently selected for the 1947 *O. Henry Prize Stories* volume.

"Homecoming" stands as the defining tale of the Elliott's eternal world, as this extended family of vampires, shape-shifters, werewolves, masters of mind control, and other outré relatives gather for a generational reunion in the family's old Wisconsin country mansion. The central consciousness belongs to Timothy, a normal human foundling who has become a much-loved child of these immortals. They love him in spite of his inability to transform or enchant, in spite of his diurnal habits and his aversion to drinking blood. They also grieve for him, knowing that someday, he will do something they cannot—he will age and die.

Dark Carnival (1947), Bradbury's first story collection, contained "Homecoming," "Uncle Einar," and "The Traveler"; a fourth Elliott tale was cut in proofs, finally reaching print forty years later in *The Toynbee Convector* as "West of October." "The April Witch," a further tale of Cecy, the teenage mind-projecting enchantress of the family, reached print in the April 5, 1952, issue of the *Saturday Evening Post*. His early attempts to present these episodic tales as an illustrated book met with no success, but it was hard for him to move on from this idea.

By the time of his mid-1990 move to Avon Books, he had a new armature concept to support full development of the Elliotts into a novelized story cycle. He was working with far fewer stories than had gone into *The Martian Chronicles* or *Dandelion Wine*, so he developed bridging interchapters to tell the back story and characteristics of certain characters. For thematic unity and dramatic focus, Bradbury turned back to the mid-century world of conformity that seemed to threaten freedom of the imagination in postwar America.

The Elliott stories were peripheral to the tales he wrote to criticize authoritarian tendencies of that day, but they represented the kind of story that he felt was most at risk: supernatural fiction, both old and new. In such late 1940s stories as "Pillar of Fire," "Carnival of Madness" ("Usher II"), and "The Mad Wizards of Mars" ("The Exiles"), Bradbury made it clear that the works of Poe, Bierce, Lovecraft, and even Hawthorne were the first that would be condemned. His own early successes with light horror and supernatural fiction were in that category, and it was only a small step to breathe the memories of those days into the structure of the new novelization.

Bradbury appropriated another *Toynbee Convector* story, "On the Orient, North," to anchor the center of the book; it dealt with a Ghastly Traveler of the supernatural who must flee the growing disbelief of the modern world. He confides his story to an elderly nurse who has been asked to tend his dying moments on the Orient Express: "With the populations and disbeliefs doubling by the day, all of my specter friends have fled. Where, I know not, I am the last, trying to train across Europe to some safe, rain-drenched castle keep where men are properly frightened by soots and smokes of wandering souls."

Along with two new bridges, "On the Orient, North" forms the central core of the emerging novelization as chapters 12–14. The two bridges bring the threat of intolerance directly into the world of the Elliott family. Many of the Elliott family members return to the shelter of the reunion home; some never left after the Homecoming at all. Mortal Timothy is the first to realize his vast adoptive family exists only because they are manifest in the human imagination and in the old cautionary tales of the great religions. In a world of disbelief, which is often a world of intolerance, they will no longer exist.

Forewarned is forearmed, but how will the Elliotts survive? Bradbury mixed a newer seventh story into the closing bridges to form two chapters; in the first of these, the family's matriarch, the Egyptian mummy known as A Thousand Times Great Grandmere, reveals the essential tragedy of their fate in the modern world: "But what have we done?" cries Timothy. "Nothing," replies the matriarch. "We have survived, is all. And those who come to drown us are envious of our lives lived for so many centuries. Because we are different, we must be washed away."

"Make Haste to Live" is the Elliott family motto. What has happened to the genre classics of the supernatural puts all creativity at risk. Here was another Bradbury echo, refashioned for the new century. The real danger isn't burning; it's indifference on one hand, willful intellectual blindness on the other. Bradbury dedicated *From the Dust Returned* to Don Congdon and Jennifer Brehl, who waited patiently until Bradbury unified these stories. Only 8 of the 23 chapters were derived from published stories, however; could the fifteen bridging chapters form an integrated whole? The *Publisher's Weekly* reviewer felt that through the sustained sense of wonderment, "the stories retain as an integrated whole their original freshness and charm."

Edward Bryant left that question asked but unanswered in his *Locus* review, and few others addressed it at all. The main concern centered on the question of balance. The Kirkus reviewer found it "A far cry from the great early stories but filled with a nostalgic charm that vitiates Bradbury's notorious rhetorical laxness and sentimentality." Writing for the *New York Times*, Mary Elizabeth Williams found it a "slim volume," but respected the "wistful meditations on the fragile preciousness of life. For Bradbury, the most bewitching force in the universe is human nature." As a young storyteller, he had found his narrative voice and truthful style exploring what makes us human. Once again, he had returned to the familiar harbor of his earliest success and found safe moorings.

37 Messages in a Bottle

Bradbury's work on his first story collection of the new century began sometime before his November 4, 1999, stroke in Palm Springs. When the stroke occurred, his longtime driver Patrick Kachurka overcame Bradbury's determination to go two hours home to Los Angeles and took him to the local hospital in time for effective treatment. Soon after his transfer to a Santa Monica hospital near his home, and while still largely immobile, he worked with his daughter Alexandra as much as his gradual recovery permitted.[1] On November 23rd, while still hospitalized, Bradbury settled on a thirty-story table of contents aptly titled, as the old century came to an end, *One More for the Road*.

In the months ahead, he and Alexandra developed a new working dynamic of long-distance dictation, transcription, and successive cycles of faxed typescript revisions that focused on the two novel-length projects that he had developed to a fairly advanced stage of composition prior to the stroke, *From the Dust Returned* and *Let's All Kill Constance!* Work on the story collection was deferred until early 2001; on January 30th, Jenny Brehl sent him a reduced twenty-story version of the contents, noting that she had restored some of her favorites, and leaving the door open for Bradbury to restore any of his favorites that might have been cut.

He moved some in and out again, finally adding five stories that had evolved from events in his adult life, rounding out a final twenty-five-title table of contents. In the process, he deferred to Brehl's suggestion that "The Year the Glop-Monster Won the Golden Lion at Cannes" (1966) might fare better as "The Dragon Danced at Midnight," an allusion to the story's twenty-four-reel film that, when re-sequenced by a blind-drunk projectionist, launches the improbably successful avant-garde filmmaking careers of two obscure producers.

For decades, Bradbury had periodically lampooned the avant-garde in literature and the arts, and the title story, "One More for the Road," offered a variation through the resurrection of the once ubiquitous Burma-Shave highway boards extended across the entire country to carry, instead, the full text of a great new novel. The cross-country construction is cheered by grassroots fans, condemned by critics and roadside landowners, pirated by the internet, and finally left unfinished as the author succumbs to a transcontinental case of writer's block.

But the title story and the few other superficially satirical stories in the volume masked the deeper revelations of the collection. On one level, *One More for the Road* represented yet another collection crafted largely, with the help of Donn Albright, around much earlier uncollected and even unpublished tales from the richly imaginative early years of Bradbury's career. "With Smiles as Wide as Summer," a latter-day attempt to recall the great bounding and smiling canines who ran with him through the wild ravine and the neighborhood yards of his Greentown, demonstrated that, once in a while, he could still effectively evoke the controlled nostalgia of Midwest childhood. Such new prose gems were few and far between, however, and would all but disappear in the years that remained to him.

Perhaps more than any of his other late-life collections, *One More for the Road* reveals an author examining moments of his personal and professional life that represented decision points for paths taken and not taken. Throughout his career, he had written about the fascinating variations in the lives of lovers, spouses, parents, and children, and his what-ifs gathered here contemplate personal moments. Can one rekindle the unconditional love for a spouse ("Heart Transplant")? Can one make amends for mistakes of the heart and earn forgiveness ("Well, What Do You Have to Say for Yourself?")? Can one draw back from the brink of uncontrolled passion ("Beasts") or unbearable heartbreak ("Fore!")? How does one deal with a father's ghost, one who cannot recognize his own son ("The Nineteenth")?

Besides his gift for metaphor, Bradbury had the true storyteller's gift of empathy, and other stories in the collection offered fundamental insights into the human condition. There is almost a catcher-in-the-rye level of compassion for the elderly Jewish woman in Ocean Park who has lost her husband ("Tête-à-Tête") and steadfast support for the friends and former lovers of friends who cannot live without guidance from the ever-patient father-author ("Leftovers"). The legendary stage performer who has no energy left for a real life ("One Woman Show") slips into a terrifying vegetative state between performances, her secret guarded by her husband. The secret life of 1939 Los Angeles after midnight ("Tangerine"), the father who disowns his son for revealing his alternate lifestyle ("My Son, Max"), and the gifted young writer who has destroyed his God-given talent ("Quid Pro Quo") all leave deep marks on the reader.

Bradbury had faced health challenges throughout the 1990s, and the stroke forced him to face the challenge of writing through the kind of pain and limitations that had ended the careers of many of the authors he had read and loved. "The F. Scott Fitzgerald / Tolstoy / Ahab Accumulator" became the latest in a series of stories dating back to 1950 in which he sought alternative endings for these writers. But this new attempt to save four authors (including Ernest

Hemingway) acknowledges, through self-humbling humor and cliché, the impossibility of the task. The story is useful, however, in revealing that he could still adapt the Hemingway style (as explored in his mid-century Mexican tales and notes) and Melville's style (an echo of his successful *Moby Dick* script for John Huston), without taking himself too seriously. Bradbury was, after all, a regular judge in the International Hemingway Competition, occasionally with Hemingway's son Jack.[2]

Donn Albright had helped unearth "Time Intervening" ("Interim," 1947), a forerunner of "A Touch of Petulance," where timelines cross to reveal a glimpse of the future to a young man and his wife. Albright also recommended the unpublished stories brought forward from deep in time, including "Autumn Afternoon" (1947), "Where All Is Emptiness, There Is Room to Move" (1949), and "One-Woman Show" (1950). Two others, relics of Bradbury's mid-century response to McCarthyism and the climate of fear, had remained unpublished more by accident than intent. "The Enemy in the Wheat" was a fable of cold war anxiety, and the tension created by constant fear of The Bomb (the father) and the parallel countervailing impulses to live through the threat (the mother) or to stand out from the enforced conformity of the early and mid-1950s (the son). "The Cricket on the Hearth" was Jennifer Brehl's favorite; it captured the nightmare of government surveillance in mid-century Hollywood, a threat that touched such good friends as his writing group colleague Sanora Babb and her husband, Academy Award–winning cinematographer James Wong Howe (Tom Lee in the story). Bradbury's principal characters, the fictitious producer John Martin and his wife, mirror the defiant response that Bradbury had offered during the climate of fear, with a twist that makes romance the casualty when the "cricket" is removed from their home.

The taste for excellent wines and the rich cultural discoveries that Ray and Maggie Bradbury regularly experienced in France for decades also percolated through the pages of *One More for the Road*. Beryl Veronique, the clinging old friend in "Leftovers," leads the thinly disguised Bradburys through memories of some of their favorite locales: Grand Cascade, country Hotellerie du Basbreau, Pierrefonds, Avillon, and such Hemingway locales as Place Vendôme and the Hotel Ritz.

These allusions provided nice biographical touches to an otherwise unremarkable story, but Bradbury developed a strikingly beautiful story of love and loss in "Diane de Forêt," based on Bradbury's actual 1989 encounter with the beautifully carved marble memorial for the eighteen-year-old "she of the forest" in the storied Père Lachaise cemetery; Bradbury created the entire story from the sculptor's inscription, carved in 1818:

So quickly she ran that only Death
could catch her.
My fortune was to know her for an hour
and love her,
in my life, forever.

The long-deceased sculptor, R.C., "Who has carved this relief | to shape her memory," was the creator of one of many memorials in this Paris cemetery that Bradbury had admired over the years, but it was the most riveting for him; his tears form a bridge with her spirit, prompting a dialog of thoughts and yearnings from both sides of the grave. Bradbury had visited the graves of the great writers and composers interred at Père Lachaise for decades—the grave of Hector Berlioz was a favorite—and he even wrote a poem about his unexpected encounter with the grave of Rock-era singer Jim Morrison, a name unfamiliar to him but known to everyone he encountered in the cemetery one day.

He did not know it yet, but all of his experiences in France, the expected and the unexpected, were now relegated to memories; he and Maggie would never be able to return. "Diane de Forêt" and "The Cricket on the Hearth" closed the new volume, and with this collection he now had published more than 380 distinct professional stories—400 tales counting his early amateur pieces. With revisions, retitling, and refashioning into story-chapters for various books over time, perhaps 600 versions of his stories existed in print. No one knew for sure.

Major reviews were few and far between for his later collections, but most reviewers of One More for the Road were mainly positive. Bradbury's rather enigmatic afterword did little to reveal the history of the sixteen unpublished stories or the nine that had appeared here and there, usually in specialized market periodicals.[3] Publisher's Weekly's reviewer found familiar themes ("memory, loneliness, childhood, love, and time"), and singled out the two childhood Greentown tales— "Autumn Afternoon" and the prose-poem qualities of "With Smiles as Wide as Summer"—as Bradbury at his best. Paul Goat Allen, writing in the very last print issue of the genre writers' magazine Explorations, noted the range of moods and the unifying exploratory nature of the collection, examining "the intricacies of the human condition . . . stamped with that unmistakable Bradbury wit and style."

Prolific Locus reviewer and critic Gary K. Wolfe observed that "Bradbury's true form is the collection more than the story," and this observation holds true for the entire range of his nonretrospective collections down through time. In the case of One More for the Road, as well as the two previous collections of the 1990s, Wolfe found the storytelling presented an archeological structure, "bent on preserving striking bits of image and dialogue even when the narrative structure to support them is barely there at all." The unity that Wolfe found in this new collection was based on a reassertion of some of Bradbury's hallmark themes—aging, survival, memory—bonded by Bradbury's increasingly detectable need to rescue the famous, the obscure, and the innocent.

Wolfe's analysis offered a way to see beneath the surface elements of Sameness in the stories of *One More for the Road*. In recent decades, other critics had fallen into the habit of simply reporting rather than interpreting a Bradbury collection before announcing a perceived thinness of material. Bradbury's collections had indeed always been carefully filled bottles, containing not one message but many related messages, washing up at intervals along the broad sands of time. Some good stories and story ideas remained; what wasn't clear was just how many bottles remained to be filled.

: : :

The spring 2002 nationwide release of *One More for the Road* coincided with events that confirmed Bradbury's enduring significance to a culture-shaping region of America that had been his home since 1934. The "One Book, One City" program, in many ways a precursor to Dana Gioia's NEA-sponsored "Big Read," had spotlighted *Fahrenheit 451* in several cities across the country. In March 2002, Mayor Richard Hahn celebrated the selection of *Fahrenheit 451* as the Los Angeles "One Book, One City" reading experience for the entire year. The ceremony was held March 13th in the downtown central library complex, now completely rebuilt after the devastating 1986 fire. Mayor Hahn presided as actor Joe Mantegna gave a very personal and substantive proclamation. Mantegna made time to meet privately with his old friend for close to an hour before the ceremony. Cell phones vibrated, but Bradbury had his undivided attention.

On April 1st, Bradbury was honored with the 2,193rd star on the Hollywood Walk of Fame, coinciding with the beginning of the monthlong "One Book, One City" events. For the ceremony he was able to stand and move about with the aid of his walker, flanked by longtime Hollywood friends Charlton Heston and Rod Steiger. Rarely does a star fall in place near an appropriate Hollywood Boulevard venue, but for many years Bradbury's star served as point of entry to a Hollywood landmark—the Larry Edmonds bookstore.

: : :

By the summer of 2002, Bradbury's third and final detective novel, *Let's All Kill Constance!*, was nearing completion. This was a short book, written in bursts between 1996 and 2003, and it represented the only novel he would begin without story antecedents since *A Graveyard for Lunatics* began to take form in the mid-1980s. These last two of his three late-life detective novels were, in fact, the only novels he *ever* wrote in this fashion, grown from a central image without the usual Bradbury evolution from short fiction origins.[4]

Legendary and reclusive silent film star Constance Rattigan is the great neo-romantic reflection of Bradbury's ultimate superwoman, evolving through the inspiration of Bernard Shaw's "Life Force" heroines found in such Shavian-Bradbury favorites as *Man and Superman*'s Ann Whitefield and Barbara Undershaft of *Major Barbara*. There is a Bradbury twist to Constance, of course, for she brings an aura of mystery, a will of iron, and unfathomable purposes to bear in all of her totally unpredictable actions throughout the three detective novels. But there is another overarching metaphor at play in this final volume, a collective fantasy that emerges from memories triggered by actually *reading*, rather than consulting, the timeworn pages of a very old telephone book.

High school yearbooks and telephone books had always represented an odd form of time machine for Bradbury. A phone book could represent comedy, as in his unpublished 1940s story, "All These Pages," where a down-and-out screenwriter manages to convince a Hollywood producer to film it with a cast of thousands. An old phone book could also trigger Bradbury's sense of sadness, as he recalled in a February 10, 1992, letter to his favorite British publisher, the aging Sir Rupert Hart-Davis:

> Maggie says to friends that I cry at telephone books. And indeed I do. My old phone books are full of lost and gone people. Why don't you throw them away, my daughters ask. I can't. I reply, it would be like a final memorial act. I imagine I want to keep the old telephone books to remember where I came from and those who helped me along the way.

As the century closed and he approached the age of eighty, Bradbury finally came to regard an old telephone book as a modern form of the ancient Egyptian Book of the Dead, a book of spells with the power to help the living navigate the dangerous journey into what Bradbury considered the eternal unknown. It was natural for him to nest the final mystery of Constance Rattigan's life in the Book of the Dead, with its origins early in ancient Egypt's New Kingdom and the time of his beloved King Tutankhamen. In Bradbury's mind, his early newspaper memory of the death mask of Tutankhamen anchored the fragile beauty of young faces he later discovered in art of the Renaissance, Neoclassic, and Romantic periods. "The young beauties fixed in place for all time," he had once described to Hart-Davis:

> The same experience we have, of course, isn't it, when we visit galleries and see the portraits of children from centuries past. The busts of men and boys

and girls from two thousand years ago in Greece and Rome especially move and hurt me. I spend a lot of time in museums finding quiet tears in my eyes. . . . I imagine it is part of the genetic gift God gave me when he sent me into the world to be his, one among many, recorder.[5]

Constance is indeed a striking beauty, aging and ageless at the same time. Her face, eyes and dark skin tone derived from memories of a high school friend from his ceramics class, a fun-loving and ever-smiling girl named Bingo. She had brown hair, brown eyes, and a richly uniform brownness to her skin tone that together fascinated Bradbury. Constance Rattigan, who swims at midnight with the playful seals of Santa Monica Sound, has the figure and features of Bingo— just Bingo, for Bradbury had uncharacteristically forgotten her last name.[6] As the novel's title character, however, Constance lives the secluded, Garbolike existence that Bradbury imagined for her in *Death Is a Lonely Business* and, very briefly, in *A Graveyard for Lunatics*.

In the first two murder novels, Bradbury gave Constance Rattigan a mysterious past, seemingly eternal beauty, and a habit of simply disappearing for long stretches of time—including half of the second novel. She represents an overarching mystery that Bradbury's writer-narrator may never be able to solve and must simply accept. Ultimately, this Modernist lack of resolution would not do for the neo-romantic author seeking to revisit the way he learned to examine the hidden depths of the human heart. As the third novel opens, Constance has disappeared, but as Bradbury's narrator-writer searches for her, he finds a trail of bodies—all people from her past. Once again, he teams up with his mentoring detective, Elmo Crumley, to find answers.

But "Young Writer" is the better detective now, and he leads the chase. Constance didn't kill the telephone people, even though they were all witnesses to the roles she played and the things she did to get those roles. She had killed all those memories once, building a mausoleum with tombs for each movie and its bitter memories, but the memories return when she is offered the one pure role she has never played—Shaw's Saint Joan. She tries but cannot kill these dark shades of her past a second time and retreats to her mausoleum of memories to die. Young Writer discovers her secret and tracks her hidden route through the great storm drains beneath Los Angeles, arriving at Forest Lawn just in time to revive her will to live.

It's an entertaining story, built on Bradbury's deep knowledge of very early Hollywood, acquired in real life by attending every film premier or revival in town and chasing down a thousand or more stars for autographs before he turned 20.[7] *Let's All Kill Constance!* is the least of the three experiments in autobiographical fiction, but it is also the most ambitious, as Young Writer brings the reader directly into his own mind. There are no clues, just the minute-by-minute experience of the writer, reported as action or dialog, and little else. What appears to be a murder story turns out to be a study of a woman in crisis, something he had not done in a sustained way since writing his early masterpieces, "The Next in Line" and "Interval in Sunlight." Less than a year after publication, he would reflect on this in private conversation:

> So the title means, not "Shall we all kill Constance?," but Constance is killing her various selves over a period of years. The book is much deeper than it seems, because it analyzes the various levels of a woman's life, and how she has to cleanse herself of all these various people that she's been until the book ends in the graveyard, where she's buried herself. She's gone there to die, and I've got to go in and convince her to come out and start a new life. And I've got to talk her out of the tomb to get her to go back down to the ocean.

He knew none of this as he began to write the novel. Writing from the same limited point of view as his characters sometimes left Bradbury with characters that did not understand their motivations and simply did not know where they were going. Sid Stebel returned to respond to the slow evolution of Constance and find the elusive ending, as he had done for the first two autobiographical mystery novels. In this way, Bradbury was able to give meaning to what had come dangerously close to becoming an emotional quagmire.

Let's All Kill Constance! was published in January 2003, and for much of the year he worked on another story collection for Jennifer Brehl. There wasn't much left to do on the old Illinois novel, maybe another year and a half or so, he figured; it would become the fifth book published since his stroke, with more projects on the horizon. The new year seemed to be opening out in promising ways.

38

The Fire Within

The spring and summer of 2003 held a surprise—one with origins almost sixty years in the past. During several weeks in October 1945, Ray Bradbury had breakfast most mornings in Mexico City with John Steinbeck. But the young Bradbury was too unsure of himself to tell Steinbeck that he too was a writer, and that missed opportunity would haunt him into the next century.

This was an improbable highlight of an improbable adventure—the twenty-five-year-old Bradbury was in the midst of a three-month odyssey through Mexico in the car of his traveling companion, Grant Beach. The two had been asked to collect Mexican masks for the Los Angeles County Museum, and Bradbury used some of the money he had earned by selling stories to three major market magazines—his first big break into the literary mainstream—to finance much of the trip. October found them in Mexico City, staying in a spacious rooming house at 76 Lerma Street.[1]

Siento Seis Lerma was perfect for an extended stay. The front courtyard was ornately gated, and the rooms opened onto a beautifully tiled patio in the rear. There was an upstairs study, but most encounters with other guests happened in the dining room. By an incredible coincidence, John Steinbeck and writer-producer Jack Wagner were staying at Siento Seis Lerma while making La Perla, a masterful Spanish language film adaptation of The Pearl. This was a challenging project for Steinbeck, but his table conversation was always easy and straightfor-ward, with the author's occasional hangover slowly dissipating in the morning air. Steinbeck's dog was also at the breakfast table, and Bradbury enjoyed the animal's obedience as well as its oddness—one eye was blue, the other brown.

He had read all of Steinbeck's works to that point, and the mark of the master storyteller he had found in those books had already inspired his own maturing style and honesty as a writer. From time to time, as his own career opened out, Bradbury thought of writing to tell John Steinbeck how much he had learned about writing from reading his novels and stories. Steinbeck's Nobel Prize came in 1962, and yet more years passed; in 1966, Bradbury was at long last preparing his letter when he heard of Steinbeck's death. This was now a circle of influence that could never be closed, the one time when his own sense of unworthiness had prevented an enduring connection with a writer he deeply respected. So often he had taken chances and reached out to make life-changing connections—John Huston, Bernard Berenson, Charles Laughton, and later Federico Fellini—but with Steinbeck he had hesitated, and all seemed lost.

Steinbeck was indifferent to science fiction, but he loved good storytelling no matter where he found it. Bradbury discovered this crucial Steinbeck trait quite unexpectedly in 2003. That spring he met Thomas Steinbeck, the older of the author's two sons, a film animator at heart who subsequently became an accomplished story writer and screenwriter. Now, at least, Bradbury could lay the ghost by telling his story of the father in the presence of the son. As Bradbury finished, Thomas Steinbeck revealed how the full connection had been made long ago; during the 1950s, John Steinbeck had read Ray Bradbury stories to both of his sons.

Thomas Steinbeck soon followed up with his own Bradbury reading chronicle, related in a five-page letter dated June 27, 2003. As young boys, he and his brother had encountered Bradbury through their father's time-honored practice of selecting readings for holidays and seasons, and the summer story was, invariably, "The Lake." After Bradbury began to publish his Irish tales in the late 1950s, John Steinbeck would read his boys "The Great Collision of Monday Last" for Saint Patrick's Day.

The Halloween story was "The Emissary," for Steinbeck dearly loved dogs, even supernatural ones, but he also felt a more direct connection; like Bradbury (and the young boy in "The Emissary"), John Steinbeck had been bedridden for a long period as a child, relying on Mr. Pins, his wire-haired terrier, to relieve the boredom, just as Bradbury had depended on his own dog to sense the smells and furborne dust and leaves of the outside world.[2] In late winter, when Hollywood honored writers and filmmakers with annual Oscars, John Steinbeck would read his boys "The Wonderful Death of Dudley Stone," Bradbury's great cautionary tale for writers who lived only for fame.

How had John Steinbeck come across Bradbury's work? It was *The Martian Chronicles*, Thomas said. "He too designed larger works from shorter stories and truly appreciated the complexity of the process." The stories and story-bridges in the *Chronicles* that described successive waves of migration out to Mars resonated with the American westward migrations fictionalized in *The Grapes of Wrath* and *The Long Valley*; the elder Steinbeck especially liked the inter-chapter bridge titled "The Naming of Names" and "The Million Year Picnic," Bradbury's closing chapter of a final return to Mars after Earth has been ravaged by war. From then on, Steinbeck followed Bradbury's career from a distance, and shared favorite tales with his sons.

Yet it was the joy of the little boys discovering Bradbury that dominated many of Thomas Steinbeck's reading reflections; here was a mirror image of a boy discovering the world of stories and longer fictions, very much like the way reading had shaped Bradbury's own growth into the writer he would become. Thomas's favorite Bradbury Halloween story was "The Scythe," and his father would allow it to replace "The Emissary" every other year for the October reading. "I think it was secretly my father's favorite, but he would read "The Emissary" to appease his own beloved ghosts." The first Bradbury story that John Steinbeck gave his elder son to read had been "The Flying Machine," from *The Golden Apples of the Sun*. Over time, it became a generational gift. "I have read it in turn to hundreds of kids over the years. The damn thing still works like a Swiss watch."

In a single moment, the revelations of Thomas Steinbeck's letter erased one of the greatest regrets of Bradbury's life. This news came as Bradbury was working with Jennifer Brehl and the Congdons on another story collection and the long-deferred Illinois novel. The unasked question would center on whether or not that novel, so closely tied to *Dandelion Wine*, would signal the return of the master storyteller of old—the storyteller that John Steinbeck had come to admire from afar. The answer would be supplied by critics and, to some extent, by the internal evidence of the stories themselves.

∴ ∴ ∴

A second surprise awaited him in the summer of 2003. Bradbury's 83rd birthday was perhaps the most memorable birthday of his later years, for it nearly coincided with a perihelic opposition of Mars—the Red Planet's closest annual approach to the sun (perihelion), coinciding with its closest approach to the Earth. In fact, this would be the closest approach of Mars to Earth in almost 60,000 years.

Bradbury had most clearly advocated, in his early fiction and in a lifetime of essays, interviews, and lectures, that *we* are the Martians of a future day. With Spirit and Opportunity only months from reaching Mars, The Planetary Society combined Bradbury's birthday and the perihelic opposition into a single celebration on August 23rd in the Jet Propulsion Laboratory at Caltech.[3] Thanks to an effective internet campaign, Bradbury received a birthday card commensurate with the combined event. It was fifteen feet long and included electronically transmitted congratulations from such space program figures as Apollo 11's Buzz Aldrin and Dr. Chris McKay at NASA Ames, cofounder of the Mars Underground research initiative. Hollywood well-wishers included Nichelle Nichols, Angie Dickinson, Charlton and Lydia Heston, George Lucas, Steven Spielberg, James Cameron, and Peter Hyams. The card was presented to Bradbury by Hyams, who was in the preproduction phase of the challenging work involved in extending Bradbury's classic time-travel tale, "A Sound of Thunder," for feature film adaptation.

Call-in greetings came from science fiction writers David Brin and Stephen Barnes; Kim Stanley Robinson attended in person, revealing to Bradbury that he, too, was a Waukegan-born Martian. Robinson's Mars trilogy of the 1980s was in the vanguard of the influential Martian novels that followed Bradbury's era, without supplanting him. Everyone was celebrating the life of a dreamer whose dreams were beginning to come true. But there was yet one more surprise— spoken, but never published. In his remarks that evening, Bradbury revealed his final dream of the Great Tale.

> Some night, a hundred years from now, there will be a boy on Mars reading late at night by flashlight, under the covers. He will look out over the Martian landscape, which will be bleak and rocky and red, and not very romantic; but when he turns out the light and lies with a copy of my book, I hope, *The Martian Chronicles*, the winds of Mars outside will stir, and the ghosts that are in my book will rouse up, and my creatures, even though they never lived, will be on Mars.

This late summer 2003 celebration came just months after Bradbury and Maggie had watched the news of the loss of *Columbia* and its crew on reentry to the Earth's atmosphere after a successful eight-day mission—a mission unknowingly doomed from the moments after launch when critical heat shield components broke loose from the left ventral wing surface. The summer birthday celebration for Bradbury, and the party's anticipation of the Spirit and Opportunity Mars landings to come a few short months ahead, provided an important moment of recovery for all. It was perhaps providential that at this moment of gratification and celebration, Bradbury did not know what was just beyond the horizon of his life—this would be the last birthday he would be able to celebrate with Maggie, who would pass away after a brief illness in November.

Theirs had been a bookstore romance; in the spring of 1946, her employer at Fowlers had asked her to watch the strange young man with his overcoat and briefcase, in case he turned out to be a shoplifter. Their romance included exchanges of books, and Bradbury soon learned to appreciate her vast passion for reading, one that was even greater than his own. She was, simply, a compulsive reader, and a wide-ranging one. She attributed this focus to being an only child, and she began to read at the age of four. She read much faster than he did, but she appreciated her husband's ability to retain what he read.[4]

Maggie also retained everything she read, and their household was richer for her knowledge of European history, literature, and languages. She was the center of the household, managing six complicated lives with wisdom and discipline. But she was also inward-turning, and there was nothing she liked better than to curl up with a good book. In the early days, Maggie typed his final submitted copy of *The Martian Chronicles* while carrying to term their first daughter, Susan. She read and critiqued his books, and he valued her opinion in ways that the public would never know. There were tensions and sometimes long silences, but love was never questioned. He missed her dearly.

: : :

The Planetary Society's Bradbury event was designed to be the prelude to the Society's next Planetfest, scheduled for January 3 and 4, 2004, to coincide with the touchdown of the rover Spirit within the Gusev Crater of Mars. The Fest's title theme was "Wild about Mars," to commemorate as well the nearly simultaneous flyby of Comet Wild-2 by the *Stardust* probe. But Spirit would be the main attraction, and Bradbury, still recovering from his wife's passing, was able to attend and enjoy this milestone at the center of events, just as he had been featured at the *Viking* 1 landing more than a quarter-century earlier.

The Pasadena Convention Center hosted "Wild about Mars," with live landing status feeds provided directly from the JPL's nearby Mission Control Center. Bradbury was present as actor John Rhys-Davies, who had participated in Bradbury's "An Evening on Mars" several years earlier, flew in from England to dramatize selections from Bradbury's works. *Star Trek Voyager*'s Robert Picardo, another "Evening on Mars" veteran, joined Bradbury on stage for a tribute to Space exploration.[5] All this culminated in the main event; Spirit's touchdown was confirmed shortly after 8:20 p.m. local time. Opportunity would reach Mars later in January; no one knew that the two rovers would have remarkably long lives, far in excess of mission planning and design specifications.

Bradbury's own dreams of Mars were now more than seventy years old, dating back to the early pulps he absorbed, along with the Martian romances of Edgar Rice Burroughs and the speculations of Percival Lowell, in the late 1920s and early 1930s. Fittingly, he was joined that evening by Forry Ackerman, who had opened up the world of science fiction fandom to him through the Los Angeles Science Fiction League chapter in 1937. Ackerman, now 87 and slowly recovering from a debilitating stroke in 2002, represented a mirror of sorts. Bradbury's own recovery from his 1999 stroke was not a level path; there were times early on when he could navigate short distances with a cane, but the two major Planetary Society events of 2003 and 2004 were navigated by walker and wheelchair. His hearing was gone in one ear, and more and more powerful hearing aids amplified what remained in the other. He had no sight in his left eye; Bradbury could sign his name once again, free of the thumbprint pad he had used for a while, and he pursued that task for his fans like a racehorse, often beyond endurance.

For the last dozen years of his public life, his bully pulpit would emanate from a chair, but it really didn't matter; the fire within still burned.

: : :

During 2004, Bradbury would publish The Cat's Pajamas, his second story collection in the span of two years. With One More for the Road, critics had tended to cast about and identify noteworthy stories, wondering if the interesting ones were older tales revised and lightly touched by the author, or newer surprises. The mystery was no longer veiled in the new collection, with stories arranged in the order of composition and titles suffixed with dates provided by long-deferred file folders or the basement office sleuthing of Donn Albright.

The title story for The Cat's Pajamas was emblematic of the household he and Maggie had shared for years with generations of cats. That story was cliché turned fiction: a young man and woman meet over a forlorn kitten lost on a seldom-used desert highway. They each claim it, and the extended argument (from highway to diner to hotel, with kitten as chaperone) extends to dawn. The story is entertaining, sentimental, playfully suspenseful, short, and almost entirely composed in dialog. It was also the norm for the later stories, varying in situation from suspense to satire, but generally anecdotal spotlights for the Bradbury style.

Ironically, most of the later stories had the feel of the early 1950s, reflecting the humor and sensibilities of his prime years. The older stories, on the other hand, were less predictable and carried deeper emotional consequences. "Chrysalis" was not the 1946 science fiction story of that title, but a study in racial intolerance dating from the same period. "The Island" is a fable of the mid-century climate of fear, a house where every member of the family lives in isolation and will not help each other when a small creature enters their individual rooms and kills them all, one by one.

Other stories from mid-century include "Transformation," a story of just consequences for a terrible hate crime, and "A Matter of Taste," which explores the reactions of a terrified Earth crew at the moment of first contact with a gentle civilization of eight-foot-tall spiders. This lost story was actually the thematic forerunner of his 1953 science fiction film, It Came from Outer Space. Once again, the older tales that Donn Albright had unearthed from the basement files accounted for half the stories in The Cat's Pajamas. As in all the collections from the 1970s on, these long-deferred stories served to fill in the gaps in Bradbury's storytelling history from a time when he was at the top of his game.

39 A Child's Imagination

"The children, knowing that their future is in space, will say to their parents, 'Do it.'"

As he spoke these words, Ray Bradbury's image was center stage on a giant screen in the auditorium of the Galileo Academy of Science and Technology in San Francisco. Galileo's gifted high school students were on spring break, however, and Bradbury was actually addressing a public audience—his image was flanked on stage by the commissioners of the 2004 Presidential Commission on Moon, Mars and Beyond. This April event was the fourth public hearing held by the president's commission, and Bradbury, speaking remotely from Los Angeles, was the lead witness on Friday, April 15th.

The commission's San Francisco session was a special hearing scheduled to gather testimony from entertainment figures closely involved with the Space Age; Bradbury's presence underlined the perspective summarized by Commission Chair Edward C. "Pete" Aldridge Jr., former Secretary of the Air Force: "I don't need to tell anyone how many people get their information about space from novels, films, and even video games." The other eight commissioners flanking Bradbury's giant image on stage included Carly Fiorina, then serving as CEO of Hewlett-Packard, other major figures in the advancement of Space technologies, three prominent planetary scientists, and astrophysicist Neil De Grasse Tyson, director of the Hayden Planetarium, who was himself beginning to move between the worlds of scientific and media-based educational endeavors.

As the day's session began, the large-screen Bradbury-centered tableau, with empaneled commissioners looking up at him from both sides of the stage, offered yet another forum for his view that religion and science were now on the same pathway in seeking answers to the mysteries of life on this planet and beyond. The scene was strangely reminiscent of other focused quests for meaning—Da Vinci's Last Supper, Raphael's School of Athens, even the initial televised press conference lineup of the original seven Mercury astronauts. In essence, this was yet another chance for Bradbury to bring his well-rehearsed clarion call into the far more pragmatic process of decision-making that would make or break the long-dormant efforts to renew human voyages beyond Earth orbit. But this hearing also documented Bradbury's last adjustments to the vision of exploration and discovery that had replaced his stories about space nearly four decades earlier.

In his last notable science fiction stories—1950s tales such as "The Gift," "Icarus Montgolfier Wright," and "The End of the Beginning"—he had captured the aspirations of children, adolescents, and young adults as they step into the very first moments of the Space Age. In the following decades, he had stepped away from fiction to revisit the great age of exploration and settlement that had, ultimately, positioned the United States for leadership in the race to other worlds. His comments before the commission went back to this vision of discovery and exploration that had created—often at great cost to the indigenous cultures—the 500-year rise of a great space-faring power. It was an abbreviated history in the traditional framework, noting (without allusion to earlier Norse explorations) that Verrazzano may have made the first continental landing near Kitty Hawk, 400 years before the Wright Brothers sparked another century of flight and space exploration on those same dunes:

> Now we are called upon, in viewing the Moon and Mars, to guess ahead 500 years. That's almost an impossible task, but we must try to do it, try to imagine that the Moon is a base and Mars as a new landing place, and a creation for civilization will burgeon in the next 500 years, 1,000 years, and 10,000 years, and become the center of a new frontier. It will move outward some day to Alpha Centauri.
>
> Why? Because life wants to exist, wants to survive, and wants to be free of the conflicts of Earth even as America when it was created was free from the conflicts of Europe. So, we're going into space to be free of the politics and conflicts of the various nations and to become one new nation on the planet Mars. I can think of nothing more exciting to all the children of the world and to their parents who are infected by the joy and the love of their children for space.

The commission's website had already received nearly four million hits, and the thousands of largely positive commentaries were still mixed with an expressed desire to solve Earth's terrestrial problems first; the commissioners' questions for Bradbury pressed gently for some pragmatic insight. "It has to be sold on an aesthetic level," he insisted, "on a level of relating ourselves to the universe and to the gift of life, which we wish to solve, and to preserve." As always, Bradbury implicitly accepted the gamble that a struggle against the universe would replace war rather than inflame conflict in a rush for riches. Quite simply, he saw planetary exploration as "a new freedom, a new movement away from the politics and the horror and the terror of Earth." He was, after all, the first Martian.

Neil De Grasse Tyson asked if there might be consequences for leaving the problems of Earth unsolved in the next great age of space exploration. Others asked Bradbury to envision practical results that might sell the concept of space travel. But Bradbury's vision worked differently; from his perspective, his job was to inspire, to follow his self-defined philosophy of "optimal behaviorism." Other prominent science fiction writers, especially those with technical and scientific backgrounds, might have envisioned the kind of selling points sought by the commissioners. There were many such "hard SF" writers, and more than a few of the younger ones had started out reading Bradbury's dreams as they began to fashion their own. Yet the commission wanted Bradbury; out of more than 180 witnesses called to the various open sessions, he was the only writer. He was a talisman, and his place in the Great Tale was based on what he meant to the younger men and women who would build and journey.

By now, Bradbury was used to this role. His testimony for President George W. Bush's 2004 Moon, Mars and Beyond commission came two decades after he testified for the NASA commission established under the Reagan administration. As always, Bradbury spoke with the voice and style of a seer, but he had no technical or scientific facility, and no way to see into the short-term consequences of the broader world of domestic and international decision-making affecting the future of the space program. Privately, and occasionally in public, he would voice his grudging hunch that the next flag planted on the Moon might just be Chinese; this possibility was made all the more irksome by his perception that China's Cultural Revolution had done as much in its own way to destroy the wisdom of culture, education, and history as any of the twentieth century's totalitarian regimes that came before.

What he could not have known in 2004, or even at his death in 2012, was that the questions he was asked by the presidential commission of 2004 reflected a major shift toward full partnership with private sector technology. It would take many years to evolve, extending throughout the decade after Bradbury's passing, but the work of this commission set the stage for a merging of NASA, military, and private sector initiatives intended to move ahead in the international race to establish a lunar base as prelude to human-capable missions to Mars.

Yet Bradbury's commentary on the power of a child's imagination was not lost on the commission. At the end of Bradbury's testimony, Chairman Pete Aldridge returned to that point: "I'm struck by the fact that one of the tasks that we've had is how do we sustain this program over decades in the future, and you reminded me that those decades will be lived by our children and we ought to listen to their vote."

: : :

His April 2004 appearance before the Presidential Commission soon became prelude to an unexpected and far more distinctive presidential honor. In mid-November, assisted by Patrick Kachurka and accompanied by three of his daughters, Bradbury traveled to the White House to receive the Presidential Medal of Arts from President George W. Bush and First Lady Laura Bush—an educator who already knew the value of Bradbury's books and stories in the lives of readers young and old. He brought the First Family a copy of his latest story collection, *The Cat's Pajamas*, covered with the fanciful dust-jacket cluster of cat faces that he himself had drawn; whimsical but controlled graphic art had been a lifelong talent that his stroke-limited hand could always overcome. Laura Bush kept *The Cat's Pajamas* with her White House readings, but the timeless summer discoveries of *Dandelion Wine* formed her favorite Bradbury experience back home in Texas. The following summer, he sent her a newer copy of *Dandelion Wine* for the White House.

Bradbury was one of seven recipients for 2004; it was a broadly inclusive honors list that recognized American dance legend Twyla Tharp, wildlife artist John Ruthven, the late sculptor Frederick Hart, architectural historian Vincent Scully, opera virtuoso Carlisle Floyd, and poet Anthony Hecht. Bradbury was the only recipient who had no formal training or education in his fields of achievement, but he had been deeply influenced by the artistic traditions represented by *every* other recipient—sometimes through the guidance of mentors such as Bernard Berenson and Charles Laughton, yet just as often self-discovered and self-studied. And like the others, Bradbury's broad cultural impact fit the foundational purpose of the National Medal of Arts—the recognition of those who "are deserving of special recognition by reason of their outstanding contributions to the excellence, growth, support and availability of the arts in the United States."

The responsibility for advisement and stewardship of the award originated with the National Endowment for the Arts. The NEA chair, award-winning American poet and writer Dana Gioia, was also present at the White House ceremony. In many ways, the broad range of award recipients represented the cultural awareness that Gioia and his staff brought to the consideration of artists and art patrons who had shaped the arts of the century just past. Gioia knew Bradbury's work well and understood Bradbury's impact as a writer who had been pivotal in the elevation of traditional genre literature into mainstream culture while also successfully adapting his work for a wide range of film, stage, and television ventures.

Gioia's recognition of Bradbury's impact on literature did not end with the 2004 White House event, however; as Bradbury received his National Medal of Arts, Gioia's recent release of the NEA's "Reading at Risk" report was already paving the way for The Big Read, the largest program in literature ever funded by the federal government. The prototype Big Read of 2006 became a fully national grant program for communities in 2007, with *Fahrenheit 451* as one of the program's initial anchoring texts.

Since the 1980s, growing concerns over literacy and dwindling library budgets had gradually elevated *Fahrenheit 451* above the story cycles of *The Martian Chronicles* and *Dandelion Wine* as the most favored Bradbury single-volume text in schools and out in the general reading public. For the next decade, *Fahrenheit* remained one of the most popular selections in NEA local community grant applications, and that momentum did not subside after the title cycled off of the primary Big Read list in 2016.

Gioia was the final significant figure in the improbable history of Bradbury's recognition in the national political arena. Decades earlier, Bradbury's space-age vision had become part of the Kennedy Administration's push for the Moon through the good offices of Pulitzer Prize–winning historian Arthur Schlesinger, serving as special assistant within the White House. Bradbury was both a personal and official highlight of Library of Congress programming during the dozen years (1975–87) that his friend Daniel J. Boorstin served as Librarian of Congress. Like his predecessors in Bradbury's Washington saga, Dana Gioia saw Bradbury as an important ally in his vision of a more literate and aesthetically aware nation in the twenty-first century, thereby adding momentum to Bradbury's continuing relevancy in the new century as well.

∴ ∴ ∴

It had been a year of transitions and unexpected honors, beginning with grief and gradual adjustment to life without Maggie, a springtime return to the NASA spotlight, and his autumn honors at the White House. Somewhere in between, the summer of 2004 brought him full circle back to one of the most deeply internalized and unfinished projects of his entire career, known to Bradbury, Don Congdon, and friends such as Bill Nolan and Donn Albright simply as "the Mexican novel."

Two long stories had emerged from his three-month 1945 excursion through Mexico: "The Next in Line," showcased as the concluding tale in his 1947 Arkham

House collection, *Dark Carnival*, and its prequel, "Interval in Sunlight," written at the same time but unpublished until 1954. These tales marked a high point of his realistic psychological fiction, allowing him to come to terms with the heartbreaking poverty and ever-present shadows of death that were his constant traveling companions. He observed other Americans in Mexico and combined them into the gradual breakdown of a marriage that had lost its vitality long before the couple entered this strange and exotic new world.

"Interval in Sunlight" brings the husband and wife deep into the mixed Catholic and native cultures of the Mohican province west of Mexico City; "The Next in Line" finds them well to the north, in Guanajuato, where the sight of the mummies preserved in the famous catacombs offers the wife a terrifying glimpse of her own future. She will die there before the next day dawns, presumably interred with the mummies like a cast-off piece of luggage by her self-centered husband. Here was a beginning, and a chilling ending, but no middle; in the early 1950s, Bradbury had composed a number of fragment pages designed to bridge the two tales, but the project never came together in its original novel form.

As sometimes happened in Bradbury's unpredictable patterns of creativity, a writer's block in one genre eventually led to renewal in another. By the 1980s, a glimpse of the Mexican novel had emerged through a stage play and a screenplay, both titled *The Next in Line*. The stage play surfaced from time to time in small-venue alternative theater productions of his Pandemonium Players in Los Angeles. Finally, in the summer of 2004, the screenplay drew the attention of Academy Award–nominated actress-turned-director Liv Ullmann.

Bradbury had met Ullmann eight years earlier, when both participated in a lecture series in Palm Springs. By the turn of the century, she was moving into directing films, and, in the summer of 2004, she was given a copy of the script by Duffy Hecht. Bradbury had worked with his father, producer Harold Hecht, in the 1950s, and the younger Hecht was now an agent; he knew about the screenplay and sensed that the script was in line with Ullmann's keen interest in strong female protagonists.

Her interest was actually engaged by Bradbury's new and surprising ending for the film, which offered a complete turnaround from the relentless death-trap of the Guanajuato catacombs found in his ever-popular story, "The Next in Line." His new ending depended, in part, on the idea of shooting the entire film through a series of contrastive colors designed to reflect the emotions of the central female consciousness. The automobile journey of husband and wife through southwest Texas would be filmed in silver and white, transitioning into the rich colors of Mexico. Tension rises through the dark tour of the catacombs, as the well-preserved mummies, disinterred for lack of annual payment on each grave, give the wife a vision of tormented souls trapped forever between life and death.

Her husband's rude and callous comments add to the horror, and when they come out into light, the visions persist through yet another color transition. "From that point on, everything's in sepia," he would reflect in a private interview. "She sees through the flesh of the mummy. The color of the mummy has colored the landscape, and the walls and the trees and the people." But in the rewritten ending, her heart will not fail, and her husband will have no chance to consign her to the catacombs. That night, she rises from bed, takes a photograph of her husband, and leaves the hotel:

> She goes up into the graveyard and she gets the grave-digger, and she goes down to the catacomb, and she puts his picture in the hands of one of the mummies there. So, she's getting rid of him, right? She's burying him in the catacomb. She comes up into the light and she looks down the hill, and down below waiting for her is a blue taxicab—it's the only color you've seen in an hour. Everything's sepia, everything around it is sepia, but this big blue taxicab is waiting for her when she walks down the hill. She gets into the cab and slams the door, and he says, "Where to?" And she says, "Mexico City." The car drives off in the night, leaving the husband's picture in the catacomb. When she slams the [cab] door, the picture falls askew in the hands of the mummy.[1]

In a bargain with his own subconscious, Bradbury always maintained the illusion that his characters wrote the stories. It was a safeguard against drifting into self-conscious thought while he wrote, but over time, this practice also left a way open for his characters to *rewrite* their stories; at least, that's what he let himself believe. This uplifting change to "The Next in Line," transformed in the process of building a screenplay out of an unfinished novel, was clearly more art than artifice. Liv Ullmann had great respect for Bradbury's work, and for a time she gave serious thought to taking an option on the property. But by the end of 2004, there was no way forward, and it was clear that the film would remain only a refashioned memory.

40 | *Farewell Summer*

By 2006, Bradbury was able to bring closure to the oldest of his unfinished projects. *Farewell Summer*, as he had eventually come to call it, represented the fertile field of childhood memories from which he had harvested *Dandelion Wine* a half-century earlier. Generations of young readers identified with his Green Town tales; early in the new century, another young reader helped him return to harvest what remained.

"My skin has grown a million new sensors to feel each touch and brush of my world." Ledah Wilcox read *Dandelion Wine* growing up in Montana, at the close of the twentieth century. In 2002, as a junior in Missoula's Hellgate High School, she penned a letter to Ray Bradbury that went, instead, directly into the popular Library of Congress–sponsored student writing competition, "Letters about Literature." There were more than 25,000 entries that year, but her Bradbury entry was the national winner in the high school division, and Montana's first national winner in the ten-year history of the prize.[1]

In her letter, Ledah focused on the inspiration of young Douglas Spaulding's firm friendship with John Huff, who must move away from Greentown during that long-ago summer of 1928. When Bradbury first saw the letter in print, he wrote to the real John Huff to say, "It looks as if you and I will live through the twenty-first century!" The two had been inseparable throughout the Tucson winter and spring of 1932–33 as seventh-graders, but it would be Bradbury, not Huff, who moved away, returning to Waukegan as his father continued to look for work during the Great Depression. They reconnected in 1970 through Huff's son, who discovered his own father in his school-assigned reading of *Dandelion Wine*.

Bradbury subsequently visited his old friend in Tucson and even lectured occasionally at the University of Arizona, where Huff was an assistant dean. He had transplanted Huff from Tucson to Waukegan in his 1957 novelized story cycle, but now it was past time to revisit that territory once again and finally finish the broken novel that had shed the stories he had woven into *Dandelion Wine* almost a half-century earlier. Bradbury had managed the same challenge in 2001, when his supernatural Elliott family tales of the 1940s and 1950s finally coalesced into another novelized story cycle, *From the Dust Returned*. The back-to-back story collections *One More for the Road* and *The Cat's Pajamas* added momentum; between 2004 and 2006, he was finally able to bring closure to the summer tales of his Midwestern youth.

Farewell Summer reflected the same power of a child's imagination that he had spoken of in his testimony for the Presidential Commission on Moon, Mars and Beyond in the spring of 2004. But this was one child's imagination, his own memories carried through a novel that had formed nearly sixty years earlier, generating one of the strongest writer's blocks that he would ever experience. In the mid-1950s, with the help of his Doubleday editor Walt Bradbury, he had eased around the block by pulling out a number of the story-chapters to form the 1957 prelude novel, *Dandelion Wine*. Now, as the book of his life slowly began to close, he was determined to finish what had been his very first sustained concept for a novel.

From its beginnings in the mid-1940s, Bradbury regarded his Illinois project as a psychological novel that would explore the profound changes he observed in the biochemical evolution of infant to child, adolescent to adult, and the slow decline into old age. He was greatly influenced by novels such as Christopher Morley's *Thunder on the Left* and *Innocent Voyage* by Richard Hughes, novels that implied profound differences between each stage of physical and psychological growth. It was the psychology that interested Bradbury, and the conflict between the young boys and the elders of Greentown had the undertones of distinctly different species at war.

It was more complicated than that, of course; from the point of view of young Douglas Spaulding, Bradbury's old men were intent on forcing metamorphosis on the children, dragging them into the adult world and thus one step closer to death. The mid-1950s extraction of the *Dandelion Wine* stories removed a great deal of town life from the original book. Only the war remained, with episodes of the boys controlling the ravine and their western side, where most of the younger families lived, and the old men holding their large homes and the downtown symbols of adult power—the courthouse with its clock, and the school. The boys attack the clock in an effort to literally stop the advance of time, and the war intensifies. At the end of the remaining 1950s structure, Lisabell's birthday party anchored the end of the war; Douglas is defeated by the discovery of young love.

From these two principal adventures, Bradbury would have to rebuild much of the book. The 1957 publication of *Dandelion Wine* diminished his motivation far more than either Bradbury or Don Congdon expected; he made some progress at great intervals, turning to it more and more frequently after 1990. The eventual title story "Farewell Summer" appeared in *The Stories of Ray Bradbury*

(1980), eventually becoming the opening of the novel—when Douglas wakes up from a strange dream, he asks his grandfather, "'Is Death being on a ship sailing and all your folks left back on the shore?' Grandpa read a few clouds in the sky. 'That's about it, Doug.'"

The war begins from that point, taking on tragicomic overtones of the Civil War. Bradbury would finally divide the novel into sections titled "Almost Antietam," "Shiloh and Beyond," and "Appomattox." A few of the thirty-seven chapters are self-contained gems—chapter 33 culminates in the first kiss as Lisabell and Douglas explore the neighborhood's haunted house.

Yet there is a thinness to the book and the internal bridging episodes. Even the kissing chapter pales in comparison to "One Timeless Spring," his 1946 *Collier's* story that is the precursor to this important moment. Other early (and admittedly more peripheral) Greentown tales could have been pulled in, but Bradbury seemed determined to stay the course with the generational war that had anchored the original concept sixty years earlier. He was a master of the short story form, and sustained works of long fiction would always be a difficult proposition.

The legacy of *Farewell Summer* would always be that of a companion to *Dandelion Wine*, which is by far the more perfect example of a novelized story cycle. But the 2006 publication of *Farewell Summer* took a great psychological burden off of Bradbury, who now only had to deal with two more deferred novellas—*Somewhere a Band Is Playing* and *Leviathan 99*. In the end, he and Jennifer Brehl would find a way to package them in a single volume under the overarching title, *Now and Forever*. These were unlikely companions at first glance, yet together they would end up showcasing Bradbury's never-ending exploration of longevity and human destiny through the microcosmic adventures of Summerton, Arizona, and the cosmic drama of the comet Leviathan. Just a few more months of work would bring both of these projects home.

: : :

Bradbury's participation in the Great Tale continued undiminished after the successful 2004 landings of Spirit and Opportunity. As the rovers extended their explorations on opposite hemispheres of Mars, Bradbury found himself connected to the ongoing missions through a range of sources. Congressman Adam Schiff presented Bradbury with a landscape composite of photos from the Martian surface, color coded with the now-familiar blue spectrum hues that the rover team scientists developed to distinguish varieties of surface rock. A broader multiple-photo landscape composite, printed in rust tones against a slightly yellowed sky, came from Caltech. In 2007 and again in 2008, NASA Mars Exploration Rover Team planetary geologist Dr. James Rice visited Bradbury with updates. On one of these visits, he presented Bradbury with a large landscape print, with signatures across the image from members of the NASA Rover team members. Dr. Rice also brought word that a rock cluster was observed near the Spirit rover, and he named the cluster "Martian Chronicles."

The reality of other worlds was now woven into the fabric of his own imagination in tangible ways. The Spirit and Opportunity landscape presentations joined gifts from earlier NASA administrations, including a famous *Lunar Orbiter 2* photograph of the massive Copernicus crater on Earth's Moon taken in November 1966, foreshortened by the oblique camera angle and deep focus lens to appear much smaller than its vast 93-kilometer diameter as seen from zenith.

Bradbury's accumulating Space Age mementos exhibited the technology of their respective times. His greatly enlarged Copernicus print—dubbed by *Life* magazine as "a photo of the century"—bore the horizontal composite scan lines of transmission back to Earth; he kept it in an old wooden frame, with no matting, but it was a treasure nonetheless. His 1976 image from the *Viking 1* Martian lander, accompanied by Mercator map projections of the Viking 1 and 2 landing sites, was a signed gift from the director of the NASA Langley research complex, given for his contributions to the 1976 Langley center's panel discussion and book, *Why Man Explores*.

By the early 2000s there were, occasionally, hands-on experiences that Bradbury cherished, including a chance to remotely target coordinates for the THEMIS infrared imaging program of Mars. His targeted image, a fascinating matrix of geological formations known to the THEMIS scientists and engineers as "The Inca Village," was given to him by the project team based at Arizona State University in Tempe. He was still able to make appearances at Caltech and the JPL, where he continued to connect with enthusiastic audiences of scientists and students who cherished his dreams of the night sky.

Many of these images from other worlds were stored in the den and the dining room, too precious to consign to the lower basement, a half-flight down from his basement office. Maggie had maintained a basic domesticity in the den and dining room and tried to limit the overflow of his treasures from the basement and garage levels. But it was a losing battle, especially after her husband's 1999 stroke, and her passing in late 2003 was compounded by the ever-increasing quantity of gifts, mementos, author's stock books, and papers associated with his works-in-progress. One imagines the home of his 1954 title character of "The Wonderful Death of Dudley Stone," a famous writer retired to a secluded family life, whose home is overflowing with the rich legacy of many books published, countless books and stories finished but left unpublished, and all the related projects they had generated.

Yet Bradbury's home was also brimming with the books of other writers who had inspired him, a house full of the art done for his books and stories, and still more art by artists of modern popular culture as well as the earlier masters he had discovered in the half-century since Bernard Berenson had fired his love of the Renaissance. His readers knew that he privileged toys as great inspirations for thinking and creativity, and his house was full of gifts from the famous as well as the grassroots readers of all ages who loved his work.

By the final decade of his life, the storyteller's entire house had become an outward representation of his own subjective reality and loves. Like Poe, who was one of his great inspirations and internalized encouragers, he was fascinated with the architectures of the mind. In stories like "The Fall of the House of Usher" and "Ligeia" Poe created edifices that fully project the inner mind of the main character. Bradbury had the same tendencies, explored in such classic tales as "The Homecoming," "Jack-in-the-Box," and "Usher II."

During the 1970s and 1980s, the overflow had been anchored in his Wilshire Boulevard office and its smaller successor; working materials also cycled back and forth between the Palm Springs weekend home he bought in the early 1980s. But by the 1990s, the residuum of nearly everything he had ever created or experienced had been compressed within the increasingly famous confines of his basement office. By the early 2000s, the house itself had become the central repository of his life's memories and accomplishments.

But there were now fewer people to connect him with the past represented in his house and his writings. Julius Schwartz, who had guided Bradbury's rise to prominence in the 1940s genre pulps, passed away in February 2004. In early April 2004, a little more than four months after Maggie's passing, his older brother Skip died. He was now the last living soul of the four children born to Leo and Esther, the last witness to the ghosts and memories of *Farewell Summer* and the many Green Town stories that radiated out across six decades from that source novel concept.

41 Samurai Kabuki

On May 6, 2005, Bradbury was able to properly send off another influential ghost from his past. In life, he had made his peace with John Huston just before Huston's death in 1987. The demanding director had tormented Bradbury throughout the dismal Irish winter of 1953–54, as they labored through the screenplay for the Warner Brothers adaptation of *Moby Dick*. In his innocence of Hollywood's ways, Bradbury had danced too close to Huston's all-consuming flame, but he always acknowledged that his ordeal had opened many doors in Hollywood for him. They had barely spoken until Bradbury took the opportunity of a chance restaurant encounter to thank him; now, nearly twenty years after their last meeting, Huston's ghost had bestowed a final gift—an honorary degree from the University of Ireland, Galway, the home of the Huston School of Film and Digital Media.

The ceremony also conferred honorary degrees on Huston's daughter, actor/director Angelica Huston, Delores Hope, and Merv Griffin. The May 6th ceremony took place at the Beverly Hilton Hotel, and represented the first time that honorary degrees had been presented by the University of Ireland on foreign soil. Dr. Garrett Fitzgerald, former Prime Minister of Ireland, presided along with the university's president. Bradbury was honored for his "outstanding achievements as a novelist, short story writer, essayist, playwright, screenwriter, and poet."

Bradbury's multi-genre degree citation was an implicit nod to the range of his Irish writings. His seven months working on *Moby Dick* with John Huston had inspired more than a dozen Irish short stories, dozens of productions of his various Irish plays adapted from these tales, and *Green Shadows, White Whale*, an overarching 1992 novel stitched together from Bradbury's Irish stories and his many months working with Huston and his production associates at Courtown House, Huston's rented manor house some miles west of Dublin, in 1953–54. His engaging but stereotypical stories, though beautifully written, had not always been well received in Ireland at first reading, but his great love of the country came through again and again as he explored, like his beloved Bernard Shaw, the profound contradictions he found in Irish culture.

In spite of his many subsequent trips to Europe and England, he could never bring himself to return to the Emerald Isle. But the degree ceremony, conducted under the watchful eye of the former Prime Minister, gave Bradbury a satisfying sense of closure. Most importantly, he could join Huston in spirit by supporting the Huston School of Film, dedicated to teaching the vocation that both men had loved all their lives.

: : :

Bradbury's long career in feature film projects was about to come full circle. In September 2005, just five months after his Huston School of Film honors, Warner Brothers distributed the last major studio film adaptation of a Bradbury story produced during his lifetime. It was almost exactly a half-century since Warner Brothers had released Bradbury and Huston's adaptation of *Moby Dick*; on September 2, 2005, *A Sound of Thunder* reached audiences after five years of development. In the end, Peter Hyams directed a strong cast (Catherine McCormack, Edward Burns, and Ben Kingsley) in an international production involving the United States, the United Kingdom, Germany, and the Czech Republic.

This 1952 story was one of Bradbury's best-known tales. The twenty-third century Time Travel Safari company has taken great pains to ensure that the past is never altered—once they scout a T-Rex that is about to die from an accident and drop out of the time line, it becomes fair game. Guide and hunters walk above the Jurassic landscape on an antigravity path, touch nothing, and even extract their bullets from the carcass. But a panicked hunter steps off the path, and the returning safari learns that even the death of a tiny butterfly can have consequences down through time.

Location filming in Prague was delayed by major storms and flooding, and the film fared no better in the post-release critical reviews. The alternate time stream triumph of rather terrifying megafauna was impressive, but the production's overall special effects were greatly diminished by loss of funding during postproduction. Critics also found fault with the underlying logic of the extended time-travel plot—the extension of a suspenseful Bradbury story into a feature-length narrative was always risky, and in this case, the need to provide plausible science fell short of the mark.

The extended structure depended on inventing a series of "time-quakes" to bring more and more disruptions to the animal kingdom's present-day chain of dominance and build toward a restorative solution that Bradbury had never intended. The new story had twenty-first-century aspects of big-business conspiracy and government collusion, but these aspects were far from Bradbury's original "now." His carefully constructed hunters and dinosaurs had been intended to highlight possible consequences of the deep political divisions leading up to the presidential election of 1952; the diverging (or devolving) evolutionary track of the extended film had an intriguing Wellsian flavor to it, but the final product was no longer a tightly structured Bradbury tale at all.

The most interesting aspect of the project played out behind the scenes, and well before production. Once again, the chance of filming a very visual and effective Bradbury tale of suspense had shown just how popular he was among Hollywood actors.[1] Before Bradbury parted ways with Rene Harlin, the original director, Pierce Brosnan was scheduled for the role of safari leader Travis. He was strongly attracted to the roll, as were the two major stars who subsequently read for the part—Arnold Schwarzenegger and Sylvester Stallone. Various complications took all three out of the actual film, but not before their strong individual interest in *A Sound of Thunder* had persuaded backers to raise the production budget to the 80-million-dollar level.

There had been no women in the original 1952 story, but Bradbury had brought a woman into the time safari for his *Ray Bradbury Theater* episode. Predictably, the casting search for the new 2005 film version was deep in A-list names for what had become a female co-lead—a scientist to match the wits of safari leader Travis.[2] In the end, the role went to British actress Catherine McCormack, with Edward Burns as Travis and Ben Kingsley as the over-the-top entrepreneurial safari company president. But strong casting alone could not carry the day, and without the Stallone or Schwarzenegger star power, the 80-million-dollar production budget would prove impossible to sustain. Diminished special effects exposed problems in the screenplay itself; Bradbury had no control over either element, and he could only imagine what might have evolved for one of the most popular stories in his literary canon.

: : :

By the early 2000s, Bradbury worked mostly from his large padded armchair in the den, a cozy space that represented the pumping heart of the house and the people who passed through it. Four doors commanded the room, including interior doorways from the bedroom hallway, the passage to a small office, and a door to the half-bath pass-through to the office. His youngest daughter Alexandra worked from the small office when she was in town; it had also been her bedroom from infancy, shared with Tina until Sue and Mona graduated from the larger bedroom on the other side of the den.

But the fourth door, opening onto the patio, was the magic one—it allowed him to catch the sounds and smells of the secluded upper terrace yard, and he kept it open as much as he could. Since his 1999 stroke, he had not been able to work in his basement office on a regular basis, and as his mobility slowly decreased, he visited mostly by proxy through family, housekeeper, aids, and visiting friends who were periodically sent down to search out a precious book or document or memento.

The patio formed a right angle between the den and the master bedroom; it was roofed, and opened out into the upper yard and garden, an area that held a charm and memories that extended beyond its relatively compact boundaries. Blackbirds patrolled the yard, and he would feed them, tossing crackers from his easy chair across the little den and through the door. By 2007, he had coaxed one or more of the boldest to hop through the doorway for the crackers. One of the cats startled the bird into sudden flight one day, and Bradbury was surprised to see the explosion of colors suddenly open out from the bird's underwings. He wrote a short poem around this momentary drama, an exercise that he called "semi-haiku":

> Blackbird in mourning
> Sad blackbird concealed
> Don't die
> But bang! Fly!
> See the bluebird revealed

He thought of this image as metaphor, a glimpse of his explosive creative process, sheltered as long as possible from the invasive nature of conscious thought or sequential logic.[3] An earlier attempt at Haiku had a more dramatic origin—one of the cats came into the kitchen with a tiny hummingbird in its mouth. Bradbury had always revered this mysterious bird, seeing in its swift and unpredictable movements the calligraphy of God. He was able to free the still form from the cat's mouth and experience one of nature's hidden wonders: "I held it cupped in my hands for a moment, and I couldn't feel the weight of the hummingbird. It was so light. But I could feel its heart beating. That's incredible. It's a religious moment."[4] He released the tiny victim, and it flew away.

The resulting haiku was not true to form, but then none of his work in any genre ever followed formal conventions. Yet these misshapen verses captured an essential human emotional paradox:

> Oh, cat that I really love,
> Oh hummingbird that I really love,
> What are you doing in the cat's mouth?

His thoughts and interest often turned to Eastern subjects and processes in these years; it was an extension of his interest in films and books that allowed him to explore foreign cultures, their politics, and their family relationships. It really didn't matter to him if these films and books were critically acclaimed or not; he was drawn to them because they taught him about other cultures on these three levels. Over the previous two years, he had explored Japanese society in this way, first by reading Noel Perrin's *Giving Up the Gun: Japan's Reversion to the Sword, 1543–1879*.

Bradbury saw the periodic Japanese Shogunate edicts against gunpowder as a science fiction story in reverse, and he would see the modernization of Japan under the Meiji Emperor as a science fictional moment as well. Idea was everything—often there was little distinction between fact and fiction in his mind. Besides, the genre was everywhere, as he saw it; he always maintained that *Singing in the Rain* was the greatest musical, a science fiction story capturing the moment when sound technology caused a quantum leap in the motion picture industry. In 2005, he saw *The Last Samurai*, a chronicle of the sudden advance in military science that represented Meiji Japan's science-fictional moment. He loved this film because it told him about the politics, the cultural subtleties, and the private lives of the remaining samurai enclaves. It didn't matter to him that Perrin's book did not reflect the actuality of sword and gun in Japanese history, or that *The Last Samurai* had its commercial side. He was learning the broad brushstrokes of Otherness again, just as he had done in imagining contact with alien cultures in the 1940s and in discovering Renaissance art under Berenson's tutelage in the 1950s.

Bradbury had used his founding leadership in the Writer's Guild Film Society to preview foreign films since the early 1960s. He had been attracted to Japanese films from the start, possibly beginning with Kaneto Shindo's nearly voiceless production, *The Naked Island* (1962).[5] Over time, his exposure extended to Chinese cinema; in 2005, he saw *Pavilion of Women*, the Chinese film adaptation of Pearl Buck's novel. "You watch the change of customs and habits as the whole family thing disintegrates under the impact of war. . . . It's a very complex movie, like *The Last Samurai*. I love that sort of thing, where I learn on three levels."[6] *Pavilion of Women* had been panned by the critics, but that didn't matter; as a Writer's Guild of America West member with screenwriting credits, he had screened films and cast Academy Award votes for decades. As in literature, his opinion did not always align with the critical consensus.

The oddness and off-trail nature of his early fictions had been one of his successful hallmarks across the genre magazines, and a touch of it returned in "Samurai Kabuki," a very visual short-short fantasy he had written in the mid-1990s and given to his friend and legendary Hollywood title artist Saul Bass, who wanted to make a short film in the manner that he had done with *Quest*, a loose adaptation of Bradbury's "Frost and Fire." Bradbury was always fascinated by electricity and power grids, seeing them as metaphors for life throughout the cosmos; "Samurai Kabuki" illuminates another imagined historical moment, when the power grid brings light to rural villages of Japan, with power lines sustained and extended on the arms and shoulders of steel-framed towers that resemble silhouettes of helmeted samurai warriors. Once one reads the story, the unintended samurai design of most high voltage towers is hard to shake.

Slowly, and then more rapidly, the samurai-shaped electric towers build themselves, strut by strut; single notes from an unseen koto, a Japanese stringed instrument, mark the placement of each new strut. These notes, and the sound of a thunderstorm, form Bradbury's imagined soundtrack as the isolated farmhouses and villages are linked by light-giving power. For a half-century, since writing his 1948 O. Henry Prize–winning story "Powerhouse," his root metaphor for the cosmos—and for humanity—had been the vast electric lights of the heavens: For each light that fades, another brightens. "Samurai Kabuki" offered a voiceless, image-centered microcosm of his grand metaphor, a remarkable echo from the earliest days of his career.

Here was the old Bradbury ability to control perception. "I discovered in my writing, years ago, if I can convince you that you're somewhere, and I surround you with the essence of that somewhere, it's a time machine. I can take you anywhere then. I'll make you believe anything."[7] But the old magic surfaced only fleetingly and didn't last long; Saul Bass died before he could make the film, and Bradbury was deeply saddened by the loss of yet another close friend.

After Bass died in 1996, Bradbury circulated the story through Tuttle-Mori, Don Congdon's sub-agents in Tokyo, to see if they could generate interest with Akira Kurosawa or other Japanese directors.[8] There was potential here to repeat the earlier Bass and Bradbury success in Japan with Quest; in Tokyo, Tom Mori felt that "Samurai Kabuki" was ideal for a short film using computer graphics. But interest waned, and the story languished until 2005, when it surfaced fleetingly as a short-story "chapbook" packaged with a very limited expanded edition of Bradbury's new story collection, The Cat's Pajamas. Only fifty-two copies of the separately bound and signed "Samurai Kabuki" circulated; it remains one of Bradbury's most elusive titles.

42 | "Nothing Has to Die"

"Naming a thing is man's greatest approach to creating it." Percival Lowell's observation appeared in *Mars* (1895), the first of his three provocative books advancing his theory of Mars as a "desiccated" world where intelligent life strove to move water around the planet through canals and oasis hubs fed by the seasonal melting of polar ice. Bradbury devoured Lowell's third book, *Mars as the Abode of Life*, at the age of ten; he saw Lowell's photographs, and studied Giovanni Schiaparelli's even earlier drawings. He began to encounter the visible Martian features through the famous and enduring names established by Schiaparelli in the 1860s, names based on the ancient waters and landmarks of the Mediterranean Sea as they were known in classical times.

Bradbury's choice of fictional names on Mars followed the pioneer tradition of America's rolling frontier, and by the first decade of the new century yet a third generation of schoolchildren knew names and places from Bradbury's Mars and names from his Waukegan of the 1920s and 1930s, which were carried forward in hundreds of anthologies and textbooks that contained his best-known science fiction, fantasy, and supernatural tales. By the early 2000s, "There Will Come Soft Rains," the penultimate story-chapter of the *Chronicles*, and "All Summer in a Day" had appeared in more than 60 textbooks each. "The Fog Horn," "A Sound of Thunder," and "The Pedestrian," all from the first two years of the 1950s, had each appeared in more than 30 textbook anthologies. In all, his stories had been reprinted more than 800 times in American textbooks, more than 600 times in American and British trade anthologies.

His characters and settings had also been interpreted by many of the best-known illustrators and graphic artists of the day—in books, magazines, and comic adaptations. These creations now had lives that could never be extinguished; he had learned this in the 1960s, when Walt Disney took him through the studio archives. "Nothing has to die," Walt told him. That was becoming true of Bradbury's legacy in the new century, and he wanted to explore the nature of immortality one more time in fiction, while he was still able to do so. For this he turned back to a long-deferred novel. In its final form, *Somewhere a Band Is Playing* is more mood piece than novel, a plot that can be summarized in a few words that nevertheless carries all the magic of Bradbury's nostalgic search for a time preserved forever out of time.

The origins predate publication by a full half-century, starting with the purchase of Stephen Leacock's Canadian novel, *Sunshine Sketches of a Little Town*. Bradbury soon began to sketch an American parallel in his own mind; initially, he thought of this new small town as a stage or screenplay, and in 1957 he turned to producer Paul Gregory for a partner. Working with Charles Laughton, Gregory had overseen Bradbury's unproduced stage adaptation of *Fahrenheit 451* in 1955. Gregory immediately joined forces with Bradbury once again, but was never able to find backing for either a stage or screen version.[1] With those doors closed, Bradbury began to build a novel around a town where time has stopped, unnoticed by the great wide world beyond.

The hard but rewarding path to the publication of *Dandelion Wine* in 1957 allowed his imagination to seek out a more fully fantasized small-town variation, but he still lacked a central character. A glimpse of her began to register in his mind the following year, when he saw Katharine Hepburn in *Summertime*, a film where (like *The Rainmaker*) she began to transform gracefully into the romantic roles of midlife. His 1974 meeting with her, and their brief moment working on the doomed possibilities of George Cukor's *The Blue Bird*, crystalized Hepburn as both a friend and a legend in his heart, and firmly placed her in the role of his emerging central character, Nef.

Initially, *Somewhere a Band Is Playing* emerged as a community where a sunflower-based elixir kept an entire town youthful, populated with young people and those entering a vigorous middle age; the graveyard would have no names on the tombstones. Too magical, perhaps; he eventually shifted to a device more in line with his old friend Robert Heinlein's *Methuselah's Children*, a town where those with longevity in their genes came together and continued the trait, with the future full of timeless possibilities.

But where would the plot begin, and how would the characters act out? For this crucial starting point, he seems to have drawn on one of the free-standing stories he had pulled into *Dandelion Wine* without its original title, "Lime-Vanilla Ice." For the new novel, the reincarnation and immortality hoped for in "Lime-Vanilla Ice" becomes more than a wish—it becomes a choice. Indeed, there are echoes of some of Bradbury's best stories throughout this slim novella, including "Mars Is Heaven!", "A Miracle of Rare Device," "The Other Highway," and "The Wonderful Death of Dudley Stone." There is the slightest hint of Bradbury playfully echoing Shakespeare's Prospero, saying farewell to the stage.

Although the roots of this novella dated back a half-century, it contains some of Bradbury's best work of later days. There is mystery and fantasy in the midst of an isolated Arizona town with orchards, and as the Eastern newspaper reporter James Cardiff is drawn deeper into these mysteries, the entire history of the timeless people unfolds with vintage Bradbury style and power. In the final chapters, he lays out the crippling limitations of fear and conformity, measured against his settled views on the power of love that nourishes both body and mind, if we take the time to feel it and know it.

There is great power as well in the way Bradbury describes the back story of these people, who have come from all time and all parts of the world, bringing the lost treasures of knowledge. "We are tomb robbers," Nef explains to Cardiff. "For the profit of the mind, the extension of the soul." This is Bradbury's Shangri-La, beautifully and sparingly reimagined. It must move, to escape the new highway. Will James Cardiff go with them in faith or return East in despair to a world where imagination is dead? *Somewhere a Band Is Playing* is built on earlier bones, but Bradbury put the best of his late-life writing into the flesh of this creation. It is a remarkable work.

: : :

The 2007 publication of the long-deferred *Somewhere a Band Is Playing* and *Leviathan 99* came in a year that also brought new national and international awards. On April 16th, Columbia University President Lee Bollinger wrote to Bradbury, through Jennifer Brehl at William Morrow/HarperCollins, notifying him that he had been awarded a Special Lifetime Pulitzer Citation for "his distinguished, prolific, and deeply influential career as an unmatched author of science fiction and fantasy." His designation as "deeply influential" and "unmatched" in science fiction and fantasy was a judgment based not on comparison with other writers, but on the way his influence spilled over into other aspects of American culture. His best works may have emerged in the first two decades of his long career, but the impact was enduring in ways that illuminated the human heart. Michael Congdon accepted the Pulitzer citation and crystal for Bradbury, who could no longer manage the rigors of cross-country travel.

As 2007 wound to a close, Bradbury received three more major lifetime recognitions. In October, a beautiful color-engraved metal plaque and matching art deco statuette arrived at his home, signed and sent by the many distinguished members of the Russian Academy of Science in St. Petersburg. It was Russia's National Olympus Award, bestowed for Bradbury's lifetime contributions to what translated as "the field of Peace, Harmony and Prosperity for Mankind." This was a reminder that Bradbury's Space Age legacy transcended superpower politics, and always had; a few years earlier he had received the annual Yuri's Night award, a broadly international celebration of all Space-Age achievements, named in honor of Russian Cosmonaut Yuri Gagarin, the first human to orbit and return safely to Earth.

On December 6th, he was able to accept in person his Jules Verne Lifetime Achievement Award from presenter Malcolm McDowell, no stranger to science fiction film roles. The Jules Verne Adventure Film Festival took place in the Shrine Auditorium, and the one-time award recognized key leaders and visionaries in the field of space exploration. Recipients included Bradbury, Apollo 11 astronaut Buzz Aldrin, and actors William Shatner and Patrick Stewart. In the award catalogue, the citations for Aldrin and Bradbury were paired under the title, "Where Science Meets Fiction."

A week later, in his Los Angeles home, Bradbury received the Honorable Pierre Vimont, French Ambassador to the United States, who presented the medal and citation of a Commandeur of the French Ordre des Arts et des Lettres. All three of these new awards went a long way toward dispelling his critical view of the intellectual establishment, but this final French honor rose above those feelings entirely. He had always had his critics in France, but he struck a chord with French writers, philosophers, teachers, and general readers that resonated with the deepest surrealist traditions in French literature.

With this honor, his thoughts inevitably turned to Madame Man'Ha Garreau-Dombasle, his friend since 1945, a seminal figure in French literary and aesthetic circles until her death at the age of 101, who had, along with his loyal agent of later days, Michelle Lapautre, and his Denoel editor, Jacques Chambon, aided his rise in French literary circles through so many of his visits to Paris since 1953. But his 1999 stroke had ended all hope of returning to France in the new century; Man'Ha, born in the spring of 1898, had died in August 1999, missing by less than five months the distinction of living in three centuries. Her granddaughter, the actress Arielle Dombasle, continued to correspond with Bradbury, and remained his last link to the remarkable woman who had perhaps started the long trail to his most important international literary award.

Fittingly, two awards of pure fantasy bracketed Bradbury's American, Russian, and French national recognitions. He had never lacked for intellectual fellowship across Old and New World Spanish cultures, and much of that fellowship derived from writers and artists—most notably Jorge Luis Borges, Aldo Sessa, and Mario Vargas Llosa—whose work had some grounding in the fantastic. In 2006, the very popular Spanish novelist Javier Marías honored Bradbury with the purely imaginary title "Duke of the Lion's Teeth."

In this way, Bradbury joined a number of internationally prominent writers granted a peerage in the uninhabited island kingdom of Redonda by Marías, one in a wayward line of "Kings" of this small dependency of Antigua and Barbuda since the mid–nineteenth century. For some years, Marías and other peers of his realm bestowed an annual literary prize. In addition to Bradbury (the only American), other winners included J. M. Coetzee, Alice Munro, Umberto Eco, Milan Kundera, and Sir Philip Pullman. The Redonda prize is perhaps the most ephemeral of the prizes awarded as tongue-in-cheek alternatives to the annual Nobel dispensations; its anti-prize status, along with the international pantheon of writers who have won it, appealed to Bradbury's ambivalent attitude toward high intellectual honors.

His other fantasy honor that year was much closer to home, and far closer to his heart. It began early in 2007, when Bradbury asked Disney's Tenny Chonin, head of artist development, to persuade the studio to film The Halloween Tree as a live-action feature. At this time, Disney was focused on feature film ideas generated from within, but Chonin offered an alternative—a Ray Bradbury seminar series of lectures where he could engage the Disney story and development staff in roundtable discussions.[2] It was, unfortunately, too late in Bradbury's life to sustain the energy required for such a seminar series, especially when there was no possibility of fulfilling his real dream of transforming his animated film success with The Halloween Tree into a live-action production.

Nevertheless, his outreach generated a fantasy honor that meant the world to him. On Halloween night, October 31, 2007, Bradbury was brought to Disneyland to dedicate a living Halloween Tree, an annual honor devised and hosted by Disney Imagineer greats Tim Delaney and Tony Baxter. The ceremonies began in Disneyland's Club 33 restaurant, where Bradbury was able to compress a fair rendering of all of his Disney stories into fifteen minutes—it was, in fact, fifty years since his initial 1957 visit to Disneyland in the company of Charles Laughton.

In his reflections that night, one deep Disney memory, seldom shared, surfaced from his years devoted to founding and leading the Writers' Guild Film Society. One year he had arranged for a children's Halloween evening of clips from the most suspenseful scenes in Snow White, Sleeping Beauty, and Alice in Wonderland, "because I wanted these children to see great scenes which combine terror with beauty." Here was a remembered moment of autumn light, harvested in counterpoint to the prolonged downward spiral of Hollywood Halloween entertainment into horror and hopelessness.

After his remarks, and after the park had closed for Halloween, he and the many guests were brought out to the Town Square of Frontier Land, where Brad Kaye had decorated a promising thirty-foot oak with illuminated jack-o-lanterns. Bradbury turned on the lights and, with emotion, he observed that "The Ghost of Walt Disney is blessing me at this very moment." Kaye had wisely selected a tree that would grow and receive more extensive light treatments every year, and that would prove to be the case. Bradbury's daughters and their families considered the living Halloween Tree a most fitting personal and public tribute; his daughter Tina, herself an Emmy Award–winning writer, would make the trip back to California for this annual renewal almost every year for the rest of her life.

: : :

The passing of years seemed to accelerate in early April 2008, when his close friend Charlton Heston passed away after a slow decline through Alzheimer's. They were friends by the 1960s and had both articulated politically active passions in support of the Democratic presidential bids of Adlai Stevenson in 1952 and 1956. Bradbury had written about racial injustice before many magazines would publish them; Heston had supported civil rights in the 1950s, and joined fellow actors such as Sydney Poitier, Harry Belafonte, and Marlon Brando in Dr. Martin Luther King's March on Washington in 1963. Both Heston and Bradbury had deep roots in traditional values as well and eventually came to support Republican presidents Nixon and Reagan.

Heston had narrated the first choral performance of Bradbury's *Christus Apollo* cantata, scored by Hollywood's Jerry Goldsmith, just before Christmas 1968. The performance at UCLA's Royce Hall was planned to coincide with the launch of the Apollo 8 Lunar orbital mission. Heston later narrated recordings of various Bradbury compositions, and never accepted payment for anything he performed for his friend. Charlton and Lydia Heston's son Fletcher had been raised on Bradbury's tales, and once told his father that Ray Bradbury was the best writer out there.

Already entering his final illness, Heston stood with Bradbury, Rod Steiger, and other longtime friends to witness the dedication of Bradbury's star on the Hollywood Walk of Fame in 2002. Their relationship was an abiding one, and in the days immediately after the April 2008 funeral service, Bradbury was driven over to the Heston home for a quiet visit with Lydia. There were too many such losses in these years, and afterward Bradbury asked his driver to take him to a place where memories of his own family and his early writing career always cheered him up. It had been a year since he had visited 670 Venice Boulevard, the little frame house on the same property with the electrical substation that he could see every day and evening from the garage window, where he sat and wrote stories from 1942 to the late summer of 1947.

The property had passed from the power and light utility to a printer, who used the beautifully trimmed brick substation as his print plant, but it had recently sold to an art gallery developer. The little house and its detached garage had been empty when he last saw it, but now the house and garage were gone. Only the repurposed substation would remain, as an extension to a new stone gallery built on the site where Bradbury had once typed and sent stories on to his New York agent Julius Schwartz for the pulp genre market—stories that would eventually find their way into *The Martian Chronicles* and *The Illustrated Man*. Here, too, he had prepared the stories that would break through into the major-market magazines after World War II ended. He could no longer contemplate his family, or that young man who became Ray Bradbury, by visiting this site.

The gallery would not long survive Bradbury himself. The bronze placard commemorating Bradbury's years in the lost house was also lost and later found; it had been paid for by friends and attached to 670 Venice Boulevard in a quiet ceremony just a few years earlier, but it no longer had a home either. His first home with Maggie, the duplex rental at 33 Venice Boulevard where they lived from 1947 to 1950, remained tucked away by the beach, just a mile to the west. The first home they owned, theirs from 1950 to 1958 on Clarkson Road in West Los Angeles, was already subsumed within an unrecognizable rebuild. His present home on Cheviot Drive, where his four daughters had grown to maturity, would survive him, but only for a few years. Bradbury Square, in front of the Los Angeles main library downtown, would become his home in a city and region that still remembered and loved that Midwestern boy who came west with his parents the summer of his fourteenth year, at the height of the Great Depression, and made a new life.

43 | Visions of Mars

The Martian library conceived and prepared in America by The Planetary Society for the doomed Russian *Mars 96* lander had been stored on a rugged but limited CD disk, representing the technology of the mid-1990s. It had included only printed text, still images, and voice recordings due to capacity limitations of the medium, but the August 2007 launch of the *Phoenix* scout lander marked a state-of-the-art American attempt to send the library time capsule as a DVD. *Phoenix* would be the first polar region Martian lander, making a successful planetfall around 68 degrees north latitude just before 5:00 p.m. West Coast time on May 25, 2008. The DVD format allowed for the encoding of motion picture images, which included an introductory montage voiced by Carl Sagan for the original project, shortly before Sagan's death in 1996.

Lou Friedman's original "ABC" concept of the early 1990s was now far more comprehensive, and the rich DVD multimedia content was titled "Visions of Mars." It had been expanded before the lost *Mars 96* mission disk was prepared, but the final *Phoenix* version still contained those core works by the ABC authors: Isaac Asimov, Ray Bradbury, and Arthur C. Clarke. The original plan to include Asimov's *I, Robot* novelization as an indirect reference to the robotic aspects of Mars mission technology was replaced by three Asimov short stories about Mars; Bradbury's *The Martian Chronicles*, and Clarke's *The Sands of Mars* remained in the final package. Jon Lomberg's introduction featured a few cover illustrations, including Michael Whelan's well-known illustration for late-century Bantam and Doubleday editions of *The Martian Chronicles*. Embedded with the digitized *Chronicles* was the well-known Spanish language introduction by Argentinian writer and fantasist Jorge Luis Borges.[1]

These works were now part of a broad tapestry that included eighty-six works of science fiction and its antecedents. Among the authors were many of Bradbury's mentors and friends from earlier times, including Leigh Brackett, Edmond Hamilton, Jack Williamson, Eando (Earl and Otto) Binder, August Derleth, Judy Merril, C. L. Moore, Fred Pohl, Ted Sturgeon, Poul Anderson, even Nobel Laureate Bertrand Russell, who had discussed his brief sojourn into science fiction tales during Bradbury's 1954 dinner at Lord Russell's home. Such younger writers as Greg Bear, Kim Stanley Robinson, Allen Steele, and Samuel R. Delany were represented, as well as writers nearly his own age who knew his work, such as J. G. Ballard, Gregory Benford, and Brian Aldiss.

The Planetary Society's founders had originated and overseen the expansion of the library, and the Society's May 2008 version of Planet Fest was timed to celebrate the landing and the first transmission of images from the high arctic landing zone. But Bradbury would not make the prime-time event. He was now almost 88 years old and did not feel well enough to attend in person. He did phone in his comments, and actor Tim Russ (Star Trek Voyager), who had read for Bradbury's "An Evening on Mars" a decade earlier, now read passages from The Martian Chronicles as the soft landing of Phoenix with its instruments and library was confirmed.[2]

By the very nature of its water-seeking objective in the frigid high latitudes, Phoenix was designed to be a relatively short-lived mission. The sun soon began to dip below the horizon of 68 degrees north, and the diminishing sunlight left Phoenix without enough power to continue transmissions after November 2, 2008. The short mission had ended, but the time-capsule mission of the tiny "Visions of Mars" disk was just beginning.

The DVD was designed to last at least 600 years, perhaps much longer. It brought literature to Mars from many nations and in many languages, as well as the audiovisual legacy of humanity's imaginings about the Red Planet. What would it prove? The late Carl Sagan's original video, a more recent video by Lou Friedman, and the introductory essay by DVD designer and artist Jon Lomberg[3] conveyed messages for a distant future where Earth's colonists, now Martians in the Bradburyian sense of The Martian Chronicles, would be curious about the purposes behind the earliest explorations.

Bradbury managed one last trip out to the Jet Propulsion Laboratory in February 2009. He enjoyed the chance to drive a Martian rover simulation and spoke briefly to an assembly of JPL scientists and staff. Fatigue led him to misremember some dates in his anecdotes, but no one cared—this man shaped their dreams, and his book was already on Mars. Bradbury had an honored place among the authors identified with the original "ABC" concept for "Visions of Mars," but his generation, as represented in the expanded Martian library, had largely returned to the dust; this late in time, he was one of the few who remained.

∶ ∶ ∶

There were more lifetime recognitions from the science fiction community during 2008. He would become one of the few Grand Masters to also receive the Rhysling Grand Master Poet Award for science fiction and fantasy verse. The University of California, Riverside, honored Bradbury with the first J. Lloyd Eaton

Award for Lifetime Achievement in Science Fiction. Small limited-edition presses continued to publish legacy works, including a complete but preliminary stage of his *Moby Dick* script (1954) and fragments from *Masks* (1947), his incomplete psychological study of modern alienation and despair started and abandoned in the immediate aftermath of World War II.

In December 2008, HarperCollins published what would be his final commercial story collection, *We'll Always Have Paris*. There were a few slight, anecdotal stories from recent decades, interesting ideas or situations not fully developed but complete. Donn Albright had harvested the great majority from the basement files for review by Bradbury, Michael Congdon, and Jennifer Brehl. A few were deferred in hopes that Bradbury could work with Alexandra to fill in gaps or rough spots. All twenty-one held interesting glimpses of the internal process he described in his introduction as "the me who watches and the me who writes." A half dozen represented examples of his old magic in Green Town memories ("Arrival and Departure"), wartime Los Angeles ("Massinello Pietro," "If Paths Must Cross Again"), the isolation of space exploration ("Fly Away Home"), weird tales ("The Reincarnate"), totalitarian nightmares ("Remembrance, Ohio"), and murder terrors, all pulled forward in time.

Exactly one year after the release of *We'll Always Have Paris*, Bradbury lost his last professional link to the old magic of his early tales, and it was a dearly personal loss as well. On November 30, 2009, Don Congdon passed away in New York, the city from which he had guided Ray Bradbury's rise into the mainstream magazines and major publishing houses—at home and abroad—for six decades. His son Michael, a partner in Don Congdon Associates for many years, had gradually eased into representation of the agency's authors, and the final transition was seamless. The elder Congdon's uncanny ability to spot talent led him to reach out to Bradbury in the fall of 1945, and by the late summer of 1947 he was Bradbury's first major market agent. For the better part of a lifetime, Don Congdon's combined abilities as a wise counselor, skilled editor, and master negotiator formed the rational half of Bradbury's headlong and highly emotional charge through the twentieth century.

: : :

Even before the loss of Don Congdon, there were hints that *We'll Always Have Paris* might represent a farewell collection. Bradbury's introduction was dictated to Alexandra, a familiar process, but this time it yielded barely 200 words that primarily showed his fascination with the younger writer he had once been. Nevertheless, the spirit was willing; Bradbury celebrated the release of *We'll Always Have Paris* with an eye toward the next collection. There was more and more urgency in his tone with each passing collection, and he was frustrated that the stories he had in mind fell short of the threshold acceptable for publication.

As Gary K. Wolfe had pointed out in reviewing *One More for the Road* in 2002, the basic unit of creativity in the collections had never been the individual story, but rather the assembled volume itself. The three collections published after his 1999 stroke—*One More for the Road*, *The Cat's Pajamas*, and *We'll Always Have Paris*—represented diaries, summaries of a writer taking stock of his own creativity at particular moments, late in life. In his late teens, he was terrified that the coming war would destroy him before he could become the writer he knew he would be; the prelude to war in 1930s Spain, where Hitler and Mussolini tried out their new air power doctrines of destruction, had given him nightmares. This sense of the proximity of death reappeared late in life, but now his determination was reinforced by his literary legacy. "With me, it's been a fight with Death since I was 12," he told a *Birmingham Post-Herald* interviewer in 1995. "Death is the enemy. So you finish a new thing and you put it in the mail, and you say, "OK, Death, one up on you, one up on you."[4]

Examples of longevity in writers and artists he admired had given him strength over the years. As ever, Bernard Shaw was a model, the Nobel Laureate who was a schoolboy before the American Civil War began and lived five years into the Atomic Age. "I remember reading him, years back, where he described himself as a scythe. He wanted to be only a thin, much used harvest blade when his years were finished."[5] Bradbury found the same disciplined perseverance in Goya, as he told Hart-Davis after traveling to Spain in the summer of 1991:

> I went on to Madrid for the first time and saw the Goyas at the Prado, which were a melancholy joy, a good many of them. Strange to consider he lived into his eighties. Looking at much of his late work makes you think it should have been impossible for him to retain his balance and do his work. Yet as soon as I say that I take it back: his work enabled him to keep his balance, even as mine does. If I go without writing for a day, I begin to feel disabled. Two or three days and if I'm not careful I am walking wounded on my way to self-crippling. The world, via newspapers and radio and TV is too much with us. I must cleanse my system as best I can, outrun the poisoners, and solve the world while it is busy wondering what to do next.

Such examples constantly renewed his abiding self-discipline; the ebb and flow of his creativity was harder to judge across the last four decades of his career, however, masked as it was by older works brought forward from earlier times. Nancy Nicholas certainly understood Bradbury's creativity during these years—she edited all three of his Knopf poetry volumes as well as the stories of

Long After Midnight and the densely written 1985 novel, *Death Is a Lonely Business*. "His genius stories were where his mind just took you places that you couldn't imagine."[6] Looking back, Nicholas sensed a combination of factors—growing financial security, the sheer volume of constant distractions in his public life, and, perhaps, a gradual loss of ability to sustain the strange and otherworldly ideas that still, occasionally, flashed through his mind.

For years Donn Albright had taken the measure of every unpublished story scattered across Bradbury's basement office and garage filing cabinets, and he worked with Bradbury to identify stories that, with some polishing and rewriting, could form yet another story collection. These went to Michael Congdon and to Jennifer Brehl, who had already seen a few of these stories considered for *We'll Always Have Paris*. In all, there were twenty worth reviewing. These were all older stories, ranging from murderous horrors to graveyard weird and Green Town memories. Four of the most promising were not quite complete. A few, such as the proposed title story "Juggernaut" and "Final Day," had appeared in magazines, but there simply weren't enough to form a major trade collection.

"Writing is like breathing for me," he confessed in his brief introduction to *We'll Always Have Paris*. And he always retained a vast library of memories to draw on. One of his last stories surfaced from a deep memory of hanging out the laundry with his mother in Waukegan during the late 1920s and early 1930s, listening to the Chicago Cubs day games on the radio. He had Alexandra leave space for the names of the great Cubs players of those years, many of them future Hall of Famers. He was sure he would get back to the story later and fill in the names; he almost succeeded.

44 | Remembrance

Harbingers of the end emerged occasionally from his typewriter, even when he was in his prime. Often this was subtle, as when he wrote a passage in his 1985 novel, *Death Is a Lonely Business*, where the reclusive silent film star Constance Rattigan is driving the Young Writer through late-night West Los Angeles in her limousine: "We managed to make all of the green lights to Vermont where we wheeled over to Wilshire and took it out as far as Westwood for no special reason, maybe because it was scenic. . . . As we prepared to turn at Westwood we passed a cemetery which was so placed that if you weren't careful, you drove into a parking lot. Or was it that some days, looking for a parking lot, you mistakenly motored between tombstones?"

There is no mistaking the landmark in this passage—Pierce Brothers Westwood Village Cemetery, where first Maggie and then Bradbury himself would be placed to rest in the next century. Their remains would rest in good company, near many of the Hollywood greats and prominent writers they had known or he had worked with, including Gene Kelly, Eddie Albert, Richard Basehart, Robert Bloch, Stan Freberg, Burt Lancaster, and James Wong Howe.

Other keyboard outbursts would be less subtle, more fully purposed. On November 2, 1964, nearly a half-century before the end of his life, Bradbury typed a gravestone inscription that he called "my obituary":

Here lies a Summer Person
Who Knew Autumn, Who Remembered Yesterday,
Who Desired Tomorrow in The Best Way,
And now accepts What Is. Forever.
R. BRADBURY
Born, August 22nd, 1920.
Died _____.

As he spoke in more and more memorial services over the years yet to come, he would usually renew his settled conviction that the universe has no beginning or end. It was, in his mind, a Forever thing, and above all he wanted mankind to be a part of it all. "We'll just keep going until the big words like immortal and forever take on meaning," says the father waiting to see the night launch of his son's rocket in "The End of the Beginning," a 1950s story that says all he ever really wanted to say about these big words:

> Since our tongues first moved in our mouths we've asked, What does it all mean? No other question made sense, with death breathing down our necks. But just let us settle in on ten thousand worlds spinning around ten thousand alien suns and the question will fade away. Man will be endless and infinite, even as space is endless and infinite. Man will go on, as space goes on, forever. Individuals will die as always, but our history will reach as far as we'll ever need to see into the future, and with the knowledge of our survival for all time to come, we'll know security and thus the answer we've always searched for. Gifted with life, the least we can do is preserve and pass on the gift to infinity.

Some part of him—his stories and books—would be part of that immortal journey. That was the easy part. The hard part was watching the early-twentieth-century world that shaped him slowly slip from living memory.

: : :

On October 20, 2009, Bradbury, now 89 years old, attended the 100th birthday gala for Carla Laemmle, one of the last silent film actresses still alive. Along with radio legend Norman Corwin, she was also one of his last living friends born in the first decade of the twentieth century. When he was five years old, Bradbury had seen Carla Laemmle on the silent screen with Lon Chaney in *Phantom of the Opera*; later, as a ten-year-old, he saw her in *Dracula* with Bela Lugosi. Her uncle Carl had founded Universal Studios in the earliest days of Hollywood, a studio that would produce two of his own works as feature films—*It Came from Outer Space* and François Truffaut's adaptation of *Fahrenheit 451*.

Bradbury himself was one of the last living moviegoers who had actually *seen* many of the lost Lon Chaney films, including the celebrated vampire classic *London After Midnight*. Documentaries of the great silent horror films often had interview footage with Bradbury, now a living witness to a lost world. He cherished an autographed movie poster reissue that Carla Laemmle had signed for him in their mutual old age. She was one of the last who had bested him in years.

Throughout his sixty years of interaction and friendships with many of Hollywood's great filmmakers and technical innovators, Walt Disney's *Fantasia* and Orson Welles's *Citizen Kane* remained Ray Bradbury's favorite films. In these judgments he was not influenced by the latter-day critics and scholars who anointed the achievement of these two films and their creators—he was nineteen when he made his commitment of love to *Fantasia* and just twenty-one when he made the same pledge to *Citizen Kane*.

Hollywood had touched his heart from his fourth year, through the successive experiences of seeing Lon Chaney project the emotion he would later understand to be one of the most tragic of all—unrequited love. *Citizen Kane* powerfully documented the price of fame and fortune for Bradbury through another deeply-felt emotion—the lost loves of childhood, remembered from a time before fame and fortune were even known concepts for a young mind.

The quest to find the true meaning of Kane's dying word, "Rosebud," shapes the entire film; the mystery is resolved for the audience only, as the closing camera shot moves in on the furnace where Kane's long-neglected childhood snow sled is slowly burning, along with its imprinted label, "Rosebud." This powerful scene held great meaning for Bradbury, whose understanding of the world was always filtered through the sights and sounds of his remembered youth. In later life, his good friend Stan Freberg, ever the comic and compassionate commentator on American culture, gave Bradbury a replica of Kane's "Rosebud" sled; in the final years of his life, the sled was prominent among the mementos around his bed.

Not surprisingly, Bradbury's earliest memories welled up in the form of photographs and music that gave texture to his world during the first five or six years of his life. His earliest remembrances, carried down through time nearly ninety years, were preliterate. At age five, he was mesmerized by some of the earliest colorized photographs in American newspaper history, special autochromes of King Tutankhamen's jeweled three-dimensional sheet-gold death mask. This vivid preliterate memory would shape his dark and golden-eyed Martians and remain as a memory bridge to the end of his days.

The memory bridges to his early life were also defined by the music of the early and mid-1920s, heard in the early days of radio in his grandparents' house next door and on the few records his mother could purchase and play on a wind-up phonograph. Little storytelling folk songs like "The Three Trees," the widely popular "Beautiful Ohio," and early comic novelty songs such as "No News, or What Killed the Dog" and "Cohen on the Telephone." Yet the greatest of these was also the most delicate memory from his deep past, "Lady Picking Tea Blossoms," played live in countless movie houses for D. W. Griffith's 1919 silent film classic, *Broken Blossoms*.

Bradbury's mother Esther had a phonograph recording of the song, and as a young child he played this beautiful melody more than any other record. The story of a young girl, caught between her brutal, prize-fighting American father and the saving but forbidden friendship of a young Chinese immigrant, would be a discovery of later years; as a child, he simply loved this beautiful song more than anything else his family owned.

Forty years later, and well established in Hollywood, Bradbury attended a special revival of *Broken Blossoms* with its surviving star, Lillian Gish, and his friends, director King Vidor and film critic Arthur Knight. During the evening's events, the studio orchestra played "Lady Picking Tea Blossoms," and Bradbury was riven by the memory. The conductor was Max Steiner Jr., who recognized Bradbury and arranged for him to have a copy of the recording as a keepsake.

In his last years, these memory bridges were never far away from his mind. Various ancient Egyptian statuaries and illustrations populated the den adjacent to the master bedroom where he spent much of his time, but the old analog recordings of these 1920s songs, along with the master-dubbed open-reel of "Lady Picking Tea Blossoms," were scattered through his basement office, his sub-basement, and the lower-level garage. But it didn't really matter; he could remember them with visitors who knew his love of these songs from another century, and he could play them in his mind. Above all, the delicate string tones—forever associated with *Broken Blossoms*—dominated. This memory predated all else that figured into his becoming Ray Bradbury, and it endured; *Broken Blossoms* was, in the final analysis, his Rosebud.

The early months of 2011 were challenging. In mid-January, Bradbury developed pneumonia, and even after his recovery he remained weak until a high-protein supervised meal plan helped him regain some weight. A springtime bout with the MERSA virus slowed his recovery for a time, but he came through it. In spite of excellent caregiver support and physical therapy, he would never regain much mobility or muscle tone. Lung capacity returned through the year, allowing him to weather another bad cold in the early fall. His favorite exercise was harmonica time; he had a good ear for it, and occasional fragments of recognizable tunes carried through the house, reminding housekeeper and caregiver that he was still a presence in his own home as he entered his 92nd year of life.

Mentally, it was often business as usual. He enjoyed the visits of family and of friends old and new, and his innate enthusiasm for life endured. Decades earlier, he had expressed the essence of the inner strength that always sustained him in the lines of one of his most controlled and purposeful poems, "Remembrance." It speaks of the imagined journey home as an older man to search an ancient tree where, as a young boy, he had left a message on a folded page, high up in a knothole:

It was a message to the future, to myself.
Knowing one day I must arrive, come, seek, return.

From the young one to the old. From the me that was small
And fresh to the me that was large and no longer new.
What did it say that made me weep?
I remember you.
I *remember* you.

In this strong and life-affirming bond with the past, he was more fortunate than many of the friends who had already slipped away. In 1973, he sent this poem within his first collection of poetry to Loren Eiseley, whose very popular reflections on time and humanity hid a deep ambivalence toward his own childhood on the Nebraska prairie:

> I will tell you that I read "Remembrance" with a kind of preternatural, nostalgic terror, knowing in advance how it would turn out. My tree, alas, was chopped down long ago, and when, as a stranger, I visited that town and stared across at my old house, . . . I turned and went hastily away, filled with inexplicable terror and loneliness. How could I tell that owner, after all of these years, about vanished objects for which I was searching, or that his house was filled with the ghosts of the dead?[1]

At the time, Eiseley was older than Bradbury and would die just three years after writing these words to his good friend, but even in his own old age Bradbury could never have given up his past. Many years later, writing "Remembrance II," he admitted that lengthening memory may no longer be accurate to reality, yet it is no less real: "But then I am | An old man now, and so perhaps I misremember | Climbing ivies, making swings. Oh, God's sweet blood, | A million-dozen multitudes of summer things!"

His continuing love of life notwithstanding, the challenges of 2011 were not over for Bradbury; the October passing of his great friend Norman Corwin was hard to bear, for Corwin, a towering influence in modern American radio broadcasting and programming, was, at the age of 101, his last living mentor. In these last years, Bradbury had been fascinated by his mentor's seemingly genetic longevity (Corwin's brother lived to 107, his father to 110). Just two years earlier, California Artists Radio Theatre presented Bradbury's radio-play version of *Leviathan 99* under Corwin's direction—a project they had intended to produce together in the early 1960s, until NBC Radio determined that this Space-Age epic would have to be broadcast in suffocating three-minute segments.

Broadcast (and recorded) on May 3, 2009, the final realization of this collaborative production of *Leviathan 99* aired in honor of Corwin's 99th birthday, and included a cast of prominent Hollywood actors, young and old, including

William Shatner, Samantha Eggar, Sean Astin, and the venerable Norman Lloyd, himself approaching the century mark. Corwin had believed in every Bradbury milestone since the 1947 publication of the *Dark Carnival* story collection, and Bradbury could not imagine a world without his friend.

There would be celebrations yet in his life, however. Steven Paul Leiva, with whom he had navigated the frustrating experiences of the doomed *Little Nemo* animated film project of the early 1980s, coordinated various 90th birthday celebrations in 2010, beginning with the Los Angeles City Council resolution designating August 22–28 as Ray Bradbury Week. While he lived, such celebrations were primarily centered in the sprawling media and cultural worlds of Southern California, where he had dreamed and worked for seventy-five years.

In December 2011, there were indications of decline in Bradbury's ability to speak and move, perhaps the result of a minor stroke. But he continued to be mentally alert and cognizant between rest periods, and over the next few months he slowly regained his voice and a limited amount of movement. Dana Gioia, former Chair of the NEA and a good friend, made his last visit to Bradbury's home in December, and spent much of the visit reading aloud, at Bradbury's request.[2] More and more, visits with friends centered on readings, usually his own stories; he never lost the ability to enjoy a good story well read and to look back in wonderment at that young writer who had written these stories so many years ago.

For nearly a dozen years Bradbury had fought back valiantly from the stroke that had felled him in his 80th year, completing—with the support of his daughter Alexandra, his agents Don and Michael Congdon, and his trade publisher Jennifer Brehl—a half dozen books in the first decade of the twenty-first century. But the old damage had consequences. His trachea and esophageal passage had been partially paralyzed by the 1999 stroke, and his ability to swallow and breathe without distress declined through the late spring of 2012. By late May he was ventilating by means of a breathing tube, with an uncertain chance that his airways might recover.

In his final days, attempts to remove the tube in the hospital succeeded for only a few hours, and Bradbury knew what he needed to do. He asked that the tube be removed a final time under medication, and that it not be reintroduced. A few hours later, just before 9:00 p.m. on June 5, 2012, Ray Bradbury passed away peacefully at Cedars-Sinai Medical Center, lucid and full of memories to the end of his time on Earth.

: : :

News of Bradbury's passing reached the media at dawn the next day, sweeping through news broadcasts hour by hour and continent by continent like an orbiting satellite aligned with the rising sun. No matter the nature of the commentary, Bradbury was *noticed* globally—his was a death observed. Countless assessments of his life and legacy followed, but that process really began while he lived, in public commentary and in many private conversations.

"I see your name so often in so many things that I read," journalist and travel writer Russ Leadabrand once observed to his good friend, "your work and ideas have so penetrated our society that I fully expect, one day, that the word/name Bradbury will have earned its way into the dictionary like Ford, or Kodak, or Xerox, or Coca Cola, or Zeppelin, or Diesel."[3] Bradbury, who was an abiding critic of the runaway consumerism that this catalog of names represented, would have seen the irony in his friend's half-humorous words.

And yet, the name "Ray Bradbury," always spoken as a single word, had indeed come to stand for edgy suspense, the unexpected twist in a supernatural tale, or the terrifying moments of unexplainable things in improbable stories of space exploration. Variations on "This is beginning to sound like a Ray Bradbury story" would punctuate television dramas from *The Twilight Zone* to *West Wing*. Homage allusions surface periodically in animated film and television, and in the music of popular performers and composers.

His unique and far-reaching kind of cultural appeal also radiated out into classrooms and libraries, touching generations of readers and preservers of the written word. Writers in all genres, as well as seminal figures of twentieth-century literature who lived in the literary mainstream, admired the best of his work. His lyrical, metaphor-rich style had illuminated the path for countless young readers and writers who continued to respect him long after they grew past his influence. "They grew up with a love of my books when they were fourteen and fifteen and eighteen," he once reflected. "So *that* love never changes."[4]

45 | Closing the Book

In his very brief but incredibly moving 1951 tale, "The Last Night of the World," Bradbury imagined the end of human life on Earth as a metaphor—no atomic holocaust, no germ warfare, no environmental disaster. "But just, let's say, the closing of a book," the husband tells his wife. "And when will it stop?" the wife asks. "Sometime during the night for us, and then as the night goes on around the world, that'll go too. It'll take twenty-four hours for it all to go." The terrifying early years of the Cold War had rarely been described in such gentle and monumentally sad terms. In the second decade of the next century, however, Bradbury's own book of life would close with far more celebration than sadness.

Planetary Society cofounder and Executive Director Emeritus Lou Friedman had planned for Bradbury to attend Planet Fest 12, scheduled to meet and celebrate the Martian equatorial zone landing of the *Curiosity* rover in Gale Crater on August 6, 2012. But Bradbury's passing left an empty place at this celebration of the Great Tale, as did the loss of Astronaut Sally Ride, whose service and achievements were also commemorated during the Planet Fest ceremonies. Bradbury's memorial would be typically supernatural, for Friedman was able to arrange for Bradbury to speak across a sea of time.

As he opened Bradbury's memorial portion of the Planet Fest ceremonies, Friedman ran one of the best-known clips of the early Mars program events, recorded at Caltech in November 1971, the night before *Mariner 9* was successfully inserted into Mars orbit. During the panel discussions with his friends Arthur C. Clarke, Carl Sagan, and future JPL director Bruce Murray, Bradbury read one of his recent poems, "If Only We Had Taller Been." It was a poem of Space-Age dreams long deferred by our various mistakes and shortcomings, culminating in the concluding lines of the poem with the celebration of the moment when, as a race, humanity achieves the first interstellar milestones, proclaiming "We're tall, by God, we're tall!"

The rousing ovation recorded on the 1971 clip set the tone for the rest of the memorial, illustrated with photos of Bradbury, Murray, Sagan, and other scientists and engineers celebrating and discussing the various mission milestones—images of Bradbury aging through time, from his athletic early-fifties image in his trademark lightweight white or pale blue suit of the 1970s Viking era, to the venerable elder Bradbury, wheelchair bound, attending his final Planetary Society honors, receiving the 2006 Thomas O. Paine Award. The Paine Award plaque featured a 3D image of *Valles Marineris*, the Grand Canyon of Mars, four times the size of Earth's great natural wonder. Bradbury knew this particular Martian topography well; during the final decades of his life, fans and supporters of the Mars missions had started to call the deepest area of the vast canyon complex, a pronounced curving *chiasma* in the southwest quadrant, the "Bradbury Abyss."

For many years, he had half-seriously asked to be buried in the sarcophagus of the Pharaoh Seti I, displayed within one of his favorite Earthbound museum settings: the marvelous treasures of the John Soane Museum in London. In later years, however, when he heard the popular mythology of the Bradbury Abyss, he opted for the future rather than the past, and declared for the Abyss whenever asked about his final journey. But the other half of his award was a flag that Thomas Paine had designed himself to symbolize mankind's universal claim on the Red Planet. This particular flag had traveled in orbit on the International Space Station, taken into orbit and returned to Earth by the Space Shuttle *Discovery*.[1]

During the final portions of the slide show, actor Robert Picardo read selections from Bradbury's Space-Age poetry. The final slide juxtaposed a formidable image of the large-payload *Curiosity* (it was nuclear-powered, and the size of an automobile) with a vintage photo of the mid-life Bradbury, exhorting an audience with one of his trademark gestures of a hand rising to indicate upward flight, framed by a caption that epitomized the memorial ceremony as well as his life's work: "The Bradbury Imperative: 'We must explore!'"[2]

Two weeks later, NASA and the JPL *Curiosity* team named the rover's Gale Crater touchdown point "Bradbury Landing." A simple name, evoking the small-town world of *Dandelion Wine*, where anyone might expect to find a point along the north shore of Lake Michigan called "Bradbury Landing." A good place to fish, or perhaps journey out beyond the sight of land to explore new horizons.

∴ ∴ ∴

What constitutes the enduring Ray Bradbury as we navigate the twenty-first century? The beginning of an answer might emerge if one considers an historical parallel. Thomas Jefferson designed his own grave marker and wrote his own epitaph; the three achievements he recorded on that stone did not include his presidency but focused instead on what he considered his three most enduring written works. Ray Bradbury, who always preferred to meditate on death's metaphors rather than its mechanics, chose a rather common conjoined marker when Maggie died in 2003, but he added a brief epitaph memorializing what he considered, late in life, to be his single greatest achievement: "Author of *Fahrenheit 451*." These words were added to his half of the stone without fanfare, and without the foreknowledge of his family and friends.

Jefferson's powerful mind centered on statecraft and technical invention, a far cry from Bradbury's dream-inspired genius. Yet both men believed in the existence of life beyond our knowledge of the cosmos. In the century between Jefferson's death and Bradbury's birth, Percival Lowell translated Schiaparelli's Martian "canali" into a master metaphor for intelligent alien life, and Edgar Rice Burroughs peopled the Red Planet with a techno-warrior cast of exotic humans. By way of Lowell and Burroughs, Mars would indeed be imprinted as overlay to Bradbury's innate desire to find life beyond Earth; he could just as easily have included *The Martian Chronicles* along with *Fahrenheit 451* on the face of the cold stone, as he contemplated his legacy for the twenty-first century.

These works clearly endure, as do the other now-classic works he created just before and just after the midpoint of the twentieth century: the edgy stories of *The Illustrated Man* and *The October Country*, the remembered past of *Dandelion Wine*, the exuberant fantasies and magical realism of *The Golden Apples of the Sun* and *A Medicine for Melancholy*, and the culminating terrors of *Something Wicked This Way Comes*. They bear the intrinsic qualities of a master storyteller, but the way that Bradbury embedded them in both popular and literary culture—at home and abroad—was a process that spanned another half century. During those later times, he also produced a few enduring prose fiction treasures in spite of the constant parade of lectures, creative consultancies, and adaptations for stage, television, and films that bled off his once broad channel of original short story production.

The enduring works of his last four decades were often nourished from the safe harbors where he had crafted his earliest stories of fantasy and suspense. The first of these, *The Halloween Tree*, represents a major affirmation of life over death that explores evolving explanations of life cycles from Neolithic times down to the twentieth century. Often mistaken as a book solely for young readers, the mythological core of *The Halloween Tree* represents one of his most illuminating later-life returns to the safe fantasy anchorages of his early years.

Bradbury's final legacy as a novelist rests just as much on the detective novels of his late career as it does on the earlier breakthrough of *Something Wicked This Way Comes*. These are fascinating experiments in autobiography that succeed in forming a true time portal back to the most important moments of his literary career: the moment at which he knew he was going to make it as a writer (*Death Is a Lonely Business*) and the moment when he knew that Hollywood would never smother him (*A Graveyard for Lunatics*). In these two experimental novels, Bradbury crafted the fascinating illusion that he is typing each story just at the moment we read it and thereby succeeds in taking the reader back for a glimpse of the perilous paths not taken.

"The Toynbee Convector" presents Bradbury's abiding goal as a writer in its most essential form. He saw Toynbee's "challenge and response" concept as the determiner of advancement or destruction for any civilization going forward. Bradbury himself is the time traveler, the one who transcends faith and makes us *know* the future will be there for us; we must not try, we must do, and thereby Bradbury succeeds in taking the reader forward in time. Certain essays share this degree of focused insight as well; these include "Beyond Eden," "Beyond Giverny," and for better or for worse, the powerful words of "The God in Science Fiction."

Certain episodes of the *Ray Bradbury Theater* have a quality equal to any author series produced in that era, but the series as a whole will endure as an enterprise that produced quality programming on a relatively small budget managed within an effective consortium of producers and broadcasters, garnering consistent award recognition throughout its six-year run.

These isolated but significant achievements from the second half of his career were punctuated by the publication of many stories and a few book-length projects conceived half a lifetime earlier. Of the long-deferred projects from his most creative years, *Somewhere a Band Is Playing* offers his last strong and sustained work of prose fiction, graced with his settled view of the choices we make to destroy or preserve the power of the imagination. These, then, of the works that he wrote or completed after the age of fifty, have lasting merit nearly to the scale of the masterful early works for which he is known in the twenty-first century.

∴ ∴ ∴

Sometime in the 1950s, the reclusive Philip K. Dick made his thoughts on Ray Bradbury privately known in a letter to noir writer James McKimmey. "I have heard STF editors rave against him," Dick observed, using the old shorthand for "scientifiction" to describe the establishment he himself never trusted. "The main thing they fear is that Bradbury is influencing the youth and therefore in a position to create the main trend in STF."[3] This was indeed the greatest Bradbury magic of all, and it extended as well to the best of his early fantasy tales. He was not alone in shaping these trends, and he accepted the fact that brighter stars would overtake and refashion what writers of his generation had seen of the world and the sky.

But there is an age in life when many who would write, or teach, or explore, still encounter Ray Bradbury. His influence on writers and teachers of fiction and the explorers of the Cosmos eventually spanned generations; to be sure, this process may have been aided by his close proximity to Caltech, NASA's Jet Propulsion Laboratory, and the great mid-century observatories on Mount Wilson and Mount Palomar, as well as the great motion picture studios that, at various times in his life, were only a roller-skate journey or a bicycle trip away from his home. Yet his explorations of the human heart, and his dreams of reaching other worlds, knew no such physical boundaries at all.

The 1960s and 1970s permanently wedded Bradbury to the Great Tale of space exploration and changed the trajectory of his role in American culture. If there was a diminished output of great short fiction across his final decades, it was not just a function of Hollywood and stage productions bleeding off his best writing efforts; it was also the result of a fundamental shift in his felt purpose in life. His true trajectory in the final four decades of his life would be that of a visionary, asked over and over again to tell us why we desire to explore, why we should go to the stars, and what we might become when we get there.

Notes

Most of Ray Bradbury's unpublished papers cited in this volume are located in the Center for Ray Bradbury Studies (Indiana University School of Liberal Arts, IUPUI); exceptions from other locations are indicated in individual note citations. The Center also holds letters to Bradbury back to the 1940s, as well as carbons or fax originals of many outgoing letters from this period of his life; many letters to Bradbury written before 1970 are privately held in the Albright Collection, with photocopies deposited in the Center for Ray Bradbury Studies. The Rare Book and Manuscript Library of Columbia University's Butler Library is the depository for Bradbury's letters to his agents, the late Don Congdon, and his successor, Michael Congdon. The University of Tulsa preserves Bradbury's letters to his British publisher, Sir Rupert Hart-Davis, in its Hart-Davis Collection. The University of Texas, Austin, curates Bradbury's letters to his Knopf editors in the Harry Ransom Humanities Center. Portions of chapter 3 were bridged and rewritten from various brief passages excerpted from my introduction to a limited press edition of Ray Bradbury's *The Halloween Tree* (Colorado Springs: Gauntlet Press, 2005). All interviews with Bradbury were conducted in Los Angeles or Palm Springs.

Chapter 1. Prometheus Bound
1 Reuters (unsigned), "What They Are Naming the Moon," *San Francisco Chronicle*, Jul. 26, 1971.
2 From three pages of typed travel notes tipped into Jan. 1967 drafts of his *Life* magazine article, "An Impatient Gulliver Above Our Roofs" (Nov. 1967).
3 Handwritten note from Col. David Scott to Ray Bradbury, undated, written on a photocopied clipping of "What They Are Naming the Moon."

Chapter 2. The Darkness between the Stars
1 Kenneth Reich (*LA Times*) to Bradbury, Apr. 27, 1972.
2 Captain Alan Bean (NASA) to Bradbury, n.d.; dated by adjacent letters.
3 Jonathan R. Eller, *Ray Bradbury: Unbound* (Urbana: University of Illinois Press, 2014), 219–220.

Chapter 3. A Teller of Tales
1 Unpublished letter, Ray Bradbury to the late William F. Touponce, Oct. 10, 1986 (photocopy in the Bradbury Center).
2 Ray Bradbury, interview with the author, Oct. 12, 1998.
3 The MGM studio research materials and Bradbury's notes are located in the Albright Collection.

4 Bradbury's copy of Edna Ruth Kelley, *Book on Halloween* (Boston: Lothrop, Lee, and Shepherd, 1919). The front endpaper, "Research for Chuck Jones 1968," is annotated in Bradbury's hand.

5 ABC (Brandon Stoddard) to Bradbury, Nov. 11, 1971. There was also brief interest from a Japanese American production company (Bradbury, interview with John C. Tibbetts, Oct. 5, 1996; in Tibbetts, *Those Who Made It* (London: Palgrave, 2015).

6 The publishing developments described in this paragraph are documented in Gottlieb to Bradbury, Jun. 25, 1971 (copy) and Sep. 24, 1971 (copy); Nancy Nicholas to Donn Congdon, Aug. 10, 1971 (copy); Ray Bradbury to Bob Gottlieb, Sep. 12, 1971; and Ray Bradbury to Nancy Nicholas, Nov. 17, 1971 (The Alfred A. Knopf Deposit, Harry Ransom Humanities Research Center, University of Texas at Austin).

7 The late insertion of the catacomb episode can be reconstructed from Bradbury's surviving manuscripts and discards in his own papers and in the Albright Collection. His recollection of the significance of this episode is quoted from Sam Weller, The *Bradbury Chronicles: The Life of Ray Bradbury* (New York: Wm. Morrow Co., 2005), 287.

8 Setting copy, with Knopf markup, the Albright Collection. Bradbury's unmediated underlayer, free of editorial markup, appears in a multiple-text limited edition of The *Halloween Tree* (Colorado Springs: Gauntlet Publications, 2005).

9 Jonathan R. Eller and William F. Touponce, *Ray Bradbury: The Life of Fiction* (Kent, Ohio: Kent State University Press, 2004), 417–423. I am indebted to my coauthor, Bill Touponce, for tracing these elements of Bradbury's authorship in the introduction to our book ("Metaphors, Myths, and Masks: Origins of Authorship in the Texts of Ray Bradbury," 1–50).

10 Leon Salanave, "1972 Summer Lecture Series Gets Huge Response!" *Mercury: The Journal of the Astronomical Society of the Pacific* (Sep.–Oct. 1972): 23; series advertisement, *Mercury*, (Jul.–Aug.): 13. Bradbury's synopsis is from the "Cosmic Evolution" lecture series flyer.

11 "Sid Stebel Blogs: Ray Bradbury & SBWC Beginnings," Jan. 21, 2001 (https://www.sbwriters.com/-blog/2017/03/the-history-of-the-santa-barbara-writers-conference-1973).

12 Mary Conrad, "The History of the Santa Barbara Writers Conference—1973," Mar. 17, 2017 SBWC (https://www.sbwriters.com/blog/2017/03/the-history-of-the-santa-barbara-writers-conference-1973). The fax of the 2005 keynote typescript is preserved in the Bradbury Center.

13 Dorf to Bradbury, Aug. 6, 1976.

Chapter 4. The Prisoner of Gravity

1 Bradbury, interview with the author, Oct. 20, 2007.

2 Bradbury, interview with the author, Oct. 25, 2009.

3 Peckinpah to Bradbury, Aug. 26, Sept. 11 and 17, 1976; Bradbury to Peckinpah, Sept. 9 (cc); Bradbury, interview with the author, Oct. 20, 2007.

4 Bradbury, interview with the author, Oct. 25, 2009.

Chapter 5. Witness and Celebrate

1 Arlen Walter, "Latin Night at the Pavilion," *Los Angeles Times*, Feb. 27, 1973, G13.
2 Bradbury, *Day at Night* television interview with James Day, Jan. 21, 1974.
3 Robert Gottlieb, *Avid Reader* (New York: Picador, 2016), 133–134.
4 Bradbury to Nicholas, Sept. 15, 1971.
5 Guy E. Coriden (Department of State) to Bradbury, Dec. 15, 1972, and May 15, 1973.
6 Parviz Davaii (Executive Secretary) to Ray Bradbury, June 4, 1973; Susan Schoenfeld (California Center of Films for Children), June 16, 1973.

Chapter 6. The Sleep of Reason

1 Goya's Capricho No. 43 is often condensed to this epigraph form.
2 Bradbury to Congdon, May 10, 1971; Alexandra Bradbury to the author, Oct. 14, 2019.
3 Bradbury, interview with the author, Mar. 14, 2002.
4 This passage from the Jan. 4, 1982, Santa Barbara lecture is transcribed in Gene Beley, *Ray Bradbury Uncensored* (Lincoln, Neb.: iUniverse, 2006), 70.
5 Bradbury, interview with the author, Mar. 14, 2002.
6 Ibid.
7 Bradbury to Nancy Nicholas (Knopf), Feb. 24, 1974.
8 "'Farm Boy'—An Album of Distant Thunder," *Los Angeles Times Book Review* (Aug. 25, 1974): 1, 10.
9 Eller, *Unbound*, 135–136.

Chapter 7. The Inherited Wish

1 Quoted from the mimeographed transcript given to Bradbury by KOAP (Albright Collection).
2 Assignment America, episode 104, "Ray Bradbury: The Fantasy Maker." The history of Bradbury's universe quotation is sourced in https://quoteinvestigator.com/2016/06/06/impossibility/.
3 Bradbury, interview with the author, Mar. 14, 2010. The meeting with Marceau and subsequent correspondence is preserved in Bradbury to Congdon, Mar. 21 and May 10, 1975.
4 Three-page carbon with titled cover-sheet. The title-page notation, "a pandemonium theatre company production," as well as a paste-up program dummy titled *The World of Marceau–Bradbury* over an old 1964 *World of Ray Bradbury* program, suggests that he hoped to coproduce with Marceau, either in Paris or Los Angeles.
5 The original actors would reunite again for a 1977 tour that included Los Angeles.
6 Belafonte to Congdon, May 3, 1977; Belafonte to Bradbury, Apr. 20, 1978.
7 Bradbury to Hart-Davis, Jan. 17, 1977.
8 NASA, *Why Man Explores* (Government Printing Office, 1977), GPO publication 0-228-449, 58–61. Subsequent quotations by Cousteau are from the same source, 70.

Chapter 8. *Long After Midnight*

1 Sid Stebel, "The Book Report: Ray Bradbury Beyond Fantasy," *Los Angeles Times*, Nov. 3, 1976, IV-3.
2 Bradbury's marked-up galleys are in the Albright Collection; the curtailed galley revisions are recorded in the Bradbury Center's *Collected Stories of Ray Bradbury*, volume 3.
3 Bradbury, interview with the author, Mar. 14, 2002.
4 The reviews cited here include Theodore Sturgeon, "Bradbury Collection to Savor," *Los Angeles Free Press*, Oct. 1, 1976; Joseph Fanzone Jr., "Sci-fi Stories: the Bester and the Brightest," *Baltimore Sun*, Oct. 10, 1976; Bruce Allen, "How Familiar This Sci-fi Seems," *Boston Globe*, Oct. 17, 1976; Charles Nicol, "Bradbury Polishes His Parrot," *Harper's* (Sep. 27, 1976); Robert LaRouche, "Views into the Unknown," *St. Louis Post-Dispatch*, Nov. 21, 1976; Beverly Friend, "Superb Tales of Lofty Speculation," *Chicago Sun-Times*, Oct. 10, 1976; Stebel, "The Book Report," IV-4; Tom Hutchinson, "Science Fiction," *London Times*, May 19, 1977, 13.
5 John Singh, "A World of Tomorrow: Inside Walt's Last Dream," *Disney Twenty-Three* 2.3 (Fall 2010): 9.
6 Sarah Englehardt (Carnegie Corporation) to Bradbury, Jul. 12, 1977. "I can tell you that 2,509 'Carnegie Libraries' were built between 1891 and 1917, when grants for buildings were discontinued."
7 Jim Korkis, "Walt's Friend, Ray Bradbury," *MousePlanet*, Jun. 7, 2012, discusses the initial post-opening edits to the Bradbury script (https://www.mouseplanet.com/10001/Walts_Friend_Ray_Bradbury).
8 "You Are . . . Renaissance People," Excerpts from two addresses by Ray Bradbury to WED and MAPO "Imagineers" on Dec. 23, 1976 (pamphlet).

Chapter 9. A Mailbox on Mars

1 Transcribed from the radio interview embedded in Bradbury's duplicate copy of the Phoenix lander's digital Martian library.
2 "Mailbox on Mars," the "Corwin on Media" column, *Westways*, Jun. 1977, 76–77.
3 JPL's "Search for Life" symposium was cosponsored with The American Institute of Aeronautics and Astronautics and the Forum for the Advancement of Students in Science and Technology.
4 Bradbury to Gottlieb, undated [Feb. 25, 1974].
5 Beley, *Uncensored*, 132. Beley's Oct. 22, 1982, interview with Peter Douglas, and his interviews with others involved in the story of this film, are preserved in Beley's journalistic biography.
6 Bradbury, interview with the author, Apr. 6, 2009.
7 Bradbury, interview with the author, Oct. 14, 2005, and Apr. 6, 2009.
8 Bradbury, interview with the author, Oct. 10, 2007, and Oct. 18, 2008. Beley's 1982 interview with Peter Douglas places the termination in January 1978, but the more likely date is January 1977. Kirk Douglas notes in his Jan. 28, 1977, letter to Charles Bronson, "in spite of David Picker's exciting reaction to it, Barry Diller said, 'No'."

9 Kirk Douglas to Charles Bronson (Bradbury cc), Jan. 28, 1977.

10 Clayton to Peter and Kirk Douglas (Bryna), Apr. 1, 1977 (from the cc to Bradbury).

Chapter 10. The God in Science Fiction

1 Jim Moore, "Reentering Bradbury's World at the Colony," *Los Angeles Times* Calendar, Jul. 24, 1977, 48. Bradbury to Kermit Christman, Aug. 8, 1993.

2 Bradbury to Congdon, n.d. (received Aug. 15, 1977).

3 Bradbury, interview with the author, Mar. 13, 2010.

4 Bradbury's program for the 1977 Allegro Ball.

5 Jonathan R. Eller, *Becoming Ray Bradbury* (Urbana: University of Illinois Press, 2011), 211–212.

6 A contemporary issue of *Foundation* included a review of *Close Encounters* by Thomas Disch that explored a similar interpretation.

7 Bradbury," Opening the Beautiful Door of True Immortality," *Los Angeles Times* Calendar, Nov. 20, 1977.

8 David McClintick, *Indecent Exposure* (New York HarperCollins,1982), 243. McClintick's passage from Bradbury also appears in Dr. R. J. Rushdoony's critique of journalistic humanism in "Religious Mentality of the Media," *Easy Chair* 32 (Nov. 22, 1982) (http://www.pocketcollege.com/transcript/ RR161A1.html).

9 From "Reflections of a Bonehunter," WNET documentary (Nebraska PBS affiliate), Jul. 1994.

10 Eller, *Becoming*, 67–69.

11 The Brackett-Bradbury collaboration on "Lorelei of the Red Mist" is described in Eller, *Becoming*, 110–111. Bradbury described his visit to the set of *The Big Sleep* in his recorded conversation with Irvin Kershner, Mar. 4, 1980.

12 Craig Miller (Star Wars Corp.) to Bradbury, Mar. 28, 1978; Bradbury conversation with Irvin Kershner, Mar. 4, 1980; Bradbury, "B&B: Bracket & Bradbury 1944," draft memorial, Oct. 16, 1998.

13 The evolution of the Kasdan-Brackett script is discussed in Laurent Bouzereau, *Star Wars: The Annotated Screenplays* (New York: Ballantine, 1997), and Michael Kaminski, *The Secret History of Star Wars* (Ann Arbor, Mich.: Legacy Press, 2008).

Chapter 11. Infinite Worlds

1 This remarkable image is recorded in Bradbury 1998 folder, "New or Un-Used, Un-published Poems!" The image is annotated "IDEA FOR A POEM, Paris, 1978. MANHA G. D."

2 Undated; possibly drafted for Bradbury jacket or liner copy and filed with his 1994 incoming correspondence. Ten years later, he remembered his words in a private conversation as: "Hold on. Everyone shut up. You're talking about the ants; I want to talk about the elephants!" (Bradbury, interview with the author, Oct. 4, 2004).

3 Elisabeth Gille (Denoel) to Bradbury, Jun. 8, 1978.

4 Alexandra Bradbury, telephone interview with the author, Apr. 20, 2019.

5   Bradbury, "The Ghost of Fellini's Wife," *Orange County Sun*, Apr. 1966.

6   Bradbury, "From Sunlit Midnights to Moonlit Noons, *Los Angeles Times Book Review* (Nov. 17, 1977): 1, 14. A review of *Fellini's Films*, Christian Strich, ed. (New York: Putnam's, 1977). Reprinted in Bradbury, *Yestermorrow* (Santa Barbara: Capra Press, 1991), 129–136.

7   Daniel Keel (Diogenes) to Bradbury (via the Intercontinental Agency, London), May 30, 1978.

8   Fellini to Bradbury, Jan. 26, 1978.

9   Bradbury to Fellini (undated carbon, ca. late February 1978); Fellini to Bradbury, Mar. 3, 1978.

10 The travel schedules for the entire trip are documented in Bradbury's copies of the French Ministry of Foreign Affairs official itinerary and the Scariano Travel Agency bookings.

11 Bradbury's self-revelation is prefaced, "'Toto'—Blind Until!" "Action!" Sees—then blind again with: "Cut!"

12 Bradbury to Congdon, Jan. 3, 1996.

13 Margaret S. Field (Writers & Artists Agency) to Bradbury (Hotel Hassler, Rome), cc Don Congdon (Columbia).

14 Bradbury to Morgan Jenness (New York Shakespeare Festival), Sept. 20, 1986. The Public Theater's directors reviewed a number of Bradbury plays during the 1980s, but none were produced.

15 Wouk to Bradbury, Aug. 17, 1978. Wouk had just completed *War and Remembrance*, his sequel to *The Winds of War*. The Sagan anecdote is recounted in Bradbury's foreword to *The Collected Poetry of Ray Bradbury* (Lancaster, Penn.: Stealth Press, 2002).

16 Bradbury to Congdon, May 28, 1978. The *Chronicles* film shooting was actually scheduled for the island nation of Malta and not the Balearic Islands of Spain.

Chapter 12. Abandon in Place

1   Nazaret Cherkezian (Smithsonian) to Bradbury, Dec. 5, 1978, citing Bradbury's unlocated letter of Apr. 22, 1978.

2   Steve Ditlea, "Does Science Fiction Have a Future on TV?" *New York Times*, Jan. 6, 1980.

3   Pacht, Ross, Warne, Bernhard & Sears, Inc., to Bradbury, Jan. 17, 1980.

4   Ben Bova (*Omni*) to Bradbury, Western Union Mailgram, Jan. 30, 1980.

5   Matheson to Bradbury, May 17, 1996.

6   The eligibility period for this Emmy cycle was June 1979 through November 1980; the Awards were presented in New York City's Roosevelt Hotel on April 13, 1981.

Chapter 13. Beyond Eden

1   Bradbury, interview with Gary Kurtz, Apr. 9, 1980. Context indicates the interview, cited here and subsequently, may have been conducted at what was then the Samuel Goldwyn Studio lot in Hollywood.

2   John Williams to Bradbury, Dec. 28, 1980.

3   Eller, *Becoming*, 114–115.

Chapter 14. Robot Museums

1 Bradbury, "Hymn to Humanity from the Cathedral of High Technology," *Los Angeles Times*, Nov. 18, 1979, K1. The probable genealogy of Bradbury's "wings" quotation is discussed in https://quoteinvestigator.com/tag/ray-bradbury/#note-3999-3 (website of "Quote Investigator").

2 James Bryant, thoughts on "Ray Bradbury and the Lost Planetarium Show," by David Romanowski, National Air & Space Museum Facebook post, Jun. 8, 2012. Bryant witnessed Bradbury's tour and lecture as a resident associate with the Natural History Museum's Insect Zoo.

3 Nazaret Cherkezian (Smithsonian Telecom) to Bradbury, Dec. 9, 1980.

4 See Eller and Touponce, *Life of Fiction*, 396–400, for a fuller discussion of the Disch review of *The Stories of Ray Bradbury* and its opposition to the Highet introduction to *The Vintage Bradbury*.

5 The draft continuation of this paragraph, mercifully edited out by Disch prior to publication, maintained that "as an artist he is callow, careless, and inept."

6 Disch would subsequently affirm his preference for these writers in his 1998 nonfiction book, *The Dreams Our Stuff Is Made Of* (New York: The Free Press / Simon & Schuster, 1998).

Chapter 15. The Great Shout of the Universe

1 David Romanowski, "Ray Bradbury and the Lost Planetarium Show," National Air & Space Museum Facebook post, Jun. 8, 2012, additional comment.

2 Ibid. "What did they expect? He's Ray Bradbury, not Arthur C. Clarke. He's a visionary, a dreamer, a romantic, a poet. Yes, in a Bradbury cosmos, the Big Bang is 'The Great Shout of the Universe'!"

3 Highlights from the individual Bradbury critiques preserved at Air & Space are noted in Romanowski.

4 A carbon of Bradbury's submitted narration text, along with the nine-page critique from Air & Space, is preserved in the Bradbury Center in a yellow folder labeled "1981 Air | Space | Wash. D.C. | Great Shout—Universe."

5 William S. Murphy, "Spacecraft, Airplanes in Exposition Park," *Los Angeles Times*, Jan. 10, 1987.

6 Thomas M. Sipos, "Ray Bradbury on Mel Gibson's Fahrenheit 451, Preaching Science, and the Universe," HollywoodInvestigator.com, Apr. 22, 2002. Bradbury's distinction between teaching and preaching is also expressed in his comments here.

7 David Boss (NFL Properties) to Bradbury, Jan. 6, 1981.

8 Bradbury's audio tape copies of the Heston narration and Hudson soundtrack are preserved in the Bradbury Center; a professional recording of the soundtrack and an illustration of the original installation can be heard and viewed at https://www.youtube.com/watch?v=lvZC20BZ6vw, apparently from the Duquette Foundation CD OPM 6602 (2005).

9 Jim Hosney (AFI) to Bradbury, Jan. 28, 1981.

10 Bradbury, AFI's conservatory seminar, Oct. 9, 1969, published in George Stevens Jr., ed., *Conversations with the Great Moviemakers of Hollywood's Golden Age* (New York: Knopf, 2006), 363 (epigraph).

11 Bradbury, AFI's Harold Lloyd seminars, Apr. 1981, or Jun. 1982, published in ibid., 375.

12 Eller, *Unbound*, 168; from Bradbury to Congdon, Jul. 29, 1961: "Going through the book I've had to sit down and work out a real background for each of the characters I did in sketch form so long ago."

13 The Theatre Vanguards in Hollywood hosted the third annual Golden Scroll awards; Bradbury's working draft of the program shows that other participants included such Bradbury friends as composer Miklos Rozsa and writers A. E. Van Vogt and Harlan Ellison.

14 Betty Givens (Academy of Motion Picture Arts and Sciences Foundation) to Bradbury, Nov. 3, 1980, with ASFFHF draft press release for the Pal Award and Lecture attached.

15 Bradbury's copy of the tribute program identifies the participants and the nature of the MHA Performance Award.

16 Eller, *Unbound*, 121.

17 Beley, *Uncensored*, ch. 7, "King Kong Pisses on 'The Mind and Supermind' in Santa Barbara," 63–77; the chapter contains a large portion of Bradbury's presentation.

18 Nils Hardin to Donn Albright, Jan. 5, 1982.

19 Bradbury to Mildred Goodnow, Jan. 25, 1982, cited in Beley, *Uncensored*, 76.

20 Barney Brantingham, "Bradbury Expletive Reduces Audience," *Santa Barbara News-Press*, Jan. 10, 1982, C-4.

Chapter 16. A Eureka Year

1 Annette McComas to Bradbury, Mar. 3, 1981, and Jan. 30, 1982.

2 Leslie Epstein (*Omni*) to Bradbury, Feb. 11, 1982.

3 Eller, *Unbound*, ch. 28, "In the Twilight Zone," 187–188.

4 John J. O'Connor, "TV Review: Ray Bradbury's Fantasy a 'Wonderworks' Film," *New York Times*, Jan. 2, 1985, C18 (national edition).

5 Bradbury, interview with the author, Oct. 19, 2002.

6 Bradbury, interview with the author, Oct. 22, 2007.

7 Murray to Bradbury, Apr. 7, 1982. Murray also gave Bradbury contact information for the JPL's senior resident at NASA to help arrange tours. Bradbury's contact with the Goddard Spaceflight Center, where he would later speak for the Goddard Awards ceremonies of 1987, may have begun during this trip.

8 A complete carbon and several discard pages of Bradbury's *Fahrenheit 451* typescript are in the Albright Collection (photocopy in the Center for Ray Bradbury Studies).

9 Bradbury to the author, Oct. 22, 2007.

10 Speakes to Bradbury, Apr. 28, 1982. A companion letter to Bradbury from Speakes's colleague Peter Roussel, also dated April 28th, noted how "Having such an offer from someone of your stature has not fallen on deaf ears."

11 Bradbury was only 20 in 1940 and could not vote in that general election. He voted for Roosevelt in 1944 but flipped to the third-party candidacy of Henry Wallace over Truman in 1948, largely for the promise he saw in Wallace's economic vision; he actively campaigned for Adlai Stevenson in 1952 and 1956, and for Kennedy in 1960, but the Vietnam War had led him away from the remaining democratic candidate field in 1968. Reagan seemed to promise economic reforms after the recession of the 1970s, and strong international leadership that just might bring down the iron curtain. His vote never depended on doctrinaire party politics (Eller, *Becoming*, 105–107, 268–272; Eller, *Unbound*, 40–44, 205–207).

12 Iris Newsom (QJLC) to Bradbury, Apr. 27, 1982.

13 Bradbury to Chaon, Apr. 30–May 1, 1982.

Chapter 17. One-Way Ticket Man

1 Beley, *Uncensored*, 87. Beley's interview with Bradbury is transcribed, but the date and place are not indicated.

2 Ibid., 125–126.

3 Korkis, *MousePlanet* online, Jun. 7, 2012. In his Bradbury memorial essay, Jim Korkis points out the poetic license that Bradbury took with Disney's words. The quotations from Bradbury's 1981 Tencennial essay were reprinted in this memorial publication.

4 Beley, *Uncensored*, 128; E. Graydon Taylor, untitled, *Time* (Nov. 8, 1982): 53 (Bradbury photo by Michael Jacobs).

Chapter 18. "My Name Is Dark"

1 Beley, *Uncensored*, 132–133.

2 Judy Smith (Spielberg) to Don Congdon, May 26, 1978 (cc Bradbury).

3 Beley, *Uncensored*, 133.

4 Phil Nichols, *The Cinema of Lost Films: Ray Bradbury and the Screen*, doctoral dissertation (Liverpool, U.K.: University of Liverpool, 2017), 228–235. His chapter 4 (190–250) represents the first archive-based analysis of the film and its precursors.

5 Bradbury to Clayton and Jeannie Sims, Aug. 31, 1981.

6 Bradbury, interview with the author, Oct. 8, 2004.

7 Steven Rebello, "Something Wicked This Way Comes," *Cinefantastique* 13:5 (Jun.–Jul. 1983): 42–43. Rebello's full article (28–49) contains a comprehensive summary of the entire project from the beginning of Disney's involvement through the remaking of the film in 1982–1983.

8 Bradbury, interviews with the author, Apr. 6 and Oct. 24, 2009.

9 Clayton to Bradbury, Apr. 4, 1983.

10 Bradbury to Howard Greene (Disney).

11 Bradbury, interview with the author, Oct. 22, 2007.

12 Alan Dean Foster, Review of *Something Wicked This Way Comes*, *Starlog* 76 (Nov. 1983): 71–73. The same issue also includes "Patching the Pandemonium of Dark's Shadow Show," a somewhat critical review of Lee Dyer's special effects by David Hutchison (65–70, 87).

Chapter 19. A Most Favorite Subject

1 Bradbury to Irish writer Patrick Skene Catling, Oct. 17, 1997.
2 Ginia Bellafante, "Suburban Rapture," *New York Times Book Review* (Dec. 24, 2008): db23, discusses the Auden introduction in her retrospective look at McGinley's life and times.
3 Eller, *Becoming*, 260.
4 Bradbury, interview with the author, Oct. 21, 2008; Bradbury, "Say Goodbye," unpublished notes, Feb. 1983.
5 Steven Paul Leiva, telephone interview with the author, May 27, 2019.
6 Lane's fantasy aircraft concepts eventually led Bradbury to have him illustrate *Ahmad and the Oblivion Machine*.
7 Bradbury, interview with the author, Oct. 8, 2004.

Chapter 20. Memories of Murder

1 Eller and Touponce, *The Life of Fiction*, 316–317; Eller, *Becoming*, 94–96.
2 Mecoy (Dell) to Bradbury, Mar. 24, 1983.
3 Ibid., Mar. 31, 1983.
4 Bradbury's 1945 carnival description is quoted in its entirety in Eller and Touponce, *The Life of Fiction*, 257.

Chapter 21. 1984 Will Not Arrive

1 Bradbury, interview with the author, Oct. 22, 2007.
2 Maryann Dadisman, "Author Ray Bradbury Returns to His Boyhood Haunts in Waukegan," *Waukegan News-Sun*, Oct. 27–28, 1984.
3 Maryann Dadisman, "Bradbury Will Help Waukegan Celebrate," *Waukegan News-Sun*, Oct. 23, 1984.
4 Ralph Zahorick, "'Bradbury' Tenants Surprised by Visit," "From A to Z" column, *Waukegan News-Sun*, Oct. 27–28, 1984.

Chapter 22. *Death Is a Lonely Business*

1 Friend and mentor Leigh Brackett spelled it out for him in early 1944: "If you gave it more length, let me meet the murderer and have several suspects to choose from, and built up your premise more fully and soundly, it would be better." Brackett to Bradbury, postcard, n.d. (postmarked Jan. 5, 1944).
2 A textual and critical analysis of *Death Is a Lonely Business* and its precursor, "Where Everything Ends," is found in Eller and Touponce, *The Life of Fiction*, chapter 6, 318–324, 340–348.
3 The phrase "death is a lonely business," typed in capital letters, first surfaced in Bradbury's correspondence in a 1963 letter to crime writer James McKimmey. It did not appear on the drafts of the new novel for some time, however; Bradbury's first working title was *Death Rides Fast*, an allusion to Gottfried Bürger's *Ballad of Lenore* and Vernet's 1838 painting, "The Ballad of Lenore, Or the Dead Ride Fast."

4   There was no single moment, of course; the October 1949 plot anchoring date radiated out into allusions to earlier moments in Bradbury's own writing and moviegoing milestones, as well as later moments in Hollywood history, ranging as far forward as the 1951 films *Sunset Boulevard* and *All about Eve*.

5   Eller, *Becoming*, chapter 28 (166–172); Eller and Touponce, Introduction, *The Life of Fiction*, 24–30, 40–43. Reconstructed portions of these failed projects have been published in limited press editions in *Masks* and in *Match to Flame*.

6   Bevington to Bradbury, Feb. 24, 1986.

7   "The Other Me" excerpt follows the draft as sent to Bevington. Publication followed in Bradbury, *Death Has Lost Its Charm for Me* (Northridge, Calif.: Lord John Press, 1987) and Bradbury, *Zen in the Art of Writing* (Santa Barbara, Calif.: Capra Press, 1990).

Chapter 23. A Poet's Heart

1   Bradbury, "There Is Life on Mars, and It Is Us!" *The Planetary Report* 6:4 (Jul.–Aug. 1986): 6–7.

2   Ibid. His only historical error is mistaking Sir Edmund Hillary as the author of George Mallory's quote, "Because it's there."

3   Cowley to Bradbury, signed postcard, Oct. 27, 1985.

4   Bradbury to Hart-Davis, n.d. (dated by content).

5   Bradbury's guest of honor address transcription, *Science Fiction Chronicle* 8:3 (Dec. 1986): 22, 31–32, 34.

Chapter 24. Forms of Things Unknown

1   Norris (National Space Club) to Bradbury, Apr. 30, 1987.

2   Gottlieb to Bradbury, Feb. 10, 1987.

3   Hourigan to Bradbury, Nov. 10, 1987.

4   Eller and Touponce, *The Life of Fiction*, 386–387.

5   Albright strongly recommended the Greentown story "All on a Summer's Night" (1950), which was instead deferred to *Bradbury Stories* (2003). Eller, "Ray Bradbury's Greentown Novels: The Stories Left Behind," introduction to *Summer Morning, Summer Night* (Hornsea, England: PS Publishing, 2007), xvii. This introduction was cut from the American edition (Burton, Mich: Subterranean Press, 2008).

6   Hart-Davis to Bradbury, Oct. 15, 1988.

7   Fellini to Bradbury, Oct. 5, 1987.

8   Bradbury to Jacques Chambon (Denoel), Feb. 1, 1990.

Chapter 25. Time Flies

1   "These may be used by any group producing the play, with the addition of your own music, thus giving your local composer a chance to prove his range." From a single-page "Author's Note," *Dandelion Wine* lyric drafts (ca. 1971–1982), in a stationery box labeled "Miscellaneous Material!"

2   Warren Seabury (Seabury & Associates) to Bradbury, Jan. 17, 1987.

3 Webb to Don Congdon, May 20, 1987.

4 Bradbury to Webb, Dec. 11, 1989 (fax).

5 Jimmy Webb to Ray Bradbury, Don Congdon, and Robert Lantz, Jan. 2, 1990.

6 Lisa Stemle, "'Dandelion Wine' Becomes Dandy of a Show," South Florida Sun-Sentinel, Mar. 5, 1993.

7 Jimmy Webb, interview with Sam Adams, Sep. 3, 2010 (https://music.avclub.com/jimmy-webb-1798221527), AVClub; abridged in Matt Cardin, "Jimmy Webb Says Ray Bradbury and SF Taught Him How to Write Beautiful Lyrics," Teeming Brain, Sep. 13, 2010 (http://www.teemingbrain.com/2010/09/13/jimmy-webb-says-ray-bradbury-and-sf-taught-him-how-to-write-beautiful-lyrics/).

8 Peter Sussman (Atlantis) to Don Congdon, Oct. 26, 1989; Sussman to Martin Leeds (Wilcox Productions), Oct. 27 (fax copy) and Nov. 21, 1989 (under fax cover ltr. from Don Congdon); Larry Wilcox to Sussman, Nov. 9, 1989, contains a counter offer; Leeds to Sussman, Nov. 16, 1989 (under Nov. 21 fax cover ltr. from Don Congdon), contains a subsequent compromise.

9 The typical working dynamics of overseas production are surveyed in Ida Yoshinaga's focused study, "Providing Direction: Lee Tamahori and The Ray Bradbury Theater," New Ray Bradbury Review 6 (2019): 68–85.

10 Cotter (Atlantis-Granada) to Bradbury, Nov. 10, 1989 (Bradbury fax copies); Bradbury to Cotter, ca. Nov. 12 and Nov. 23, 1989.

11 Peter Sussman (Atlantis) to Butch Fries (Fries Entertainment), Nov. 9, 1989, Bradbury to Sussman, Congdon, and Cotter, re the Eisner call; Sussman to Robin Russel (Disney), confirming Eisner's call (Bradbury fax copies).

Chapter 26. Beyond the Iron Curtain

1 Bradbury to Nancy Evans (Doubleday), Jan. 6, 1990.

2 Matt Schudel, "Josef Skvorecky, Czech Writer and Publisher of Dissident Works, Dies at 87," Washington Post, Jan. 7, 2012.

3 Bradbury to Jacques Chambon (Denoel), Feb. 1, 1990. A Jan. 25, 1990, postcard from Prague, possibly written by his friend Bob McCabe (International Herald Tribune in Paris), describes lobbying for more Czech editions of Bradbury's works and noting the ongoing rebuild of the post–Cold War Czech state.

4 Bradbury to Jacques Chambon (Denoel), Dec. 12, 1991; Judith Green, "A Few Words with Ray Bradbury" (interview), San Jose Mercury News, Oct. 30, 1993.

5 Rafael Motamayor, "Before Home Alone, There Was the Cult Boy-vs.-Santa Film Dial Code Santa Claus," Dec. 13, 2018 (https://www.polygon.com/2018/12/13/18138333/dial-code-santa-claus-theaters-blu-ray).

6 Bradbury to Jacques Chambon (Denoel), Feb. 1, 1990.

7 Bradbury to John Phillips (International Herald Tribune), Apr. 21, 1990.

8 Bradbury, "For Ray Bradbury, Proud of a Case of Mistaken Identity," Los Angeles Times (special to the Times, Oct. 26, 1991) (http://articles.latimes.com/1991-10-26/entertainment/ca-315_1_gene-roddenberry).

9 Bradbury's personal file folder, "Soviet Gorbachev Luncheon May 31 1990."

10 Lois Romano, "The Luminaries' Lunch," *Washington Post*, Jun. 1, 1990, B2.

11 Eller, *Unbound*, 145–146; Bradbury to Anthony Boucher, Nov. 6, 1957: "F.451 sold 500,000 copies in Russia before they found it really criticized them, too." Original in the Lilly.

12 Mikhail Iossel, "Ray Bradbury in the U.S.S.R," *The New Yorker* (Jun. 8, 2012).

13 Douglas Fairbanks included his address, so that Bradbury could send him a photo of Fairbanks taken by Bradbury, then a young fan of fifteen, on Sunset Boulevard in 1935. Fairbanks to Bradbury, Aug. 8, 1990.

14 Bradbury, interview with the author, Oct. 22, 2007.

Chapter 27. *A Graveyard for Lunatics*

1 Bradbury, interview with the author, Mar. 14, 2002.

2 Eller, *Becoming*, 266–267; Eller, *Unbound*, 167–168.

3 Fritz Lang had come to Bradbury on Halloween 1950 to discuss the possibility of filming *The Martian Chronicles*. James Wong Howe had been Bradbury's friend even longer; in the late 1940s, Bradbury and Sanora Babb, Howe's wife, became founding members of Dolph Sharp's writer's group, which initially formed around local area writers who had been published in the annual *Best American Short Stories* volumes.

4 It was no coincidence that Bradbury and Harryhausen had been inspired as young men by Howard Roark, the uncompromising architect of Ayn Rand's 1943 novel *The Fountainhead*.

5 Principal reviews include anon., *Publisher's Weekly*, Jul. 1, 1990; Patrick Skene Catling, "The Return of the Beast," *The Spectator*, Oct. 6, 1990.

6 Bloch to Bradbury, undated postcard (postmarked Oct. 12, 1990).

Chapter 28. Disputed Passage

1 Steven Muller (President, JHU) to Bradbury, Apr. 25, 1990; William A. Eames (USIA) to Bradbury, Apr. 30, 1990.

2 Deborah and Thomas Shuster (Waukegan Parks District) to Bradbury, Aug. 12, 1990.

3 Nick Austin (Grafton) to Abner Stein (agent), Aug. 30, 1990.

4 This was not the first overseas World Con he had declined to visit when close by; he and Maggie and their family had been in Paris late in the summer of 1957, when the London Con was just across the English Channel.

5 Bradbury to Don Congdon, Jul. 6, 1991.

6 Bradbury, "The Voyage to Far Metaphor and Elephant India," *Yestermorrow*, 5–6.

7 Guinzburg to Bradbury, Apr. 2, 1991; "Background," Turner Publishing Press Release, Jun. 3, 1991 (Turner Publishing FAX to Bradbury, Jun. 5, 1991).

8 Edwin McDowell, "Judges in Turner Award Dispute Merits of Novel Given a $500,000 Prize," *New York Times*, Jun. 5, 1991, C21.

9 David Streitfeld, "Judges Denounce Turner Prize," *Washington Post*, Jun. 5, 1991; "Turner Flap," *USA Today*, Jun. 5, 1991. Bradbury's oppositional comments are quoted in the same article.

10 Bradbury, interview with the author, Los Angeles, Mar. 11, 2002.

11 Bradbury to Hart-Davis, Jul. 20, 1991; Fellini, transcribed telephone message to Bradbury, Jun. 28, 1991. Bradbury to Jerry Weist (fax, n.d., circa 2001) includes a photocopy of Bradbury's last photograph with Fellini.

12 Bradbury to Don Congdon, n.d.; dated by content references and adjacent filed correspondence to Spring 1991.

13 Bradbury to Congdon, Jul. 6, 1991.

14 Bradbury to Hart-Davis, Jul. 30, 1991 (Tulsa; Bradbury's photocopy).

15 Bradbury, "Voyage to Far Metaphor," 14. Expanded privately in Bradbury, interview with the author, Oct. 24, 2002: "In one of the introductions that I wrote for one of my books recently, I quoted the words to 'Toyland, Toyland | Beautiful Girl and Boyland | Once you pass its portals, you can never return again.' And my response is, bullshit, you know. If you do that, you're sunk. . . Because we can do both—you don't have to give up anything."

Chapter 29. *Green Shadows, White Whale*

1 Dr. Baliunas (Mt. Wilson Observatory) to Bradbury, Aug. 8, 1991.

2 Bradbury to Congdon, Aug. 12, 1991 (original with hand corrections).

3 Bradbury to Abe Grossman (representing Cosmopolis), Aug. 9, 1991 (cc).

4 Marilyn Beck, "Ray Bradbury Rushes to Clarify Huston Legend," Los Angeles *Daily News* LA Life section, Jan. 4, 1988, 17.

5 Bradbury to Don Congdon, Oct. 24, 1991. Bradbury also knew that the Huston inserts would give more balance to the book: "The best thing about these additions, of course, is that they give us some much needed relief from Finn's pub and its semi-comedy grotesques."

6 Most of Bradbury's commentary that day became the introduction to David Alexander's *Star Trek Creator, the Authorized Biography of Gene Roddenberry* (New York: ROC/Penguin, 1994), xiii–xvi, the source of this and subsequent citations in the text.

Chapter 30. The ABCs of Science Fiction

1 Entry on the initial unsuccessful *Mars Orbiter* is at https://nssdc.gsfc.nasa.gov/planetary/chronology_mars.

2 Louis Friedman to Bruce Murray and Carl Sagan, Apr. 22, 1992 (Bradbury fax).

3 Louis Friedman to Isaac Asimov, Oct. 23, 1991 (faxed Apr. 22, 1992).

4 Mikhail Iossel, "Ray Bradbury in the U.S.S.R." *The New Yorker* (Jun. 8, 2012).

5 Bradbury to Congdon, Apr. 30, 1992.

6 Entry on Russia's failed *Mars 96* mission is at https://nssdc.gsfc.nasa.gov/planetary/chronology_mars. Jon Lomberg's introduction to the Phoenix DVD-version of the disk noted that some of the debris landed in the South Atlantic Ocean.

7 The identity of the attendees is based on commentary by Larry Brooks, a principal historian of Disney's *20,000 Leagues* adaptation, preserved in a third-party email sent to Bradbury in 1993 (sender unknown).

8 Bradbury to Roy E. Disney, Jan. 9, 1992 (photocarbon).

9 Bradbury to Kathy Hourigan (Knopf), [Apr. 11, 1992] (Texas; dated by context).

10 Bradbury to Michelle Lapautre (Paris agent), Jan. [1992].

11 Bradbury to Mary Kahn and Tom Cotter (Atlantis Films), Feb. 20, 1992, and Bradbury to Tom Cotter, May 26 and Jun. 2, 1992. News of the ACE Award nominations is documented in Bradbury to Kahn, Nov. 20, 1992.

Chapter 31. An American Icon

1 Sharon J. Salyer, "Board Votes 'Martian' Book Can Be Required," Everett, Washington *Herald*, Mar. 14, 1989, 1B, 4B. These cases involved Haines City, Florida (1982), Newton-Conover High School, North Carolina (1987), and Mukilteo, Washington (1989).

2 Robert Duncan to Roy Disney, Feb. 22, 1996 (cc Bradbury).

3 Bradbury to Turner (n.d.), dated to 1992 by content (FAX master with cover note to Alexandra Bradbury).

4 Bradbury to Mary Dawn Early and John Noaks, Nov. 3, 1992; Bradbury to Pamela Wesson, Nov. 13, 1992. In the Wesson letter, Bradbury used the term *abysmal fracture* to describe Maggie's ankle break, but there is no such term; an avulsion fracture is the most likely intended meaning.

5 Jan and Gordon Lawrence (Paris) to Bradbury, Feb. 11, 1993 (fax); Bradbury to the Gordons, Feb. 14, 1993.

6 Colleen Phillips (Challenger Center) to Bradbury, Jul. 6, 1993; "Ray Bradbury Lands on Mars," *Challenger Log* 5.2 (Summer 1993): 1–2.

7 Bradbury quoted in Jeffrey Staggs, "Honoring the Spirit of Challenger Crew," *Washington Post*, May 4, 1993, E2.

8 Leonard Klady, "Restored 'El Cid' Kicks Off 7th AFI/LA Fest," *Variety* (Jun. 10, 1993); Nancy Blaine (AFI) to Bradbury, Jun. 29, 1993. The schedule and notes for Bradbury's films were documented in the *Los Angeles Times* Calendar section F, Jun. 16–17, 1993.

9 Tom Rooker (Malpaso Productions) to Bradbury, Jul. 29, 1993.

Chapter 32. Harvest Time

1 "Fellini and Halloween," in *October Dreams* (New York: Cemetery Dance, 2002); rpt. in *Halloween Horrors* (New York: Fall River Press, 2010), 287–288. The original typescript (ca. 1999) is preserved in the Bradbury Center.

2 Bradbury to Congdon, Jan. 3, 1996.

3 Bradbury to Kirshner, Peluso, and Young (Hanna-Barbera), Jun. 29, 1992 (FAX original).

4 Bradbury, interview with the author, Los Angeles, Oct. 5, 2004.

5 John Hench (Disney) to Bradbury, Nov. 16, 1993: "Some of the scenes are unforgettable. Like the meeting [of the costumed children] under the swinging light at the street intersection and the circus-papered barn wall."

6 Eller, *Unbound*, 55, 168; Bradbury, Introduction, in *Forbidden Planets* (New York: DAW Books, 2006), 1.

7 Bradbury's bound copy of Silliphant's *Forbidden Planet* script is dated Oct. 1, 1993; Bradbury's initial (and only known) revisions package is dated Oct. 10.

8　Arthur C. Clarke to Bradbury, May 12, 1994.

Chapter 33. A Promise of Eternity

1　Mark Rhodes (IMAX Ridefilm Corp.) to Bradbury, Mar. 6 and Apr. 7, 1995; Bradbury's copy of the revised Ridefilm storyboards, Apr. 7, 1995.

2　Bradbury to Mary Dawn Earley, Jul. 6, 1995.

3　Bradbury to Lawrence Gordon, Jul. 6, 1995 (fax).

4　Eller, *Becoming*, 12, 82–83.

5　Bradbury's radiological report of Jan. 8, 1996, with comparisons to the previous Oct. 10, 1995, report, Saint John's Hospital Department of Medical Imaging, Santa Monica, Calif.

Chapter 34. Séances and Ghosts

1　Anon., "Aldo Sessa Archive: 1958–2018: Sixty Years of Images," Museo de Arte Moderno de Buenos Aires (https://www.museomoderno.org/en/exposiciones/aldo-sessa-archive-1958–2018–60-years-images), Mar.–May 2018. In the early 1960s, Sessa studied film and color photography in Los Angeles with Sydney Paul Solow.

2　This passage was the only portion of his lecture preserved in the newsletter for the Society of Children's Book Writers and Illustrators, a major sponsor of the National Book Fair. Maria Brandán Aráoz, "A Touching Ray Bradbury at the Book Fair in Buenos Aires," *Argent News* 3:2 (Winter 1997).

3　"Menem, Con Bradbury y Vargas Llosa," *Diario Clarín*, Buenos Aires (Apr. 29, 1997): 41; "Bioy Casares y Bradbury Querian Conocerse," *Diario Clarín* (May 4, 1997): 15.

4　Bradbury to Kathy Hourigan (Knopf), May 15, 1997.

5　Sessa to Bradbury, May 10, 2002. Sold, along with Sessa's 2002 box of photographs, as Lot 247 in the Bradbury Estate auction, Nate D. Sanders, September 2014. Sessa's 1997 photographs and cover letter are preserved in the Bradbury Center ("Aldo Sessa May 1997" file folder).

6　Sessa to Bradbury, May 10, 2002.

7　"Gibson, WB in Hot Talks." Bradbury's undated and unattributed clipping dates from the time of location shooting for *Braveheart* (Jun. 6–Oct. 28, 1994).

8　Bradbury to Don Congdon, Oct. 31, 1997.

9　Nichols, *Cinema of Lost Films*, 184–188.

10　Roy E. Disney to Bradbury, Jan. 29, 1987; Disney to Stuart Gordon, Aug. 9, 1994.

11　Bradbury to Stuart Gordon (Disney), Dec. 29, 1995.

12　Bradbury to Michael Eisner, Feb. 23, 1998; Roy E. Disney to Bradbury, Feb. 26, 1998; Eisner to Bradbury, Mar. 18, 1998.

Chapter 35. An Evening on Mars

1　Eller, *Unbound*, 224.

2　Frederik Pohl to Bradbury, Aug. 31, 1998; Bradbury to Pohl, undated, after returning from DragonCon in Atlanta (cc).

3　Bradbury to Bob McCabe, Sep. 16, 2004 (fax original).

4 Bradbury, interview with the author, Mar. 14, 2002.

Chapter 36. "Make Haste to Live"
1 Eller, *Unbound*, 40.
2 Bradbury to Neil Baldwin, Nov. 7, 2000 (fax). Baldwin returned the fax, noting "Ray, our prayers are with you."
3 "Ray Bradbury Accepts the 2000 Medal for Distinguished Contribution to American Letters," transcribed by the National Book Foundation (https://www.nationalbook.org/ray-bradbury-accepts-the-2000-medal-for-distinguished-contribution-to-american-letters/); Weller, *Bradbury Chronicles*, 323–324; Donn Albright, various discussions with the author.
4 Mike Connolly, "Rambling Reporter," *Hollywood Reporter*, Aug. 27, 1954, 2. A 1959 FBI informant report, released (with redactions) in the early 2000s through Sam Weller's Freedom of Information request, also alludes to Bradbury's words at the 1954 WGAW meeting. Eller, *Unbound*, 146–147.

Chapter 37. Messages in a Bottle
1 Bradbury's stroke and immediate aftermath is summarized in Weller, *Bradbury Chronicles*, 321–322.
2 Bill Higgins, "It Was Bad Writing at Its Very Finest," *Los Angeles Times*, Mar. 22, 1995.
3 Principal reviews include: Roland Green, *Booklist* 98:15 (Apr. 1, 2002): 1312; *BookPage* (Apr. 2002): 28; *Chronicle* 23 (Apr. 2002): 48; *Kirkus Reviews* 70:4 (Feb. 15, 2002): 227; [Unsigned.] *Publishers Weekly* 249:10 (Mar. 11, 2002): 51; [Unsigned.] "Fiction," *Toronto Star*, Apr. 21, 2002, D17; Gary K. Wolfe, *Locus* 48:4 (Apr. 2002).
4 *Death Is a Lonely Business*, the first of these three murder mysteries, had opened out from an early unpublished murder tale, "Where Everything Ends" (1944; published 2009), just as the entire plot of *Something Wicked This Way Comes* had emerged from "The Black Ferris" (1945; published 1948).
5 Bradbury to Hart-Davis, Sep. 9–10, 1988 (Tulsa; Bradbury's photocopy).
6 Bradbury, interview with the author, Oct. 5, 2004, contains a description of Constance and the features that Bradbury transferred from her real-life antecedent Bingo.
7 Three wooden file boxes of these signatures, carefully documented on the back of each card, were preserved for more than sixty years.

Chapter 38. The Fire Within
1 Details of the Mexico City lodgings and his interactions with John Steinbeck are from Bradbury, interviews with the author, Oct. 20, 2007, Oct. 18, 2008, Apr. 8 and Oct. 24, 2009; Bradbury, interview with Donn Albright (for the author), Mar. 2008.
2 For Bradbury, the long illness was whooping cough; Steinbeck's childhood illness was rheumatic fever.
3 "Help Ray Bradbury Celebrate a Martian Birthday," Planetary Society press release, Aug. 5, 2003; "Last Chance to Celebrate Mars Day with Earth's Favorite Martian," Planetary Society press release, Aug. 25, 2003.

4 Maggie Bradbury, interview with the author, Mar. 11, 2002.

5 "'Go Wild about Mars' with the Planetary Society," Planetary Society press release, Dec. 29, 2003; anon., "My Personal Martian Chronicles" (https://musingsofamiddle agedgeek.blog/2018/06/12/my-personal-martian-chronicles/).

Chapter 39. A Child's Imagination

1 Bradbury, interview with the author, Oct. 6, 2004.

Chapter 40. *Farewell Summer*

1 By 2014, as the submitted letter pool rose to 50,000 for the Letters about Literature contest, junior high national honor winner Jane Wang reflected on *Fahrenheit 451* in her winning letter to the late author. Erin Allen, LC blog at https://blogs.loc.gov/ loc/2014/07/letters-about-literature-dear-ray-bradbury/.

Chapter 41. Samurai Kabuki

1 Karen Howard (Crusader Entertainment) to Bradbury, Sep. 20, 2000.

2 Crusader's top choices for the female lead had been Nicole Kidman and Charlize Theron before Catherine McCormack emerged as the final choice. Brad Pitt had shown interest in the Travis role but considered the film to be more of a commercial venture than he wanted to engage at that time.

3 Bradbury, interview with the author, Oct. 22, 2007.

4 Mitchell Diggs, "Bradbury's Ahead of Death," *Birmingham Post-Herald*, Mar. 7, 1995, B4.

5 Bradbury knew *The Naked Island* at least as far back as the early 1970s, when he described this film in his August 25, 1974, book review of Archie Lieberman's *Farm Boy*.

6 Bradbury, interview with the author, Oct. 13, 2005.

7 Bradbury, interview with the author, Mar. 14, 2002.

8 Susan Ramer (Congdon) to Bradbury, Mar. 10, 1997 (fax); Bradbury to Tom Mori (Tuttle-Mori), Mar. 11, 1997; Mori to Bradbury, Apr. 1, 1997 (fax).

Chapter 42. "Nothing Has to Die"

1 Bradbury, interview with the author, Mar. 10, 2012.

2 Bradbury to Tenny Chonin (Disney), Feb. 21 and 23, 2007; Chonin to Bradbury, Feb. 26, 2007 (email).

Chapter 43. Visions of Mars

1 The history of the "Visions of Mars" disk, and its context among many other message disks and plaques sent out on various missions, is recounted in Damond Benningfield's "'Hi! I'm From Earth!'" *Air & Space Magazine*, Oct. 2015.

2 Bradbury's proxy presence at Planetfest '08 is described in "My Personal Martian Chronicles," preserved at https://musingsofamiddleagedgeek.blog/2018/06/12/ my-personal-martian-chronicles/.

3 The words of Sagan, Friedman, and Lomberg are among the few components of the disk that are readily accessible, because not all of the many authors or estates would authorize broader distribution of the whole.

4 Mitchell Diggs, "Bradbury's Ahead of Death," *Birmingham Post-Herald*, Mar. 7, 1995, B1, B4.

5 Bradbury to Hart-Davis, Jul. 30, 1991.

6 Nancy Nicholas, interview with the author, May 2001.

Chapter 44. Remembrance

1 Loren Eiseley to Bradbury, Jan. 11, 1974.

2 Dana Gioia to the author (email), Oct. 29, 2012. When Gioia arrived, Bradbury asked him to read aloud the introduction and first chapter of *Becoming Ray Bradbury*, the first volume in the present biographical trilogy, and the only volume Bradbury would live to see in print.

3 Leadabrand to Bradbury, May 16, 1982. Leadabrand along with Norman Corwin, may have brought Bradbury's work into the pages of *Westways*, the nationally circulating magazine of the California Automobile Association.

4 Bradbury, interview with the author, Mar. 14, 2002.

Chapter 45. Closing the Book

1 The 2006 Thomas O. Paine Award, the Mars flag, and Bradbury's photographic mementos from this event are preserved in the Center for Ray Bradbury Studies.

2 A comprehensive series of Planet Fest 2012 photos is archived on Sebulia's Flickr site: https://www.flickr.com/photos/18703657@N03/albums/72157630935488944/page2.

3 Jason Star, "Writing Is a Lonely Business: James McKimmey, Philip K. Dick, and the Lost Art of Author Correspondence," *Los Angeles Review of Books*, Nov. 3, 2014 (online).

Index

and, 104; *We'll Always Have Paris* and,
296; *Wonderful Ice Cream Suit* and, 28–32;
Zigler agency and, 86
Congdon, Michael, 289, 298, 304
Congdon, Sally, 197
Conrad, Barnaby, 24
Conrad, Charles "Pete," Jr., 230
Conrad, Mary, 24
Cooke, Alistair, 73
Copland, Aaron, 44, 52, 72, 92–93
Corwin, Norman, 63, 64, 300, 303–304
"Cosmic Evolution" lecture series, 23–25
Cosmogonias, 233
Cosmos, 165
Cotter, Tom, 162, 179–180, 215
Cotton, Joseph, 26
Cousins, Norman, 54
Cousteau, Jacques, 54
Coward, Noel, 29
Cowley, Malcolm, 163, 244
Craven, Wes, 182
"Creatures That Time Forgot, The," 100,
143–144
Crichton, Michael, 137
Cronkite, Walter, 124
Crowther, Edward, 115
Crumley, James, 141, 154–155
Cukor, George, 42–43, 112, 288
Culp, Robert, 180
Cunningham, Walt, 36, 122
Curiosity rover, 1, 306
Curiosity Shop, The, 21

Dadisman, Maryann, 149
Daley, Tyne, 215
Dandelion Wine, 3, 7, 33–34, 104, 151, 152,
170, 209, 220, 253, 265, 272, 276, 288,
308; 1960s/1970s performances of,
28–31, 52–53; 1989 performance of,
176–178; read in schools, 273; "The
Night" in, 106
Dannay, Frederic, 171

Darabont, Frank, 238
Dark Carnival, 51, 104, 129, 143, 146, 170,
253, 274
DaVinci, Leonardo, 92
Davis, Abraham, 150
Davis, Marc, 11–12, 60, 88, 124
Day, James, 44, 50
Day at Night, 44, 50, 63, 73
Day the Earth Stood Still, The, 226
Death in the Family, A, 152
Death Is a Lonely Business, 3, 154–157, 164,
189, 193, 298, 299; dedications of, 158;
ghosts collaborating the final writing
of, 157–158
"Death Wish," 57
DeCuir, John, Jr., 60
DeCuir, John, Sr., 60
De Curtis, Antonio, 83
De Grasse Tyson, Neil, 269, 271
De Havilland, Olivia, 26
Delaney, Tim, 291
Delany, Samuel R., 294
Delerue, Georges, 133
Dell Publishing, 142
De Mille, Agnes, 44
Dench, Judi, 125
Denoël, publishing in, 181
Derleth, August, 294
Destination Moon, 113
detective fiction, 141–143, 153–155,
259–262
Detective Tales, 141
Dial Code Santa Claus, 182
Dick, Philip K., 309
Dickinson, Angie, 265
Diller, Barry, 65
Dime Mystery, 141
Dinosaur Tales, 136–137, 138, 140
Dirty Harry, 36
Disch, Thomas M., 105–106
Disney, Roy E., 125, 214, 218, 238–239
Disney, Walt, 123, 287

JONATHAN R. ELLER is a Chancellor's Professor of English at Indiana University-Purdue University in Indianapolis, the senior textual editor of the Institute for American Thought, and director of the Center for Ray Bradbury Studies at IUPUI. His books *Becoming Ray Bradbury* and *Ray Bradbury Unbound* were each finalists for the Locus Award in the Nonfiction category.